Social Care, Health and Welfare in Contemporary Scotland

Edited by

Gerry Mooney
Senior Lecturer and Staff Tutor in Social Policy at the Open University in Scotland

Tony Sweeney
Senior Lecturer in Social Sciences at Glasgow College of Nautical Studies

Alex Law
Lecturer in Sociology at the University of Abertay, Dundee

Contributing writers

Jason Annetts
Joyce Cavaye
Colin Clark
Sue Dumbleton
Gesa Helms
Jan Law
Patricia McCafferty
Mo McPhail
Mary Munro
Jan Nicholson
Gill Scott

Kynoch & Blaney

Kynoch & Blaney Limited
Registered Office: Sherwood House, 7 Glasgow Road, Paisley PA1 3QS.

© Kynoch & Blaney Ltd, 2006
© The rights of Gerry Mooney, Tony Sweeney, Alex Law, Jason Annetts, Joyce Cavaye, Colin Clark, Sue Dumbleton, Gesa Helms, Jan Law, Patricia McCafferty, Mo McPhail, Mary Munro, Jan Nicholson and Gill Scott to be identified as the authors of their separately and/or collaboratively authored chapters of this Text have been asserted by them in accordance with the Copyright, Designs and Patents Act 1988.

First published 2006.

British Library Cataloguing in Publication Data
A catalogue record for this book can be obtained from the British Library.

ISBN-13 digit: 978-0-9553973-0-1
ISBN-10 digit: 0-9553973-0-8

Text formatting designed by Kynoch & Blaney Ltd.
Photograph of Princes Street, Edinburgh and cover design by Brian Paul.
Printed and bound by Bell and Bain Ltd., Glasgow, UK.

Contents

Notes on Contributors

Dr Jason Annetts is a Lecturer and the Sociology Division Leader at the University of Abertay Dundee and teaches modules on health, sexuality and social movements and political protest. His current research interests are focused on sex education and he has just completed a Scottish Executive funded research report that considered the support needs of teachers delivering sex and relationships education in primary schools.

Joyce Cavaye is a Lecturer and Regional Manager in the Faculty of Health and Social Care at the Open University in Scotland. She previously taught social policy at the University of Glasgow. Prior to moving into academic life, she worked for many years as a community nurse. Her research interests in health and social care, service users, informal carers and older people, stem from her experience of working in the community. She is currently editor of a series of books on policy and practice in health and social care in Scotland.

Dr Colin Clark is a Senior Lecturer in Sociology in the Department of Geography and Sociology at the University of Strathclyde, Glasgow. Before moving back to Scotland in 2005, he taught Sociology and Social Policy at the University of Newcastle upon Tyne for nine years. The majority of Colin's research and writing is in the area of 'race' and ethnicity and he is author (with Margaret Greenfields) of *Here to Stay: the Gypsies and Travellers of Britain* (UHP, 2006).

Sue Dumbleton is a Staff Tutor in the Faculty of Health and Social Care at the Open University in Scotland. Sue has previously taught in schools, the college sector and in adult education. She has many years experience in the social care sector and has a particular interest in services to children and adults who have a learning disability.

Dr Gesa Helms is a Research Fellow in the Department of Urban Studies at the University of Glasgow. Her current research interests include critical social theory, political economies of urban restructuring, policing and surveillance, and social regulation. Her forthcoming book, *Towards safe city centres? Remaking the spaces of an old-industrial city* will be published in 2007 by Ashgate.

Dr Alex Law is a Lecturer in Sociology at the University of Abertay, Dundee. He has published on class, national identity and the mass media and, along with these areas, other research interests include social, cultural and technological change, and culture and social inclusion.

Jan Law is a Research Fellow at the Department of Education and Social Work, University of Dundee. She has worked as a social science teacher in most Scottish universities.

Dr Patricia McCafferty is a Lecturer in the Department of Geography and Sociology at the University of Strathclyde. Her current interests include exploring the impact of the modernisation and reform of public services on working lives in the public sector. She is interested in all aspects of work under New Labour in the devolved Scotland and has also been involved in the 'Neo-Liberal Scotland?' project with Professor David Miller of the University of Strathclyde.

Mo McPhail works as a Regional Manager and Lecturer in the Faculty of Health and Social Care at The Open University in Scotland. She has been involved in social work and social work education in Scotland for over 12 years in various college and university settings. Mo currently chairs the introductory level course in Health and Social Care at the OU. Her practice as a social worker was based in the voluntary sector, with the Family Service Unit and the international children's organisation, Save the Children. Her areas of special interest are children's rights, service user and carer participation and promoting anti-racist and anti-oppressive practice in social work education.

Dr Gerry Mooney is a Senior Lecturer and Staff Tutor in Social Policy with The Open University in Scotland. He has co-edited and authored several publications in social policy and urban geography and has particular research interests in the impact of New Labour's agenda as it applies to Scotland. He has written widely on issues relating to urban studies and social policy, and with Gill Scott he is co-editor of *Exploring Social Policy in the 'New' Scotland*, The Policy Press, 2005.

Mary Munro is a former solicitor and probation officer in the north-east of England, Mary is now a freelance researcher and an associate lecturer with the Open University. She has also lectured in criminology at Strathclyde and Caledonian Universities. Mary founded and also runs the CjScotland website (www.cjscotland.org.uk), a key source of information about criminal justice in Scotland.

Jan Nicholson has lectured in Criminology at the Universities of Strathclyde and Glasgow and has also taught with the Open University. Currently at Glasgow University, she is researching the Law of Evidence in Sexual Offence Trials, focusing on the use of sexual history and character evidence in evaluation of the 2002 Sexual Offences (Scotland) Act. Her co-authored report on the baseline study can be viewed at http://www.scotland.gov.uk/Publications/2005/09/13144738/ 47390. Other research interests include sentencing, youth crime, crime and gender.

Professor Gill Scott is Professor of Social Inclusion and Equality in the School of Law and Social Sciences at Glasgow Caledonian University. She is also Director of the Scottish Poverty Information Unit. She has published widely in the area of poverty and is currently researching the role of advice services in the transition from welfare to work. Gill is co-editor, with Gerry Mooney, of *Exploring Social Policy in the 'New' Scotland*, The Policy Press, 2005.

Tony Sweeney is Senior Lecturer in Social Sciences at Glasgow College of Nautical Studies and an Associate Lecturer in Social Sciences with The Open University in Scotland. He has published in areas such as social class and work and employment and has undertaken several educational appointments to the Scottish Qualifications Authority as a moderator and writer for HNC/HND Social Sciences sociology Units, as an external marker for Higher Sociology and as a vetter for examinations papers.

Acknowledgements

The authors and editors of this Book, along with Kynoch & Blaney, would like to thank all those involved in the development, writing and publication of this Book. Every effort has been made to trace and contact copyright holders for resources and materials used in the production of this Book. If any resources or materials have been incorrectly acknowledged, the publishers would be pleased to make corrections at the earliest available opportunity.

Specifically, Mo McPhail would like to thank 'George' and his foster carer for their generous contribution and various colleagues across Scotland for their contribution to her chapter.

Grateful thanks is attributable to Brian Paul for providing various covers for the Book and then, when the final cover was decided upon, making periodic changes whenever asked to by the publishers. Andy Boyd of Printcare has been very helpful in working with the publishers in the design of the flyer for this Book and for general help in preparing for the print run, so deserves a thank you. Thanks, too, to Gerry McQuillan (and his assistant, Paul) of Kelvin Books, Glasgow, who, as the distributor of *Social Care, Health and Welfare in Contemporary Scotland* has also been exceptionally helpful in the marketing of this Book and will also be in its distribution.

Eleanor Ramsay, Qualifications Manager for Care Scotland at the Scottish Qualifications Authority also looked (in a personal capacity) at an early draft, so to Eleanor we would also like to say thank you. There are too many other people who have been supportive and helpful in the development of this Book to name in the space provided here, so we would like, on behalf of all of those involved in its writing and editing, to thank you – you will know who you are!

Finally, without diminishing all the input, help, support and even acquiescence of the aforementioned, the editorial team would like to especially thank the authors of each of the chapters for their hard work, patience and excellent contributions, and Kynoch & Blaney for publishing this Book, including the wide ranging and substantial work associated with this. You have all done a great job!

Gerry Mooney
Tony Sweeney
Alex Law

Editorial Team
Paisley, Glasgow and Dundee, October 2006

Preface

Social Care, Health and Welfare in Contemporary Scotland aims to provide an exciting and engaging, comprehensive and accessible coverage of many of the key social policy-making areas in Scotland. Each of the chapters provides a detailed outline of the history, key policy developments, innovations and practices and an informed discussion of their impact on different groups in Scottish society. The chapters are linked by a shared consideration of the ways in which these policies either reinforce or address issues of exclusion and disadvantage. The chapters address pertinent issues in areas such as poverty, health, social policy, criminal justice, class stratification, urban policy, the welfare of children and young people, care of older adults, learning disability, work and welfare, family, education and ideology.

Taking into account the commitment of Scottish education to demonstrating the importance of benchmarking all higher education against the Scottish Credit and Qualifications Framework (SCQF), we would point out that this Book is written with students studying at SCQF levels 7 and 8 in mind. In lay-persons' terms, this Book will be an invaluable tool for students in years 1 and 2 of a Bachelors Degree, as well as those undertaking Higher National Certificates (HNC), Higher National Diplomas (HND), Certificates in Higher Education (CertHE) and Diplomas in Higher Education (DipHE) in the following areas:

- Social Work
- Social Care
- Social Policy
- Health and Welfare
- Nursing
- Youth and Community Studies
- Child Care and Education
- Education
- Teacher training
- Sociology
- Politics
- Social Sciences

Social Care, Health and Welfare in Contemporary Scotland is written by a wide range of experienced lecturers, researchers and practitioners from a rich variety of backgrounds in social work, social care, social policy, sociology, health and welfare. Each brings their own first hand experience of working with service users and students in their field, which should contribute significantly to making this Book an invaluable learning and teaching resource. This Book has been written in an accessible yet challenging and comprehensive way, in order to provide necessary support to those learners who need it but will also challenge even the keenest students at this level. Authors have used relevant Scottish case studies*, statistics, examples and research in order to help students engage with issues impacting on daily life in contemporary Scotland. Students are encouraged to use the text as a means of understanding and evaluating issues relating to social care, health and welfare in their own communities and beyond.

As well as the important contribution made to this Book by all of the authors, it is important to point out the work of the three editors, whose contributions have been invaluable to this project. It would be remiss, however, to say the least, not to give special mention to Gerry Mooney's contribution. Gerry has, quite frankly, directed this project from start to finish and deserves special mention here.

We hope this text proves to be useful to students of social care, health and welfare on Scottish courses as well as to professionals and activists, and we would welcome your feedback. Please send any comments to Kynoch & Blaney at the registered address.

Good luck with your studies!

Kynoch & Blaney, October 2006

---

*All names in all of the case studies in this Book have been changed to ensure the confidentiality and protection of individuals.

Section 1:

Approaching the Study of Health, Care and Welfare in Scotland

Chapter 1

Introduction: Social Care, Health and Welfare in the Devolved Scotland

Gerry Mooney, Tony Sweeney and Alex Law

Introduction: 'Scottish Solutions to Scottish Problems'

A convincing argument can be made that **devolution** is inseparable from issues relating to social care, health and welfare. As is now well known, much of the 'push' for devolution for Scotland came on the back of rising demands for some degree of 'self-governance', for a greater 'say' for Scots in issues that mattered to 'Scotland'. There was widespread expectation across Scotland, perhaps unreasonably so, that devolution would result in policies that were more in tune with 'Scottish needs'. Such sentiments were also used to help justify devolution. Developing '*Scottish solutions for Scottish problems*', to borrow from the language used by successive First Ministers, would be the main rationale for the re-established Scottish Parliament at Holyrood in Edinburgh, following devolution in 1999 (Mooney and Scott, 2005; Stewart, 2004). Speaking in 1998, the (first) First Minister, the late Donald Dewar, commented thus:

> "We have a proud tradition in Scotland of working to tackle social division. We have developed innovative responses to social problems, many of which are now being promoted within the UK as models of good practice. We have a body of people [...] who are committed to creating a fairer society in Scotland. And in the not too distant future we will have a Scottish Parliament, which will give us the opportunity to develop Scottish solutions to Scottish needs, and to bring the arm of government closer to the needs of the people. Devolution matters. It will let us take the decisions that matter here in Scotland. It is an end in itself: but it is a means to other ends, and none more important than the creation of a socially cohesive Scotland" (Scottish Office, Press Release, 3 November, 1998).

In order to facilitate the decisions that matter here in Scotland, a range of 'powers' – 'devolved powers' – were made available to the new Scottish Parliament. The majority of these powers were related to policy-making in the fields of social care, health, housing, education, area regeneration and so on. In other words, the Scottish

Parliament was largely concerned with what, in general terms, are referred to as welfare and/or social policies. Of course, prior to devolution, many areas of social policy in Scotland came under the control of the Scottish Office, notably in relation to health care, education and housing (see Law, **Chapter 3**). In a number of other areas, for instance, criminal justice, the distinctive legal system that exists in Scotland is reflected in Scottish-specific policies, such as in relation to youth justice. On top of this were a range of extensive organisational and institutional differences that gave the **welfare state** in Scotland a sense of distinctiveness – even if this was more apparent than real for the most part.

The main aim of this Book is to introduce you to many of these key social policy making areas – often referred to as 'sites' of social and welfare policy making. We focus on a number of the important 'sites' that have occupied much of the work of the Scottish Parliament since 1999. There is little doubting that the Scottish Executive has been busy in the first seven years of devolution across a wide range of health and welfare policy making areas. The task that falls to this Introductory Chapter is to present some of the key concepts, ideas and approaches that will inform the discussion, to outline the main themes of the Book and to outline the structure of the Book itself, introducing the different chapters in the process. ***Social Care, Health and Welfare in Contemporary Scotland*** also encourages you to engage with the study of social care, health and social policy in Scotland in particular ways and to understand these as part and parcel of the wider fabric of Scottish society, as central to the social structures, social divisions and social inequalities that shape modern Scotland.

Devolved and Reserved Powers

What do we mean by social or welfare policy? One of the difficulties that face us here is that there is no one agreed upon definition of social policy. As in many other areas of the social sciences, there are a range of different and sometime competing views and ideas as to what the study of social policy might involve. The existence of a large and seemingly ever growing number of books on social policy is perhaps testament to some of these differing 'takes' on what constitutes the study of social policy. Social policy is *not* taught in Scottish schools – though a range of different subjects (from modern studies, sociology, economics, human geography and history to social psychology) will often focus on issues that are of interest and concern to those who are studying and researching in the field of social policy, health and social care.

Social Care, Health and Welfare in Contemporary Scotland explores a range of the key sites of social and welfare policy making in Scotland today. To quote Richard

Titmuss (1976), who in the post-1945 era was one of the main academics that worked to establish social policy as a legitimate area of social scientific investigation:

> "We are concerned with the study of a range of social needs and the functioning, in conditions of scarcity, of human organisation, traditionally called social services or social welfare systems, to meet those needs" (Titmuss, 1976: 20).

However, one of the limitations of an approach that focuses exclusively on 'sites' is that it is possible to neglect some of the key factors that shape and influence the delivery of social and welfare policies. Further, how many 'sites' are there? In this Book – following on from the approach adopted by many academics and researchers across Britain in recent years – we include health policy, welfare to work/workfare, urban and community policy, care for the elderly, approaches to learning needs, social work, family policy and education as important sites. Perhaps more contentiously, for some commentators at least, we also include criminal justice policy. There have always been close interconnections between social and criminal justice policy making in Scotland. However, following the election of New Labour in 1997 and devolution in 1999, the links between such policies have been taken to new levels. The development of 'pragmatic', 'joined-up' thinking has been a key element of New Labour's approach to policy making across the entire UK (Lavalette and Pratt, 2006; Powell, 2002). This is reflected in important areas of policy making in Scotland, for instance, the Scottish Executive's Joint Future Agenda from 2000, which is concerned with providing more integrated community care provision (see Cavaye, **Chapter 11**). Focusing on sites alone, irrespective of how many we include, potentially may result in important links between them being neglected. Issues of **social inclusion**, of poverty, ill-health, of who gets access to care and who is excluded, are issues that take us beyond a concern with 'sites' of social policy and to questions and issues about the structure of Scottish society itself. We return to this below in relation to the main themes of the Book.

As we have already highlighted, devolution for Scotland is intertwined with social policy making in important ways. The Scotland Act 1998 (otherwise known as the 'Devolution Act') *devolved* powers to the Edinburgh Parliament in areas such as health, education, housing, social work, local government and criminal justice, among others. However, the same legislation 'reserved' 11 key areas of policy making to the Westminster Parliament, including employment, social security, immigration and nationality policy, trade and industry, industrial relations and so on. Immediately it can be seen that this too includes areas of social policy making – for some, *the* key areas of social policy making. Notable here is, of course, social security, which encompasses the main welfare benefits.

Policy Tensions Between Holyrood and Westminster

Obvious tensions can potentially arise over political and policy objectives and decision making between Holyrood and Westminster. Arguably, it is the existence of a New Labour government in London and a New Labour dominated Scottish Executive (in coalition with the Liberal Democrats, at least at the time of writing in late 2006) that has worked to minimise such 'tensions'. However, there are visible signs that they do exist and that they have the potential to seriously disrupt relations between the two Parliaments. In some areas, such as benefit entitlements, the existence of reserved and devolved powers might inevitably be expected to lead to conflict between both governments. Housing benefit, for instance, is a reserved power, but housing policy is devolved. In other areas, perhaps more unexpectedly, other conflicts have emerged.

In relation to immigration and asylum policy, for example, the Immigration and Asylum Act 1999 and the 2002 Immigration, Asylum and Nationality Bill, frame policy in these important areas across the entire UK. The Scottish Parliament has no powers over such matters. However, this has not prevented growing demands for 'Scotland' to have more 'say' in policy making in this area (and indeed this has proved to be an unexpected part of calls for 'greater' devolution to Scotland). These demands were fuelled to a large extent in autumn 2005 by the forced detainment of asylum seekers at the Dungavel detention centre in Lanarkshire. That such detainments involved children, frequently taken along with their families in dawn raids, generated a widespread outcry and demands that the Scottish Executive 'intervene'. Concerns were voiced also by Scotland's Children's Commissioner, who, along with others, claimed that dawn raids together with the forced detainment of children breeched the Children (Scotland) Act 1995 . The Commissioner had commented a year earlier:

> "My job is to promote and safeguard the rights of all children and people in Scotland. Immigration may well be a reserved issue, but the children aren't" (quoted on BBC News Online, September 13, 2004: www.bbc.news.co.uk).

'Fresh Talent'

As a result of this and other related areas of controversy, the Scottish Executive has been required to respond to public concerns that the forced detention of children, namely that the internment of asylum seeker children at Dungavel was not, in some sense, *'the Scottish way'*. The dispute also highlighted the tensions that exist between the Scottish Executive's flagship **'Fresh Talent'** policy, and UK immigration and asylum legislation (Scottish Executive, 2004a).

'Fresh Talent' was developed amidst growing concerns with Scotland's demographic 'time bomb'. Demography refers to population measurements and analyses of trends in population levels. In Scotland, the population is forecast to decline further in the next half century and more, with one estimate predicting a fall from 5.08 million in 2004 to 3.5 million by 2074 (Registrar General for Scotland, quoted in *The Herald*, 21 October 2005). Introduced in 2004, Fresh Talent sought to stem population decline and attract both expatriated Scots as well as encouraging others to settle in Scotland. The main aspect to the policy was the encouragement to foreign students to stay and work in Scotland with a two year visa extension the lure, with a further application for permanent residency on the basis of the securing of permanent employment.

Fresh Talent shows that there is a real gap between the ambitions of UK asylum and immigration policy and the reality of population decline in Scotland. As such it is a useful illustration of some of the tensions that are thrown up by and through devolution, albeit in this instance somewhat unanticipated ones. Other potential sources of conflict can arise when both Parliaments 'go their separate ways' in relation to policy making. While, as we have noted, there is a New Labour government in the UK Parliament in London that legislates for the entire UK, devolution for Scotland, Wales and Northern Ireland has provided the basis for potential 'divergence' in social policy making. The devolved administrations could then act as "policy laboratories" (Jeffrey, 2005: 5).

Divergence and Convergence

There are important and continuing debates around the degree of 'divergence' or 'convergence' between policy-making in different parts of the UK (see *Critical Social Policy*, 2006; Mooney and Scott, 2005). While we do not have the space to consider these in full here, nonetheless one of the main promises of devolution was that it would lead to greater policy divergence – *Scottish solutions* – not least in those key social and welfare policy sites. While there has been considerable scepticism and perhaps even disappointment that the level of divergence *from Scotland* has been limited, some recent research suggests that if anything, divergence is being driven *in England* by a more radical New Labour agenda for the restructuring of public services and social policy, including the introduction of 'top-up' fees for students, foundation hospitals and new policies for schools that will result in an erosion of local authority control (Adams and Schmueker, 2005; Wincott, 2006). It is notable that once again it is in relation to key areas of social policy where divergence has arguably been at its greatest, both from England and from Scotland.

One important and much discussed example of this is the case of free personal care for older people. The Scottish Parliament introduced this in 2002 following the 'majority' recommendations of the Sutherland Commission on the future of long-term care (Royal Commission on Long Term Care, 1999). The Community Care and Health (Scotland) Act 2002 has been termed one of "devolution's major successes" (McCabe, 2004). The Act introduced free personal and nursing care for the elderly, funded by taxation, based on need and free at the point of use, with all costs to be covered by the state (for a fuller discussion see Stewart, 2004). Such a policy was not introduced in England.

Policies for the funding of students in higher education in Scotland have also taken a different direction from those in England and Wales (see Clark, **Chapter 13**). Since late 2000, students on full-time higher education courses in Scotland's colleges and universities have not been required to pay tuition fees up front.

It would be mistaken to ignore the controversy that surrounded both the philosophy and implementation of such policies. In both areas there has been considerable argument over the effectiveness of these respective policies. In addition, while they highlight important differences in the approach of the Scottish Executive compared with other parts of the UK, there remain UK-wide concerns about costs and the sustainability of such policies.

Social Care, Health and Welfare in Contemporary Scotland: **Book Themes and Structure**

Our main goal in producing this Book was to provide an accessible introduction to many of the debates and issues that surround both the discussion and policy-making outcomes of a diverse range of welfare sites in contemporary Scotland. As we note above, the Scottish Executive has been active across the range of policy-making areas in which it has a major degree of devolved responsibility and, together with the continuing drive of New Labour – across the entire UK – to reshape public services and social policy, these work in Scotland to provide a sense of the changing context within which social care, health and welfare are being approached and understood.

Importantly, this is *not* a Book that attempts to provide a detailed examination of each and every welfare site and how these might have changed since devolution in 1999. We do not devote a separate chapter to housing policy, for instance (though this is discussed in passing in Mooney, **Chapter 12**). Likewise, we do not provide a chapter that focuses on the activities of the voluntary sector and the growing contribution that this makes in the delivery of a range of social and welfare services across Scotland. However, the chapters here do offer a picture of a world of welfare and social policy (in its widest sense) that is undergoing profound and far-reaching change.

It is hoped that you will grasp that the 'welfare mix', that is the contribution of the state, private sector and voluntary/third sectors to general social policy and welfare provision, is subject to constant change. Otherwise referred to as the mixed economy of welfare or **welfare pluralism**, it is evident from the discussions offered in many of the chapters in this Book that the private sector ('the market') has come to play an ever increasing role in the delivery of so-called 'heartland' welfare services. This is no accident, but is a deliberate policy on the part of Conservative and New Labour government's to 'modernise' public services and to introduce the methods and practices of the private sector. Such measures have proved to be highly controversial to say the least and, therefore, it will come as little surprise that where relevant the authors of the chapters in this Book offer critical examinations of these developments.

The topics that are discussed in the chapters that comprise this Book were identified as particularly important, not least because of their centrality to the developing debates and policy-making agendas of the Scottish Executive since devolution in 1999. We also provide a chapter that explores the historical development of welfare in Scotland (Law, **Chapter 3**) and another that considers the impact of a predominantly Westminster-driven policy making agenda – **'welfare to work'** (Helms, **Chapter 6**).

All too often in books of this kind there are no apparent links between the chapters or across the entire collection. We have attempted to overcome this by:

- Requiring each author to address a series of themes as they focus on their particular topic areas: *social divisions and differentiation*, *social inclusion and exclusion*, *care and control* and *continuity and change*.

- Building-in cross-chapter links and connections in each chapter.

- Asking authors to write in a way that highlights and draws out the inter-connectedness of policies across a range of different 'sites'. This offers a key map of the Book as a whole.

The way that each author addresses these points will differ depending on the approach that they take and, of course, the particular issues and debates that are thrown up by the topic that they are discussing. This is particularly the case with the Book-wide themes outlined above. While each of the chapters will relate to these –

the extent to which each or all of them are accorded importance will, of course, vary. The themes play a particularly important role in this Book other than as a means of providing some book-wide linkages and connections. The contributors who have written the chapters share a variety of concerns, interests and approaches to the study of social care, health and welfare. Indeed, one of the things that make edited collections such as *Social Care, Health and Welfare in Contemporary Scotland* so potentially rich and valuable is that they bring together different perspectives and ways of thinking (these are explored more fully in Sweeney, **Chapter 2**).

However, and this is where the themes are of particular importance, the dominant approach adopted by each of the authors involved here is one that is concerned to discuss and understand social care, health and welfare in relation to *wider* issues of social difference, division and inequalities – all of which are of major importance for those of us who are interested in making sense of different areas of social life in contemporary Scotland (Best, 2005). Therefore, we provide a chapter that considers social class related differences and discussions elsewhere that focus on gender relations and the family. These are, of course, inter-related in multiple and diverse ways. In part through the themes and in part through the relevant policy-related issues themselves, each of the discussions relates in a variety of ways to this overall concern with divided and unequal Scotland.

The idea of Scotland as unequal and divided is by no means novel. That Scotland is marked by massive inequalities and a gulf in **life chances** between different social groups is also recognised – albeit to a limited extent – by the Scottish Executive. In part, this has been reflected in the Scottish Executive's Social Justice Strategy and more recently in its concern to 'Close the Opportunity Gap' (Scottish Executive, 2004b). The promotion of **social justice** has been a priority for the Scottish Executive since devolution in 1999. In *Social Justice...A Scotland Where Everyone Matters*, the Scottish Executive first set out its wide ranging social justice strategy (Scottish Executive, 1999). While no clear definition of social justice was offered here (or subsequently), this was presented as "the most comprehensive framework ever for tackling poverty in Scotland." This strategy was founded on a 'life cycle approach' that focused on both people and places. Ten long term targets were identified for achieving a more socially just Scotland. These targets included defeating child poverty within a generation (thereby reflecting the commitment given the previous year by New Labour in Westminster), ensuring that every 19 year old was in education, training or work; full employment and reducing inequalities between different communities across Scotland. The targets were supplemented by 29 'milestones' that would be measured annually to show how far progress had been made in meeting the long term targets. A Social Justice Annual Report was to be published detailing progress. Three such Reports were published in 2000, 2001 and 2002 (available at www.scotland.gov.uk).

Following the second Scottish Parliament elections in 2003, the Social Justice Strategy was subject to review and the outcome was a revised approach (Scottish Executive, 2003, 2004b). 'Social Justice' was 'dropped' as the term describing anti-poverty policy, replaced by *'Closing the Opportunity Gap'* (CtOG). CtOG had three broad aims:

- To prevent individuals or families from falling into poverty.
- To provide pathways out of poverty.
- To sustain individuals or families in a lifestyle free from poverty.

Poverty is widely seen as a prime example of a 'social problem'. However, we need to be careful how we use this label. We have asked authors to avoid the type of approach that is driven by a concern 'to do something about' the 'problem' of this or that. This is *not* a Book that will argue that youth crime, for example, 'must' be tackled in such and such a way or that urban regeneration 'must' take on board *x* and *y*. What it does argue for, however, and this is implicit throughout, is that we need to avoid simply taking for granted the idea that there are 'problems' that 'everyone' in Scotland accepts and wants to see addressed in the same ways.

We are, just in case you get the 'wrong' idea, not saying that that Scotland is free from major social problems – far from it! What we are saying, however, is that how 'social problems' are identified – *and by whom* – is an important way of making sense of social policy. Therefore, if poverty is seen as a problem caused by the inadequate spending habits and lifestyles of the poor the obvious solution would be to cut benefit entitlements. By contrast, in seeing poverty as a consequence of inequality and of extreme wealth, the preferred policy would be one that would tend to favour the large scale redistribution of wealth and income. 'Need', in a general sense, is often taken for granted as self-explanatory, but this is also subject to competing and contrasting definitions and explanations as to who *should* or *should not* get access to welfare and social policy services (Langan, 1998). Need, therefore, is **'socially constructed'**.

The identification and definition – or social construction – of a particular issue or set of issues as a 'social problem' does not happen by accident. It reflects a series of assumptions, beliefs and values about individuals, groups, behaviours, about what is 'right' and 'wrong', and about society itself (Saraga, 1998). This is not a neutral process, but involves the objective interests of particular social groups and subjective value judgements and political judgements. The shared argument in this Book is that the dominant ways through which social problems come to be constructed reflects the power of specific groups in society today.

A **'social constructionist'** approach can help us to avoid 'common sense' ('what everyone knows') understandings of social issues – that present, in a taken for granted way, the *construction* of a particular issue, behaviour or phenomenon as 'a problem'. This approach also encourages us to be *sceptical* and *critical*. A critical and questioning approach – of the kind adopted by each of the authors in this Book – is to be welcomed and valued as a means by which we aid our understanding of an issue. To help with this each of the chapters also provides a series of questions or activities asking you to *'pause for thought'*, to help you engage with the discussion being presented. We will come back to this shortly.

Social constructionism is an important approach in a critically informed social science. However, such an approach is much more limited when it comes to explaining why it is that certain activities and groups come to be defined, often repeatedly so, as a 'problem' in some way or another. Therefore, we would urge you to keep in mind the contrasting perspectives that are outlined in **Chapter 2**, in particular. We are also concerned to build upon this by locating the discussion of different sites of social and welfare policy within the overall context of social divisions and inequalities. In other words, it is argued across this Book that social policy is also about power and about the processes and social relations of inclusion and exclusion, advantage and disadvantage, wealth and poverty. The famous American sociologist, C. Wright Mills, argues that in order for us to develop an informed understanding of how particular social issues come to be defined and constructed as a problem, the wider social context must be considered (Mills, 1959). Mills argued that 'personal troubles' and 'public issues' are closely inter-related. Therefore, in addition to providing an exploration of key policy developments in each of the topic areas considered, there is also a concern to offer some analysis and explanation.

The Book is structured in *three* main sections as follows:

- **Section 1**, including this chapter, provides a general introduction to the Book and to the study of social care, health and welfare in contemporary Scotland; in **Chapter 2** Tony Sweeney provides an exploration of many of the key theoretical approaches that feature prominently in any analysis and explanation of the issues that concern us and, finally, the section also offers in **Chapter 3** by Alex Law, an account of the development of the welfare state in Scotland.

- **Section 2** is primarily concerned to explore some of the key dimensions of social division and inequality in Scotland today. **Chapter 4** by Alex Law and Jan Law discusses some of the key ways in which Scotland continues to be structured by inequalities of social class. In **Chapter 5** Gill Scott analyses poverty and social exclusion, while in **Chapter 6** Gesa Helms provides a critically informed discussion of what is arguably *the* key New Labour social policy – welfare to work.

- In **Section 3** the focus moves to a discussion of policy developments and social issues in specific welfare sites. The chapters here also illustrate in other ways some of the key aspects of divided and unequal Scotland and in other ways they build upon **Chapter 2** by offering other explanations of the issue at hand. In **Chapter 7** Jason Annetts considers a key area of social policy making, family policy, while in **Chapter 8** Mo McPhail examines some of the main ways in which social work policy making for young people has been developing in the devolved Scotland. In **Chapter 9** the focus of attention moves to that area of social policy making that is all too frequently in the media and public spotlight, health policy. Here, Tricia McCafferty examines some of the main ways in which New Labour policies have been 'restructuring' health care provision, in the process reconstructing the traditional meanings of public health care. In **Chapter 10** Sue Dumbleton, by contrast, discusses policy developments in a field that has often received scant attention, learning disability. **Chapter 11** by Joyce Cavaye includes an examination of one of the key early policy developments of the Scottish Executive, free personal care for the elderly. The concern of **Chapter 12** by Gerry Mooney is developments in community and urban policies in the devolved Scotland, while in **Chapter 13** Colin Clark focuses on that other 'great' area of social policy making – educational policy. Finally, in **Chapter 14** Mary Munro and Jan Nicholson provide a detailed discussion of some of the key developments in criminal justice in modern Scotland.

Finally…How to Use this Book

This Book can be used in a variety of ways. It is a ready resource that can be used to support your studies on a range of courses. It may form an important part of a particular module/unit and it can be used to supplement other books and sources that you may want to use. We remind you that this Book is meant to offer an introduction to a range of social and welfare policy issues as they 'matter' in contemporary Scotland. You may want to follow up some of the debates and discussions that are provided here and, to that end, each of the main chapters provides some guidance as to further resources (books, journal articles, newspapers, internet resources, government reports/web pages and so on), each being fully referenced (and all too often such references and sources are overlooked yet they provide a wealth of material that can only be of help to your studies).

We have already mentioned the activities that are provided in each chapter. These are questions that encourage you to reflect upon key issues and arguments that are discussed in the chapters. You may wish to tackle these on your own or with your student colleagues or as guided by your lecturer. However, do please try them as they will help to consolidate your understanding of the material that is being presented.

A number of the chapters also utilise what is termed a case study method of learning. Case studies provide a particularly engaging and illuminating approach that encourages you to closely study a particular example or illustration of a particular issue or problem, focusing on the way it affects an individual or group. While any case study will be selective, nonetheless it contributes to your understanding and ability to use a range of conceptual tools, such as critical reflection.

We do hope that you will find this an interesting and thought provoking Book and that it will prove to be an invaluable aid to your studies.

Further Reading

Health Scotland (2005) *Understanding the Policy Maze: A Guide to Social and Health Policy in Scotland* (3ʳᵈ Edition), Edinburgh, Health Scotland
Mooney, G. and Scott, G. (eds.) (2005) *Exploring Social Policy in the 'New' Scotland*, Bristol, The Policy Press

Useful Websites

Scottish Executive: www.scotland.gov.uk
Scottish Parliament: www.scottish.parliament.uk
Unity for the Study of Governance in Scotland: www.ed.ac.uk/usgs
Scottish Council Foundation: www.scottishcouncilfoundation.org
Joseph Rowntree Foundation: www.jrf.org.uk
Scottish Poverty Information Unit (SPIU): www.povertyinformation.org
ESRC Devolution and Constitutional Change Programme: www.devolution.ac.uk
Scottish Centre for Research on Social Justice (SCRSJ): www.scrsj.ac.uk

Bibliography

Adams, J. and Schmueker, K. (2005) *Devolution in Practice 2006*, Newcastle Upon Tyne, Institute for Public Policy Research (IPPR) North (www.ippr.north.org)
Best, S. (2005) *Understanding Social Divisions*, London, Sage
Brown, U., Scott, G., Mooney, G. and Duncan, B. (eds.) (2002) *Poverty in Scotland 2002: People, Places and Policies*, London/Glasgow, Child Poverty Action Group/Scottish Poverty Information Unit
Critical Social Policy (2006) Special Issue on Devolution and Social Policy, *Critical Social Policy*, 26 (3)
Dewar, D. (1998) Scottish Office Press Release, Edinburgh, Scottish Office, 3 November, 1998
Ferguson, I., Lavalette, M. and Mooney, G. (eds.) (2002) *Rethinking Welfare*, London, Sage
Health Scotland (2005) *Understanding the Policy Maze: A Guide to Social and Health Policy in Scotland* (3ʳᵈ Edition), Edinburgh, Health Scotland
Jeffrey, C. (2005) *Devolution: What Difference Has it Made?* Swindon , ESRC Research Programme on Constitutional Change, www.dev.ac.uk (accessed on 20 January 2006)
Langan, M. (ed.) (1998) *Welfare: Needs, Rights and Responsibilities*, London, Routledge

Lavalette, M. and Pratt, A. (eds .) (2006) *Social Policy: Theories, Concepts and Issues* (Third Edition), London, Sage

Levitas, R. (2005) *The Inclusive Society? Social Exclusion and New Labour* (Second Edition), Houndsmills, Palgrave MacMillan

McCabe, T. (2004) www.scotland.gov.uk/News/Releases/2004/09/28111008 (accessed 25 November 2004)

Mills, C.W. (1959) *The Sociological Imagination*, Oxford, Oxford University Press

Mooney, G. and Johnstone, C. (2000) 'Scotland Divided: Poverty, Inequality and Scottish Parliament', in *Critical Social Policy*, 63

Mooney, G. and Scott, G. (eds.) (2005) *Exploring Social Policy in the 'New' Scotland*, Bristol, The Policy Press

Powell, M. (ed.) (2002) *Evaluating New Labour's Welfare Reforms*, Bristol, The Policy Press

Saraga, E. (1998) *Embodying the Social: Constructions of Difference*, London, Routledge

Scottish Executive (1999) *Social Justice... a Scotland Where Everyone Matters*, Edinburgh, Scottish Executive

Scottish Executive (2003) *Closing the Gap: Scottish Budget for 2003-2006*, Edinburgh, Scottish Executive

Scottish Executive (2004a) *Fresh Talent Initiative*, Edinburgh, Scottish Executive

Scottish Executive (2004b) *Closing the Opportunity Gap*, Edinburgh, Sco ttish Executive, www.scotland.gov.uk/closingtheopportunitygap

Stewart, J. (2004) *Taking Stock: Scottish Social Welfare After Devolution*, Bristol, The Policy Press

Sutherland Report (1999) *With Respect to Old Age: Long Term Care – Rights and Responsibilities*, Report by the Royal Commission on Long Term Care, London, The Stationary Office

Titmuss, R. (1976) *Commitment to Welfare*, London, Allen and Unwin (first published in 1968)

Wincott, D. (2006) 'Social Policy and Social Citizenship: Britain's Welfare States', in *Publius: The Journal of Federalism*, 36 (1)

Chapter 2

Theories of Welfare

Tony Sweeney

Introduction

People are often put off by the thought of studying theory. The term itself sounds a bit daunting and dry, but we all use theories in our everyday lives – even if they are not the academic types that we will consider here. Any type of theory is basically an attempt to provide a framework against which information can be *interpreted*. Theories attempt to *explain* as well as *describe*. They seek to develop knowledge by making sense of information through the linking of related ideas and concepts. Whilst raw data, statistics or other information help describe *what* might be occurring in any situation, theories attempt to explain *why* things might be occurring.

We all use theories in our everyday thoughts and conversations. For instance, I may ponder over the real reasons behind my reluctance to do the garden in an attempt to build a theory, or explanation, to present to anyone who might criticise me. In doing so I may use a set of ideas and concepts that will support my theory. These may include the notion that gardening can put your back out, or be boring, or even cause death if you were to hack through an electric cable when trimming the hedge, for example. I might link these ideas and concepts, then, in such a way as to attempt to explain *why* I am quite happy to see the grass rise to tropical proportions.

Similarly, you might use theories to explain things in your life. For example, in conversation with friends you might speculate as to why your partner decided to end a relationship with you. You would also use linked ideas and concepts to support your theory. These might include your claim that she became aware that she could not possibly reach your high standards, or that his feet were too smelly or that you were far too interesting for her or him in the first place. You would then link these ideas and concepts in such a way as to attempt to explain *why* you were jilted.

The types of theory that we will consider here are *social*. They all, to varying extents, attempt to explain something about the social world in general and social welfare in particular. They seek to explain our lives as individuals and the societies in which we live. Some theories are very broad in scope – those that analyse the nature of wider social systems, for example. Others are narrower in scope and tend to focus on specific social phenomena. Many competing theories exist and there is no single theory that there is general agreement on. Also, whilst some theories regularly present themselves as entirely separate from others, often it is the case that theoretical concepts and arguments overlap. As well as theories differing in terms of their explanations, they also differ in terms of what they describe and so some theories cannot be measured directly against some others since they focus on different things – they seek to explain different things.

You may note a number of things about theories. These apply to all types of theory:

- Theories use linked ideas and concepts in an attempt to explain something.

- Theories include some ideas and concepts and not others and are therefore to some extent *selective*.

- Theories can only explain things that relate to the ideas and concepts that they embrace.

- Usually there are competing theories on any aspect under investigation.

- Theories differ in terms of how competent or useful they are at explaining things.

This chapter serves to introduce you to some of the more prominent theories of welfare that influence the study of social care, health and welfare. It is by no means a comprehensive account of all available theories, but intends to help you to understand the theoretical backgrounds, or origins, of many of the theories highlighted in individual chapters in this Book. Whilst it is important to study various theoretical traditions and the ideas and concepts they employ, it is also very important to *evaluate* the theories – to weigh up their usefulness by examining their strengths and weaknesses. This is not something that has been done for you here, but is something to bear in mind as you read the chapters in this collection.

What is presented below is essentially an introduction to some of the key groups of theory that are referred to throughout the book though in some chapters different authors utilise other theories. A number of things should be noted here:

- First, it is important to realise that many ideas and concepts used by various theorists overlap and the labels applied to their theoretical works are often applied by others in order to simplify differences between theories.

- Second, in a volume such as this, it is neither possible nor desirable to include all theories of welfare and so what follows is, quite deliberately, a dipping of the toe into the water of what is a very wide and deep pool.

- Third, whilst theoretical traditions have their roots in particular historical times and events, theoretical positions and the ideas and concepts they use move in and out of fashion according to the government in power (or other world events, such as the collapse of 'Communism' in Eastern Europe in the 1980s and 1990s, seen (by some) as a setback for Marxist theories), and are often modified, reformulated and represented in other guises. In other words theoretical traditions undergo a process of *continuity and change* alongside the systems of welfare they analyse.

- Fourth, just because a theory exists and, indeed, continues to exist over a prolonged period of time, this does not necessarily make it a sound theory. This is because welfare theories are linked to political ideologies and may therefore appear more or less attractive depending on the dominant ideas at the time.

- Fifth, and perhaps most importantly, welfare theories often differ most fundamentally in terms of how they view human nature, the relationship between the individual and the state and the role of the state and/or the market (private firms) in providing welfare. It is important to seek out these differing views in welfare theories as they are crucial to an understanding of the assumptions on which they are based.

Pause for thought
- Think of some theories that you have used in your own life recently. What are their strengths and weaknesses?

With all this in mind then we can begin our introductory journey around some key theories of welfare. We can start by considering a prominent set of ideas and concepts known as **liberalism**, which has significantly influenced many governments in the Western world in recent times.

Liberalism

The establishment of what might be described as a coherent body of ideas of liberalism dates from the late 18th century. It is a universal theory or group of theories in that it claims that all societies contain **'natural laws'** or processes that function best when incorporating the free participation and interaction of all citizens. Stable and just societies are the *outcome* of the successful exercise of these *processes*. As such, **liberals** *tend* to reject any form of external interference with social processes, such as welfare provision, which would be viewed as artificial manipulation of 'the natural'.

Liberals, therefore , reject any artificially constructed ideas about what societies *ought* to be like. They reject **utopian** ideals of the 'good' society or designs and plans for the shaping of society and its members' behaviour. Accordingly, they reject theories or initiatives based on state intervention, including welfare provision, wealth redistribution and production planning. This was apparent in their wholesale rejection of communist centrally-planned economies or large scale state intervention and the nationalisation of industries in post-1945 British society.

Liberals assume that all members of liberal society are in all respects 'free', including the 'freedom' to be wealthy or poor. One manifestation of this is the concept of 'freedom of expression', which they claim is essential since no external moral values exist, only opinions. In a feat of blind optimism, they assume that if these opinions are freely expressed they will aggregate toward the self-evident 'truth'. Citizens should have equal rights to perform a good or evil act, which effectively grants individual liberty preference over notions of right and wrong. Liberals believe in formal equality among citizens in terms of ability to engage in societal *processes* – in other words, they should have equal *opportunities* – but believe that natural (even biological) differences will inevitably lead to inequality of *outcome*.

The Free Market

A key component of liberalism is its focus on the freedom of individuals to engage with the operations of the **free market**. The free market requires competition, as well as exchange or trade transactions, which creates the **'market force'** of pressurising competing sellers to lower product prices. Such a force is viewed as a naturally occurring and unconscious act on the part of participants. It is a natural *process* of market economies, with satisfactory *outcomes* for all. Provision of human need through welfare *automatically* emerges from free engagement with a system of exchange that is assumed to be fair and natural. Individuals need not be tied to the state for provision of welfare. Thus liberals place great value on the operations of free markets and primarily on the entrepreneurs who sustain them.

The formal development of the liberal school of economics stemmed from the publication of the Scottish economist, Adam Smith's, *The Wealth Of Nations* in 1776. Along with other commentators of the time, he advocated the abolition of government intervention in economic affairs. National economies would best develop if market forces were left unfettered; that is, were left free from external restriction and interference. Individuals are best left to make their own rational calculations and economic transactions in a free market without restriction or regulation. The accumulation of such private transactions at the micro level would result in stable and ordered relationships at the macro level. In other words, societies would flourish when individuals were 'liberated' from undue influence from governments. For Smith, the **'invisible hand'** of free market operations would naturally lead to the common welfare of all. Since human nature yields a degree of sympathy for others, when we act due to 'self-interest' in the free market we will naturally tend towards others' welfare at the same time. Therefore, the efficient operation of market mechanisms is dependent on the consistent rational calculations of participants and on the non-intervention of the state.

Pause for thought
- Do humans always act rationally?
- To what extent do you think your actions are motivated by self-interest?

Some key aspects of liberalism can be summarised as follows:

- Free market relations are viewed as consistent with human nature, which in turn is viewed as competitive, self-interested and rational. It is, therefore, assumed that individuals should be responsible for their own welfare and that participation in the free market guarantees adequate levels of provision.

- The fact that individuals are free to participate in so-called 'natural' social processes legitimises the outcome. In free market societies, market transactions are the primary process and a liberal society is the outcome. Therefore, liberal societies may be characterised by significant differences in income and wealth, if that is what market forces produce.

- All social interaction should be underpinned by the principle of **rationality**. In other words, individuals should make decisions in their own interest based on a cost/benefit analysis. Therefore, no government agency should make decisions for them.

- Market mechanisms ensure that liberal societies are self-regulatory. Liberals are therefore opposed to external interference from the state, in the form of **social policy**, for example, which they assume would artificially override natural processes and destroy market equilibrium (balance).

Therefore, although liberalism interprets the free market as the activities of competing individuals, it may be alternatively viewed as being a form of social organisation in itself. It is neither naturally or spontaneously occurring nor fundamental to the human condition, since for thousands of years before the establishment of classical liberal theory, it did not exist. The modern free market was created around the political demands of market liberals and enforced by **the state**. Despite the claims of liberals that the market is naturally occurring and, therefore, non-utopian, the model is essentially **socially constructed** and **ideologically driven**. It is utopian since it is based on a desire to produce purely rational market transactions in an often irrational world. It is ideological in that it privileges entrepreneurs over other social groups and establishes them as an **'elite'** group.

Challenges to Economic Liberalism

The influence of this type of **'economic liberalism'** prevailed in general terms in many Western societies up to the early 20th century when the economist, John Maynard Keynes, in *The General Theory of Employment, Interest and Money* (1936), developed a theory that challenged liberalism as the dominant economic framework for capitalist economics. At the core of his theory was a challenge to the prevailing orthodoxy of the time that full employment was a naturally occurring order, which was apparently undergoing a temporary period of disruption in the **Great Depression** of the 1930s in the United States (US), with similar developments in Britain and elsewhere in the Western world. Unless direct and significant governmental intervention occurred, he claimed, chronic episodic unemployment would persist and would result in mass long-term unemployment, which would inevitably destroy future economic growth in capitalist economies.

These claims took on significant political appeal in such times of economic hardship. They greatly influenced the creation of President Franklin Roosevelt's 'New Deal' programme in the United States in the 1930s, which improved the standard of living for many poor Americans (Timmins, 2001). In Britain they underpinned the 1944 White Paper on Employment Policy, advocating a commitment to full employment as a government aim:

"[This] can be seen as the most important single event in the construction of the British welfare state achieved by successive British governments in the 1940s [and] signalled the dawn of a new collectivist age with an active interventionist government at its heart" (Pratt, 2006: 11).

Thus, the idea that it should be the role of government to advance citizen welfare became widely accepted.

However, significant circumstances have led to what some have described as a 'capitalist crisis' over the last 30 years or so, which has heralded something of a revival of classical liberalism in the form of **'neo-liberalism'**.

Neo-Liberal Approaches to Welfare

'Neo-liberalism' is a term most readily used by its critics, but describes a set of social and economic policies whose influence has become widespread since the mid-1970s in Western democracies. The post-war productivity boom and its attendant **political consensus** had given way alongside a collapse of the **Bretton Woods** system of fixed exchange rates, which had previously ensured free and ordered trading relationships between liberal states. Commodity prices rocketed, especially for oil, and rapid technological change, coupled with deliberate government policy from 1979 on, ensured widespread **de-industrialisation**. Such events created the conditions for the introduction of new policy prescriptions distinct from the prevailing orthodoxy, which was increasingly being viewed as unable to cater for the rapidly changing economies of the time.

Instead of a new set of policy prescriptions, however, governments in Britain and the United States in particular have reasserted a somewhat newer version of an older and largely discredited one. Whereas its predecessors had advocated the market model for the production of goods and services, this newer brand extends market relations into all aspects of social life, including social policy and individual behaviour. Neo-liberals speak of **'market societies'** rather than 'market economies'. Like its predecessor, though, it is both a philosophical as well as economic (and, therefore, political) set of beliefs.

The main tenets of neo-liberalism as relevant to social policy include the following:

- **Reducing public expenditure on public goods and social services:** This includes state benefit provision, education and health care. Reducing and, in some cases, eliminating state benefits for those considered to be the

'undeserving poor' who have become part of a **'culture of dependency'**, no longer self-reliant and engaging in rational market transactions (see Scott, **Chapter 5**). Reducing state provision for public goods such as housing provision, transport and so on.

- **Industry deregulation:** Reducing government regulation of industry in all areas that may impact on profit maximisation, including controls on **monopolisation**, pollution, workers' terms and conditions and health and safety.

- **Privatisation:** The wholesale jettisoning of state-owned industries, goods and services and the partial jettisoning of welfare to private investors in an attempt to have them run subject to market forces and rational efficiency. The effect of this is to greatly concentrate wealth in a relatively small band of worldwide investors and shareholders and often to increase prices for goods and services previously politically accountable. Also, to create public costs where none previously existed, as is the case with the water supply and toll bridges and subcontracting of some welfare services in the UK.

- **Redefinition of notions of 'social problems' as problems for individuals:** Notions of **'rights'** and **'responsibilities'** become couched in legal and political terms, rather than automatic rights to welfare. In return for **civil rights**, individuals should take responsibility for their own predicaments and finding their own solutions. Blame is attached to those who do not (or, indeed, cannot) do so. Social justice is an illusory and normative concept and cannot be achieved by interventionist means. Welfare states should only remain in a residual form providing minimum assistance for those who simply cannot compete in the market – the **'deserving poor'**. Poverty is also seen as a result of the non-entrepreneurial and, therefore, irrational behaviour of the poor, which is transmitted generationally rather than through structural inequalities (this is explored further in Scott, **Chapter 5**).

- **View of the state:** Marquand (1987) claims that the single most significant departure neo-liberalism made from its predecessors is contained in its rejection of the state as inherently neutral and competent. The problem of 'excessive' government intervention, commonly labelled as 'big government', has become much more pronounced than market failure, for which it was originally meant to compensate.

Pause for thought
- For each aspect of neo-liberalism stated above, can you think of how it impacts on modern welfare provision?

Whilst neo-liberalism rarely exists in any 'pure' form, its influence has been felt on a global scale due to its adoption by liberal democratic governments and powerful financial institutions like the **International Monetary Fund (IMF)** and the **World Bank**. It is evident in the so-called **'Washington Consensus'**, which refers to the neo-liberal international policy agenda for Latin American aid as subscribed to by Western liberal states, including Britain. Arguably, New Labour has been significantly influenced by its terms, concepts and values and has jettisoned much of the social democratic principles on which it was founded. It is to this latter set of beliefs that we now turn.

Social Democracy

Social democracy is a political philosophy that spans a range of ideas and approaches. It partly emerged in the late 19th century from **'reformist' socialists** who believed that the transition to a socialist society could be achieved through democratic evolutionary means, rather than the revolutionary method advocated by classical Marxists. For others, though, social democracy meant not **socialism** as such, but a more 'humane', managed and regulated capitalism. It advocates gradual political, governmental and legislative reform of the capitalist system in order to compensate for the worst excesses of the free market economy. To this end, social democrats campaigned for the achievement of social and economic goals, such as the equitable distribution of wealth, income and **'life chances'** – goals that would have to be achieved through deliberate and direct state intervention on an otherwise disinterested economy.

Central to the achievement of these ends was the creation in the years immediately following World War II of the **welfare state**, which was founded on so-called social democratic principles (see Law, **Chapter 3**).

- First of these is the principle of **freedom**. Individuals should enjoy freedom at the personal, socio-political and cultural levels, which means that they should be free to make their own informed choices, to access basic standards of welfare, education and employment and be free from discrimination, abuse and maltreatment.

- Second are principles of **equality** and **social justice**, which should guarantee equality of opportunity for all regardless of level of ability and degree of disadvantage.

- Third is the concept of **solidarity**, which means 'unity' or 'togetherness'. It promotes collective action based on notions of duty to, unity with, and compassion for, the victims of injustice and inequality.

Social democrats are resolute in their defence of civil rights as enshrined in **representative democracies**. They claim that principles of political democracy, such as universal suffrage, should be extended to include social and economic democratic principles, such as equal rights to education, health care, adequate employment terms and conditions and state benefits, where necessary. Assuming that the state can act as a neutral arbiter providing for the regulation of industry and equitable distribution of wealth and income, they encourage extensive active state intervention to provide for the common welfare.

Key Principles of Social Democracy

In general, then, Social Democrats support:

- Regulatory systems over public and private industries designed to protect the interests of workers and consumers. Examples might include health and safety initiatives and controls on pollution.

- An extensive and universally available system of social security, designed to counter the worst excesses of capitalist economies, such as low pay and unemployment.

- Government-owned or subsidised programmes in fields such as industry, provision of goods and services and education, health care and child care for all citizens.

- High rates of government expenditure funded by moderately high taxation based on ability to pay, i.e. progressive taxation.

Pause for thought
The British Labour Party (now 'New Labour') was arguably founded on social democratic principles. Think of these various principles as outlined above.

- To what extent do you think New Labour has moved away from 'Old' Labour values?

The Third Way – 'New' Social Democracy?

In recent times, Prime Minister Tony Blair has frequently referred to his search for a 'third way' in British politics between capitalism and socialism. This is presented as a necessary response to the "demand for a new politics" in the wake of the "failed pasts" of the pro-state and anti-market left and the pro-market and anti-state right. Blair's particular version is laid out thus:

> "The Third Way is a serious reappraisal of social democracy, reaching deep into the values of the Left to develop radically new approaches [based on the values of] democracy, liberty, justice, mutual obligation, and internationalism" (Blair, 1997: 1).

The Sociology professor, Anthony Giddens, whose work has influenced New Labour thinking, provided something of a theoretical backdrop to Blair's ideas. He makes the claim that:

> "No one has any alternatives to capitalism – the arguments that remain concern how far, and in what ways, capitalism should be governed and regulated" (Giddens, 1998: 26, 44).

Thus he declares the death of socialism and makes redundant 'old' social democracy. For both Blair and Giddens, the term, 'the Third Way', is used to describe a *reformed* version of social democracy in the face of increased **globalisation** of the market, which, they assume, necessitates reform toward the **'enterprise society'** – one where welfare is tied to the needs of economic competitiveness.

Accordingly, central to the presupposed need for a newer version of social democracy is the need to "modernise" welfare by tying it to paid work (Blair, 1997). This would not dismantle the welfare state but reform it "based on a new contract between citizen and state" (Blair, 1998: v). This revaluation of the role of the state in welfare Giddens refers to as the "social investment state" (Giddens, 1998: 117) where the state hires out welfare services to private agencies and "takes on an enabling function, rather than the mass provider that characterised the social democratic state" (Ferguson *et al*, 2002: 167). Most notable here is the similarity with neo-liberal principles and policies, leading many to interprete the Third Way as significantly closer to the Thatcherite New Right than 'Old' Labour left (Jones and Novak, 1999; Callinicos, 2000; Ferguson, Lavalette and Mooney, 2002).

Therefore, although New Labour has been popularly associated with the term, third way, the concept itself lacks credence as a distinct theoretical category. In any case, some analysts have noted their associations with other, older theories stemming from the academic discipline of sociology.

New Labour and 'Old' Functionalism

Many of the ideological terms and concepts used by New Labour have been based on their self-proclaimed aim of creating a society based on the maxim "fair is efficient" (Brown, 1994). Prior to the 1997 General Election victory, this was to be brought about through the 'stakeholding economy' built on competitiveness, efficiency and profitability, entwined with "freedom" and "choice" (Thompson, 1996: 42). This not only signalled New Labour's sympathies with the neo-liberal ideas adopted by the two previous Conservative administrations (as noted above), but was significantly reminiscent of arguments emanating from largely discredited theories initially advanced by North American **functionalist** sociologists in the years between the 1940s and 1960s (Prideaux, 2005).

An examination of New Labour rhetoric provides useful comparisons with the language used in functionalist theories (Prideaux, 2005). New Labour's apparent acceptance of terms such as efficiency, competition and the market economy implies that they also accept the inequalities in terms of distribution of wealth, income and life chances that go along with such **stratified** societies (see Law and Law, **Chapter 4**). Back in 1945, the structural functionalists, Kingsley Davis and Wilbert E. Moore similarly proclaimed that stratification was an inevitable, even essential, characteristic of modern society (Davis and Moore, 1967), since through this system of structured inequality ordered societies could efficiently 'allocate' position and 'motivate' its individual members.

New Labour's focus on equality of 'opportunity' as opposed to an equality of 'outcome' (i.e. wealth, income, life chances and so on), betrays an apparent acceptance of inequality and a stratified society. Their stated aim is to create a **'meritocracy'** – a model of society that rewards effort and a honing of talent that takes the form of a competitively functional hierarchy motivated by 'aspiration'. This, too , is reminiscent of the functionalist concepts advanced by the US sociologist, Robert K. Merton (1968), who argued that stratification promotes individual aspiration through the provision of opportunities to be upwardly socially mobile. The French sociologist, Emilé Durkheim (1858-1917), shared these premises when he asserted that human fulfilment can be found through finding one's 'niche' in the **division of labour** characteristic of labour markets in complex industrial societies (Durkheim, 1933).

Notably, this focus on equality of opportunity rather than outcome betrays another aspect of New Labour's view on welfare. The redistribution of wealth, for example, would take the form of the allocation of resources so as to provide 'opportunity' for all. Gone would be any commitment to redistribute financial resources to the poor, since available resources would be ploughed into helping individuals get back into the labour market. Gordon Brown, when Shadow Chancellor, said as much when he declared that the welfare state should, and could, be reorganised to provide "pathways" out of unemployment, poverty and, ultimately, crime (1994: 4-5). This strategy of government providing the means for individuals to meet their "aspirations" has the by-product of reorganising welfare so that many individuals are removed from welfare provision and into work (see Scott, **Chapter 5**). Again, this echoes Merton's (1968) prescription for the use of 'governmental avenues' as a way out of 'functional failure'.

New Labour and 'New' Functionalism

Etzioni and Communitarianism

Amitai Etzioni (1998) has more recently resurrected and further developed other functionalist notions and ways of thinking. In *The Essential Communitarian Reader* (1998), for instance, he attempts to explain how modern society can regain what he sees as a lost cohesion and morality. Elsewhere, he advocates that social equilibrium can be restored through a unique blending of some elements in "tradition (order based on virtues) with elements of modernity (well protected autonomy)" (Etzioni, 1997: xviii). Indeed, he goes on to argue that theses elements are required in order to "restore balance between individual rights and social responsibilities" (Etzioni, 1998: x).

Modern day social relations have 'gone wrong' for Etzioni, which has major implications for our understanding of modern welfare. In *The New Golden Rule* (1997), he yearns after the 'social ideal' of 1950s America when, he argues, core values "were relatively widely shared and strongly endorsed" and so helped to promote a situation where members "of society had a strong sense of duty to their families, communities and society" (1997: 61) as a whole. Stable social relations were generated through morality and a "common sense order" (1997: 61). Etzioni (1997: 65) enthuses over this past society, where:

> "There prevailed an overarching sense of obligation, which has since been replaced by a rising sense of entitlement and a growing tendency to shirk social responsibilities."

To establish the means through which this erosion of society can be reversed, Etzioni re-emphasises the need to amend the existing imbalance within society. This can be done through the propagation of a renewed, suitably modernised moral education (Etzioni, 1995: 15). With the necessary revival of the highly functional institutions of family, school, neighbourhood and community, this moral education would start with the reassertion of family values and subsequently continue through the support, and reiteration, given during formal education and future life in a vibrant communal atmosphere.

Such a society would promote a sense of mutual responsibility where community members would "gently chastise those who violate shared moral norms and express approbation for those who abide by them" (Etzioni, 1995: ix). Interestingly, Etzioni cites the examples of Scotland and Wales which, for him, are two countries that have already managed to embrace the **communitarian** ethic!

Communitarianism Apparent in New Labour Welfarism

Etzioni's communitarian rhetoric can be seen to influence New Labour's renewed emphasis on community and their reliance on work in terms of satisfying individual aspiration and as the main means toward social inclusion. However, as well as **'New Deal'** initiatives offering (limited) financial incentives to come off welfare and into work, they are ensconced in terminology that has undoubtedly moral underpinnings reminiscent of Etzioni's analysis of previously implemented North American examples in social engineering.

Examples include the constantly reoccurring rhetorical themes of 'education/re-education', 'community spirit', 'mutual' and 'individual' obligation', 'responsibility', 'self-reliance' and 'social exclusion' (Levitas, 2005). In return for state provision of 'opportunities' in an increasingly 'meritocratic' society, 'dysfunctional' individuals (and communities) are seen as duty bound to cooperate by taking up their 'responsibilities' as well as their rights.

Prideaux (2001) notes how New Labour's general policy direction appears firmly tied to 'new communitarianism'. This is evident in the original but prevailing New Labour concept of the 'stakeholder society' and its invitation to individuals to take an active 'stake' in a society or community (as if the problem was that they had previously simply not thought to do so). It also influences the underlying principles of New Labour's project concerning a 'partnership' between people, communities and government. Lastly, the 'moral judgementalism' of Etzioni and New Labour is apparent and Levitas (2005) particularly notes the prominence given to the twin concepts of 'family' and 'community' as sites for learning and social control.

It is these communitarian emphases upon family, community, duty, obligation and responsibility, then, that underpin New Labour's **welfarism**. This approach stands in sharp contrast to our next theory of welfare – **Marxism**.

Marxism and Welfare

Marxism adopts a 'totalising' theory of society, which is to say that it views components of capitalist society as contributing to, and shaped by, the *whole* of the capitalist system. This applied to social policy and social welfare means that we cannot understand these as autonomous spheres of activity. Rather, we must locate them within the totality of an integrated, coordinated and functioning capitalist system. In order for us to analyse welfare from a Marxist perspective, then, it would be prudent to consider some of the key relevant aspects of Marx's critique of the capitalist system. Central to this is Marx's focus on class struggle (see Law and Law, **Chapter 4**).

The Class Struggle

For Marx, exploitative class relations are the key to understanding any society:

> "The history of all hitherto existing society is the history of class struggle" (Marx and Engels, 1848 [1973]: 1).

The **class struggle** under capitalism comes from the fact that the ruling class – the owners of the **means of production** (factories, machinery and resources) or **bourgeoisie** – exploit the wage labour of the subject class – the non-owners or proletariat (the working class). Under previous **modes of production**, such as slavery or feudalism, exploitation was visible and often physical. Under capitalism, however, the worker is free out with the terms of the labour contract. S/he is not subjugated to the capitalist in the way the slave is to the master, or the serf to the lord. Exploitation is economic and takes the form of **'wage slavery'**, since the worker does not own the means of production:

> "The silent compulsion of economic relations sets the seal on the domination of
> the capitalist over the worker" (Marx, 1867 [1976]: 899).

The vast majority of workers who lack the will, resources or opportunities to be self-employed are forced to work for those who control the means of production and, therefore, adhere to terms and conditions set by employers. Since capitalist employers are driven by the maxim of profit maximisation, they force workers to work longer than is necessary to meet their wages, thus creating **'surplus value'** (profit) from their labour. Since this relationship appears to be voluntary, its exploitative nature, no matter how real, remains concealed.

The Role of Ideology

For Marxists, this class struggle and the role of ideology are crucial to our understanding of modern welfare provision. If people have, since the end of primitive tribes, lived in class societies, then this means that it is important for the ruling class to persuade the direct producers (workers) to accept their situation. This acceptance can take a variety of forms. It can be simply *resignation*, based on the belief that the ruling class is too strong to overthrow. This type of resignation may explain, to some extent at least, modern voter 'apathy' in vast sections of the British electorate. It can, however, be the positive belief that the present social order is just, legitimate and even desirable. The Italian Communist, Antonio Gramsci, labelled this form of persuasion 'hegemony'; a situation where:

> "[...] Dominant groups in society, including fundamentally but not exclusively
> the ruling class, maintain their dominance by securing the 'spontaneous
> consent' of subordinate groups, including the working class, through the
> negotiated construction of a political and ideological consensus which
> incorporates both dominant and dominated groups" (in Strinati, 1995: 165).

In either case, the direct producers' beliefs play a crucial role in their acceptance of the status quo.

Thus, ideologies themselves (with the obvious exception of Marxism!) in this way keep the existing mode of production going by persuading people to form mistaken views about the nature of society. Marx believes that ruling class ideologies prevail among the masses as a result of the economic and political power of the ruling class:

> "The ideas of the ruling class are in every epoch the ruling ideas: i.e. the class
> which is the prevailing material force of society is at the same time its ruling

intellectual force" (Marx and Engels, 1845 [1968]: 61).

It follows then that the systematic beliefs that people have about the world, ideologies, can only be understood from the standpoint of their role in the class struggle (Callinicos, 1983). In other words, they have to be analysed in terms of their contribution to sustaining or undermining the prevailing relations of production. We must apply the same conditions to a Marxist analysis of welfare.

Since capitalism is a uniquely dynamic mode of production dependent on the productive capacities of its workforce, it requires them to be increasingly educated, trained and healthy. To this extent, then, capitalism 'needs' adequate welfare provision. From another standpoint though, we could interpret welfare as a political concession to working class power. The creation of the welfare state in the immediate aftermath of World War II may have been an attempt to maintain the status quo against revolutionary fervour, given the experience of workers in the depressions of the 1930s and participation in a bloody world war. The subsequent post-war political consensus could be viewed as a concerted attempt to reconstruct the capitalist infrastructure – the reproduction of capital – and the morale of a dejected workforce – the reproduction of class relations. Increased public expenditure provided for investment in the building and resourcing of hospitals, schools, roads and railways and the expansion of welfare provision served to pacify the masses. Developments since 1979 could be viewed as an attempt by capital to reassert dominance over labour. It should be no surprise, then, that welfare provision should be cut from then on and indeed under New Labour, who have to all intents and purposes extended many political initiatives undertaken under the Thatcher led Conservative governments. Either way, welfare state provision bears the hallmark of capitalist class relations.

Moreover, welfare provision in capitalist societies provides much needed ideological 'legitimation' for a system that produces many obvious downsides. The exploitative nature of capitalist relations of production, although often hidden, is disguised or compensated for if the system can be perceived to offer 'free' benefits to all. However, the dominant values expressed in specific welfare policies and who they provide for, act to transmit dominant ruling ideas to the masses. In other words, to determine how we think about welfare and related social issues and how we behave. The reorganisation of welfare under New Labour to provide 'incentives' for the unemployed to work and the 'transference' of benefits from the 'undeserving' to the 'deserving poor' carry with them definite value systems relating to how people should live and behave. If it is incumbent on capital to reduce the 'welfare burden' then these measures do so under the veneer that there are those who do not deserve benefits in the first place – in tabloid newspaper terms, welfare 'cheats' and 'scroungers'. This way welfare provision is used for the purposes of **social control**.

The fact that the social institution of the family is a central plank of the sustenance, reproduction and regeneration of future capitalist labour forces has not escaped the attention of capital. This, arguably, explains the growth of family related social policy over the course of the 20th century, but with ever more fervour under the Conservative and New Labour administrations of recent years, which have viewed recent developments, such as the growth of lone parenthood, as threatening the very fabric of the family as a 'cornerstone' of civil society (Lavalette and Mooney, 1999). The growth of welfare provision in this area is not philanthropic, but rather meets what the Marxist historian, John Saville (1983: 11), calls the "social requirements of an increasingly complex industrial society."

Pause for thought

Marx claimed that human need could be met by the maxim, "from each according to ability, to each according to need."

- How do you think welfare would be organized in a society based on this idea?

Another group of theories that place significant emphasis on the relationship between family and welfare are known as 'feminist'.

Feminist Theories of Welfare

The post-war construction of the welfare state was based on the **nuclear family** model, which assumes that men are the primary breadwinners and women the primary caregivers (see Annetts, **Chapter 7**). It has to this extent been based on stereotypical and traditional notions of gender roles. This, along with significant social trends such as the massive expansion of women in the labour force, increases in the divorce rate and the accompanying growth in female lone parenthood, has had disproportionate impacts on women.

Social constructions of **'gender'** define masculinity and femininity, which vary over time and place. Here, we consider how gender relations profoundly shape the character of welfare states. This is evident in how gender – notions of masculinity and femininity – is interpreted in areas such as the **'sexual division of labour'**, **'compulsory heterosexuality'**, discourses and ideologies of **'citizenship'**, and 'motherhood'. In turn, the nature of policy provision and the welfare institutions created from it affect gender relations in a variety of ways. Indeed, a proper understanding of gender relations is not possible without an appreciation of welfare politics and policy, since states play a significant role in constituting gender relations. The interplay between the state, market, family and social class reinforces important aspects of gender differences (Bussemaker and Kersbergen, 1994).

The main analyses of gender have come from theorists known as feminists. Weedon (1987) defines feminism in the following way:

> "Feminism is a politics. It is a politics directed at changing existing power relations between men and women in society. These power relations structure all areas of life, the family, education and welfare, the worlds of work and politics, culture and leisure. They determine who does what and for whom, what we are and what we might become" (Weedon, 1987: 1).

To suppose that there is a singular, all-encompassing feminist approach to the study of social welfare would, however, be overly simplistic, indeed mistaken. Instead, Woodward (2006) prefers the plural term, 'feminisms', to describe the wide variety of perspectives in this area.

Types of Feminism

- **Liberal feminists** have tended to focus on achieving gender equality through the establishment of equal rights in public policy and legislation. They advocate reform of currently existing practices and institutions in order to achieve their goals.

- **Radical feminists** have focused on how welfare states and welfare provision are **'patriarchal'** – male -dominated. Welfare provision is simply another avenue through which male power over women is exercised. Women are oppressed by men through the use of gendered concepts, such as 'maternalism' – the assumption that mothers are natural caregivers, and 'compulsory heterosexuality' – the view that women are naturally subservient partners for men.

- **Socialist/Marxist feminism** combines the two branches of theory referred to in their titles. Arguably, classical Marxism failed to account for women's position in capitalist societies and this brand of feminism claims that the oppression and inequality that capitalism generates universally exploits women. They advocate revolutionary overthrow of capitalism rather than reform.

- **Black feminism** has openly challenged the (white) **ethnocentrism** apparent in welfare provision and its critiques and advances arguments based on notions of 'multiculturalism' and ethnic 'difference' (Lewis , Gewirtz and Clarke, 2000).

- **Postmodern feminists** do not see men and women as exclusive groups. Instead they highlight that women differ from each other as well as from men and are more likely to share common cultural experiences than a common material identity.

Pause for thought
- How would each type of feminism resolve problems of welfare provision, in your view?

However, despite a tension between how the various types of feminism, or feminisms, perceive issues such as equality and difference, the contributory factors to gender inequality and how to eradicate gender division, there are significant overlaps between them. These include:

- A primary focus on 'women's issues'.

- An examination of how welfare states adopt gendered definitions of 'social problems' and policy intervention.

- Analyses of differences between men and women and among women in terms of opportunities and outcome.

- Advocation of strategies for gender equality.

Another key overlap, in general terms, among feminist analyses of welfare is a varying focus in terms of the relationship between the welfare state and gender (Orloff, 1996). Despite an admission by many theorists that the welfare state has to some extent ameliorated some of the worst affects of gender inequality, the most prominent contention is that the welfare state contributes in one way or another to the *social reproduction* of gender hierarchies.

The Social Reproduction of Gender Hierarchies

Social policies regulate gender relations and contribute to the social reproduction of gender inequality through a variety of mechanisms (Orloff, 1996). As modern welfare states emerged they extended the scope of patriarchal domination from the private and personal level to the public and structural. Feminists have been among the fiercest critics of the **Beveridgean** male breadwinner model of welfare. In particular, socialist feminists have employed neo-Marxist theories of the state to claim that welfare states have contributed to the reproduction of patriarchal capitalism. Through an assessment of social welfare policies, we can see how the state organises domestic life through the gendered model it has adopted since Beveridge. These feminists claim that state support provides a microcosm of socially controlled gender relations in wider society and, as such, reflect patterns of inequality in women's labour market participation, the **'feminisation of poverty'**, the domestic division of labour and family and household forms (Millar and Glendinning, 1987).

In this model, key mechanisms for the maintenance of gender hierarchy are identified, including:

- **Gendered divisions of formal and informal labour**, with women still concentrated in 'women's jobs' and responsible for caregiving and domestic labour as well as human reproduction.

- **The family wage system**, in which men's relatively superior wages, terms and conditions are justified partly in terms of their supposed responsibility for the support of dependent wives and children.

- **Women's continued economic dependence** on men due to low wages and domestic commitments.

- **Traditional marriage and prevailing notions of motherhood**, where women are 'given away' to a husband by their father, for example, who they promise to "love, honour and *obey*", and assume the principal or entire caregiving role for dependent children.

- **Compulsory heterosexuality**, in which women are perceived as being 'naturally' subservient partners for men.

For Abramovitz (1988) all of these mechanisms operate together by means of a "family ethic" that serves to present gender hierarchies as 'normal' for women, in much the same way as the **Calvinistic 'work ethic'** presents paid work as normal and dutiful for men. However, whilst these mechanisms contribute to the reproduction of systemic gender relations, Lister (1992) notes that welfare states can also use them to provide critical support to those suffering from the family "failures" they imply.

The essence of welfare provision has been based on the assumption that *women bear ultimate responsibility for care work,* the continuing dependence of society on women's (paid and unpaid care work) and the ways in which welfare states reward care work less well than the paid labour that characterizes men's lives (Land and Rose, 1985; see also Cavaye, **Chapter 11**). These various mechanisms also serve to ensure women's exclusion from *political power* (Nelson, 1984).

The social reproduction analysts have tended to highlight the ways in which welfare states, through their regulatory or social-control practices, reinforced pre-existing (traditional) gender roles and relations. When explaining why the welfare state oppresses women, socialist feminists are united in viewing the Beveridgean welfare state as culpable. This was achieved via *three* means (Orloff, 1996):

1. Beveridge specified that married working women should pay reduced National Insurance contributions and, as a result, receive lower benefits. Beveridge established this rule on the grounds that the woman was being supported by the man, who was paid a **'family wage'**.

2. Beveridge made arrangements for married working women, if they chose to, to be exempted from paying National Insurance, which had the longer term effect of reducing their benefit entitlement. Although the married women's option was finally phased out in 1978, Land and Rose (1985) maintain that it will be well into the next century before the majority of married working women who work full-time will be covered by National Insurance.

3. Most importantly, feminists criticise Beveridge for assuming that the majority of women would abandon paid work to be financially supported by a male bread-winner upon getting married. This meant that if married/co-habiting women were deserted or became lone parents, they could only claim means-tested national assistance (now Income Support).

In a similar vein, Abel-Smith and Townsend (1965: 77) contend that "Beveridge made married women into social security dependents on a scale unequalled today by the vast majority of social security schemes in the world," and that Beveridge's insistence that married women should be regarded as dependents, rather than individuals, has reinforced resistance to reform. This continues to pose a problem in the modern British welfare state, since the Beveridgean model still underpins contemporary policy, if in modified form.

More recently, analysts have looked at how state practices themselves constitute gender stereotypes. The patriarchal construction of gendered citizenship and assumptions of male 'independence' based on paid work and female 'dependence' create gender-differentiated social provision (Lister, 1992). Full rights of citizenship can only be secured through formal employment, which favours those able to pursue careers. Additional domestic responsibilities tend to preclude many women from doing so.

Others note how state provision, such as welfare benefits, produces gender differentiation. Men's benefit provision is based on their role as workers, whereas women's benefits are primarily targeted at their roles as wives and mothers before that of workers. This allows Bryson (1992) to refer to a "men's welfare state" and a "women's welfare state", claiming that *significant* inequality of provision accompanies the gender differentiation.

All in all, these various processes and mechanisms are viewed as reproducing hierarchical gender relations. Any advancement to women's material position is to be seen as relative to men's and in the context of reinforcing women's status as wives, mothers and primary caregivers.

Conclusion – Where to From Here for Welfare Theories?

It should be clear by now that theories of welfare all attempt to explain, as well as describe, some fundamental aspects of human nature, human need, the relationship between the state and the individual and the role of the state in welfare provision. They also prescribe how societies and economies should be organised. All do so to varying extents and with varying degrees of success, but all, at least in some way, contribute to the numerous debates – past, present and, no doubt, future – around social care, health and welfare. It will also be apparent by now that particular theoretical ideas and concepts have come to the fore under different governments and that they often reappear in modified, even disguised, forms. Most theories do *not* stand as entirely separate entities from others as has been noted above. Rather, theoretical ideas and concepts often merge at various points. One exception to this is Marxism, which distinctively does *not* merge with or embrace other approaches (though Marxist feminism may give an appearance otherwise).

One more recently developing group of theories that have (arguably) not had a fair hearing here are known as **postmodernists**. They are merely referred to here since they propose a significant departure from the focus of the theories presented above.

Although 'postmodernism' is essentially an ambiguous and elusive concept, with multifaceted aspects that make it difficult, if not impossible, to define, they do pose challenges for the future direction of welfare theory (Widdowson, 2006).

Postmodernists such as Foucault (2001) reject notions of ultimate principles, such as *state welfare, equitable distribution of wealth, human need* and *human progress*. They reject optimistic notions of there being any scientific, philosophical, or religious truth that explains the world and advocate prescriptions for progress towards a 'better world'. Their influence was late to arrive with regard to welfare theories and indeed their impact may already be redundant. However, at the time of writing, with New Labour entering a period of near or imminent transition at the level of party leader, it would appear that there are no real reasons to expect significant ideological change that would necessitate the development of new theoretical constructs to explain that which can be explained perfectly well through the use of 'old' ones. Whilst *ideologies* of welfare prevail, *theories* of welfare are needed to explain them.

Further Reading

Alcock, P., Erskine, A. and May, M. (2003) *The Student's Companion to Social Policy*, Oxford, Blackwell Publishing

Ferguson, I., Lavalette, M. and Mooney, G. (2002) *Rethinking Welfare*, London, Sage

Lavalette, M. and Pratt, A. (eds .) (2006) *Social Policy: Theories, Concepts and Issues*, London, Sage

Useful Websites

Spicker, P. (2006) *An introduction to social policy*, Aberdeen, The Robert Gordon University: http://www2.rgu.ac.uk/publicpolicy/introduction

Internet for Social Policy: http://www.vts.intute.ac.uk/he/tutorial/social-policy

Social Policy Virtual Library: http://staff.bath.ac.uk/hsstp/world3-menu.htm

Bibliography

Abel-Smith, B. and Townsend, P. (1965) *The Poor and the Poorest: a new analysis of the Ministry of Labour's Family Expenditure Surveys of 1953–4 and 1960*, Occasional Papers on Social Administration, No.17, Bell, 1965

Abramowitz, M. (1988) *Regulating the lives of women: Social welfare policy from colonial times to the present*, Boston, MA, South End Press

Alcock, P., Erskine, A. and May, M. (2003) *The Student's Companion to Social Policy*, Oxford, Blackwell Publishing

Bean, P., Ferris, J. and Whynes, D. (eds.) (1985) *In Defence of Welfare*, London, Tavistock

Bendix, R. and Lipset, S.M. (eds.) (1967) *Class, Status and Power* (2nd edition), London, Routledge & Kegan Paul

Blair, T. (1997) *The Modernisation of Britain*, Speech to the 1997 Trade Union Congress, London, TUC

Blair, T. (1998) *The Third Way*, London, The Fabian Society

Brown, G. (1994) *Fair is Efficient – A Socialist Agenda For Fairness*, London, Fabian Tract, No. 563

Bryson, L. (1992) *Welfare and the State*, London, Macmillan

Bussemaker, J. and Kersbergen, K. (1994) 'Gender and Welfare States: Some Theoretical Reflections', in Sainsbury, D. (ed.) (1994) *Gendering Welfare States*, London, Sage

Callinicos, A. (1983) *The Revolutionary Ideas of Karl Marx*, London, Bookmarks

Callinicos, A. (2000) *Equality*, Cambridge, Polity Press

Davis, K. and Moore, W.E. (1967) 'Some Principles of Stratification', in Bendix, R. and Lipset, S.M. (eds.) (1967) *Class, Status and Power* (2nd edition), London , Routledge & Kegan Paul

Durkheim, E. (1933) *The Division of Labor in Society*, translated by George Simpson, New York, NY, The Free Press

Etzioni, A. (ed.) (1998) *The Essential Communitarian Reader*, Oxford, Rowman and Butterfield Publishers Inc

Etzioni, A. (1997) *The New Golden Rule: community and morality in a democratic society*, London, Profile Books Ltd

Etzioni, A. (1995) *The Spirit of Community. Rights responsibilities and the communitarian agenda*, London, Fontana Press

Ferguson, I., Lavalette, M. and Mooney, G. (2002) *Rethinking Welfare*, London, Sage

Foucault, M. (2001) *Madness and Civilisation*, London, Routledge

Fraser, N. and Nicholson, L.J. (1990) 'Social Criticism without Philosophy: An Encounter between Feminism and Postmodernism', in Nicholson, L.J. (ed.) (1990) *Feminism/Postmodernism*, New York, NY, Routledge Chapman & Hall, Inc

Giddens, A. (1998) *The Third Way*, Cambridge, Polity Press

Gramsci, A. (1971) *Selections from the Prison Notebooks*, London , Lawrence and Wishart

Hayek, F.A. (1996) *Individualism and Economic Order*, Chicago, University of Chicago Press

Heron, E. (2001) 'Etzioni's Spirit of Communitarianism: Community Values and Welfare Realities in Blair's Britain', in *Social Policy Review*, 13

Jones, C. and Novak, T. (1999) *Poverty, Welfare and the Disciplinary State*, London, Routledge

Keynes, J.M. (1936) *The General Theory of Employment, Interest and Money*, Cambridge, Cambridge University Press

Land, H. and Rose, H. (1985) 'Compulsory Altruism for Some or an Altruistic Society for All?', in Bean, P., Ferris, J. and Whynes, D. (eds.) (1985) *In Defense of Welfare*, London, Tavistock

Lavalette, M. and Mooney, G. (1999) 'New Labour: New Moralism: The Welfare Politics and Ideology of New Labour Under Blair', *International Socialism*, 85

Lavalette, M. and Mooney, G. (eds.) (2000) *Class Struggle and Social Welfare*, London, Routledge

Lavalette, M. and Pratt, A. (eds.) (2006) *Social Policy: Theories, Concepts and Issues*, 3rd Edition, London, Sage

Levitas, R. (2005) *The Inclusive Society? Social Exclusion and New Labour* (2nd edition), London, Palgrave Macmillan

Lewis, G., Gewirtz, S. and Clarke, J. (eds.) (2000) *Rethinking Social Policy*, London, Sage

Lister, R. (1992) *Women's Economic Dependency and Social Security*, Manchester, Equal Opportunities Commission

Loney, M. *et al* (eds.) (1983) *Social Policy and Social Welfare*, Milton Keynes, Open University Press

Marx, K. (1844 [1975]) *Early Writings*, Harmondsworth, Penguin

Marx, K. (1844 [1975]) 'Economic and Philosophical Manuscripts', in Marx, K. (1844 [1975]) *Early Writings*, Harmondsworth, Penguin

Marx, K. (1867 [1976]) *Capital*, Volume 1, Harmondsworth, Penguin

Marx, K. (1894 [1974]) *Capital*, Volume 3, Harmondsworth, Penguin

Marx, K. and Engels, F. (1848 [1973]) 'The Communist Manifesto', in Marx, K. (1848 [1973]) *The Revolutions of 1848*, Harmondsworth, Penguin

Marx, K. (1848 [1973]) *The Revolutions of 1848*, Harmondsworth, Penguin

Marx, K. and Engels, F. (1845 [1968]) *The German Ideology*, Moscow, Progress Publishers

Marquand, D. (1987) 'Beyond Social Democracy', in *The Political Quarterly*, Volume 58, Issue 3

Merton, R.K. (1968) *Social Theory and Social Structure* (Enlarged Edition), New York, NY, Free Press

Millar, J. and Glendinning, C. (1987) *Woman and Poverty in Britain*, Brighton, Wheatsheaf

Nelson, B. (1984) 'Women's poverty and women's citizenship: some political consequences of economic marginality', in *Signs*, Vol. 10, No. 21

Nicholson, L.J. (ed.) (1990) *Feminism/Postmodernism*, New York, NY, Routledge Chapman & Hall, Inc

Orloff, A. (1996) 'Gender and the Welfare State', in *Annual Review of Sociology*, Vol. 22

Pratt, A. (2006) 'Neo-liberalism and Social Policy', in Lavalette, M. and Pratt, A. (eds.) (2006) *Social Policy: Theories, Concepts and Issues*, 3rd edition, London, Sage

Prideaux, S. (2005) *Not So New Labour*, Bristol, The Policy Press

Prideaux, S. (2001) 'New Labour, Old Functionalism: The Underlying Contradictions of Welfare Reform in the US and the UK', in *Social Policy and Administration*, Vol. 35, No. 1 (March)

Sainsbury, D. (ed.) (1994) *Gendering Welfare States*, London, Sage

Saville, J. (1983) 'The Origins of the Welfare State', in Loney, M. *et al* (eds.) (1983) *Social Policy and Social Welfare*, Milton Keynes, Open University Press

Smith, A. (1776) *An Inquiry into the Nature and Causes of The Wealth Of Nations*, London, Methuen

Strinati, D. (1995) *An Introduction to Studying Popular Culture*, London, Routledge

Thompson, N. (1996) *Political Economy and the Labour Party*, London, UCL Press

Timmins, N. (2001) *The Five Giants: A Biography of the Welfare State*, New York, NY, Harper Collins

Weedon, C. (1987) *Feminist Practice and Post-structural Theory*, Oxford, Blackwell

Widdowson, B. (2006) 'Cultural Turns, Post-structuralism and Social Policy in Social Policy: Theories, Concepts and Issues', in Lavalette, M. and Pratt, A. (eds.) (2006) *Social Policy: Theories, Concepts and Issues*, 3rd edition, London, Sage

Woodward, K. (2006) 'Feminist critiques of social policy', in Lavalette, M. and Pratt, A. (eds.) (2006) *Social Policy: Theories, Concepts and Issues*, 3rd Edition, London, Sage

Chapter 3

Evolution of the Welfare State in Scotland

Alex Law

Introduction

Justifiably or not, Scotland has acquired a reputation for being a caring society. Throughout its history this myth states that 'Scotland' has always taken care of the least fortunate members of the lower classes. The emergence of the **welfare state** in the 1940s and the Scottish Parliament in 1999 are sometimes seen as continuing a deep Scottish tradition of the collective provision of care and welfare. This is reflected across many of the different policy areas that are explored throughout this Book. Despite some continuity with the past, in the most fundamental ways the setting up of the welfare state in the 1940s represented a sharp break. Although the welfare state could be and has been criticised, for millions of working class people in Scotland it marked a radical improvement to what had gone before.

While you may be drawn to particular chapters in this book that are more directly relevant to your specialised area of practice-based training or study, it is essential that you can place your own interests in the wider historical context of how you arrived here in the first place. In other words, history matters to all students of social welfare and care. This chapter claims that an historical perspective on welfare and care in Scotland gives us some sense of why the bureaucratic, cumbersome, creaking welfare state that many of us experience on a regular, sometimes daily basis, has survived these past 60 years or so. What went before depended not on care and welfare as a *right* of being a British citizen. Instead, a confused parochial mess of middle class charity and mean-minded local parishes, also controlled by middle class ratepayers, saw the condition of poor working class people as a personal and moral failing on the part of the individual.

An historical approach, therefore, provides a crucial context for understanding some legacies of such thinking in theories of 'the underclass' (see Scott, **Chapter 5**). It also helps explain the continuing popularity of the idea that the state should fund and provide care and welfare support, delivered in an equitable way by qualified specialists across the board. This chapter, therefore, addresses the following:

1. It sets out the main *changes* in social care and welfare over the past century.

2. Despite the many changes that have taken place in welfare, it also looks at strong *continuities* in the provision of care and welfare services, some going back to at least the 19th century.

3. The continuity of deep social *divisions* in Scotland that welfare provision has been unable to alter fundamentally.

4. The view of the poor and the disadvantaged as a 'problem' to be *controlled* by welfare institutions.

5. Despite the fact that in the second part of the 20th century the state became the main welfare and care institution, other non-state organisations have also been historically involved in welfare functions.

In this respect, Scotland is no different from many other societies where the poor and other marginal groups have been frequently viewed as a social problem to be regulated and managed, first by their social 'betters' and later by qualified 'experts'. Yet the history of welfare provision in Scotland has certain features that are distinctive. At the heart of this has been the changing role played by the state. As we will see, the state operates at local, regional and national levels. Welfare services have also been provided by other organisations apart from the state, including private philanthropists, voluntary bodies and private businesses. As was highlighted by Tony Sweeney in **Chapter 2**, the exact mixture of state and non-state providers differs according to the prevailing historical circumstances and ideas, often about what is good for the economy, as well as the nature of care and welfare being provided, whether it be housing, health, education, social security, or the other areas of services covered by this Book.

Welfare in Scotland *before* the Welfare State

Despite romantic images of a pre-modern or feudal Scotland of happy, rural communities, clad in tartan and living high on the fat of the land through a self-supporting clan society, the poor were vulnerable to especially harsh treatment from their social superiors. From the 1570s onwards, unemployed labourers, the destitute and gypsies became subject to a series of legal measures that gradually grew into the **Scottish Poor Law** (Mitchison, 1974). A distinction was enshrined by these laws that would last well into the 20th century between the infirm, the sick, the insane, abandoned children and the elderly, who were deemed deserving of public support by local burghs, and the 'able-bodied', who were not. Parishes took care of those who could not care for themselves, if not quite from cradle to grave, at least from the **poorhouse** to a pauper's funeral. Parishes supported the old and the sick by providing pensions, placing or 'boarding' orphans and destitute children in respectable households, paying for the education of the poorest students, and burying paupers.

On the other hand, the 'able-bodied', a 19th century term, referred to those who were homeless or workless. Defined as 'vagrants' and 'beggars', they were forced into **serfdom** to work for manufacturers by the 1663 amendment to the Poor Law. This was added to in 1672 with a law that allowed local parishes to set up **workhouses**. Landlord power ensured that the poor and the needy had little in the way of legal rights that could be enforced to provide social care in times of hardship or difficulties. There was no legal recourse at all for unemployed labourers, who out of necessity turned to vagrancy and begging, which although illegal was tolerated in some parishes for a limited period. Where families depended on the incomes of waged labour that was set at or below subsistence-level, they could expect no additional support from parish funds.

As it evolved, relief for the poor was highly localised and voluntary (Mitchison, 1988). From another vantage point, the rural parish system of custom, tradition and hierarchy could be idealised by later reformers like Dr W.P. Allison:

> "In a perfectly simple, and at the same time educated and civilised state of society […] where all the high orders who are to give, and all the low orders who are to receive, are aware of their duties, and are known to one another, and, as long as the proprietors are resident, of charitable disposition, and attentive in their duties, th e burden may be sufficiently equalised among the former, and the benefits sufficiently secured to the latter, without the intervention of the law […]" (quoted in Campbell, 1985: 159).

Practices varied from parish to parish depending on the influence of the Kirk, local landowners, the judiciary and the 'middling sorts' in society. Not the least factor affecting poor relief was the level of taxation that wealthy landlords were prepared to pay to support local poor relief. Clan chiefs may have supported their tenants during poor harvests but local customs could vary greatly. Clan -based systems of social responsibility also came with the authoritarian powers for powerful landowners to impose cruel penalties on tenants under their jurisdiction, a system that went into sharp decline after the ill-fated rising of the Jacobites in 1745 led to the abolition of landowner privileges known as the 'heritable jurisdictions' (Davidson, 2003).

When a severe crisis crashed down on society, such as a bad harvest or a serious downturn in trade, the system of poor relief was put to a stern test. Usually , just about enough was done to ward off the social devastation of widespread famine. By the 19th century, however, a new set of principles, th ose of capitalist political economy, transformed more traditional ways of providing care for the needy (see Sweeney, **Chapter 2**). Although these ideas were of recent vintage, they were typically couched in terms of tradition, antiquity and an unchanging human nature. Political economy formed a rigidly dogmatic way of middle class thinking. It argued that no relief could be provided for the poor where it might contradict the now inviolable laws of the free market. In 1844, the Royal Commission into the Poor Law could claim that:

> "[T]he important distinction made by the poor laws of Scotland between the
> respective titles of able-bodied and impotent paupers, was held for centuries to
> be the distinguishing excellence of these laws" (Mitchison, 1988: 261).

The point was that the unemployed should not be supported by the rates levied on the parish because that would interfere with the efficiency and economy of market forces in setting wage levels and providing employment. On the other hand, those not involved in labour market competition like the elderly or the insane could be supported on a voluntary basis since that would have no effect on market efficiencies. Contrary to the myth of a caring, collectivist Scotland through the ages, the Scottish Poor Law took a much harsher approach to alleviating deprivation than the (slightly) more relaxed Poor Law system that operated in England.

Rights or Charity?

By then the nature of society had been transformed. The main labouring class in society had gone from that of a rural **peasantry** to that of the urban **proletariat.** As 18th and 19th century Scottish landlords tried to make agriculture more profitable, efficient and rational, a surplus labour force gravitated from the country into Scotland's towns to find waged employment, leaving the traditional forms of social solidarity and support structures behind them. Victorian reformers argued that Scotland had some of the worst urban slums in Britain. In cities like Glasgow indescribable misery was concentrated among the masses of impoverished communities. At the same time a new kind of individualism expected 'able-bodied' adults to support themselves and their families by their own efforts and not depend on public assistance. Individuals were forced to support themselves often at a miserly rate of income supposedly set by the impersonal workings of the market. The central issue was that of giving incentives to encourage individual self-help and punish individuals who became dependent on the parish by making the alternative to hard labour and poverty wages even worse.

In many areas charitable organisations were set up on a voluntary basis to assist particular causes. These included infirmaries, orphanages, district nursing and homes for 'fallen women', like the now notorious Magdalene Institutes (Mahood, 1989). Charities provided welfare support in highly arbitrary ways, often through religious bodies, and were choosy about the kind of 'creatures' they looked after (or rejected). They often seemed more intent on making judgements about the moral outlook of the poor and needy than in remedying deep-seated social iniquities. Middle class philanthropists kept the pressure on the Poor Law to keep to strict definitions of the 'unfortunate' poor and the 'degraded' poor, and to keep subsistence at levels low enough so that it would be seen as a call of last resort and would disabuse the 'idle' poor that they could get indiscriminate support from the state. Making personal claims on middle class run charities for help could seem like the final indignity and degrading act for many impoverished and helpless supplicants. Despite the glaring failings of humiliation, stigma and condescension for the poor, charity had the beneficial side-effect for the middle class who claimed that voluntary donations and good works allowed local rates, which were overwhelmingly borne by the middle class, to be abolished. It was also seen as morally uplifting by the middle class for the poor to call on charity than to depend on public assistance.

As well as appalling urban squalor, Scotland also had some of the worst rural poverty. Economies like the Highlands were so basic that they barely provided a subsistence level existence. Many communities were highly prone to famine. Such societies were close to famine in every decade down to the 1870s (Richards, 2000). During the 1846-1851 potato famine in the west Highlands and Islands, for example, the relief effort organised by voluntary bodies averted any repeat in Scotland of the mass starvation that took place in Ireland at the same time. It also helped to justify a new round of Clearances from the land, since it could not secure even the most basic welfare of rural communities. A new cycle was thus set in train of forcing rural populations to migrate to Scotland's urban centres, where they would find themselves the poorest of the poor.

With huge pools of unemployment being created by 'trade depressions' in the 1840s, the Kirk-led voluntary relief system was further threatened by the Great Disruption of 1843, when the Church of Scotland split into rival factions. In response, the Scottish Poor Law was reformed in 1845, the terms of which would remain well into the middle of the 20th century. Unlike the **English Poor Law**, before 1845 there was no legal entitlement for hardship support in Scotland and contributions were not compulsory but voluntarily collected by the church (Crowther, 1990). The 1845 Poor Law (Scotland) Act created new parish boards that were obliged to relieve the poor through setting local rates. Ratepayers, typically middle class owners of property, elected the parish boards and so had some influence over the level of the rates and the generosity or, more usually, the parsimony of poor relief. It was shown later that Scottish ratepayers constantly contributed much less per head of population to poor relief than their English counterparts (Crowther, 1990). A national Board of Supervision based in Edinburgh was also created to manage the system overall. Locally in the parishes, an Inspector of the Poor assessed the claims for poor relief.

Nor did the 1845 Scottish Poor Law resolve the tension between the statutory rights of the poor and the charitable discretion of the middle classes. Middle class groups in Scotland operated under the idea that harsher treatment of the 'profligate', the unemployed and the disabled would re-moralise them to become self-sufficient and industrious. Anything else would undermine respectable Christian values of work and moral order. The Reverend Thomas Chalmers of Glasgow continued a guerrilla campaign against the Poor Law on the basis that statutory relief was un-Christian and undermined personal independence and family responsibility. In 1909 a Royal Commission on the Poor Laws was divided on this question, with a 'majority report' accepting the force of the argument for voluntary efforts while a 'minority report' argued for a more systematic implementation of statutory care. As Ian Levitt (1988), an historian of social welfare in Scotland, put it, for the majority report:

> "Poverty was still grounded in a moral defect of character which, without the regulation of some social institution would destroy 'man's capacity for self-management'" (Levittt, 1988: 69).

Both sides of the argument struggled to balance the *positive* right to adequate welfare support and the *negative* right to individual liberty.

> "The majority had cloaked their concept of 'care' in the terminology of the 19th century – stigma, moral discrimination and paternalistic, middle class rule – and the minority their concern about a person's social development in the illiberality of a mechanistic bureaucracy" (Levitt, 1988: 70).

Pause for thought
- Do you think that the right balance can be struck in a welfare and care system that meets both the right to individual liberty and public intervention? Give examples for you answer.

No group in Scotland was more stigmatised and discriminated against than the Irish. As recent immigrants they suffered racist and religious indignities and lacked the most basic rights of residency to even apply for such social welfare as was on offer to most poor Scots. The endemic poverty of the Irish ghettoes was seen by Scots to be indistinguishable from their race, nationality and Catholic religion. This sea of enmity against Irish immigrants was compounded by the Poor Law residence qualification of five years in a parish before any relief could be offered. Such hostility and Poor Law discrimination encouraged the Irish to huddle together in overcrowded slums, where they might at least organise their own subsistence on a voluntary basis. It was these pressures that led, for example, to the founding of the football club, Glasgow Celtic, in 1888 as a charitable organisation to provide relief to the impoverished Irish Catholic parishes of the East End of the city.

From the Poorhouse to Specialised Care

Still the Poor Law reforms failed to give the 'able-bodied' any rights to receive relief during periods of unemployment. Their only option was exceptionally to enter the dreaded poorhouse. Poorhouses were designed to make only the most desperate and vulnerable people to apply for help. In Scotland the poorhouse was more usually reserved for the sick, the insane and the disabled poor, or, as defined by the Old Poor law, "cruikit folk, blind folk, impotent folk and waik folk" (cited in Levitt, 1988: 12). However, the 'disreputable' classes of people accepted by the poorhouse were defined by a strong dose of middle class moralism. As the Board put it in their evidence to the 1909 Royal Commission:

> "It is hurtful in practice to grant relief otherwise than in the poorhouse to the following classes:
>
> 1. mothers of illegitimate children, including widows with legitimate families who may have fallen into immoral habits;
> 2. deserted wives;
> 3. persons having grown-up families settled either in this country or abroad;
> 4. persons having collateral relatives in comfortable circumstances;
> 5. wives of persons sentenced to terms of imprisonment;
> 6. in general, all persons of idle, immoral or dissipated habits" (quoted in Crowther, 1990: 275).

Poorhouses were organised on a much more parochial basis than in England. This reduced the effectiveness of central control and monitoring and kept the size of the poorhouses smaller and less well resourced. It also meant, as the quote above indicates, that poorhouses had to fulfil a confusion of functions, from providing accommodation for the homeless to rudimentary care for the sick and the insane.

Only gradually did physical and mental medical care functions become specialised and separated. In the poorhouse there was little segregation by medical condition. Care began to be separated from the Poor Law with the Lunacy (Scotland) Act 1857, which placed asylums for the mentally ill under the control of the Board of Lunacy. However, the emerging medical ideals of specialised care, classification, purpose-built facilities and qualified, trained staff was simply out of the question for most small, parochial poorhouses. Where specialised and segregated medical welfare was developed, for instance in the magnificent Victorian Royal Infirmaries in Glasgow and Edinburgh, it depended on voluntary subscription. Such voluntary infirmaries were exclusively for the care of the urban poor. Not until the 20th century did a more extensive medical hospital system begin to be developed, with Glasgow leading the way with Stobhill Hospital in 1902. The 1909 Minority Report had argued that more specialised and preventive methods of care were evolving over time and that these principles needed to now be placed at the heart of the relief of the poor. This was still some decades away from being organised in a systematic, coherently planned manner.

Pause for thought

Compare how the following six categories have changed by considering how they are defined and treated by the welfare system today:

1. Single mothers.
2. Deserted wives.
3. Elderly people living alone.
4. Individuals with rich relatives.
5. Families of prisoners.
6. The 'idle', 'immoral' or drug and alcohol addicts.

*   Have any other groups been added since then?

Poor health, slum housing and poverty are always bound together. Scotland's overcrowded slums were hell on earth, places where contagious disease festered and spread with ease through the weakened, undernourished bodies of the poor. In poor communities, infants and the elderly were particularly susceptible to being struck down. Entire poor families were crushed into a single room, where life and death occurred side by side. As the Glasgow Medical Officer for Health's own research showed in 1898:

> "Of all the children who die in Glasgow before they complete their fifth year, 32 per cent die in houses of one apartment; and not 2 per cent in houses of five apartments and upwards. There they die, and their little bodies are laid out on a table or a dresser, so as to be somewhat out of the way of their bothers and sisters, who play and sleep and eat in their ghastly company" (quoted in Crowther, 1990: 283-4).

Only towards the 1870s was an effective, rational, centralised, statutory sanitary policy enacted (Campbell, 1985). Until then efforts by medical officers and civic bodies to campaign for hygienic public conditions, clean water supplies, efficient sewers, public parks, hospitals and better living space had little impact beyond voluntary good works locally. Of course, there was little control of the industrial pollution that spewed out of factories and into the slum tenement streets and canals nearby. Similarly, parish doctors could provide free rudimentary treatment but were unable to treat the wasted bodies already pulverised by debilitating poverty.

Welfare Struggles and the Labour Movement

Certain groups of workers organised their own response to the hardships of urban capitalism. First, in the face of violent repression workers like weavers formed combinations, early trade unions, to resist threats to their livelihood, organising a General Strike in 1820 and a strike among cotton spinners in the 1830s. In the decades that followed miners would be at the forefront of building union organisations locally to provide for the welfare, and protect the employment conditions, of its members. Second, the co-operative movement was a way for workers to try to control access to the necessary items of consumption at affordable prices. This was taken further by Robert Owen's attempt to create a harmonious, cooperative community at New Lanark in the early decades of the 19th century (Owen, [1813 and 1821] 1970). Finally, workers began to form their own political parties. These were influenced by a range of ideas about socialism, ranging from the idea that society could be gradually and peacefully reformed through to the necessity for its revolutionary overthrow. At the start of the 20th century, the Labour Party was making itself felt as a reformist political force that would eventually re-shape welfare in Britain.

As the working class gradually won the vote they could begin to elect radicals to the more democratic parish councils. To start with these were mainly drawn from the middle class until the Labour Party began to break through. Even before then, in the 1900s, the threat posed by the Labour Party ensured that idea of state reform of welfare was already being entertained by radical Liberals. Conservatives and Liberals were also becoming worried that the children of the poor were so physically stunted that the racial superiority of the British to rule over its Empire was being placed in mortal danger and urged state intervention to prevent the "race" from "degenerating" (Levitt, 1988: 58). The common sense ideas of liberal individualism (see Sweeney, **Chapter 2**) seemed a much less secure basis on which to organise child welfare now that the ruin of the Imperial 'race' was being threatened.

On the other hand, the demands of socialists for working class adults to have a right to state welfare were rejected. From the parish elections of 1907 Labour increased its representation in places like Leith and the coalfields of Fife. In 1919 Labour controlled ten parishes in Scotland and exerted a strong presence in many more. Socialists were ideologically starting from a different position than middle class ratepayers. Socialist councillors were unimpressed by the operation of free 'choice' and moral independence in an unequal market economy. They viewed public assistance to the victims of the free market as a universal right not a haphazard outcome of voluntary charitable efforts. Not that Labour councillors advocated revolutionary policies. In terms of poor relief their demands were for equality and dignity: equitable treatment for all; an end to middle class moralising at working class mothers on how to raise their children; professional care in specialist units to avoid stigmatisation; and state funding of the Poor Law, which should be made available to all hardship cases, *including* the able-bodied (Levitt, 1988). A much more comprehensive scope for medical care and national insurance was demanded by the Labour Party. However, such demands would later be moderated as Labour MPs tried to create a consensus with other political parties.

Outside of the growing influence of the Labour Party independent working class protest resulted in more immediate challenges to welfare reform. Most famously in Scotland were the Red Clydeside events (Gallacher, 1936; Milton, 1973). Unrest during the First World War (1914-1918) on the Clyde took the form of industrial and community protest. Housing, specifically the exorbitant increases in rent, was the spark for a rent strike in 1915 led by women in working class districts like Glasgow's Govan, which was actively supported by striking munitions and shipyard workers (Melling, 1983). Against the imperative of market forces a Rent Restriction Act was passed to control rents, bypassing the Scottish Office that was nominally responsible for housing matters. This represented a sharp break with the incontrovertible rights of private property and markets forces.

While the state had been at war from 1914 to 1918 National Insurance covered all industrial workers in Britain. After the war, however, unemployed workers in Scotland reverted to the unequal treatment of restricted access to Poor Relief compared to England. The first test came with the miners' strike of 1921. In line with 19th century Poor Law precepts, relief tended to be denied to miners' families unless they were threatened with absolute destitution. As the post-war recession began to generate mass unemployment in Scotland the situation became radicalised. So long as most workers, most of the time, were in paid employment they could afford to ignore the Poor Law. Once they were forced to call on it for support in times of widespread hardship they soon discovered how exposed they were to the legacies of the 19th century social policy.

Serious rioting broke out in Dundee in September 1921 after the parish had failed to grant relief. "During three days of disturbances, the parish offices were sacked and with the unemployed chanting the 'Red Flag', the city centre was looted" (Levitt, 1988: 114). Assistance was immediately granted. Other forms of direct action followed in the industrial centres of Scotland. Edinburgh parish granted assistance after a march to the Board and the parish offices. Serious rioting followed a large march in Aberdeen. In Glasgow large demonstrations took place, with the authorities fearing the influence of John McLean and the communists (Milton, 1973). In response, the Poor Law Emergency Provisions (Scotland) Act 1921 was rushed through to allow the unemployed in Scotland to be put on Poor Relief temporarily.

While the action and unrest of unemployed workers forced the state to intervene the Poor Law was not abolished and replaced by a universal and equitable system of public assistance as the socialists had earlier demanded. It gave the Poor Law a new lease of life that would linger until 1948 when it was at last put out of its misery. Labour-controlled parishes had running battles with the Board over what counted as adequate levels of assistance. Indeed, more generous parishes like Blantyre decided that it would bring up the wages of low paid workers to the same level that those on the parish roll were getting. As the parish chairman argued:

> "What man was entitled to more money for going about through unemployment compared to a man who was employed, and who could not even earn sufficient to bring him up to the pauper standard" (quoted in Levitt, 1988: 117).

Pause for thought
The above situation described in Blantyre could also be considered the forerunner to more recent attempts to provide a minimum wage and family tax credits.

- Do you consider this a fair way to guarantee a basic minimum level of income for all?

Similarly, shipyard workers placed on temporary works at Lithgow's yard in Port Glasgow went on strike because they were being paid less for doing relief work than unemployed workers were getting on assistance. As the level of relief remained depressed and claimants became frustrated by the officiousness of the Charity Organisation Society, serious disturbances broke out. Protests spread to nearby Greenock, where only after the storming of parish offices by local communists did the councillors immediately reverse their previous decision to cut the level of benefit. Elsewhere parish meetings were politicised internally and confronted by demonstrators outside. In this atmosphere, parish election voters swung to the left to make more generous payments with less humiliation. In one case, Bonhill parish council illegally refused to deduct war disability pensions from relief payments.

Such struggles had turned the Scottish Poor Law on its head by giving relief to the able-bodied unemployed and even, on occasion, to low paid able-bodied workers. It also brought into focus the class differences between middle class ratepayers, who operated a low cost system to keep their own rate payments down, and the unemployed working class, who demanded more comprehensive and adequate forms of relief. This also drew the central state into underwriting parish relief. However, the humiliating means test was left intact as a central plank of the Poor Law, even after Parish Councils and the Board of Supervision were abolished in 1929. It was precisely over the **'Means Test'** that the communist-led National Unemployed Workers Movement mobilised thousands of unemployed workers in the 1930s on the 'Hunger Marches'. Thus the struggles from below of unemployed workers and left-wing movements in Scotland between 1921 and 1934 re-shaped the terrain on which the post-war British welfare state would be founded.

The Road to 1948 – the Establishment of the British Welfare State

As part of the effort to secure popular support for Britain's war aims, the 1942 Beveridge Report into *Social Insurance and Allied Services* set out a plan for social welfare in the UK (Timmins, 1995). Beveridge extended his remit to plan a comprehensive social policy that did not only narrowly look at social insurance, but also at what he called 'the Five Giants' that periodically afflicted working class lives. Beveridge's 'Five Giants' were:

1. 'Want' (poverty).
2. 'Idleness' (unemployment).
3. 'Disease' (health).
4. 'Squalor' (housing).
5. 'Ignorance' (education).

Beveridge stressed that state intervention was essential to maintain full employment, provide family allowances and build a comprehensive health service. On the basis of a single weekly insurance contribution, Beveridge planned to provide a 'cradle-to-grave' welfare system comprising a range of benefits for sickness, medicine, maternity, u nemployment, old age, industrial injury, even funeral benefits. These were conceived as positive *rights* to welfare and social care rather than negative *freedoms* from state interference in the economy and society.

While Beveridge's report was hugely popular in Britain it was not universally endorsed. Indeed, the wartime leader, Winston Churchill, saw it as falsely raising expectations that the state could not deliver. He said:

> "Ministers should in my view be careful not to raise false hopes as was done the last time by speeches about 'Homes for Heroes', etc. […]. It is because I do not wish to deceive the people by false hopes and airy visions of Utopia and Eldorado that I have refrained so far from making promises about the future" (quoted in Fraser, 1973: 203).

Despite the fact that both the main political parties (Labour and Conservative) agreed substantially on the need for welfare reform, Churchill lost the 1945 General Election to a landslide Labour government. The electorate recalled the privations of the inter-war (1918-1939) decades only too well and distrusted the Conservatives, even those like Harold Macmillan who advocated a 'middle way' between socialism and capitalism that was virtually identical to Labour Party policies. According to the historian, John Saville (1977), *three* main factors came together to create the welfare state:

1. The struggles of working class movements demanded it.

2. The post-war capitalist economy needed a trained and productive workforce that the welfare sate would ensure.

3. Moderate reforms were a price worth paying by the governing elite to ensure political stability.

However, these conditions could and would change by the 1970s, challenging the welfare settlement of 1948. As Saville (1977: 9) argued, "there exists within any capitalist society strong and powerful tendencies offsetting egalitarian measures."

Although the Labour government of 1945 is often seen as a golden age of far-reaching reforms, it was less radical in practice. The reforms Labour introduced fell short of what Beveridge – an upper-class Liberal MP – had argued was essential. On the 'giant' of *squalor*, Labour's house building programme was modest compared to the numbers being built just before the war started. On *ignorance*, Labour failed to raise the school leaving age to sixteen as the 1944 Education Act had expected, and the building of schools, colleges and nurseries became a lower priority for Labour than increased military spending for the Korean War. Cold War rearmament also hit that other 'giant', *disease*, with prescription charges being placed on medicines, spectacles and false teeth, leading to the resignation of the architect of the National Health Service (NHS), Aneurin Bevan, in 1951. Throughout the post-war period, the over-riding emphasis was on paid work as the normal method of maintaining workers and their families. Welfare support was seen as a temporary measure or only appropriate in extreme cases where paid work of whatever kind could not be undertaken, an assumption that continues to underpin welfare services to this day (see Helms, **Chapter 6**).

Nor was health wholly nationalised or centralised by Labour. Community health services came under local authorities, though in Scotland some services devolved onto the Scottish Office. Bevan managed to preserve the principle of universal, free and comprehensive health service without any recourse to a Means Test in the National Health Service Act 1946. He did, though, have to fight a rearguard battle with the vested interests of the medical profession represented by the British Medical Association (BMA). He 'bought off' elite consultants by:

> "stuffing their mouths with gold […]: Consultants were to be allowed to work part-time in the hospitals for high salaries while continuing private practice as well and, more important, were to have their own pay-beds in hospitals for private patients, without limit on the fees that could be charged" (Fraser, 1973: 218).

More than 60 years later some commentators argue that the legacy of medical elites "stuffing their mouths with gold" continues to haunt the NHS (see McCafferty, **Chapter 9**). Doctors wanted the state to buy their practices, i.e. lists of patients, from them, which Bevan rejected on the basis that patients were not to be sold like cattle. However, Bevan refrained from imposing fixed state salaries on doctors when the NHS began on 5 July 1948. Even a radical reformer like Bevan saw a need to take a pragmatic approach to challenging powerful vested interests. Such moderation may help explain why Labour lost the 1951 election to the Conservatives despite the welfare reforms, which the **Tories** accepted and, indeed, went on to strengthen.

Sixty Years of the Welfare State in Scotland

Popular demand for NHS services like medical treatment, prescriptions , dentist services and opticians greatly exceeded what had been anticipated, reflecting decades of national neglect for the health of millions of British citizens. Another area where demand was set to grow was social work services, previously undertaken by voluntary agencies. Social work gradually became professionalized and came under local authorities that had acquired statutory obligations for the care of children, the homeless and the mentally ill. Legislation such as the Mental Health Act 1959 and the Chronic Sick and Disabled Persons Act 1970 marked a further step in caring for marginalised groups of people who had suffered grievously through centuries of neglect and hostility (see Dumbleton, **Chapter 10**). Yet laws are one thing and unforgiving institutional habits are another, as episode after episode of abusive institutional practices that have been uncovered over the past four decades demonstrate.

Welfare policies cannot be divorced from the social and political circumstances from which they are enacted. The social revolts of the 1960s and 1970s around the demand for humane values, respect and civil rights for oppressed groups continues to inform the revulsion against abuses of the weak and vulnerable by people with institutional authority in places like children's homes, asylums and borstals (see McPhail, **Chapter 8**). In an earlier age such abuses would have been ignored or hushed up, as the brutal treatment of young women in the Magdalene Institutes (Mahood, 1989) – an episode recently put into the spotlight by Peter Mullan's film, *The Magdalene Sisters* (2004) – illustrates.

Throughout the 1970s an atmosphere prevailed that the welfare state was 'failing' the people it was set up to help. As the economy slid into crisis in the early 1970s and unemployment began to rise steeply, more people were claiming social security benefits and fewer were contributing to general taxation to pay for this. A **'poverty trap'** also existed where people who took up paid work would lose benefits for every extra pound of income they earned, producing a strong disincentive to take low paid work of the kind that was all too prevalent in Scotland. Spending on health in Britain was also proportionately lower than in comparable advanced economies. The NHS and the Social Security system could feel like an impersonal bureaucracy, made deliberately complex, indifferent and remote for the people that used it (see McCafferty, **Chapter 9**). The housing supply had grown so that there were record numbers of dwellings, complete with inside toilets and bathrooms, but much of the public housing stock in Scotland was barely habitable and the built environment deteriorated in the peripheral schemes (see Mooney, **Chapter 12**). Scotland was the only area of the UK where more than half of the total housing stock was rented from the council. It also had the lowest levels of owner-occupancy.

For much of the past century Scotland had been near the bottom for most welfare measures indicators, including health, housing, income and employment. Despite this, the welfare state remained hugely popular in Scotland. True, it had singularly failed to redistribute society's wealth from the rich to the poor. Instead of a strategy for greater equality the welfare state had become, despite its best intentions, a strategy for preserving existing levels of inequality (Le Grand, 1982). It had, though, also prevented things from worsening, from relapsing to pre-war levels of hardship and suffering. It ensured a minor transfer of wealth to the poor in the form of paid benefits, which were funded by the taxation of higher income earners. It also provided transfers in kind, for instance, health care that required no payment from the patient. So, the welfare state had, at best, a mildly redistributive effect overall but, more immediately, had a huge personal effect for the working class families who relied on it.

Thatcherite Reforms

Even such mild forms of redistribution were anathema to a new, harsher, right-wing Conservatism that emerged in the 1970s. **Thatcherism**, as it became known after Margaret Thatcher, the Tory leader, sought to emulate Victorian values of thrift and self-help in the late 20th century. State intervention was thought to interfere with the natural efficiency of free market economics. A supposedly excessively generous welfare state spawned what the Tories called a **'dependency culture'** and what their tabloid supporters called 'scroungers'. Under Conservative rule the welfare state adopted a more austere approach to welfare users and used private models in an attempt to improve the efficiency of welfare providers (see Sweeney, **Chapter 2**). The former principle was enshrined in the Social Security Act 1986, which seemed deliberately designed to discourage benefit take-up in the guise of encouraging personal independence and self-help. For instance, the take-up of family credit was only around 40 per cent of its potential. As one social historian put it:

> "The forms to be filled in for family credit were long and complex, and a formidable deterrent in themselves. It was the right-wing Adam Smith Institute that remarked in its paper *Needs Reform*, published in January 1989, that the 'chosen course of all governments would appear to be rationing by squalor – that social security should be sufficiently difficult, sufficiently degrading and sufficiently inconvenient to limit the numbers that will have access to it'" (Marwick, 1996: 355).

The parallels of the modern system of "rationing by squalor" with the earlier principle of discouraging claimants in the Scottish Poor Law seems to continue a legacy that welfare reformers like Beveridge and Bevan thought would be left behind as the relic of an unenlightened society. Policy determined that many of the functions of the welfare state should be turned over to private property or 'market forces' (see Sweeney, **Chapter 2**). This took various forms, including:

- Privatisation (for instance, selling off council houses).
- Personal health and pension schemes.
- Contracting out of ancillary services.
- Competitive tendering.
- Stand alone cost centres.
- Managerialism.
- Internal markets in the NHS.
- Redefining clients and patients as 'customers'.

- Proclaiming individual 'choice' of service provider.

Yet this remained limited compared to the ideology espoused by the Prime Minister Margaret Thatcher and **'think tanks'** like the Adam Smith Institute. A key reason for this is that politicians want to be re-elected and so long as the welfare state was held in great affection across Britain its full privatisation and re-voluntarisation on the United States' model proved electorally impossible.

The deepening unpopularity of the Conservatives in the late 1980s and early 1990s was in large part due to the widespread belief that they wanted to dismantle the entire state welfare system and return to 19th century models of provision. At a minimum there was a sense that the health service was becoming a two-tier system, with a lavish private sector for the rich and a run-down public service for the rest (see McCafferty, **Chapter 9**). This was despite the fact that spending on the NHS was at record levels and constant Tory claims that the 'NHS is safe in our hands'. A general sense existed that the social fabric made possible by the welfare state was being left to decay beyond repair. Some made handsome profits from the re-sale of council houses at the same time as record numbers were reported homeless; destitution, long thought to be consigned to the dustbin of history, was no longer a marginal feature of a rich, enlightened society. Young people especially were caught in a trap they had no control over (see McPhail, **Chapter 8**). As property prices rocketed they found it increasingly difficult to simply afford basic accommodation let alone become part of the 'property-owning democracy' promoted by Thatcherism. Once homeless, it would prove impossible, without a home address, for a young person to get a job, sign on for benefits, or even get onto government training programmes such as the Youth Training Scheme (YTS).

After winning a third successive General Election in 1987 a gap opened up between the Tories and the political realities of a Britain still broadly committed to the values of progressive redistribution represented by the welfare state. The **Poll Tax**, as it became (un)popularly known, was introduced by the Conservatives in response to Scottish middle class protests in 1986 over domestic rates revaluation. Hence the Poll Tax was introduced in Scotland in 1988, a year before England and Wales, not as an anti-Scottish measure as was widely believed at the time, but to appease the Scottish middle classes, as well as to curtail left-wing Labour councils with wide-ranging public services (Lavalette and Mooney, 1989). Its principle was that every adult occupant of a property should pay a fixed amount towards funding local services regardless of ability to pay and value or type of property. This was a *regressive* form of taxation, with a poor family in a dilapidated council house potentially required to pay more than a single landlord on his country estate. Such unfairness galvanised a mass campaign of non-payment of the tax, where millions of non-payers broke the law of the land (Lavalette and Mooney, 2000). After protests in towns across Britain, the Poll Tax revolt culminated in a huge demonstration in Trafalgar Square, London, which erupted into a serious riot against the police and the symbols of property nearby. Soon afterwards Mrs Thatcher resigned and the Poll Tax was abolished in 1990 and replaced by the far from popular Council Tax.

Thatcher may have been gone from office but Thatcherism, which was now called **'neo-liberalism'**, continued with her successors, John Major and Tony Blair (see Sweeney, **Chapter 2**). Full employment, the underlying basis of the classical welfare state, was no longer a priority for government. Housing was largely removed from the local state in many parts of the country, except for the poorest groups in the most disadvantaged areas of cities like Glasgow and Dundee. A largely unsuccessful attempt was made to resurrect a private rented sector (see Mooney, **Chapter 12**). Education was under constant pressure to conform to private 'choices' and league tables, though Scotland's separate education system was largely exempt from the more zany attacks on local authority control seen in England (see Clark, **Chapter 13**). Other matters like social security affected Scotland as much as elsewhere in the UK. For instance, while Prime Minister, John Major introduced a **Citizen's Charter** that attempted to re-cast the relationship between the state and the citizen as if it was similar to that between a consumer and a seller in a market-style contract relationship (see Sweeney, **Chapter 2**). In Scotland, the consumer model of citizenship cut little ice since the very nature of the relationship between democracy and the British state was itself under question. The die had been cast by the Poll Tax experience and pressure grew for some form of self-governing constitutional change for Scotland. This was delayed only until the Tories evacuated Downing Street in 1997.

Conclusion

So, just how distinctive was (and is) welfare in Scotland? Before the Second World War political pressures had already built up to organise welfare on a different basis from the Scottish Poor Law. Ian Levitt (1988: 201) sums up the growing need to break with the 19th century Scottish Poor Law:

> "In particular, the failure of the voluntary movement to maintain a hospital service, the inability of local authorities to infuse their welfare services with a philosophy of non-discriminatory care and the expanding nature of material needs to be met, meant that there was bound to be considerable pressure on Government to take the initiative in formulating new welfare policy."

Instead of parochial councils the welfare state would be centrally controlled. Instead of a mix of voluntary and parish provision the state would become the main focus. Labour MPs had been ambivalent about the abolition of parish councils. One MP argued that the ending of parish control was "alien to the Scottish character" (cited in Levitt, 1988: 203). Some socialists were also suspicious about the loss of local democratic control and autonomy compared to the growing middle class control of a centralised, bureaucratic welfare apparatus.

Yet it is precisely the retention of autonomy and control over the new welfare state in Scotland that some have argued characterises what is distinctive about Scotland as a nation (Paterson, 1994). In most accounts, however, the welfare state is seen as a uniformly British institution (Fraser, 1973; Thane, 1982). As the historian, R.H. Campbell (1985: 235) said of the 1909 Royal Commission and the welfare state some four decades later:

> "By then, though a few aspects of the poor law had distinctly Scottish features, its administration, and the problems of social welfare more generally, were cast in a British mould. With one major exception of housing policy, the rise of the welfare state was not a uniquely Scottish affair."

Clearly, the education system in Scotland has some highly distinctive features while social security has few, with housing, social work and health somewhere in between. However, for Paterson (1994) the key issue is that Scotland has had its own separate welfare bureaucracy through the Scottish Office. Welfare professionals – doctors, social workers and teachers – maintained the sense of a distinctive Scottish nation more than any other aspect of society. Scottish nationalism in this account is a creature of the professionalized welfare state:

> "Whole new sections of that class were produced in the new state institutions such as health, education, social work and the nationalised industries. Middle class people staffed the boards and committees in the policy network, reaching these positions through technical competence rather than the capacity to win elections" (Paterson, 1994: 113).

This form of 'welfare nationalism' (Law, 2005) was maintained by the Scottish middle class based not on popular democracy, but on the kind of professional specialisation that, as we saw, began to undermine the Scottish Poor Law.

Most advanced economies produced something resembling the welfare state after 1945 and the system in Scotland did not differ greatly from that covering the rest of Britain. Scotland was different only in the details of how it implemented reforms; only the *means* differed, not the *ends*. For instance, housing required more public subsidy than England; social work was affected by the distinctive Scottish legal system (though how far "a Scottish social ethic" influenced practice is difficult to say (Paterson, 1994: 127)); and health was managed by a specifically Scottish structure.

An historical analysis lets us begin to assess how far middle class professional groups advanced the cause of welfare in Scotland. It also indicates the continuing grip on Scottish society of the legacies of the past in the form of endemic poverty, sickness, slum housing, malnourishment, abusive relationships, homelessness and racism towards immigrants and asylum seekers. The history of welfare shows that there was much in the traditional Scottish approach to the Poor Law, the poorhouse, charitable voluntarism and mean, small-minded parochialism that, frankly, still casts a dark cloud over Scottish society. There were other aspects that helped moderate the damage done to the poor by capitalist economics and middle class morality, such as the activity of working class Scots to demand a more civilised life for themselves, their families and communities.

Scottish society is today often criticised by Tories and newspapers like the *Daily Mail* and *Daily Telegraph* for being 'too dependent' on the central and local state to provide welfare services. As we have seen, to the extent that this claim has any validity, it has its roots in the historical experience of the failure of small-scale, voluntary efforts and the lack of legal rights to welfare support under the Poor Law, something that survived until it was finally abolished by the British welfare state. As one historian argued:

> "If there is any truth in this, then the explanation may lie in the excessive burdens placed on small communities in the nineteenth century – burdens which many were happy to hand over to the state" (Crowther, 1990: 287).

As we saw in Sweeney, **Chapter 2**, state welfare remains under fire in the 21st century. Ye t, a n historical understanding reveals the limits and failures of the alternatives to provide adequate care and welfare in Scotland in a coherent, enlightened manner.

Further Reading

John Saville's (1977) essay 'The welfare state: An historical approach' dates from the 1950s but is still an excellent short account of the rise of the welfare state. For a short introduction to the history of popular struggles for political change and welfare reform in modern Scotland see Chris Bambery's (1999) overview in his essay 'Two Souls of Scotland', in the book he edited, *Scotland, Class and Nation*. For a more detailed examination of history of welfare in Scotland leading up to the creation of the British welfare state see Iain Levitt's (1988) *Poverty and Welfare in Scotland, 1890-1948*. See Nicholas Timmins' (1996) book, *The Five Giants*, for a highly readable account of the setting-up of the welfare sate. For an account of the relationship between nationalism and welfare in Scotland for the period since the 1940s, see Lindsay Paterson's (1994) *The Autonomy of Modern Scotland*.

Bibliography

Bambery, C. (ed.) (1999) *Scotland, Class and Nation*, London, Bookmarks
Bambery, C. (1999) 'Two Souls of Scotland', in Bambery, C. (ed.) (1999) *Scotland, Class and Nation*, London, Bookmarks
Campbell, R.H. (1985) *Scotland Since 1707*, Edinburgh, John Donald
Crowther, M.A. (1990) 'Poverty, health and welfare', in Hamish Fraser, W. and Morris, R.J. (eds.) (1990) *People and Society in Scotland, Volume II, 1830-1914*, Edinburgh, John Donald
Davidson, N. (2003) *Discovering the Scottish Revolution, 1692-1746*, London, Pluto Press
Devine, T.M. and Mitchson, R. (eds.) (1988) *People and Society in Scotland, Volume I, 1760-1830*, Edinburgh, John Donald
Fitzgerald, M., Halmos, P., Muncie, J. and Zeldin, D. (eds.) (1977) *Welfare in Action*, London, Routledge and Kegan Paul/The Open University Press
Fraser, D. (1973) *The Evolution of the British Welfare State*, London, Macmillan
Gallacher, W. (1936) *Revolt on the Clyde*, London, Lawrence and Wishart
Hamish Fraser, W. and Morris, R.J. (eds.) (1990) *People and Society in Scotland, Volume II, 1830-1914*, Edinburgh, John Donald
Lavalette, M. and Mooney, G. (eds.) (2000) *Class Struggle and Social Welfare*, London, Routledge
Lavalette, M. and Mooney, G. (1989) 'The struggle against the poll tax in Scotland', *Critical Social Policy*, 26
Lavalette, M. and Mooney, G. (2000) '"No Poll Tax Here": The Tories, social policy and the great poll tax rebellion, 1987-1991', in Lavalette, M. and Mooney, G. (eds.) (2000) *Class Struggle and Social Welfare*, London, Routledge

Law, A. (2005) 'Welfare nationalism: Social Justice and/or entrepreneurial Scotland?' in Mooney, G. and Scott, G. (2005) *Exploring Social Policy in the 'New' Scotland*, Cambridge, Polity Press

Le Grand, J. (1982) *The Strategy of Equality*, London, Allen and Unwin

Levitt, I. (1988) *Poverty and Welfare in Scotland, 1890-1948*, Edinburgh, Edinburgh University Press

Mahood, L. (1989) 'The domestication of "fallen" women: The Glasgow Magdalene Institution, 1860-1890', in McCrone, D. Kendrick, S. and Straw, P. (eds.) (1989) *The Making of Scotland: Nation, Culture and Social Change*, Edinburgh , British Sociological Association

Marwick, A . (199 6) *British Society Since 1945*, New Edition, Harmondsworth , Penguin

Melling, J . (1983) *Rent Strikes: Popular Struggle for Housing in West Scotland 1890-1916*, Edinburgh, Polygon

Milton, N. (1973) *John Maclean*, London, Pluto Press

Mitchison, R . (1974) 'The making of the Old Scottish Poor Law', in *Past and Present*, 63

Mitchison, R . (1988) 'The Poor Law', in Devine, T.M. and Mitchson, R. (eds.) (1988) *People and Society in Scotland, Volume I, 1760 -1830*, Edinburgh , John Donald

Mooney, G. and Scott, G. (2005) *Exploring Social Policy in the 'New' Scotland*, Bristol, Policy Press

Owen, R . (1970) *A New View of Society and Report to the County of Lanark*, Harmondsworth, Pelican Books (originally published 1813-14 and 1821)

Paterson, L . (1994) *The Autonomy of Modern Scotland*, Edinburgh , Edinburgh University Press

Richards, E. (2000) *The Highland Clearances*, Edinburgh, Birlinn

Saville, J . (1977) 'The welfare state: An historical approach', in Fitzgerald, M., Halmos, P., Muncie , J. and Zeldin, D. (eds.) (1977) *Welfare in Action*, London , Routledge and Kegan Paul/The Open University Press

Thane, P. (1982) *The Foundations of the British Welfare State*, London, Longman

Timmins, N. (1996) *The Five Giants*, London, Fontana

Section 2:

Divided and Unequal Scotland

Chapter 4

Class and Social Stratification in Contemporary Scotland

Alex Law and Jan Law

Introduction: Neds and Class

Any occupation concerned with social care and working with people in a welfare capacity will be dealing with the symptoms of an unequal, class-divided society. Yet we are constantly being told that class is becoming irrelevant to the modern world. So, rather than starting with general theories of class as is traditional in introductory chapters like this, it might be better to explore class in the context of a social 'problem' that most people in Scotland will be very familiar with: 'ned culture'.

In the past few years you may have noticed that the problem of 'ned culture' has become a burning issue for the mass media, policy-makers and politicians in Scotland. **Neds** are seen as responsible for many of society's ills like youth crime and violence (see Munro and Nicholson, **Chapter 14**). As such, the 'ned problem' has been addressed by demands for a greater use of **anti-social behaviour orders (ASBOs)**, more visible and aggressive policing, social work interventions and more severe punishments by Scotland's courts (Croall, 2006; see also McPhail, **Chapter 8**).

Much of the discussion of ned culture in Scotland is based on a limited form of 'common sense' thinking. Common sense thinking typically accepts that 'what everybody knows' is sufficient grounds for making sound judgements about social groups outside of our own immediate circle of friends and family. Common sense accepts the ideas that are dominant in society at any one time as self-evident, true and immutable (see Mooney, Sweeney and Law, **Chapter 1**). Such thinking typically identifies a *problem* – in this case, youth crime and urban squalor, attributes *blame* – 'nedish' behaviour and attitudes – and poses *solutions*, tougher law and order policies. Neds are, therefore, diagnosed by common sense thinking as one of the key factors that *cause* social inequalities and deprivation in the streets of Scotland's poorest areas (Law and Mooney, 2006a).

Pause for thought
- What do you take to be the main characteristics of ned culture?
- How does your list compare with the one below?
- Describe how each of the following characteristics might apply to neds:

  - Class
  - Gender
  - Neighbourhood
  - Dress style
  - Behaviour
  - Social group
  - Attitude
  - Age
  - Education
  - Speech
  - Employment

Once you have completed your answer compare it to the one that we came up with (which you find at the end of this chapter). We tried to identify what we thought might be considered the most common features (we should perhaps add that we do not actually subscribe to this picture of working class youth in Scotland).

Some of these features appear to be based on *objective* facts – age, gender, neighbourhood, education, employment. On the other hand, certain negative features are *subjectively* attributed on the basis of culture – dress, attitude, behaviour, speech. The latter set of features mainly deploys 'lifestyle choice' and social identity to define neds as a stereotyped social group. Ned dress codes, for instance, Burberry checks and tracksuits, are seen as evidence of their 'bad taste'. That neds are often made into figures of fun, as well as fear, in television comedy shows in Scotland like *Chewin the Fat*, the daily press, websites and paperback books shows how common sense stereotypes can become circulated across society (Law, 2006; Law and Mooney, 2006a). This mixture of characteristic ned-ish traits builds up a picture of a stereotyped view of young working class people in Scotland that helps to distinguish and differentiate them from other social groups like, for instance, respectable middle class adults.

Class stereotypes are also a way of inflicting what American sociologists have called "the hidden injuries of class" (Sennett and Cobb, 1977). In a society based on inequality, entire groups of people in the lower and inferior classes in society are made to feel like failures. Respect and dignity always seem to be out of their grasp and in the hands of other people who control and order their lives, such as bosses, bureaucrats, politicians, and welfare professionals. Such stereotypes may influence welfare policy-makers as well as the day-to-day practices of welfare delivery by categorising social groups into 'deserving' and 'undeserving' ones.

The 'hidden injuries of class' are often seen as a failure of the working class to have 'good' cultural taste, lifestyle and identity. For instance, you might have noticed how many middle class presenters there are on so-called reality TV programmes telling their largely working class viewers how they should dress, eat, decorate their homes, and so on. These are key ways in which social difference and distinction are asserted, as we shall see in the discussion of the ideas of the sociologist Pierre Bourdieu later on.

For the moment it is important to recognise that a poor or tasteless 'lifestyle' is often taken as the *cause* of social inequalities, limited job prospects, impoverished housing schemes and low educational attainment. On the other hand, a social science approach would see these as a *consequence* of wider social and economic relations, processes and structures. Therefore, in order to understand the division of society into unequal social groups, we need to look not just at *subjective* issues to do with group identity, but also at *objective* issues to do with how society is structured into classes, as well as other social categories like gender, ethnicity and sexuality.

An understanding of class and stratification helps to put social categories like neds in a much wider social context. This combination of objective and subjective elements is a key way that society becomes divided – or stratified – into various social groups. Social groups like neds can be better understood by the more systematic approaches of social science towards class and stratification, rather than leaving it to the prejudices of common sense stereotypes.

In many accounts class and stratification are treated as if they referred to the same thing. However, there are vast differences between these two concepts. In one sense, they are indeed referring to the same thing: how *inequalities are structured over time*. However, in another sense, each concept directs us to examine, describe and explain different kinds of things. Unpacking and clarifying what we mean by these terms is the main purpose of this chapter. The key themes of this chapter are:

1. **Social divisions and differentiation:** How and why is society divided unequally?

2. **Inclusion and exclusion:** How do certain social classes maintain their power and pass it on through the generations?

3. **Continuity and change:** To what extent has the class structure of society changed?

Class and Stratification

Unpacking Social Stratification

This seems an appropriate point to begin to define the key terms that you will come across in this chapter. A good place to start when defining unusual concepts like stratification and social class is to consult a specialised dictionary.

Pause for thought
In your library or on the web look up any *Dictionary of Sociology* for the entry for the term **'social stratification'**.

Interestingly, in the *Collins Dictionary of Sociology*, edited by David Jary and Julia Jary (1995), the entries for class and social stratification were cross-referenced to each other. This suggests that they are closely-related concepts. To quote the first few lines of the entry for social stratification:

> "**Social stratification** The hierarchically organized structures of social inequality (ranks, status groups, etc.) which exist in any society. As in geology, the term refers to a layered structuring or strata, but in sociology the layers consist of social groups, and the emphasis is on the ways in which inequalities between groups are structured and persist over time" (Jary and Jary, 1995: 621).

Jary and Jary (1995) pack rather a lot into this definition and this is just the first paragraph of it! If we move through it one step at a time, though, we can begin to unravel what exactly they are getting at.

1. Social stratification refers above all to *social inequality*.

2. Social inequality is not something haphazard and random that happens to some unlucky individuals (even if it feels that way sometimes). Stratification is a *system* of inequality, expressed in a stable social structure that gets reproduced over time to create patterned inequalities.

3. This structure is organised vertically in a *hierarchy*, so that some social

groups appear at the top, some in the middle and some at the bottom.

4. The term, 'stratification', is borrowed from the geological study of layers of rock formation and applied as a metaphor to provide us with a clear image of how society is *layered* or sedimented into social groups.

Now look up **'status'** in your *Dictionary of Sociology*.

Jary and Jary (1995: 655) provide the following definition:

> "**Status** [T]he positive or negative honour, prestige, power, etc., attaching to a position, or an individual person, within a system of social stratification [...]. In modern societies status positions tend to be more fluid."

Status refers to the subjective and unequal attribution of respect and distinction that flows from our social position and standing in the wider community. However, when we look at social status we find that it tends *not* to be fixed but can be quite fluid. Status is only part of a wider system of social stratification. So, we can work out that stratification is the widest possible category with social status (and social class) referring to particular positions within the stratification system.

Our idea of social status owes a great deal to the German sociologist, Max Weber (1946). Status, Weber claimed, could be used to exclude inferior social groups from honourable and prestigious professions like the clergy, teaching, medicine, law and so forth. This is often done through a strategy Weber called **'social closure'** (Parkin, 1979). Status can be and usually is based on some arbitrary trait like skin colour, nationality, gender, religion, speech, lifestyle, consumption and so forth. Women, national and ethnic minorities and the poor can find that their ability to get access to certain jobs, institutions and organisations is restricted by practices that discriminate on the basis of their perceived lowly status.

Pause for thought
- Can you think of occupations, institutions and organisations that are restricted to people of a certain status?
- Why might this be the case?

For Weber (1946) status groups are related to social class through economic conditions, especially the ownership of property and wealth. However, status is not identical to class or wealth, or always directly related to it. For instance, a working class nurse may have considerable status in society, but she may not be rewarded for this in her pay packet. In the pre-modern period, landowning aristocracies with inherited titles had high levels of wealth and property that corresponded to high social status at the apex of society. In the modern period, though, aristocratic power certainly declined, but they retained considerable social prestige and status.

Let us return briefly to our neds example. Except perhaps among their own peer groups, neds clearly are at the bottom of the end of the social status hierarchy. Neds have low or nil prestige and little social power or control over their social standing. By being placed at the bottom of the status hierarchy neds are also subject to social closure and exclusion from more prestigious occupations, institutions and professions. In contrast, other social groups with greater amounts of prestige and social rank like journalists, politicians, policy-makers, teachers, judges, police offers, social workers and so forth have the hierarchical power to define neds as an inferior and dishonourable social group.

Street gangs can operate for young working class people as an alternative means of acquiring status among themselves by inverting the values of the dominant status groups in society. Using the approach of stratification neds can be located as falling into the bottom layer of society. This has been called **'the underclass'** by the conservative sociologist, Charles Murray (1990). We will consider the idea of the underclass later in this chapter. For now it is important to keep hold of the image of society in theories of stratification as one of unequal layers of social groups sitting on top of each other.

Unpacking Class

It was earlier noted that class and stratification are often confused and that they need to be understood as quite different approaches to social divisions and differences.

Pause for thought
Again, look up your *Dictionary of Sociology* for the entry for the term 'class'.

Jary and Jary (1995: 77) define class as follows:

"**Class 1** The hierarchical distinctions that exist between individuals or groups (e.g. occupational groups) within a society. In this general sense class is an alternative general term to social stratification."

They then go on to set out the different approaches taken to class by Weber and Karl

Marx. Any discussion of class needs to take these two approaches into account. These are considered the two major theories of class.

Theories of Class

The Marxist Theory of Class

Marx approached the issue of class in two ways that are fundamentally different from Weberian stratification theory:

1. Classes are a product of historical development.

2. Marxist class theory starts from a more general understanding of capitalist society itself rather than from individual social groups.

So, where stratification theory tends to measure the groups of people in fixed positions in the social hierarchy, Marxist class theory views different classes in society as dynamically related to each other and subject to change. One class of people, say slaves, would not exist without another class of people, that of slave owners. Also, whole societies based on slave labour declined in importance over time. Just as social relations between certain classes of people come into existence so they may well also, like slave society, go out of existence.

Marx claimed that each society as it emerged historically was distinguished by the totality of what he called the **'mode of production'**. This refers to the way in which production in society is carried out and what sorts of social relations between the main classes are involved. These relations are based on the exploitation of one class by another, what is sometimes called 'the two-class model' (Sweeney, Etherington and Lewis, 2003). One main class produces the wealth that supports the non-producing class. For instance, in societies like ancient Rome slaves were captured, bought and sold by slave owners to undertake domestic and field labour for the slave owners. In Europe in the middle ages, peasants worked the land that was owned by a land-owning class, such as the lairds in Scotland, to whom they handed over an amount of what they produced as payment in the form of rent.

In modern society the mode of production is known as **'capitalism'**. It is based on the reality that most people out of material necessity need to sell their labour power in return for wages. Capitalist society is similarly divided into *two* main classes. One, the working class, is based on **wage labour** and the other, the capitalist class, is based on the ownership of the **means of production** like factories, offices, call centres and so forth. Extra (or surplus) value over and above what workers are paid

75

in wages is produced in the work that they do in these workplaces. Marx called this the **'labour theory of value'** where wage labour creates the profits that flow to the owners of the means of production.

Class relations in capitalism are therefore quite different from all earlier societies. These societies used force to directly seize the product of the producing class like slaves or peasants only after they had produced some finished good like wheat, milk or beef. Under capitalism, force is replaced by the freedom of workers to sell their ability to labour in exchange for wages. It is during the work process itself that extra or **surplus value** is produced by labour rather than after the work is completed, as with slaves or peasants. This process is wonderfully described in Robert Tressell's (1965 [1955]) novel *The Ragged Trousered Philanthropists*, which you can read for an engaging account of 19th century working class life in England.

Classes are not pictured by Marxist class theory as layered in rock-like formations of social groups, sitting vertically on top of each other (Gubbay, 1997). Instead, the main classes in society are always inter-related by exploitative and conflictual social relations. Marxists tend to emphasise class struggle. As workers do not have an independent income they need to find some kind of paid employment as an absolute necessity. Therefore, workers and capitalist are both dependent on each other. At the same time, they also have opposing interests. Employers seek to pay labour as little as they can while squeezing the greatest amount of work out of their workers in the time that they are employed. Workers seek to get the highest wages possible for the fewest hours that they need to work. Since individual workers are in a weak position of power compared to their employer, workers often form collective organisations like trade unions and political parties, such as the Labour Party, the Scottish Socialist Party, or Solidarity, to defend and advance their interests.

In the objective sense of class structure, the position that most people find themselves in as a wage labourer means that they form what Marx called a **'class-in-itself'**. In the subjective sense of how people think of themselves and others in a similar position to them, workers develop what Marx called **'class consciousness'**. They begin to have a more active sense that they have separate class interests as opposed to the ruling capitalist class. They become what Marx also called a **'class-for-itself'**.

In this sense Scotland is seen as a particularly working class country, with strong traditions of working class movements, collective action, class consciousness and support for the **welfare state** (Gall, 2005). **Table 4.1** measures the proportion of workers belonging to trade unions, 'union density', in Scotland and the UK over the past decade. It shows that Scotland consistently has a slightly higher percentage of trade unionists, a third of all workers, than the average for the UK as a whole, although this tends to be slightly lower than other regions like the north of England, Wales and Northern Ireland.

Table 4.1 Trade union density: 1995-2004

Year	Scotland	UK
2004	33	29
2003	35	29
2002	34	29
2001	35	29
2000	35	29
1999	35	29
1998	35	29
1997	36	30
1996	36	31
1995	39	32

(Source: Gall (2005: 47) *The Political Economy of Scotland: Red Scotland? Radical Scotland?* Cardiff, University of Wales Press.)

Trade unions are not the only expression of class conflict, however. Marx predicted that society would split increasingly into two fundamental classes – wage labourers and capitalists – and that this process would result in the revolutionary overthrow of capitalism. It is seen as a particular weakness of Marxist class theory that neither **class polarisation** nor social **revolution** has occurred in developed capitalist countries. Subjectively, class has declined as a key form of identity for many people and, objectively, the class structure has become more complex, splitting into numerous groups who enjoy unprecedented prosperity, social mobility, cultural identities and advanced education. In this context the prospects for class struggle, class consciousness and revolution have been forestalled. We will return to examine some of the evidence for these claims later on.

Key terms of Marxist class theory:

1. Mode of production.
2. Capitalism.
3. Wage labour.
4. Working class.
5. Surplus value.
6. Labour theory of value.
7. Class in itself/class for itself.
8. Class consciousness.

9. Class struggle.
10. Revolution.

The Weberian Analysis of Class

Foremost among the critics of Marxist class theory have been sociologists in the Weberian tradition. As we have seen, for Weber, social class was only one variable in a complex system of hierarchical stratification. Weber's approach to stratification has been viewed as a more refined way of dealing with unequal social groups than Marxist class theory. Weberian class analysis treats social class as only one, albeit highly important, variable amongst many others.

Weber (1946) identified class as the **'life chances'** that are shaped by the economic position that a large number of people share in common. In Weber's view, class reflects the position of social groups in the labour market. Class is also shaped, as we have seen, by status differences and **'party'**, by which Weber did not mean support for specific political parties but the general moral and political outlook of individuals. Status and class often, though not always, go in hand in hand. As an individual's market position rises so their status tends to also increase and, *vice versa*, as their status rises so their market position improves.

Weberians and Marxists thus have contrary starting points. Marxists take the totality of class relations in an historically given mode of production as their starting point. In contrast, Weberians start from the individual who, through the opportunities that exist in the labour market, joins different social classes. Individuals can therefore move through a range of class positions in their lifetime as they change their market position, for instance, by getting higher educational qualifications. Weberians also place greater stress on the subjective ideas, beliefs and meanings held by individuals and social groups. Marxists, on the other hand, tend to stress that individuals in society first of all have to deal with the objective existence of a class structure, or 'class in itself', as preceding subjective class consciousness, or 'class for itself'.

Weberian class analysis is able to more narrowly and precisely identify a range of market and status differences between individuals in social groups. For some social scientists, this is seen as a *strength* since it accurately reflects the changing types of occupations and lifestyles in society. For others, like Marxists, it seen as a *weakness* since it merely describes a range of positions open to individuals in society without setting this in a wider explanation of the dynamic of exploitation in the workplace, profit and class struggle that drives capitalist society (Allen, 2004).

In order to evaluate these approaches to class we need to examine how the class structure in Scotland has changed and how this has been explained by social scientists coming after Marx and Weber.

Key terms of Weberian class analysis:

1. Social stratification.
2. Hierarchy.
3. Inequality.
4. Social class.
5. Status group.
6. 'Party'.
7. Market position.
8. Social closure.
9. Social mobility.
10. Life chances.

Developments in Stratification and Class

The 'Goldthorpe Occupational Scale'

The study of class has always been the subject of fierce debate and controversy. Arguably, the dominant approach in British social science is the Weberian tradition of **empirical class analysis**. The key sociologist responsible for developing empirical class analysis has been John Goldthorpe. For Goldthorpe (1980; 1987) class corresponds to the bunching of occupational categories of people who roughly share the same market situation in terms of qualifications, income, social mobility in the form of career prospects and secure job contracts. What has become known as the 'Goldthorpe occupational scale' identifies *seven* main social classes, subdivided into 11 social groups (see **Table 4.2**).

Such scales have the great merit of being able to measure the size of social groups based mainly on their *objective* situation in terms of occupation. Similar scales are also used by official surveys such as the **Registrar-General's** collection of census data every ten years based on a simple five-class model (see **Table 4.3**).

Using the analytical categories of class in **Table 4.2**, Goldthorpe (1980; 1987) has been able to show that there has been very little social mobility in Britain from the class of origin (that is, your parent's class) and the present class position of most people. Social closure continues to exert an influence over who gets what kinds of jobs. In terms of occupational structure and despite changes in the type of jobs, class is marked with strong continuities. Britain is not an 'open' society in the sense that anyone of ability can rise to any position of prestige and authority in large organisations. Public (private) school and other social networks ensure that the leadership positions in society, for instance, at the top of the civil service, the armed forces, the diplomatic corps, the BBC and so forth, are drawn between the generations from a narrow class of privileged elites. So, even though the nature of jobs has shifted dramatically from manual to non-manual ones, class remains the key shaping factor in people's life chances.

Table 4.2 The 'Goldthorpe occupational scale'

Class	Occupations
Class I Higher service class	1 High-grade professionals 2 Owners of large firms 3 Senior managers of large organisations
Class II Lower service class	4 Lower-grade professionals 5 Managers of small businesses 6 Supervisors and middle managers of white collar workers
Class IIIa Routine white collar employees	7 Non-manual workers in administration and commerce (office workers)
Class IIIb Routine white collar employees	8 Non-manual personal services
Class IVa Petite bourgeoisie	9 Small business owners with few employees
Class IVb Petite bourgeoisie	10 Self-employed small business owners ('own account workers')
Class IVc Petite bourgeoisie	11 Self-employed farmers and fishermen
Class V 'Labour aristocracy'	12 Lower-grade technicians 13 Supervisors of manual workers
Class VI Skilled manual workers	14 Skilled manual workers
Class VIIa Semi- and unskilled manual workers	15 Semi- and unskilled manual workers (non-agricultural)
Class VIIb Semi- and unskilled manual workers	16 Agricultural manual workers

Many critics have noted that Goldthorpe's (1980; 1987) class scale is graded in terms of a hierarchy, from Class I at the top to Class VIIb at the bottom. This depends on a *subjective* evaluation of the social status of different occupational groups. It also tends to class together different kinds of jobs within the same social group. Missing from such a classification based on occupation are the people not in paid work, such as the unemployed, housewives and voluntary workers who are often at the heart of social care and welfare services. Also missing are the super-rich who live off the dividends and interest from stocks and shares. Also, if class is defined according to the male 'head of the household' where does that leave women as housewives or paid workers in their own right?

Pause for thought

- Using Goldthorpe's (1980; 1987) class scale, which class do you think that the following welfare occupations fall into?

    - Nurse.
    - Social worker.
    - School janitor.
    - Minister for Work and Pensions.
    - GP.
    - Home help.
    - Classroom assistant.
    - Director of Social Services.
    - Chair of NHS Trust.
    - Benefit worker.
    - Care home manager.
    - Nursery nurse.
    - Hospital porter.
    - Voluntary carer.
    - Community worker.
    - Consultant.
    - Head teacher.
    - Cleaner.

Table 4.3 Registrar-General's five class model

Class I	Professional occupations
Class II	Intermediate occupations
Class III	Skilled occupations
Class IV	Semi-skilled occupations
Class V	Unskilled occupations

Wright's Marxist Class Analysis

Marxists have been criticised by Weberians for adopting a two-class model that is far too simplistic to capture the rich complexity of the changing occupational structure. Marxists also tend to over-emphasise class conflict and struggle and ignore how individuals slot into different market situations. Finally, the Marxist approach to class tends to be too theoretical and historical and insufficiently empirical and analytical.

In response to criticisms like this, some Marxists such as the American sociologist, Erik Olin Wright (1979; 1985 ; 1997), adopted a more empirical and analytical approach to class categories. Wright (1979) began with the express intention of keeping Marxism free from the "contaminating" influence of Weberianism, but ended up adopting a classification scheme that even he conceded did not differ that much from the one "used by Goldthorpe" (Wright, 1997: 37). In keeping with the Marxist focus on exploitation, Wright (1985) identified *three* types of exploitation:

1. Exploitation based on *ownership* of capital assets.

2. Exploitation based on the *managerial control* and *supervision* of organisational assets.

3. Exploitation based on *skill or credential* (qualifications) assets.

This gave rise to a *twelve* class model as represented in **Table 4.4**.

Table 4.4 Wright's twelve class model

Basis of exploitation	Class
Ownership	Large capitalist employers
Ownership	Small capitalist employers
Ownership	Petite bourgeoisie
Control	Expert managers
Control	Semi-credentialed managers
Control	Uncredentialed managers
Supervision	Expert supervisors
Supervision	Semi-credentialed supervisors
Supervision	Uncredentialed supervisors
Non-managerial	Expert employees
Non-managerial	Semi-credentialed employees
Non-managerial	Uncredentialed employees

Do not worry about trying to remember all of the names that Wright gives to each of his classes. The important point to recall is how Wright shifted his Marxist analysis much closer to a Weberian concern with market position in terms of:

1. *Qualifications* (or the lack of them).

He also maintained the more traditional Marxist concerns with:

2. *Ownership* of the means of production (or lack of).
3. *Control* over the work process itself (or lack of).

By using such criteria, Wright was able to identify social groups that had what he called **'contradictory class locations'** between the three traditional classes in Marxist theory: capitalists, workers and the self-employed **petite bourgeoisie**. The main classes caught in a contradictory class location were those who did not own the means of production themselves, but possessed considerable control and autonomy over what they did during the working day. This discretion at work was often related to having high levels of credentials like a higher university degree, as found in the groups identified in **Table 4.4** as 'expert managers', 'expert supervisors' and 'expert employees'. These social groups form what Wright called 'the new middle classes'. Expert researchers, elite academics and those in leadership positions have considerable autonomy over how they carry out their work. In contrast, most **white collar workers** have no or little autonomy over their work environment and so remain part of the working class.

Pause for thought
- Is the welfare state increasingly controlled by a 'new middle class' as Wright conceives it?

Well, this depends on the degree of autonomy they have in organising the work of others and themselves. If they have considerable autonomy to do this then they *are* part of the new middle class. Which groups do you think this applies to? If, on the other hand, their work is tightly controlled and monitored from above then they may be more like traditional supervisors or line managers.

From Underclass to Social Exclusion

One group that is definitely *not* part of the new middle class is the so-called 'underclass'. This term was coined in the 1980s to refer to a social group who are defined by a dependency relationship to the welfare state:

> "In some definitions the underclass consists of individuals who are unemployed, living on welfare, or existing off criminal activity; in other definitions the underclass consists of family units who live off welfare" (Jary and Jary, 1995: 703).

The idea of an underclass emerged at a politically expedient time when the Conservative governments of the 1980s and early to mid 1990s were seeking to 'roll back the state', cut income taxes and make individuals as self-sufficient as possible. Welfare claimants were seen by such politicians as part of the **'undeserving poor'** who lived off generous welfare benefits while the **'deserving poor'** uncomplainingly went out to work each day for low wages or when the sick or old depended on subsistence level benefits. The idea of 'deserving' and 'undeserving' cases for public services is a theme that runs through many of the chapters in this Book.

Sociologists who were sympathetic to **Thatcherite** ideas, such as Charles Murray (1990), fluctuated between a *structural* explanation and a *culturalist* one. The structural account of the underclass argued that because benefits and/or criminal activity were so profitable, it was rational for the underclass to avoid poorly paid work. Hence, petty crime needed to be punished even more severely and welfare benefits cut back to an even lower level to give the underclass an incentive to take low paid work. The culturalist account stressed the way that work-avoidance values were being passed on culturally from one generation to another. Whether due to socio-economic structures or cultural values and practices, a sizeable group of people, said to be as much as one-third of the population, were cut-off from the **values**, **norms** and work commitment of the rest of society on which they had become a 'parasitical drain' (see Scott, **Chapter 2**).

Pause for thought
- Can structural and cultural explanations of class be separated in this manner? Give reasons for your answer.

Empirical research has failed to find evidence of an underclass as a social group completely divorced from the rest of the working class. The idea of an underclass lacked credibility and was seen as a flagrant right wing attack on the poorest sections of society. It compounded the 'hidden injuries of class' and fell into disuse among social scientists, although some journalists and policy-makers continued to use it as a shorthand way of speaking about the poor, criminality and deprived housing schemes (see Mooney, **Chapter 12**).

From 1997, with the setting up of New Labour's Social Exclusion Unit, the language of politicians and journalists became increasingly one of **'social exclusion'** rather than the underclass. Although the term 'social exclusion' seems more neutral and less **stigmatising** than 'underclass', the same types of delinquent traits, behaviour and values continue to inform its underlying assumption. Even 'class' as a descriptive category has been removed from the re-conceptualisation of poverty as 'social exclusion' (see Scott, **Chapter 5**). New Labour talks about social *inclusion* rather than the structures of a society based on class divisions that give rise to poverty and deprivation. Moreover, the language of social exclusion already presupposes that class is largely irrelevant for tackling endemic poverty and acute social inequalities in British society.

Social exclusion tends to involve a poorly understood version of Weber's idea of social closure as discussed earlier. Here, the socially excluded suffer from a disreputable social standing that keeps them out of 'mainstream society'. However, this does not make much sense unless the idea of class, in terms of an individual's market position and the wider wage relationship, is also addressed. Instead, the category of the 'socially excluded' shifts attention away from class inequalities and antagonisms that already exist across society, even amongst those New Labour views as the 'socially *included*'.

Bourdieu, Class Habitus and Cultural Capital

The final contribution to recent debates about class comes from the French sociologist, Pierre Bourdieu. In developing a distinctive approach to class Bourdieu drew on Marx and Weber, as well as the sociologist Emile Durkheim (1947). Bourdieu's (1987) main idea was to see class as something shaped by both *objective* structures and *subjective* culture. This led him to explore the way that class inequalities are reproduced in society through cultural practices.

People's whole way of life, how they walk, talk and feel, is profoundly shaped by what Bourdieu called **'class habitus'**. Habitus is concerned with how our practical sense of what is possible in any situation is structured by our earlier class-based internalisation of social habits and norms, for instance when, where and how we can be assertive about our feelings or views or need to be deferential to our social superiors. Class conditioning is further reinforced but also slightly altered by later adult social interaction. We acquire instinctual class habits or 'a feel for the game' about what to do and how to conduct ourselves. Through these unconsciously learned habits we tend to reproduce the class structures that we have inherited as if it was part of the natural order of things to live like this.

Common sense tends to reflect our class habitus. Middle class children seem to find higher education or fine art as things that they can effortlessly understand because they have already acquired the necessary skills and aptitudes through their class habitus. Working class children, perhaps brought up in a situation where money is tight and where art and books might be seen as a luxury or a waste of time, tend to have lower educational and cultural expectations and aspirations and need to make a greater conscious effort when it comes to studying.

Bourdieu (1984) uses another term to help explain how class seems to be reproduced so naturally, **'cultural capital'**. The *Sociology Dictionary* gives the following definition:

> "**Cultural capital** Wealth in the form of knowledge and ideas, which legitimates the maintenance of status and power" (Jary and Jary, 1995: 137).

Cultural capital develops Marx's idea of economic capital and Weber's idea of social status. Like economic capital, cultural capital in the form of advanced education or a refined appreciation of art can be used by its owners to get control over resources. Like social status, cultural capital is concerned with how social inequalities are legitimated and perpetuated. Class inequalities will continue, Bourdieu argued, as long as cultural capital can be 'cashed in' for economic capital and economic capital can buy the time and space that is necessary to acquire higher levels of cultural capital.

A key way that the class structure is reproduced is through the education system. The education system prizes the kind of abstract knowledge that middle class groups acquire from birth and undervalues the practical skills that working class groups are immersed in. High levels of cultural capital enable middle class children to succeed in school, college and university and so acquire high educational capital. However, when working class children begin to succeed in higher levels of education and qualifications begin to be more equally distributed across society they lose their economic value as a badge of privileged access to middle class occupations. Then, Bourdieu argues, the middle class switch away from educational capital to new kinds of social closure. They get privileged access to elite occupations through their cultural capital of having been at a 'good school' or studied at an elite university.

Bourdieu's research disputes the idea that society is based on merit and ability. Instead, inherited social and economic privileges and cultural advantages give each generation of middle class children an edge to maintain themselves in high prestige and well paid occupations like medicine, the arts, finance and law.

Class in Scotland Today

For two centuries Scotland has been viewed as a working class nation. This was due to its early **industrialisation** in the late 18th century and the resulting creation of a new class of wage labourers. By the early 19th century wage labour was the dominant way that people supported themselves in Scotland. The working class were mainly employed in heavy manual work, such as coal mining, engineering and shipbuilding. Or, at least, working class men were employed in these industries. Many working class women were employed in domestic service, though other women worked in factories and mills, for instance, the mainly female workforce in Dundee's jute mills.

The industrial past that shaped Scotland as a class society has largely disappeared. Many people, including social scientists, reach the conclusion, therefore, that class is no longer as important as it once might have been. Class is often seen as less important in shaping life chances than status indicators like gender, religion, ethnicity or sexuality. People are more preoccupied with consumer choice, lifestyle and taste, so the argument goes, as markers of social difference, to concern themselves with the tedious and seemingly old fashioned ideas of class, class consciousness, class conflict and class interests (Giddens, 1994).

The restructuring of the economy and the workforce of the past two decades, it is further claimed, has led some to argue that while inequalities are still with us this has little to do with class as Marx and Weber understood it. Instead, it has more to do with the way that society has been broken up and fragmented down to the level of individuals, who are left to fend for themselves in a society defined not by class but by the growing number of 'risks' – economic, environmental, personal – that people now face. For the main theorist of a **'risk society'**, Ulrich Beck (1992: 88), we now live within "capitalism without classes." Today, when the risks and hazards of social inequality have been thoroughly 'individualised' according to Beck (1992), it makes no sense to keep talking about social groups facing a common situation as we do about class.

This rejection of class, either in terms of Marxist class theory or Weberian class analysis, has thrown the baby out with the bathwater. In Scotland, class has not declined as the primary determinant of people's life chances or their collective identity (Law and Mooney, 2006b). A look at some of the statistical data on class in Scotland will allow us to pinpoint some of the changes and continuities in class inequalities over the past few decades.

1. What Kinds of Industries do People Work in?

First, let us look at the changing industrial structure of employment. **Table 4.5** shows that fewer people work in jobs where they make things. Manufacturing fell from nearly one quarter of the Scottish workforce to around an eighth. On the other hand, there were large rises in service sector employment in finance, estate agents and business management services in the private sector. In the public sector employment has also risen, especially in health and social work. Such sectors also tend to have a higher proportion of female workers.

Table 4.5 Industrial employment in Scotland 1981-2001

Sector	Year		
	1981	**1991**	**2001**
Agriculture	2.9	2.5	2.1
Fishing	0.4	0.5	0.3
Mining, quarrying	2.1	1.7	1.2
Manufacturing	24.1	18.5	13.2
Construction	8.6	8.2	7.5
Wholesale, retail and motor trade	14.5	14.6	14.4
Hotels and restaurants	4.5	4.5	5.7
Transport, storage and communication	6.9	6.6	6.7
Financial	2.7	3.5	4.6
Real estate and business activity	3.7	6.2	11.2
Public administration and defence	7.0	7.9	7.0
Education	7.2	7.6	7.3
Health and social work	9.5	11.5	12.4
Other community, social and personal	3.8	4.4	5.2

(Source: Adapted from Paterson *et al* (2004: 47) *Living in Scotland: Social and Economic Change Since 1980*, Edinburgh, Edinburgh University Press.)

2. What Kinds of Jobs do People do?

So, it is clear then that the type of workplaces that people work in is changing. What are the kind of jobs they are employed in? From **Table 4.6** we can see that around 10 per cent more people are working in 'managerial and professional' positions and around 14 per cent less are working in what are often referred to as 'traditional' manual working class jobs, since 1981.

Table 4.6 Socio-economic group, 1981-2001

Percentage in columns	Year		
Socio-economic group	1981	1991	2000
Employers and managers, large establishments	4.4	4.2	9.3
Employers and managers, small establishments	4.4	8.5	7.1
Professionals, self-employed	0.5	0.8	1.1
Professionals, employees	2.9	3.9	5.1
Total managers and professionals	**12.2**	**17.4**	**22.6**
Intermediate non-manual	10.2	14.5	16.2
Junior non-manual	19.3	21.0	18.9
Personal service	6.1	4.7	6.1
Foremen and supervisors	2.6	2.4	4.4
Total non-manual	**38.2**	**42.6**	**45.6**
Skilled manual	19.3	14.2	10.5
Semi-skilled manual	12.4	10.8	9.6
Unskilled manual	7.7	7.0	5.1
Total manual	**39.4**	**32**	**25.2**

(Adapted from Paterson *et al* (2004: 85) *Living in Scotland: Social and Economic Change Since 1980*, Edinburgh, Edinburgh University Press.)

These figures have led a group of leading sociologists at Edinburgh University to claim that Scotland is *not* a predominantly working class society. Instead, they argue that Scotland is becoming a 'professional society' (Paterson *et al*, 2004). The Edinburgh social scientists see class in broadly Weberian terms based on the classification of occupations. As they put it:

"Simply put, social class refers to the structuring of power, mainly but not exclusively economic power, power in the marketplace, which differentiates people according to the skills and resources they are able to bring to the market, and the rewards they derive from it" (Paterson, *et al*, 2004: 81).

However, the figures can be interpreted quite differently from the conclusion that the market power of individuals today can be characterised as 'professional'. It is true that just over one-fifth of employees have some kind of senior responsibility inside the organisations that employ them. On the other hand, the majority of the rest of the workforce have significantly less power and control over their working conditions. This would seem to place them firmly in the Weberian category of the working class. Except that the Edinburgh-based Weberians tend to identify the working class on a narrow basis with the manual working class only and see non-manual work as an indicator of social mobility up the hierarchy of status and market situation.

Marxists looking at the same data would emphasise the continuing structuring of wage labour as subordinate to and exploited by managers in the sectors identified in **Table 4.5**. So, although the specific occupations and workplaces have changed, most Scots still have no option but to sell their labour power and to come under the control of a management hierarchy in the workplace to produce surplus value. Marxists would also tend to look at the totality of how the working class has been restructured on a global scale, with the manufacturing work formerly done in Scotland being transferred to newly developing economies like South Korea and China.

3. How Equally is Wealth Distributed?

If Scotland was truly becoming a 'professional' middle class society and if the Weberian assumption that status, market position and wealth tend to go together, then we might reasonably expect that Scots would be not only more prosperous as individuals but that wealth would begin to be spread more evenly across society. **Table 4.7** shows the distribution of wealth in the UK. From this it is clear that wealth is very unequally spread across society. Indeed, society is becoming more, not less, unequal. The top few per cent of the richest people in the country have amassed even greater personal fortunes for themselves, with the top five per cent going from owning just over one third in the mid-1980s to approaching half of all the personal wealth in the country by the 2000s.

One source of this growing inequality is a regressive taxation system that compels most wage earners to pay contributions to the Inland Revenue at a set rate while the very rich and special categories of earners can avoid or reduce taxation by using various accountancy loopholes and tax dodges. Even famous celebrities who campaign against world poverty can take advantage of this to add to their already huge fortunes. For instance, multi-millionaire Mick Jagger's pop group the Rolling Stones managed to pay only 1.6 per cent tax on earnings of £81 million in 2005, the same year as the giant Make Poverty History march in Edinburgh and the Live8 pop concerts. Anti-poverty campaigner Bono's band U2 similarly moved their business interests to the Netherlands in order to avoid paying higher taxation rates in Ireland.

Even Irvine Welsh, the best-selling author who became notorious for writing about the Scottish 'underclass', was listed by the Irish Revenue Commission as not paying any tax between 1998 and 2002 thanks to an 'artistic exemption' scheme (Dalgarno, 2006).

On the other hand, the proportion of wealth owned by the bottom half of society, who make regular taxation and national insurance payments and receive standard state benefits, has declined from ten per cent to six per cent. So, the distribution of wealth has changed to become even *more* unequal under New Labour than under the Conservatives. This suggests that class remains central to explaining worsening inequalities.

Table 4.7 Concentration of wealth among adult population, UK, 1986-2000

Year	Percentage of wealth owned by					
	Top 1%	2%	5%	10%	25%	50%
1986	18	24	36	50	73	90
1991	17	24	35	47	71	92
1996	20	27	40	52	74	93
1997	22	30	43	54	75	93
2000	22	29	42	54	74	94

(Source: Paterson *et al* (2004: 178) *Living in Scotland: Social and Economic Change Since 1980*, Edinburgh, Edinburgh University Press.)

4. Do People see Themselves as Working Class?

As we have seen, class can be considered not just as an objective fact based on occupation or wage labour. It also has an important subjective aspect. It is one thing for social scientists to categorise people into classes based on a classification scheme like Goldthorpe's (1980; 1987). This is an important way of finding out how class is changing. However, it is limited if no account is taken of how people actually see themselves in class terms. Past research found that some working class groups like routine office workers categorised themselves as belonging to the 'middle class' on account of the fact that they do not carry out manual labour. Other people in working class jobs may have a university degree or own their own homes and this might lead them to see themselves in status terms as 'middle class'.

In Scotland, exactly the reverse has happened. Employees in occupations that social scientists class as middle class 'professional' overwhelmingly see themselves as belonging to the working class. **Table 4.8** asked people to state which class they saw themselves as belonging to. It then compared their answer to the class that social scientists would place them in. Remarkably, more professionals saw themselves as 'working class' (51 per cent) than 'middle class' (43 per cent). At least two-thirds of all other social groups saw themselves as 'working class'. While this may or may not reflect the fact that most of these apparently 'professional' occupations have become more 'working class' in one way or another, working class identity in Scotland is stronger than ever even though the occupational structure has undergone dramatic changes since 1979 (Law and Mooney, 2006b).

5. Are Class and Education Connected?

As Bourdieu (1984; 1987) argued, class inequalities are at least in part maintained by the education system. **Table 4.9** shows a strong relationship between educational qualifications and the jobs that people end up getting. People in professional and skilled non-manual occupations tend to be educated to degree level. On the other hand, people in unskilled manual jobs, which have been declining over the past two decades, have much lower and fewer qualifications. In Scotland, therefore, educational attainment or failure remains central to the reproduction of class inequalities.

Table 4.8 Self-perceived class by broad socio-economic group, 1979 and 1999

Per cent in rows within year	Year			
	1979		1999	
Self-perceived class	Working class	Middle class	Working class	Middle class
Broad socio-economic group				
Professional and managerial	42.2	50.0	51.8	43.5
Intermediate non-manual	52.8	30.3	56.1	38.8
Junior non-manual	71.6	19.3	72.6	26.1
Skilled manual	78.4	10.8	82.8	14.6
Semi-skilled manual	84.2	10.5	79.1	15.7
Unskilled manual	81.3	6.3	79.6	15.3
All	62.8	20.9	69.2	26.9

(Source: Paterson *et al* (2004: 99) *Living in Scotland: Social and Economic Change Since 1980*, Edinburgh, Edinburgh University Press.)

Table 4.9 Highest educational qualification by socio-economic group in 2000

Per cent in rows	Highest educational attainment					
Socio-economic group	First degree, higher degree, professional qualification	HND, HNC, etc.	Higher Grade, A level, etc.	O Grade, Standard Grade, etc.	Scotvec modules, CSE, etc.	None or no answer
Professional and managerial	41.3	14.2	18.5	15.6	5.1	5.3
Intermediate non-manual	44.0	15.0	16.3	13.6	5.4	5.8
Junior non-manual	7.0	11.8	31.3	28.9	8.2	12.8
Skilled manual	2.6	6.2	25.7	41.2	12.8	11.5
Semi-skilled manual	3.3	6.7	17.1	32.8	16.6	23.5
Unskilled manual	1.1	1.6	11.7	26.7	20.6	38.2
Unclassified or armed forces	6.7	4.9	16.5	25.6	12.2	34.0

(Source: Paterson *et al* (2004) *Living in Scotland: Social and Economic Change Since 1980*, Edinburgh, Edinburgh University Press.)

Conclusion

Overall, we can say with some confidence that Scotland remains a society that is fundamentally shaped by class inequalities. While we need to register all the many changes that have happened to the kinds of industries and jobs people work in, we also have to ask whether this is a matter of degree or a matter of kind. In other words, are the changes to the structure of class so fundamental that we can talk of a society where class today is relatively unimportant?

Class has been declared 'dead and buried' time and time again. Curiously, the end of class is always announced by people like politicians, journalists, or academic social scientists, in other words people who occupy a very definite position in the class structure (Bourdieu, 1984). This chapter demonstrates that class remains at the heart of any adequate understanding of society. Recall how easy it was for common sense to stereotype working class youth as 'neds'. There are different ways to understand the class nature of Scottish society. Let us recap what we have covered in this chapter.

1. One, the Weberian approach, mainly emphasises *subjective* factors like social status and market situation.

2. Another, the Marxist approach, mainly emphasises *objective* structures of exploitation of wage labour and capitalist society.

3. A range of more recent approaches have tried to build on these traditions:

   i. Goldthorpe's class scheme.
   ii. Wright's contradictory class locations.
   iii. Bourdieu's ideas of class habitus and cultural capital.

4. Still others talk about class and poverty in the stigmatising language of 'the underclass'.

5. Finally, New Labour's concept of 'social exclusion' manages to ignore the class basis of poverty altogether.

Then we went on to look at some of the changes to class in contemporary Scotland. We found out the following about class:

1. People in Scotland tend to work in the service sector rather than manufacturing.

2. People tend to work in non-manual occupations.

3. More women are working than ever before.

4. The rich are getting richer and the poor are relatively poorer.

5. People in Scotland overwhelmingly tend to see themselves as working class.

6. There is a strong relationship between educational qualifications and the kinds of jobs people do.

What does all this mean for the study of social care and welfare policies? There is a widespread recognition in social policy and social welfare debates that we live and function within a class-divided society. Social policies are determined by unequal types of political power that tend to reinforce existing social divisions. For some social groups marginalisation or exclusion leads to discrimination, sometimes unintentionally, in their receipt of services. The structure of welfare provision might even reinforce class divisions (Ferguson *et al*, 2002). Earlier, we saw this with how taxation policies reinforce wealth inequalities.

Welfare can become a tool of social control over classes with low economic capital, low social status and low cultural capital. We have seen how ideas of 'neds', the underclass and social exclusion have been used in this way. Such groups become even more marginalised and disadvantaged so long as the structural basis of class inequality exists. For instance, welfare benefits might be used to bring people above the poverty level but still leave the wider class structure untouched. It is therefore important to critically examine the role of class in the restructuring of the welfare state and the role of the wider economy in reproducing an unequal and divided society in Scotland.

Further Reading

An excellent starting point for an introduction to theories of social class is the relevant chapter in Tony Sweeney, John Lewis and Neil Etherington (eds.) (2003) *Sociology and Scotland: An Introduction*. You might also look at any of the many introductory sociology textbooks that are aimed at students like yourselves. A good critical introduction to the ideas of Max Weber can be found in Kieran Allen's (2004) book of the same name: *Max Weber: A Critical Introduction*. A useful discussion of the Marxist approach to class as it applies to welfare is available in chapters 3 and 4 of Iain Ferguson, Michael Lavalette and Gerry Mooney's (2002) book, *Rethinking Welfare: A Critical Perspective*. On class in Scotland, two recent books have plenty of relevant data. Lindsay Paterson, Frank Bechhofer and David McCrone's (2004) *Living in Scotland: Social and Economic Change Since 1980* contains a CD-Rom full of interesting statistics. Their book takes a broadly Weberian approach to class, while Gregor Gall's (2005) *The Political Economy of Scotland* is more sympathetic to Marxism. You can find up-to-date material on class in the 2001 Census online (www.statistics.gov.uk/census/) and for wealth try the Inland Revenue website (www.hmrc.gov.uk/).

Useful Websites

2001 Census online: www.statistics.gov.uk/census/
Inland Revenue (HM Customs and Revenue): www.hmrc.gov.uk/
Registrar General: www.gro.gov.uk/
Registrar General for Scotland: www.gro-scotland.gov.uk/
Registrar General's Department: www.rgd.gov.jm/

Bibliography

Allen, K. (2004) *Max Weber: A Critical Introduction*, London, Pluto Press
Beck, U. (1992) *Risk Society: Towards a New Modernity*, London, Sage
Bourdieu, P. (1984) *Distinction: A Social Critique of the Judgement of Taste*, London, Routledge
Bourdieu, P. (1987) 'What makes a social class? On the theoretical and practical existence of groups', in *Berkeley Journal of Sociology*, 32
Croall, H. (2006) 'Criminal Justice in post-devolution Scotland', in *Critical Social Policy*, 26(3)
Dalgarno, P. (2006) 'Welsh: tax break wouldn't tempt me back', in *The Sunday Herald*, 13 August, p.11

Durkheim, E. (1947) *The Division of Labour in Society*, New York, NY, The Free Press

Ferguson, I., Lavalette, M. and Mooney, G. (2002) *Rethinking Welfare: A Critical Perspective*, London, Sage

Gall, G. (2005) *The Political Economy of Scotland: Red Scotland? Radical Scotland?* Cardiff, University of Wales Press

Giddens, A. (1994) *Beyond Left and Right: The Future of Radical Politics*, Cambridge, Polity Press

Goldthorpe, J.H. (with Llewellyn, C. and Payne, C.) (1980) *Social Mobility and Class Structure in Modern Britain*, Oxford, Oxford University Press

Goldthorpe, J.H. (with Llewellyn, C. and Payne, C.) (1987) *Social Mobility and Class Structure in Modern Britain* (Second Edition), Oxford, Oxford University Press

Gubbay, J. (1997) 'A Marxist Critique of Weberian class analysis', in *Sociology*, 31(1)

Jary, D. and Jary, J. (1995) *Collins Dictionary of Sociology* (Second Edition), Glasgow, HarperCollins

Law, A. (2006) 'Respect and hatred: the class shame of "Ned" humour', in *Variant*, 25, Spring, http://www.variant.randomstate.org/pdfs/issue25/nedhumour.pdf

Law, A. and Mooney, G. (2006a) 'From the 'Underclass' to 'Neds': Continuity and Change in Class-Based Representations of Working Class Youth', Paper to British Society of Criminology, Annual Conference, Glasgow, July 5-8

Law, A. and Mooney, G. (2006b) ''We've never had it so good': The 'problem' of the working class in devolved Scotland', in *Critical Social Policy*, 26(3)

Murray, C.A. (1990) *The Emerging British Underclass*, London, IEA

Paterson, L., Bechhofer, F. and McCrone, D. (2004) *Living in Scotland: Social and Economic Change Since 1980*, Edinburgh, Edinburgh University Press

Parkin, F. (1979) *Marxism and Class Theory: A Bourgeois Critique*, London, Tavistock

Sennett, R. and Cobb, J. (1977) *The Hidden Injuries of Class*, Cambridge, Cambridge University Press

Sweeney, T., Etherington, N. and Lewis, J. (2003) 'Social Class', in Sweeney, T., Lewis, J. and Etherington, N. (eds.) (2003) *Sociology and Scotland: An Introduction*, Paisley, Unity Publications

Sweeney, T., Lewis, J. and Etherington, N. (eds.) (2003) *Sociology and Scotland: An Introduction*, Paisley, Unity Publications

Tressell, R. (1965) *The Ragged Trousered Philanthropists*, London, Granada (first published in 1955)

Weber, M. (1964) *The Theory of Social and Economic Organization*, New York, NY, The Free Press

Weber, M. (1946) 'Class, status and party', in Gerth, H.H. and Mills, C.W. (eds.) (1946) *From Max Weber: Essays in Sociology*, New York, NY, Oxford University

Press

Wright, E.O. (1985) *Classes*, London, Verso

Wright, E.O. (1979) *Class, Crisis and the State*, London, Verso

Wright, E.O. (1997) *Class Counts: Comparative Studies in Class Analysis*, Cambridge, Cambridge University Press

Answers to *'Pause for thought'*

Characteristics	Describe how this applies to neds
Class	Poor working class
Gender	Mainly male but also female 'nedettes'
Neighbourhood	Housing scheme
Dress style	Tracksuit, trainers, caps
Behaviour	Threatening, violent, gang member, Buckfast drinker, exaggerated swagger
Social group	Street gang member
Attitude	Aggressive, belligerent
Age	Teenager
Education	Low attainment, expelled
Speech	Slang, swearing, slurred
Employment	Menial work, unemployed, petty criminal

Chapter 5

Poverty and Disadvantage in Contemporary Scotland: Examining the Policy Responses

Gill Scott

Introduction

The idea that poverty matters and that the public cares about it cannot be in doubt when we consider the high profile achieved by the Make Poverty History campaign in 2005 and the public acceptance of the End Child Poverty strategy of government in the UK and Scotland since 1999. However, when we start to evaluate poverty and the true extent, nature and impact of anti-poverty measures, the complexity and the politics of such measures become apparent. Poverty and relative disadvantage remain key features of UK society. Poverty affects the lives of millions of people despite the material success of the UK economy. It involves not only a lack of resources, but reflects patterns of power, reduces life expectancy and impacts on social cohesion. For readers of this Book, key themes that need to be addressed with relation to poverty are **social inclusion** and **social exclusion** and **continuity and change**.

Relevant questions that need to be asked, therefore, are: 'why does poverty persist?' and 'why do poverty and disadvantage remain a major starting point for any student of health and welfare?' As **Chapters 1, 2** and **3** highlight, students of welfare need to think carefully about not only the conditions that policy and welfare services attempt to address, but also about the different ways in which 'conditions' come to be seen as *problems* that need to be addressed. In this chapter that approach will be taken as a starting point for the analysis of poverty and social disadvantage and the policy responses in Scotland. In particular this chapter will attempt to:

- Examine and explain the recent 'rediscovery' of poverty amongst policy makers.

- Consider the politics and values underlying anti-poverty policy.

- Assess the changing landscape of poverty and poverty reduction policies in the 21st century.

- Explore the significance of current policy settlements for poverty reduction and the overall discussion of social justice.

Poverty – A 'New' Policy Issue Since the 1990s

The newly formed devolved Labour-led government (which included the Liberal Democrats) that took office in Scotland in 1999 inherited levels of poverty and inequality that were the highest amongst the industrialised countries of Europe. Levels of poverty that had been reduced in the 1960s and 1970s reappeared as unemployment rose in the 1980s and as public services and benefits came under pressure from the Thatcher governments (1979-1990). The response from the Scottish government was in many respects similar to that of New Labour in the UK as a whole – reducing poverty was to be a key policy aim for the next ten years (Mooney and Scott, 2005) . Where Tony Blair claimed in an article in *The Independent* in 1996:

> "If the next Labour government has not raised the living standards of the poorest by the end of its time in office it will have failed" (28 July 1996).

Donald Dewar claimed, just prior to his move to First Minister in the new Scottish Parliament, that a Scottish Labour government was committed to:

> "[A] more inclusive, cohesive and ultimately sustainable society" (quoted in *The Herald*, 3 February, 1998).

As we examine how this rhetoric has been transformed into policy we can explore why poverty and social inclusion re-appeared in policy discussions, how it relates to longer traditions of social justice in welfare settlements and what impact recent policy has had on the gap between Britain and Scotland's levels of poverty and those of other European countries.

A Political Issue

There can be little doubt that poverty is a political issue. For centuries the poor in the United Kingdom have been defined by the *non poor* in political debate as lazy, criminal and responsible for their circumstances, i.e. as disreputable, whilst demands from *the poor* often had political expression through the labour movement. What lessons can be learned from this? Problems associated with poverty are *not* always with us, are *not* always accepted and may have as much to do with those who are *not* as poor as the poor. At times, though, it appears as if policy makers and members of the public are happy to see poverty increase and, according to Saul Becker (1997), to ignore the part that all citizens, including the poor, can have in discussions about poverty and welfare.

Poverty can be seen as only referring to a lack of resources available to an individual or household. However, it tends to be identified as a much wider issue and addressed through a number of policies that link both poverty and **social exclusion**. Much of the politics of poverty sees its expression in different ways of thinking and talking about poverty, each of which carries ideas about causes and ways of dealing with the problem (Howard *et al*, 2001). *Three* key values can be seen to have shaped policy in Scotland since the late 1990s. These include:

- The belief that **social exclusion** and social injustice rather than simply low income or material poverty should be addressed.

- A belief that anti-poverty strateg ies should be directed at those who are **willing to help themselves**.

- And, finally, a belief that there are **anti social values** held by some families and communities that prevent anti-poverty strategies working effectively.

Each of these is discussed below.

Social Exclusion

Social exclusion is a term that has largely been adopted throughout the European Union (EU) as a way of conceptualising poverty (Berghman, 1995). It represents a dynamic and wide-ranging definition of the processes and relationships involved in poverty and extends thinking beyond simple measures of material deprivation. Walker and Walker (1997: 8) argue:

> "Poverty is about a lack of resources, especially income, necessary to participate in British society. Social exclusion refers to the dynamic process of being shut out, fully or partially, from the systems which integrate a person into society."

There is an implicit promise in the notion of social exclusion to examine all of the processes contributing to poverty, including, for example, racism and sexism, but as some critics point out the term does raise questions of "who includes whom, on what terms? And in what are they included?" (Levitas, 1998). In Scotland and Wales, the concept of 'social justice' has also been used when thinking about poverty and has added a further dimension to ideas about social exclusion and **social inclusion**. It often, but not always, directs attention to issues of inequality not merely disadvantage and exclusion. There is no doubt that 'social justice' is a difficult term to define (Bevir, 2005; Pearce and Paxton, 2005). It is often used to argue for a fairer distribution of goods, resources and opportunities as well as for policies covering wider indicators of wellbeing. In many ways the concept of social justice also encourages a stronger reflection on the role of political and social institutions than the term social inclusion. The promotion of social justice as a key feature of a 'new' devolved Scotland is clear in early statements from the (first) First Minister:

> "The commitment to social justice lies at the heart of political and civic life in Scotland. We need to harness the efforts of many to the greater good of all, and establish social justice as the hallmark of Scottish society" (Donald Dewar, First Minister, 'Foreword', in *Social Justice: A Scotland Where Everyone Matters*, Scottish Executive 1999).

Similarly in the other established devolved nations of the UK, such as Wales, a multi-faceted dimension of social justice is highlighted by the Welsh Assembly's *Social Justice Report 2004*, when it states that:

> "Social Justice is about every one of us having the chances and opportunities to make the most of our lives and use our talents to the full. Social Justice touches on all aspects of life – from our health as babies to our care as older people" (Welsh Assembly, 2004: 4).

Pause for thought
- How would you define 'social justice'?

However, we need to recognise that there are sharply contrasting views about what is meant by a 'fair' or 'just' distribution 'social justice', what the basis of a 'fair' distribution should be and how institutions can address injustice most effectively.

Brian Barry, a contemporary philosopher who has spent much time trying to define the modern term social justice points out the following:

> "The modern concept of social justice emerged out of the throes of early industrialisation […] it was the rallying call of social democratic parties everywhere in Europe" (Barry, 2005: 12).

He is referring to early 20th century ideas. Today the conception of social justice is clearly on the political agendas of politicians, but it is less clearly identifiable with a commitment to social redistribution of resources than in the past, when 'problems' of poverty were seen to be closely related to 'problems' of affluence and power. Nevertheless from 1999 the idea was increasingly used by politicians and policy makers to describe strategies to reduce poverty and develop an 'inclusive' society in Scotland. Indeed, in both Scotland and Wales, a Minister for Social Justice was appointed to bring together strands of social policy across areas such as education, urban regeneration, health, childcare and social care. Important steps were taken to develop a 'social justice strategy' in Scotland and statements of intent and policy, providing indications of how the strategy, has been rolled out. These are particularly evident in *three* documents:

- *Social Justice: a Scotland where everyone matters* (Scottish Executive, 1999).

- *'The Partnership Agreement'* (Scottish Executive, 2003a).

- *Closing the Gap: Scottish Budget for 2003-2006* (Scottish Executive, 2003b).

All were characterised by cross party support and targets were identified that made delivery of the strategy more specific. The strategy was founded on a 'life cycle approach' and focused on both people and places. Ten long term targets were identified for achieving a more socially just Scotland. These targets included, defeating child poverty within a generation (thereby reflecting the commitment given the previous year by Prime Minister Blair and New Labour at Westminster); ensuring that every 19 year old was in education, training or work; full employment; and reducing inequalities between different communities across Scotland. The targets were supplemented by 29 'milestones' that would be measured annually to show how far progress had been made in meeting the long term targets. A Social Justice Annual Report was to be published detailing progress. Three such Reports were published in 2000, 2001, and 2002 (Scottish Executive, 2000, 2001, 2002 – all available at www.scotland.gov.uk).

Those Willing to Help Themselves

The second belief shaping anti-poverty policy has been that anti-poverty strategy should be directed at those who were willing to help themselves. It is most clearly seen in discussions about widening opportunities and the value of prioritising entry or return to work as a key anti-poverty policy direction. Labour's strong focus on employment has seen what McNight (2005) calls a shift from *employment for all* to *employment opportunity for all*. **Welfare to Work** is often used to describe the shift in emphasis that has occurred and which highlights a change to a welfare contract where citizens must prove that they are contributing as much as they can if they are to receive support from the state. The concept of social exclusion here is that it is largely but not solely exclusion from paid employment – and, in turn, social inclusion is principally dependent upon entering paid employment. Active labour market policies and tax credit policies directed at helping adults in workless households towards work have been the result. In fact the importance of a job lies at the centre of anti-poverty policy across Europe (see Helms, **Chapter 6**).

The UK is not different, although the level of compulsion and relationship to benefits does differ markedly between countries (Scott, 2006). Unlike the ideas of social exclusion and social justice, this view of the problem of poverty concentrates on the barriers to participation and not the distribution of resources. It is a very powerful idea in current policy development.

Anti Social Values

Finally, but quite importantly, a view of poverty that has been particularly strong from the political right is the idea that the problems of poverty lie in the anti social values of significant sections of the poor. Debate about the future of welfare in Britain became increasingly focused on morality, behaviour and personal character in the late 20th century. It continues today. In important respects, recent welfare 'reforms' have drawn on the rhetoric of an **'underclass'** and have been as much about forging fundamental changes in the relationship between the individual and the state, as they have been about developing new ways of tackling poverty or social exclusion (see Helms, **Chapter 6**).

The concept of an 'underclass' is one employed by commentators across the political spectrum, although definitions vary widely. The American writer, Charles Murray (1994), argued that belonging to the 'underclass' is a matter of choice made possible by an over-accommodating welfare state; people *choose* to depend on benefits because it is a rational thing to do. However, benefits act as a disincentive to work, so the appropriate response from the state should be to withdraw benefits so that people would have no alternative but to try to find employment. A different approach is taken by Mead (1986), who argues that people who become part of an 'underclass' do so because they are feckless or unwilling to work, because they have become detached from the values of their society. The answer to this is not to withdraw benefits, but to make them conditional on fulfilling certain requirements, in order to *re-condition* people to the *obligation* to work. This has typically meant carrying out some form of work or training in return for benefits – thus giving rise to the name **'Workfare'**. Whatever the approach, the 'underclass' is generally another name for the groups the Victorians called **'the undeserving poor'**. That is, people whose poverty is generally felt to be self-inflicted and who are perceived not to conform to the **'norms'** of society. Others, however, point out that "the term expresses more about the fears of the rest of society than about the reality it seeks to describe" (Oppenheim, 1998).

The result of the belief in an underclass, for policy, is that the language of, and emphasis on, 'responsibilities' and 'duties' to what are seen to be 'common values' has come to be a consistent feature of many social and welfare policies. This is often linked to the idea of the 'greater good': that individuals have important duties to family, community and to society as a whole. There is seldom an analysis of what that 'greater good' is and who it serves, but it does mean that for those who are seen by policy makers as seeking to side-step their social responsibilities, an increasing range of penalties have developed, as in, for example, the withdrawal of benefits for those neglecting to take up work.

Poverty and Social Justice in Scotland: Facts and Figures

Changing views of the nature of society and political will are important in understanding why poverty has moved up the political agenda in different ways at different times. Also significant to the amount of resources devoted to addressing the issue, is the evidence on the extent and causes of poverty. The evidence has proved a powerful incentive for change in the last few years in Scotland. Despite the conclusion of Paterson, Bechhoffer and McCrone (2004) in *Living in Scotland* that Scotland is "a more affluent, comfortable and pleasant place than it was in 1980," the 'darker side' of change is also evident when we examine figures in more detail. Poverty is no mere residual phenomenon in Scotland: 1.1 million people in Scotland (22 per cent) in 2002-2003 were living in low-income households (defined as less than 60 per cent of median income, after deducting housing costs). Drawing on government and academic research since 1997 we can get a clear picture of the extent of social exclusion, income deprivation and **worklessness** (see Helms, **Chapter 6**). A less clear picture is available for the issues that a wider definition of social justice would demand, i.e. the *extent* of inequalities. Nevertheless in the next few sections we will look at some of the key questions for any student of poverty and anti-poverty policy. These are:

- Which groups are vulnerable to poverty?
- Where are they located?

- What is the impact of poverty on the poor?
- What are the key responses?

Which Groups are Vulnerable to Poverty?

Pause for thought
- Thinking about contemporary Scottish society, which groups do you feel are most vulnerable to poverty?

The risks of poverty are not spread evenly and they are dependent on a number of factors. These include:

- Discrimination.
- The ability to meet the extra costs of a child.
- The ability to meet the extra costs imposed by disability.
- Unequal access to the labour market.
- Geographical location.
- Age.
- Gender.

The likelihood of experiencing poverty varies across the life cycle and over time. Remember that no group is homogenous; factors such as gender, disability, ethnicity and class need to be taken into account (Brown *et al*, 2002). Key groups where risks of poverty are high in Scotland include:

- **Female headed households, particularly lone parent.** Poverty amongst lone parents has reduced, but lone parents remain twice as likely to be poor when compared with couples with children. They are also more likely to experience persistent and severe poverty even when they are working (One Plus, 2004). Over half of the lone parents surveyed in a 2003 Scottish Household Survey (Scottish Executive, 2003) reported an annual income of between only £6,000-£10,000. Thirty seven per cent of lone parents in the same survey reported 'not managing very well', having some financial difficulties or deep financial difficulties, over twice the proportion of households generally. Lone parents in remote rural areas are particularly likely to struggle financially.

106

- **Children:** Using the headline measure of children in households with income below 60 per cent of the median British household income after housing costs, in 2003/2004 some 25 per cent of children in Scotland were living in relatively low income households (Department for Work and Pensions (DWP), 2005). To put this indicator into context, for a couple with two children (aged five and 11) the cash value of the 60 per cent median threshold for 2003-2004 after housing costs was £262 per week, and £182 for a single parent with two children (aged five and 11). The figures over the last five years suggest that the lives of children from low income households have improved. However, the Scottish Executive's own figures (Scottish Executive, 2005) suggest that advances in educational achievement and health seem to reach children from low income households more slowly than children in affluent households and inequalities of opportunity across generations remain a major problem.

- **Disabled:** Poverty relates strongly to the incidence of limiting long term illness. Individuals with limited long-term illness are at greater risk of poverty than those who have no limiting long term illnesses: 40 per cent of those with limiting long term illnesses compared with 21 per cent of the general population in 2004. Figures collated in 2004 also show that the disabled are less likely to be able to access employment: they have a 30 per cent employment rate compared with the rate of 85 per cent for all adults of working age (Riddell *et al*, 2005).

- Some groups who have a high risk of poverty may not appear in great numbers. Although we may have little detailed information about such groups, partly because they are the least likely to be surveyed, when evidence does appear it is clear that their poverty can be extreme, for example, gypsies/travellers, minority religions, ex-offenders, the homeless, refugees and asylum seekers. One study of asylum seekers and refugees found, for example, that destitution was a significant issue for asylum seekers in Scotland and was exacerbated by administrative procedures (Marsden *et al*, 2005).

What of the groups most likely to be affected by the newer integrated economic and social policy? Has work proved a successful route out of poverty for all? The recent Joseph Rowntree Foundation report (Palmer *et al*, 2004), *Monitoring Poverty and Social Exclusion in Scotland 2004*, found that the number of indicators of poverty showing improvement in the last decade is more than double the number that have grown worse. Nevertheless the researchers identify *two* groups who, despite the supposed integration, are bearing the costs of poverty:

- **Working age adults *without* dependent children:** The percentage of children and pensioners in low-income households has been falling, but the rate among working-age adults without dependent children has been rising. Looking at households where no working-age adult has a job, three out of four are single people or couples without dependent children. This situation is compounded by the fact that security for this group does not appear to have been a matter of priority: out-of-work benefits for this group have stayed unchanged in real terms for a decade, whereas benefits for pensioners and families have risen by a third since 1998.

- **Low paid workers:** Although work reduces the risk of poverty, it does *not* eliminate it. Thus, two out of five Scottish people living in poor working-age households include at least one adult who is in paid work. One in three Scottish workers is paid less than £6.50 an hour, the majority of them women. Half the working population aged 25 to 50 without Higher grade qualifications earns less than £6.50 an hour. The extent of mobility up and down the earnings distribution has also fallen sharply. Low paid workers are increasingly likely to remain low paid workers.

Where are the Risks of Poverty Located?

We know that place as well as social position is also related to poverty and its risks. What is the distribution in Scotland? Looking at the geographical patterns of deprivation across Scotland the highest concentrations of households in poverty are found in areas where economic growth has passed them by: Glasgow, Dundee, Inverclyde and West Dunbartonshire (Scottish Executive, 2005a). There has, moreover, been a long running negative impact on urban conditions of concentrated poverty within deprived areas. The multiple problems of deprived neighbourhoods are nothing new, but since the late 1990s there has been recognition that some of these problems have been getting worse. Life expectancy is poorer in areas of deprivation (see McCafferty, **Chapter 9**), car ownership and access is lower, literacy rates and internet access are lower. Overall, it appears that opportunities for work, social activities, environmental justice and good health are limited in areas of deprivation. The report, *Social Focus on Deprived Areas* (Scottish Executive, 2005a), found that 16 of the 20 most deprived areas in Scotland were in Glasgow and more than half of that city's wards were in the poorest 10 per cent for Scotland as a whole.

Much of this relates to geographic patterns of unemployment over the last 20 years; however, it is not solely due to lack of work. When we examine patterns of low income we can see that poverty and place do not simply reflect unemployment or economic inactivity. The Joseph Rowntree Foundation/New Policy Institute's (Palmer *et al*, 2004) *Monitoring Poverty and Social Exclusion in Scotland 2004* highlighted distinct patterns of low pay related to geography. Low pay as a source of low income is particularly prevalent in rural areas such as the Borders and Dumfries and Galloway, as well as areas where traditional industry has declined, such as Inverclyde and West Dunbartonshire.

Geographic distribution, then, is well documented and often reflects the distribution of work. However, policy can also contribute to spatial divisions if the areas of deprivation become seen as 'problem areas' and the people in an area become **'labelled'** as problems themselves. Economic growth in inner city areas, for example, is sometimes seen as more important than the people who have traditionally lived in them:

> "Improving local economies often exposes existing communities to displacement and increased surveillance" (Mangen, 2005: 203).

What is the Impact of Poverty on the Poor?

Poverty means diminished **'life chances'**. For some it may entail going without essentials such as sufficient food, adequate housing, heating and enough clothing. For many it will also mean having to live without access to the services or social activities that others consider normal; in effect being excluded from taking part in society. Some of the impacts identified by Palmer *et al* (2004) include fuel poverty, debt and poor health. Drawing on a range of reports their study shows the following:

- Around three in 10 households cannot keep warm at a reasonable cost. Living with fuel poverty has serious consequences for health. It may also mean making cuts in other areas such as food or social activities. Living in poverty means going without necessities. Those in poverty spend half the average on food and 75 per cent lack two or more necessary items of clothing.

- Living on a low income also brings with it the threat of falling into unmanageable debt. Low income households most frequently fall behind on payments of basic household bills, such as rent and utilities – debts that incur the harshest of sanctions.

- When it comes to health there is abundant evidence that Scotland's poor suffer poor health as well as low income. McCafferty (**Chapter 9**) deals with this in some depth, but it is worth noting here that the highest **mortality** rates, by a considerable degree, are seen amongst those with persistently low incomes. Looking at the most deprived areas we find that men die 14 years younger than the national average, women seven. Both spend the last 13 years of their lives in poor health.

Pause for thought
- What impact do you think poverty has on those who suffer it?

Just as important as these quantifiable impacts of poverty on the life experienced by the poor, is the growing evidence (such as in McKendrick *et al's* (2004) *Life in low income families in Scotland* and Ridge's (2005) *Childhood poverty and social exclusion*), that poverty is in many ways a socially unacceptable world, heavily imbued with stigma and prejudice. For Richard Wilkinson (2005) it is the psychological impact of relative poverty, i.e. the differences in resources between those at the bottom and top of the income and resource ladders that is the most concerning for welfare analysts. He argues (Wilkinson, 2005) that whilst material living standards *do* contribute to health inequalities, the stresses of low social status and self esteem attaching to relative poverty are major contributors to poor health. Poverty *and* inequality are powerful determinants of long term health and social well being.

Causes and Policy Responses

Julian Le Grand (1999) states that if one individual is deprived relative to another due to social factors beyond their control, then that situation is unjust. Crucial to an understanding of poverty and the means to overcome it, is an analysis of those social factors, the processes and institutions that give rise to and exacerbate poverty and social exclusion. Some writers suggest that those most at risk of poverty are the casualties of industrial and social change. McGregor (2003) comments:

> "Research in the 1980s and 1990s had built up a picture of the social impact of economic change. The evidence pointed strongly in the direction of a process of cumulative disadvantage. Those in insecure labour market positions suffered from a series of major disadvantages in terms of personal welfare" (McGregor, 2003).

The intergenerational and life course transmission of social exclusion and poverty have also been explored: the part that early experiences and behavioural patterns play in social exclusion has been researched by a number of studies (Hobcraft, 1998; Gregg *et al*, 1999).

Some studies, though, see politics as the root of the problem, i.e. those who are powerful and privileged appropriate the resources and opportunities in both national and international arenas (Townsend, 2000).

There is no doubt that public policy can have an impact on the experience if not the cause of poverty. Policy responses vary. They are not always effective. Urban policy, criminal justice policy, employment policy, educational policy (see Mooney, **Chapter 12**, Munro and Nicholson, **Chapter 14**, Helms, **Chapter 6** and Clark, **Chapter 13**, respectively) can sustain social divisions as well as reduce them. However, it is clear that New Labour north and south of the border have tried to develop a new and wide ranging set of policies aimed at many of the drivers of poverty and social exclusion during the last decade. The **New Deal** and **Working Families Tax Credit** are examples of policies aimed at macro economic change; increases in Child Benefit and policies such as **Sure Start** aim to reduce intergenerational sources of exclusion; extra resources have been put into education and training; the work of the Social Exclusion Unit in England has been aimed at reducing community based poverty. Rather than redistribution, there has been much evaluation of the distinct approach adopted in the UK and a range of judgements regarding the effectiveness of the centrality of work and opportunity as the preferred route out of poverty (Walker, 1999; Pantazis and Gordon, 2000; Powell, 2002; Toynbee and Walker, 2005). The rest of this chapter will examine the reach of policy in Scotland in 2005.

Scotland and Anti-Poverty Policy

As we reported at the beginning of this chapter, the Scottish Executive has prioritised anti-poverty policy since its establishment in 1999 and has developed clear strategies and targets for change. In its first four years' assessment of policy, an impact was felt by many in government to be restricted by the existence of targets that were linked to national as well as devolved government policy. As the Labour led devolved government in Scotland entered its second and perhaps more confident term in 2003, policy responses became more targeted. Policies to prepare people for work and ease their entry to work, sometimes called **'activation policies'** had become established at UK level, as in the rest of Europe, as the most important policy tool for reducing poverty, but they were increasingly likely to be developed and delivered in consultation with the devolved government and local authorities.

The term **'social justice'** had been adopted in 2001 by the Scottish Executive as a means of describing anti-poverty policy, but the difficulties in clearly defining the term, when there was no great potential to redistribute resources in the devolved settlement, led to its replacement by a more explicit commitment to promoting equal *opportunity* rather than equality of *outcome*. This can be seen in the more 'New Labour' inspired phraseology of the Scottish Executive (2005), *Closing the Opportunity Gap* (CtOG), which describes the Scottish Executive's anti-poverty strategy. Positive changes could be seen in the strengthening of cross departmental work taken forward by the Closing the Opportunity Gap Cabinet Delivery Group. The result was that targets for reducing poverty and social exclusion were set that focused more clearly on the interventions of Scottish rather than UK government. They included:

- Reducing economic inactivity in the areas of highest economic inactivity.

- Reducing the proportion of 16-19 year olds not in education, employment or training (**'NEET'**).

- Increasing the employment and employability of those economically inactive or unemployed through creating jobs in the NHS.

- Tackling a significant aspect of health inequalities.

- Providing an integrated package of support for the most vulnerable children.

- Improving educational attainment at age 16 for the lowest attaining pupils across the country.

- Improving educational outcomes for 'looked after' children (i.e. in care).

- Improving access to high quality services in rural areas.

- Tackling community regeneration by improving the local infrastructure in the most disadvantaged communities.

- Reducing the risk of financial exclusion and multiple debt for low income families.

Specific targets have been set for each of the above. The targets for reducing economic inactivity rates, for example, were agreed with local Community Planning Partnerships in 2005 and a date for review set for some two years later.

These targets were selected because they were deemed to have the potential to have the greatest impact on poverty in Scotland. The high level objectives of the Scottish Executive's (2005) *Closing the Opportunity Gap* approach include:

- 'Providing routes out of poverty'.
- 'Preventing new generations from falling into poverty'.
- 'Supporting the most vulnerable'.

They were clearly about widening opportunities and reducing the impact of poverty. We can see too that the targets are, as in the rest of the UK, largely focused on work as the route out of poverty for this and the next generation. Indeed, the first year of developing service delivery for these targets largely focused on employability issues. In achieving the targets, partnerships between different Scottish Executive departments, local authorities, Community Planning Partnerships and national organisations, such as the Department for Work and Pensions, are crucial. Strategies to achieve the targets are devolved to local partners, but in drawing up the targets the Scottish Executive is highlighting that the distribution of funds and service delivery agreements are to be set more clearly.

Generally, the targets were received well by the Scottish Parliament and by the anti-poverty network in Scotland. Anti-poverty agencies at local and national level and in both the public and voluntary sectors saw them as evidence of a commitment to a distinctive social welfare in Scotland. Nevertheless, there have been some concerns about the lack of attention paid to the increase in low paid work in Scotland and whether measuring target achievement is possible (Poverty Alliance, 2005). Whilst there has been some recognition that the Scottish Executive has relatively little power to change the pattern of inequality, some would argue that it should still be central to policy development and communications between Whitehall and Holyrood.

In reality, what distinguishes Scottish anti-poverty policy from that of the rest of the UK, are the delivery agencies rather than its content. Until very recently one of the most dominant features of the British welfare state was its highly centralised nature, particularly in the policy areas of employment and social security – critical policy areas for addressing poverty. Like many countries, however, there is a growing realisation that even anti-poverty measures such as the **'activation'** of unemployed people – specifically social assistance recipients – may benefit from decentralization (Finn, 2000; see also Helms, **Chapter 6**). There was a widespread view that devolution for Scotland would shape the development of innovative and 'more inclusive' social policies and the development and delivery of the *Closing the Opportunity* targets suggest that, in the devolved parts of the UK, policy can enhance support available to disadvantaged groups. However, the analysis above suggests that the content of anti-poverty policy does not differ markedly from the rest of the UK. Child poverty is foregrounded, work and enterprise are seen as essential elements of progress, and inequality is hardly mentioned.

Policy Impact?

What has been the result of change in anti-poverty policy in Scotland? Some key criticisms of anti-poverty policy generally over the last 20 years have been that: policy can create new barriers in the reduction of poverty; connections between policy areas are not adequately understood or exploited; and policy has not been informed by what works, either in the short or long term and auditing has not been built into the process (Sanderson, 2000). Can these criticisms be levelled at anti-poverty in Scotland?

It is difficult to answer, as many of the challenges of effective anti-poverty policy involve both the direct policies of a Scottish Executive and the fiscal and social security issues of Westminster. They highlight the need and value of an integrated UK and Scottish approach to poverty. Nevertheless there is room for 'Scottish *solutions* to Scottish *problems*'. The last five years have provided invaluable experience of an integrated approach to policy development and delivery within the new devolved Scotland. This is not to suggest that the understanding of poverty and the impact policy could make was not available prior to devolution. Rather, t he clearer targets for poverty reduction, the growing confidence of the devolved government and far more accurate, robust data at Scottish level, provide a more effective, but by no means complete, base for evaluating policy and trends in poverty that are affected by the Scottish Executive and UK government.

On the basis of the information that is available it does seem as though, despite some disputes over the figures, anti-poverty policy has begun to be more integrated and effective. **'Absolute' poverty** has fallen, poorer pensioners have done far better, and the numbers living in households with less than 60 per cent of 1998 median income have fallen.

Nevertheless there are areas where policy makers could still focus their attention if social injustice is to be addressed and a fairer society developed. These include:

- A need to identify the situations and times when risks of poverty are high for particular groups and the identification with these groups of what would 'work'. Poverty is complex and multi-dimensional. Greater understanding of those complexities would help to effectively focus interventions.

- A need to support people making the transition into employment. This can include initiatives like the Lone Parent Student Childcare Support Grant (Ballantyne *et al*, 2003), but could also include the provision of advice and guidance services relating to employment and training rights, money and debt advice, as well as childcare information.

- The asking of key questions about sustainability and quality of services. Identification of long term plans and commitments is needed, rather than 'media friendly' initiatives that can lead to disappointment and anger amongst the electorate.

- Improvements in key public services, particularly childcare and housing. These remain major areas where the Scottish Executive can make a difference to people at various stages of their lives, particularly households with children, the working poor without children, the economically inactive and the elderly.

- A recognition that inequality of resources as well as opportunities exists and can have a long term effect on areas such as health, but also on social cohesion. (Doing so can help demand attention be paid to social justice.)

Pause for thought
- What are the main dimensions of current anti-poverty policy in Scotland?

Conclusion

Throughout this chapter the point has been made that understanding poverty and deprivation in Scotland today involves an examination of the factors that contribute to their distribution and to the policy responses that have been adopted. It is clear from this review that, despite economic growth, poverty has *not* disappeared. The risks of poverty have been reduced for some but many continue to experience living conditions and levels of financial hardship that are not compatible with good health or social cohesion.

A key question for health and welfare workers is, 'what creates and maintains poverty in a relatively prosperous industrial society such as Scotland?' Individual explanations have been eschewed in this chapter – more emphasis has been placed on the potential of macro level explanations for students of health and welfare. Economic and social change has occurred that explains some shifts in the distribution of risk, particularly shifts in the Scottish jobs market . However , the politics of poverty policy has been highlighted as an area worthy of further examination if we are to understand why the aim of reducing child poverty has been prioritised and why achievements have not been as great over the last decade as many had hoped. Earlier chapters have examined the historical context in which welfare in Scotland has developed. In this chapter this has been combined with a short analysis of the key perspectives on poverty that have informed policy, and students are advised to compare this analysis with the theories on welfare introduced by Tony Sweeney in **Chapter 2**.

Of particular importance is the need to reconsider why social justice and attempts to address social inequality have not really appeared in recent policy responses. As Kitty Stewart (2005) notes in a review of poverty in Europe, the UK's position did improve from the worst to fifth from the bottom between 1998 and 2001 and in Scotland the number of indicators of poverty showing improvement since 1997 is more than double the number that have grown worse in Scotland (Palmer *et al*, 2004). However, this has largely been achieved by concentrating on raising the floor: improving the economic and social position of the poor in absolute terms and concentrating on the most vulnerable – children and pensioners. It is still not the case that anti-poverty policy is effective for all of those 'at the bottom'. A number of groups have not seen an improvement and are increasingly bearing the costs of poverty, particularly working age adults without dependent children and low paid workers. Even more worrying for those who are interested in relative poverty is the picture of inequality that has accompanied what Kitty Stewart (2005: 304) calls:

> "[T]he importance attached to a job that lies at the heart of anti-poverty policy across Europe."

The 'making work pay' element of anti-poverty policy has meant increased vulnerability for working age adults not in work or in low paid employment, and is accompanied by increasing inequalities in the workplace. Lower paid workers may have seen some improvement; wage growth for them has been keeping up with middle earners. High earners, however, continue to move further ahead of middle earners and single non-earners have experienced greater rates of poverty. In fact, Scotland's inequalities of income have risen and the UK's inequality ranking in Europe has worsened as those at the top of the income distribution have moved further away from the middle. In 2002, for example, average pay in Britain rose by 3.2 per cent but chief executives' pay rose by 23 per cent. It is not just inequalities of income that bear witness to a failure to fully address **'relative' poverty**. Inequality of opportunity remains; the life chances of individuals today are still significantly

116

affected by the economic and social position of their parents, and public services have not really mediated the inequalities in housing or environment.

In much of continental Europe the goals of social solidarity and social cohesion are matched with concerns about the relief and prevention of poverty. Adrian Sinfield (2005) argues that prevention appears neglected in anti-poverty strategies in current UK policy debates. It frequently forms part of broad statements of intent in combating poverty and social exclusion, but it is given less attention in the detailed discussion of policy and its impact. In general, there is much on lifting groups out of poverty, a little on preventing poverty from recurring and even less on preventing poverty in the first place. Perhaps it is time the poverty debate in the UK started to embrace such ideas if we are to avoid the growing decline in **social mobility** and the increasing depth and length of poverty that exist for some of our citizens.

Further Reading

Levitas, R. (1998)   *The Inclusive Society? Social Exclusion and New Labour*, Houndsmills, Palgrave Macmillan
Lister, R. (1994) *Poverty*, Cambridge, Polity Press
Wilkinson, R.G. (2005) *The Impact of Inequality*, London, Routledge

Useful Websites

Child Poverty Action Group Scotland (CPAG): http://www.cpag.org.uk/scotland/
Joseph Rowntree Foundation: www.jrf.org.uk
Scottish Executive: www.scotland.gov.uk
Scottish Poverty Information Unit (SPIU): http://www.povertyinformation.org/show.php?Con tentid=6

Bibliography

Adelman, L., Middleton, S. and Ashworth, K . (2002) *Britain's Poorest Children*, London, Save the Children
Ballantyne, F., Hendry, C. and Leishman, R. (2003) *Impact of Childcare Support for Lone Parent Students*, Edinburgh, Scottish Executive Social Research
Barry, B. (2005) *Why Social Justice Matters*, Cambridge, Polity Press
Becker, S. (1997) *Responding to Poverty: The Politics of Cash and Care*, Harlow, Addison Wesley Longman
Berghman, J. (1995) 'Social exclusion in Europe: policy context and analytical framework', in Room, G. (ed.) (1995) *Beyond the threshold: the measurement and analysis of social exclusion*, Bristol, Policy Press
Bevir, M. (2005) *New Labour: a critique*, London, Routledge
Brown, U., Scott, J., Mooney, G. and Duncan, B. (eds.) (2002) *Poverty in Scotland 2002: People, Places and Policies*, London/Glasgow, Child Poverty Action Group /Scottish Poverty Information Unit
Department for Work and Pensions (DWP) (2005) *Households below average income 1994/5-2003/4*, London, Department for Work and Pensions, http://www.dwp.gov.uk/asd/hbai/hbai2004/contents.asp (accessed on 16-17 June 2005)
Ellison, N. and Pierson, C. (eds.) (2003) *British Social Policy 2*, Houndsmills, Palgrave Macmillan
Finn, D. (2000) 'Welfare to Work: the local dimension', in *Journal of European Social Policy*, 10(1)

Gregg, P., Harkness, S. and Machin, S. (1999) *Child Development and Family Income*, York, Joseph Rowntree Foundation

Hills, J. and Stewart, K. (eds.) (2005) *A more equal society? New Labour, poverty, inequality and exclusion*, Bristol, The Policy Press

Hobcraft, J. (1998) *Intergenerational and Lifecourse Transmission of Social Exclusion: Influences of Childhod Poverty, Family Disruption and Contact with the police*, CASE paper 15, London, LSE

Howard, M., Garnham, A., Finister, G. and Veit Wilson, J. (2001) *Poverty: the Facts*, London, Child Poverty Action Group

Keating, M. (2003) 'Social inclusion, devolution and policy divergence', in *Political Quarterly*, 74(4)

Kemp, P., Bradshaw, J., Dornan, P., Finch, N. and Mayhew, E. (2004) *Routes out of poverty: A research review*, York, Joseph Rowntree Foundation

Le Grand, J. (1999) 'Conceptions of Social Justice', in Walker, R. (ed.) (1999) *Ending Child Poverty*, Bristol, Policy Press

Levitas, R. (1998) *The Inclusive Society? Social Exclusion and New Labour*, Houndsmills, Palgrave Macmillan

Lister, R. (1994) *Poverty*, Cambridge, Polity Press

Mangen, S.P. (2004) *Social Exclusion and Inner City Europe: Regulating Urban Regeneration*, Houndsmills, Palgrave Macmillan

Marsden, R., Aldeghern, E., Khan, A., Lowe, M., Strang, A., Salinas, E. and Thiri, J. (2005) *"What's Going on?" A study into the destitution and poverty faced by asylum seekers and refugees in Scotland*, Glasgow, Oxfam

McCormick, J. and Oppenheim, C. (eds.) (1998) *Welfare in Working Order*, London, Institute for Public Policy Research

McCrone, D., Paterson, L., and Bechhofer, F. (2004) *Living in Scotland: Social and Economic Change since 1980*, Edinburgh, Edinburgh University Press

McGregor, S. (2003) 'Social Exclusion', in Ellison, N. and Pierson, C. (eds.) (2003) *British Social Policy 2*, Houndsmills, Palgrave Macmillan

McKendrick J., Cunningham-Burley, S., Backett-Milburn, K. (2004) *Life in low income families in Scotland: research report*, Edinburgh, Scottish Executive

McKnight, A. (2005) 'Employment: tackling poverty through "work for those who can",' in Hills, J. and Stewart, K. (eds.) (2005) *A more equal society? New Labour, poverty, inequality and exclusion*, Bristol, The Policy Press

Mead, L. (1986) *Beyond Entitlement: the social obligations of citizenship*, London, Basic Books

Mooney, G. and Scott, G. (eds.) (2005) *Exploring Social Policy in the 'New' Scotland*, Bristol, The Policy Press

Murray, C. (1994) *Underclass: the crisis deepens*, London, IEA Health and Welfare Unit

Newman, J. (ed.) (2005) *Remaking Governance*, Bristol, Policy Press

One Plus (2004) *Annual Report 2003*, Glasgow, One Plus

Oppenheim, C. (ed.) (1998) *An Inclusive Society: Strategies for Tackling Poverty*, London, Institute for Public Policy Research

Oppenheim, C. (1998) 'An overview of poverty and social exclusion', in Oppenheim, C. (ed.) (1998) *An Inclusive Society: Strategies for Tackling Poverty*, London, Institute for Public Policy Research

Oppenheim, C. (1998) 'Wefare to work: Taxes and benefits', in McCormick, J. and Oppenheim, C. (eds.) (1998) *Welfare in Working Order*, London, Institute for Public Policy Research

Paterson, L., Bechhofer, F. and McCrone, D. (2004) *Living in Scotland: Social and Economic Change since 1980*, Edinburgh, Edinburgh University Press

Palmer, G., Carr, J. and Kenway, P. (2004) *Monitoring Poverty and Social Exclusion in Scotland 2004*, London, Joseph Rowntree Foundation/New Policy Institute

Pantazis, C. and Gordon, D. (eds.) (2000) *Tackling Inequalities: where we are now and what can be done?* Bristol, Policy Press

Pearce, N. and Paxton, W. (eds.) (2005) *Social Justice: Building a Fairer Britain*, London, IPPR Politico's

Percy-Smith, J. (ed.) (2000) *Policy Responses to Social Exclusion*, Buckingham, Open University Press

Poverty Alliance (2005) *Briefing 3: Closing the Opportunity Gap: the Objectives and Target*, Glasgow, Poverty Alliance

Powell, M. (ed.) (2002) *Evaluating New Labour's Welfare reforms*, Bristol, Policy Press

Riddell, S., Banks, P. and Tinklin, T. (2005) *Disability and Employment in Scotland: A Review of the Evidence Base*, Edinburgh, Scottish Executive

Ridge, T. (2002) *Childhood poverty and social exclusion: from a child's perspective*, Bristol, The Policy Press

Room, G. (ed.) (1995) *Beyond the threshold: the measurement and analysis of social exclusion*, Bristol, Policy Press

Sanderson, I. (2000) 'Evaluating Initiatives to address social exclusion', in Percy-Smith, J. (ed.) (2000) *Policy Responses to Social Exclusion*, Buckingham, Open University Press

Scott, G. (forthcoming) 'Active labour market policy and the reduction of poverty in the 'new' Scotland', in *Critical Social Policy*, Special Issue: Devolution

Scottish Executive (1999) *Social Justice: a Scotland Where Everyone Matters*, Edinburgh, Scottish Executive

Scottish Executive (2003) *Living in Scotland: An Urban-Rural Analysis of the Scottish Household Survey*, Edinburgh, Scottish Executive Environment and Rural Development Department, Social Research

Scottish Executive (2003a) *A Partnership for a Better Scotland: Partnership agreement between the Scottish Labour Party and Scottish Liberal Democrats*, Edinburgh, Scottish Executive

Scottish Executive (2003b) *Closing the Gap: Scottish Budget for 2003-2006*, Edinburgh, Scottish Executive

Scottish Executive (2005) Closing *the Opportunity Gap: Social Justice Milestones*, Edinburgh, Scottish Executive, http://www.scotland.gov.uk/Topics/People/Social-Inclusion/17415/milestones (accessed on 8 February 2006)

Scottish Executive National Statistics (2005a) *Social Focus on Deprived Areas.* Edinburgh, Scottish Executive

Sinfield, A. (2004) 'Preventing Poverty in Market Societies', Paper presented at the ESPANET annual conference 2004, http://www.apsoc.ox.ac.uk/Espanet/Espanet Conference/papers/ppr.13B.AS.pdf

Sterling, R. (2005) 'Promoting democratic governance through partnership', in Newman, J. (ed.) (2005) *Remaking Governance*, Bristol, Policy Press

Stewart, K. (2005) 'Changes in Poverty and Inequality in the UK in International Context', in Hills, J. and Stewart, K. (eds.) (2005) *A More Equal Society? New Labour, Poverty, Inequality and Exclusion*, Bristol, The Policy Press

Sutherland, H. and Piachaud, D. (2001) 'Reducing Child Poverty in Britain: An Assessment of Government Policy 1997-2001', in *Economic Journal*, Vol. 111

Townsend, P. (2000) 'Ending World Poverty in the 21st Century', in Pantazis, C. and Gordon, D. (eds.) (2000) *Tackling Inequalities: Where are we now and what can be done?* Bristol, Policy Press

Toynbee, P. and Walker, D. (2005) *Better or Worse? Has Labour Delivered?* London, Bloomsbury Publishing

Walker, A. and Walker, C. (e ds.) (1997) *Britain Divided: The Growth of Social Exclusion in the 1980s and 1990s*, London, Child Poverty Action Group

Walker, R. (ed.) (1999) *Ending Child Poverty: popular welfare for the 21st century*, Bristol, Policy Press

Welsh Assembly (2004) *Social Justice Report 2004*, Cardiff, Communities Directorate, Welsh Assembly Government

Wilkinson, R.G. (2005) *The Impact of Inequality: how to make sick societies healthier*, London, Routledge

Chapter 6

Work to Welfare: Welfare to Work?

Gesa Helms

Introduction

The aims of this chapter are to:

1. Problematise notions of work and worklessness in contemporary social policy.

2. Examine key trends in work and employment in Scotland in recent decades.

3. Explore the social and individual consequences of worklessness.

4. Discuss and evaluate current initiatives to tackle worklessness.

The importance of work and employment for **social inclusion** has been a central plank of New Labour's vision of contemporary British society (Levitas, 1998). In doing so, the policy focus has moved away from the management of relatively high levels of unemployment since the early 1970s to what has been called **welfare-to-work** or **workfare** policies. The latter term refers strongly to the punitive elements of such policies since non-compliance often leads to sanctions imposed on the unemployed, such as having benefits stopped. This shift in the approach to people's entitlement to unemployment benefits is seen as part of a much broader shift in the whole field of social policy and welfare, and will be explored through current benefits such as **Jobseekers' Allowance (JSA)** and **Working Tax Credits (WTC)**. In so doing, this chapter connects with the themes of this book in terms of the 'inclusion and exclusion' of particular social groups and/or individuals as well as questioning the extent to which social policies actually *care* for people or attempt to *control* them. Furthermore, it addresses the theme of 'continuity and change' by examining the changing definitions of work and **worklessness** in British social policy in the following section.

After examining the key changes in work and unemployment over the past 30 years in Scotland (and beyond), the chapter explores the *individual* and *social* consequences of being unemployed at the beginning of the 21st century. The next section discusses some of the recent national initiatives to deal with worklessness, before turning to the range of measures designed to address worklessness. These range from national initiatives such as WTC or the **New Deal** to more localised projects such as 'Glasgow Works' and other training schemes. Here, the chapter focuses on *three* case studies – the New Deal, Employment Zones and Glasgow Works – in order to examine different approaches, tensions and outcomes in contemporary work-related social policy.

In the discussion of social policies of work and employment we can look more closely at the ways in which the economy and economic policy shape social policy. We also begin to understand how particular strategies, policies and practices are framed by social and political considerations. So, in order to understand particular social policies, we need to be aware of the relevance that class, poverty and disadvantage carry for contemporary Scottish society (see Law and Law, **Chapter 4** and Scott, **Chapter 5**).

From Welfare to Workfare? Changing Social Policies of Work

Pause for thought
Discuss the differences and similarities between Jobseekers' Allowance and Unemployment Benefit.

Let us begin by considering the following statement:

- 'Job Seekers' Allowance (JSA) is the money that is being paid to the unemployed in the UK.'

While there seems not much wrong with this simple statement, it is important to look at it more closely. Twenty-five years ago, an unemployed person would have been *entitled* to *Unemployment Benefit*. Looking at the terms respectively we can begin to understand some of the key changes that have taken place in Scottish (and British) social policies of work. In order to qualify for receipt of JSA, each applicant signs a contract with the Jobcentre Plus in which they agree to a set of tasks relating to how they will seek employment. Many of these conditions seem common sense, such as looking for jobs in the newspapers or on the internet or signing up with 'temping' agencies. Nonetheless, this process marks a significant change in the delivery of benefits for the unemployed. It makes the provision of benefits *conditional* on the cooperation and willingness of the recipient.

Worklessness has over recent years become the term to describe those without paid work. Part of the reason for talking about worklessness rather than unemployment is the definitional problems that arise from the renaming of unemployment benefit to JSA. If you, as an unemployed person, fail to 'sign on', strictly speaking you would not count as unemployed according to one the measures of unemployment in the UK, the 'unemployed claimant rate', which only includes those who signed on over the past fortnight. Worklessness instead is a more inclusive measure as it includes not only those in receipt of JSA, but also those who are actively looking for work as well as those who are economically inactive – those of working age who are not actively looking for work due to illness or incapacity or for other reasons. At the same time, however, worklessness in itself is also a moralistic term that echoes the Victorian Poor Laws and the 19th century Poor House (see Law, **Chapter 3**).

In this brief overview, the central role *work* plays in much of social policy is becoming clear. Work and the understanding of what work constitutes, is central to the payment of unemployment benefits to only those who sign on once a fortnight in the Jobcentre. It also is central to related benefits such as the Working Tax Credits or Incapacity Benefits. Post-World War 2 (WW2), British social policy has always centred on work, yet we can identify a range of changes in the ways in which it is being defined and, also, with rising worklessness, the ways in which the lack of work is being 'targeted' by social policies.

These changes in the ways that social policy regards work-related benefits payments have been described and explained in a number of ways, including: **activation**, **welfare-to-work** or **workfare**. Again, it is worthwhile to look carefully at these different terms since they identify key aspects of British social policy and signify different responses to the problem of worklessness.

Social Policy and Work-Related Benefits Payments

Activation

Labour market activation is regarded as a means by which policy *enables* individuals to move into employment. Such an *enabling* role of the state is emphasised as distinct from a traditional managerial and paternalistic role of the welfare state, which is often viewed as creating dependency among citizens. Strongly based on the view that social groups are marginalised within society and suffer from social exclusion, labour market programmes and policies are designed to strengthen individuals' positions within the labour market and help them into work; thereby helping to overcome **social exclusion**. Many of these measures specifically target social groups such as single mothers, ex -prisoners, ex -addicts or those with mental health problems by providing support to overcome barriers to employment. This support may come in the form of childcare or counselling, for example. As such, these measures often focus on improving the individuals' skills and characteristics through training so that people compete better and more successfully in the labour market.

Activation is the most positive of the three concepts as it regards the state and its services as focused on individuals and their needs, enabling them to become included through participation in the labour market.

Welfare-to-Work

Welfare-to-work describes the pathway of individuals who are moving away from welfare to paid employment. Similar to activation, welfare -to-work denotes an enabling approach, yet, at the same time, an element of *compulsion* is clearly visible. Most UK policies are described as welfare-to-work, with the New Deal being the best-known one since its introduction in 1997. Here, every long-term unemployed person between the ages of 18 and 50 – after six months for 18-24 year olds and after 18 months for over 24 year olds – have to take part in a variety of programmes, or otherwise face the threat of having their benefits stopped (see below for more detail). After almost a decade of active labour market programmes such as the New Deal, these programmes have begun to cast a wider net. In recent months (2006) these moves have increasingly focused on those people who receive incapacity benefits, often promoting welfare-to-work as a means of achieving social inclusion. Yet, if we follow public debates (*The Guardian*, 29 October 2005), calls for putting a stop to 'benefit cheats' are often not far away. These recent initiatives to enable people on incapacity benefits also introduce sanctions for those deemed to be able to work but appear to be unwilling.

Workfare

The third term most clearly denotes the element of compulsion and threat of sanctions for non-compliance: workfare, a term consistent with the intention to replace welfare as a universal right by making it conditional upon work. The concept is most commonly used for active labour market programmes in the United States (US), from where many of the early ideas surrounding initiatives such as the New Deal originate. Within the US model of welfare, relatively little social security is offered and is often means-tested and tied to fulfilling certain requirements (Peck,

2001).

It is clear then from examining the meaning of the terms activation, welfare-to-work and workfare that they assume varying degrees of responsibility on the part of the individual for their unemployment. While activation denotes a more enabling approach, workfare, at the other end places both *blame* and *responsibility* on the individual. Yet, if we regard worklessness as a social problem, tensions exist over the degree to which individuals can actually resolve their situation on their own.

Pause for thought
- How is 'work' being defined in current social policy?

In all these debates about work, there is the implicit assumption that work is not just any productive activity but *paid* employment. This focus on **wage labour** is a significant one as it in fact excludes a whole range of other work and activities that are unpaid. Unpaid work has traditionally not been included in the definition of work and **feminists** point out that 'housework' is in fact crucial in reproducing the ability of workers to actually go and do paid work at the workplace. Yet, at the same time, such social reproduction is often hidden away, invisible to the actual labour process (Mitchell *et al*, 2004). So, in order to understand policies of work, we need to consider how a particular society defines and shapes notions of work and non-work. Therefore, current definitions of employment, unemployment and economic inactivity need to be set in relation to their particular society. Understanding these is crucial to the study of, and the working in, the field of social policy and care.

In the context of care and welfare workers, these debates carry particular significance due to:

1. The importance that is attributed to work for the social inclusion of particular groups, not only, for instance, the unemployed but also lone-parents, the disabled, the homeless and ex-prisoners.

2. The shift from social policy based on welfare entitlements to more contingent rights based on individuals' willingness to seek and accept work.

3. The increasing numbers of voluntary sector organisations (such as welfare rights, advocacy and anti-poverty groups) involved in not only delivering but also modifying and contesting this equation of 'welfare = workfare'.

Key Trends in Work and Employment in Scotland in Recent Decades

Unemployment became a serious problem for many Western industrialised countries in the wake of the international oil crisis of the early 1970s, which signalled an end to post-WW2 economic growth and threw into question the then-existing model of economic growth and welfare, the **Beveridgean-Keynesian** welfare state. Based on government spending to promote investment and consumer spending, this economic model was also based on the establishment of a national welfare system, including the NHS, state pension and social security. This system of welfare was essentially based on a 'family model' where the male was the main breadwinner (see Sweeney, **Chapter 2** and Law, **Chapter 3**).

Pause for thought
- Can you identify wider economic and political reasons behind the current importance of work for social policy?

Deindustrialisation and Worklessness in Scotland

Sparked by the crisis of the early 1970s, however, the international competitiveness of many of the traditional industrial sectors in Great Britain such as coal, steel and heavy manufacturing was seriously compromised. While this was not the first time this had happened – arguably poor competitiveness of key British industries has hindered the British economy from as early as the start of 20th century – it was only in the 1970s that wide-scale **deindustrialisation** took hold all over the UK. This deindustrialisation meant that production was down-scaled and factories were closing. While much of the British economy was affected by the decline of manufacturing industries, it was the heavily-industrialised cities and regions such as South Wales, South Yorkshire, Merseyside , Teeside and Clydeside that were particularly badly hit. These were the regions that were strongly dominated by traditional industries, while regions in the South East of the UK, for example, have been less dependent on manufacturing (Allen and Massey, 1988).

Most obvious is the deindustrialisation of the Scottish Central Belt where heavy industries and manufacturing have all but disappeared. Thereby the composition of the economy has changed dramatically over the course of 35 years. For social policies of work, such change is very significant as it is first and foremost expressed through the large-scale unemployment suffered by those whose companies closed down. Furthermore, many of these old-industrial regions not only have relatively high unemployment rates in comparison to other parts of the country but they also have high rates of economic inactivity, which means that a large part of the population of working age does not participate in the labour market. Many of these economically inactive receive incapacity or disability related benefits. In particular, the number of men receiving sickness related benefits has risen drastically over the past 20 years in the UK. Fothergill (2001) points out the correlation between the distribution of job losses due to the restructuring of old industrial regions and the rise of sickness in men and estimates the level of hidden male unemployment to be around 750,000 for the UK. The job loss in those regions disproportionately affected older, unskilled and less healthy men. By means of the benefits system and employment services, these men were then diverted into sickness-related benefits rather than unemployment benefits (Beatty *et al*, 2000). For Glasgow, the rate of people receiving incapacity benefits was as high as 16.9 per cent in February 2005 (Office for National Statistics, 2005). The drop in employment rates for men in Glasgow, in comparison to other Scottish and UK figures, is displayed in **Figure 6.1**.

Figure 6.1 Employment rates in percent between 1970 and 2000

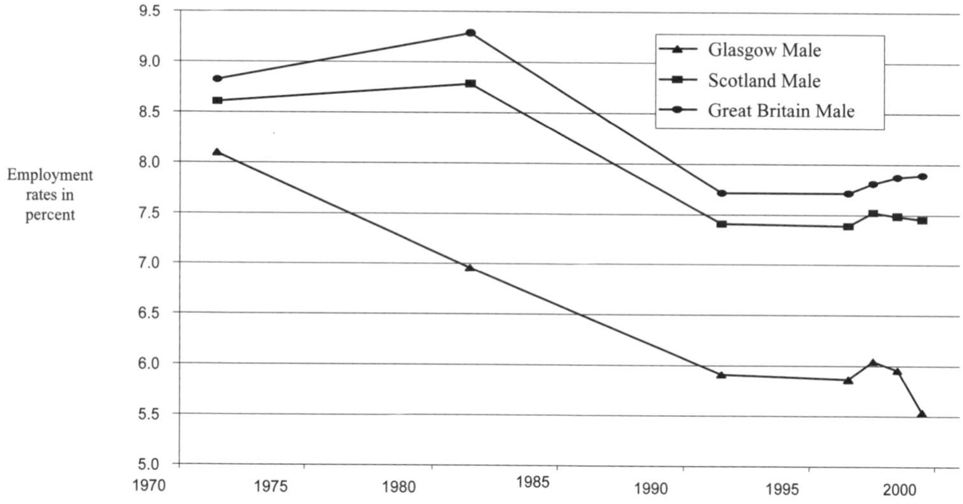

(Source: Census 1971, 1981, 1991, Labour Force Survey)

Examining the high prevalence of incapacity benefits in these old-industrial regions demonstrates the value of looking at worklessness rather than unemployment. If we were to discuss unemployment in places such as the West of Scotland, the true scale of deindustrialisation and the impacts this has on individuals and communities would be difficult to grasp. The strong overall decline in the male employment rate – which in the early 1970s was at a similar level as the overall Scottish and British rates – and also the subsequent failure to attain any recovery, both display the sustained problems of economic restructuring in the city (see Mooney, **Chapter 12**).

Traditional working class communities have borne the brunt of these developments with large numbers being unemployed, poor and increasingly isolated in peripheral housing schemes (see Law and Law, **Chapter 4** and Mooney, **Chapter 12**). Yet, trying to locate these developments is more complicated than pointing to peripheral housing schemes such as Easterhouse in Glasgow, the Central Belt or even throughout Scotland, since these are not the only places that have experienced similar developments. Hence, we need to investigate the role of *global* changes as well as *national* ones within the economy to understand how the benefits payments of, for example, young single mothers in Easterhouse, are changing.

The 'Rise' of the Service Sector in Scotland

Deindustrialisation has meant that large numbers of skilled manual workers (most of them men) have been made redundant. Alongside the loss of two-thirds of manufacturing employment between 1981 and 2002, the share of service sector jobs has risen to 87 per cent of Glasgow's total employment over the same period. However, given the devastating impact of deindustrialisation, the total number of jobs has only risen by around 30,000. Service sector employment largely consists of part-time jobs, often taken on by female workers. Also, a **polarisation** of employment opportunities can be found: at the bottom end we find insecure jobs that offer little in terms of pay and employment conditions, with many of these located in the new 'boom' industries such as retailing, catering and service jobs like call centre operations. At the higher end, much attention of economic development has heralded the birth of a **'knowledge economy'** in which 'good' qualifications are seen as the entry point to highly specialised professional employment. Such polarisation is especially significant for those workers who had previously been employed in manual employment. As many of their workplaces are being closed down or relocated abroad, often the only jobs available are those at the lower end of the labour market – meaning that their skills and experience are neither drawn upon nor remunerated. Ritzer (1993) has called this the **'McDonaldization'** of jobs, a process whereby a growing proportion of jobs become routinised, deskilled and devalued (Toynbee, 2003).

The Scottish working age population experiences these changes in various ways. Examining these experiences more closely allows us to place the significance of work/worklessness within the context of social policy and social care, since client-focused practitioners will encounter people with various experiences of large-scale economic restructuring.

For people of working age living in Scotland, the most significant changes are marked by different job profiles found in the new industries. Here, the technical manual expertise and craftsmanship that skilled workers within manufacturing and heavy engineering possessed have been seen as of little value to the new industries that emphasise a whole set of 'soft skills' based around communication, customer-orientation and 'good manners' to deal with customers within retailing, catering and the service sector. These soft skills are often regarded as 'feminine' skills and such gendering accounts for some of the changes, whereby female participation outgrows male participation in the labour market by 52.5 per cent to 47.5 per cent in 2002 (see **Table 6.1**).

Table 6.1 Components of change in the Glasgow labour market 1981-2002

Sectoral change	1981 (% of total)	2002 (% of total)	% change 1981-2002	Net job growth
Manufacturing industries	23.2	7.4	-66.3	-58,219
Services	68.0	87.0	+34.5	+88,616
Gender composition of change				
Male	54.3	47.5	-7.6	-
Female	45.7	52.5	+20.2	-
Male full-time	52.0	40.9	-17.3	-34,054
Male part-time	2.3	6.9	+208.8	+18,525
Female full-time	29.3	28.6	+2.4	+2,675
Female part-time	16.4	23.7	+51.9	+32,139
All full-time	81.3	69.4	-10.2	-31,379
All part-time	18.7	30.6	+71.6	+50,664
Total jobs growth			+5.1	+30,000

(Source: Nomis database, www.nomisweb.co.uk)

Historically, many more women were economically inactive compared to today, mainly due to the **gendered division of labour** within family households. In terms of gender relations, these shifts reverberate beyond the workplace and into communities, as men are strongly affected by worklessness. Some of these men are, for instance, older manual workers who lost their jobs when workplaces closed, but there are also young men who have been unemployed since leaving school and who often possess relatively few or no formal qualifications.

Along with the new service sector economy, Scottish (and British) society has witnessed a systematic cut-back of the welfare state and social security for the workforce, most notably through the above restrictions on benefits for those out of work. Previously, employment rights had been protected within traditional workplaces through strong bargaining positions and high levels of unionisation, which safeguarded access to sick pay, holiday entitlements, overtime pay and final salary scheme pensions. With the closure of those companies, the rise of new, often non-unionised industries and the Conservative government onslaught against organised labour, many new employment contracts are marked by flexibility, little protection from redundancy and little access to many employment rights for the workforce. This rising employment insecurity affects many households across the UK (Gallie *et al*, 1998).

Being without Work in Scotland Today: Social and Individual Consequences

Pause for thought
- Why do we need to examine both the *social* and *individual* consequences of worklessness?

Deindustrialisation, unemployment and wider economic inactivity has been experienced by large groups of the Scottish population and, since this process has taken place over the past 35 years, there are households that are affected by unemployment across generations. In the course of these processes, household models based on a male breadwinner have been largely outdated. In addition to the material consequences of poverty, a whole range of problems arise for those who are out of work often over long periods of time, including poor physical and mental health, and social isolation.

There exist a number of specific problems caused by worklessness in British society:

1. A high concentration of worklessness by household.
2. Child poverty in these households.
3. Long-term unemployment.
4. Prevalence of incapacity benefits.
5. Particular localities suffer most.

We can see that worklessness does not only affect the individual, but instead extends across families and households and also into wider localities or communities. Grint (2005: 39) outlines how mass unemployment created by factory closure through to large scale deindustrialisation impacts on many people at the same time, but nonetheless leaves people to "experience unemployment as an individual, not as a member of a social group." Here, the effects of social structures and social problems impact as *individual* problems and failings. As we will see in the approaches to tackling worklessness, notions that it is the problem of the individual are often reinforced. Let us look at the specific problems in more detail.

While the UK has a relatively high employment rate in comparison to other countries, the incidence of whole household unemployment is far higher than in any other **OECD** (Organisation for Economic Cooperation and Development) country (Nickell, 2004). Thus, while unemployment is relatively low, when it occurs it tends to affect all members of working age within specific households. In such instances all household income is accrued from state benefits.

This concentration at household level also goes some way towards explaining the high presence of child poverty in the UK, as many of the children living in **'relative poverty'** can be found in those workless households. While about one-third of British children in 2000/2001 lived in relative poverty, 80 per cent of these were living in workless households (Nickell, 2004). It also pinpoints a strong link between poverty and unemployment in the UK, where in 1988 48 per cent of unemployed households fell below the relative poverty line. At the same time only three per cent of Danish unemployed households experienced relative poverty (Andersen and Halvorsen, 2002). While this data is relatively old, it still gives a useful indication of international differences between unemployment and poverty (see Scott, **Chapter 5**).

Among the unemployed, a large group of people have been without employment for more than a year. Such long-term unemployment points towards the structural nature of the British employment problem. For the long-term unemployed being continually out of work means that their skills are decreasing, making their chances for future work smaller still. Furthermore, it is among the long-term unemployed that the physical and mental health problems that affect people without employment are most concentrated. Since the classical study of an unemployed community in 1930s Austria (Jahoda *et al*, 1972), these profound implications of unemployment on personal well-being have been well researched and, as such, have influenced the formulation of social inclusion strategies and the measures by which a reintegration to the workplace should be achieved. Most strongly, this is encapsulated in the 'activation' approach, but the existence of households in which successive generations, often of fathers and sons, are without work shows the limited success of these measures.

Many of the workless households are in receipt of *incapacity* benefits, rather than *unemployment* benefits. Inactivity rates among working age men over 25 were at the beginning of the new millennium almost four times higher than in the 1970s. Around 40 per cent of these were due to limiting health problems and particularly affected men with relatively low skills levels (Faggio and Nickell, 2003).

While these experiences are directly suffered by the affected individuals, they can be attributed to wider economic restructuring and the consequences affect society as a whole. On a purely economic level, income tax revenue is lost, but questions also arise over social justice and the distribution of wealth within society. Moreover, despite the feelings of individual failure experienced by many unemployed, many of the origins of unemployment and worklessness are *structural* social problems rather than *individual* ones.

Part of the wider impacts of worklessness is its concentration within particular *localities*. As mentioned earlier, old-industrial regions and cities particularly suffered from deindustrialisation and the ensuing rise in unemployment, worklessness and economic inactivity. So, while many cities and regions are doing relatively well in the new economy, many of the previously heavily-industrialised places still struggle to deal with the concentration of worklessness. In the UK, this has furthered the uneven development between the North and South, with the latter being dominated by a relatively strong, often service-based high technology economy (Allen and Massey, 1988).

Social care, welfare and voluntary sector organisations are confronted with the experience and costs of unemployment and its consequences, often primarily through their work with those people affected by it and in trying to redress these experiences, their wider origins as well as consequences surface and demand attention.

Tackling 'Worklessness'

Initiatives and programmes to tackle worklessness operate in *two* ways:

- First, they can target the demand side of the labour market, which means that the availability of jobs would be increased – and if there are more jobs, more people can move from unemployment into employment.

- Second, initiatives can focus on the supply side of the labour market (which means focussing on the labour supply), by trying to improve the attributes of those individuals who seek work.

This latter approach regards the individual who is unemployed as not being competitive enough in the labour market to obtain a job. From the Conservative government of 1979 onwards, worklessness has almost exclusively been tackled by labour supply-oriented approaches. We can see this in various programmes that focus on the characteristics of the unemployed, whose so-called 'lack of skills' have been at the centre of training initiatives to improve job specific vocational skills as well as in many cases, key skills in literacy and basic maths. Such a focus on specific skills for the unemployed has become known as **'employability'**. Interestingly, many individuals who are targeted here are highly skilled former 'old industry' workers. What they lack are skills for the available 'new' service sector jobs.

Pause for thought
- What are the advantages and disadvantages of focusing labour market policies on the individuals who are seeking work?
- What are these policies and initiatives trying to do?
- Do they offer social inclusion and the possibility of 'activating' dormant skills in willing workers, so that people can realise their potentials?

A wide range of initiatives exist to retrain the unemployed and provide supported entry points for these people into the labour market. These range from European programmes (such as the European Social Fund) and national initiatives such as the New Deal and Employment Zones to small-scale local projects such as 'Glasgow Works', set up by Scottish Enterprise Glasgow.

New Deal

In the UK under the New Labour government, the shift towards the conditional delivery of welfare benefits has been encapsulated in the Welfare-to-Work agenda and the New Deal programme that the Labour government introduced shortly after it won power in 1997. Initially focussing on young people and the long-term unemployed, the New Deal presents a **supply-side** labour market tool that focuses on basic skills training and job placement as a means of moving the unemployed and low-skilled into work. In effect, the move into more coercive forms of labour market policy under previous Conservative regimes has been consolidated into a much broader and more comprehensive attempt to integrate social policy and labour market policy (Tonge, 1999).

As has been noted by Sunley *et al* (2001), the local impact of these schemes has varied considerably, reflecting both the uneven nature of economic restructuring processes (see above for the dramatic impact this restructuring has had on old-industrial places such as Clydeside and Glasgow) and the difference of local organisations and actors contributing to policy agendas.

Almost 10 years since the start of the programme, it is now expanding to focus on groups that are even more marginalised in the labour market than young people; namely the long-term unemployed and lone parents. Thus, increasingly , these projects access client groups such as ex-prisoners, people with mental health issues and disabilities; social groups that often constitute the classic client groups of social work practitioners.

Employment Zones (EZs)

As early as the New Deal, but initially with much less publicity, New Labour also first piloted and then rolled out from April 2000, 15 **Employment Zones (EZ)** in areas with consistently high levels of long-term unemployment. Specifically to address *local* problems to do with worklessness, these Zones were to provide more tailored and flexible approaches to suit individuals' needs to find employment (see www.dwp.gov.uk). The long-term unemployed who live in an area designated as an EZ have to participate in the programme or otherwise risk losing benefit entitlements. This compulsory participation is similar to the New Deal as is the client group, which consists of young people, long -term unemployed and lone parents. Many of the Zones are located in inner-city and old-industrial areas, although Glasgow City is the only Scottish one.

Again similar to the New Deal, the EZ programme consists of *three* stages:

1. Upon entry, a personal adviser draws up an individual action plan for the client.

2. The 'client' follows this action plan up by undertaking training and finding employment over a period of up to 26 weeks.

3. The client then moves into paid employment with an employer where s/he

receives support from the EZ team for the first few weeks.

On the introduction of the EZ programme, many commentators seemed optimistic since, unlike the New Deal, this approach appeared to be more flexible, both to individual needs but also to the actual labour markets found in the area. Such flexibility was seen as one important means to address some of the low success rates of placing people into employment that national programmes such as the New Deal had. However, Jones and Gray (2001), when writing just at the end of the EZ pilot programme, were sceptical over the prospects of the programme. They particularly raised concerns over the nature of mandatory participation, which effectively undermines flexibility and attention to individual needs by forcing the individual to participate. Furthermore, they are concerned that much of the training provided for the EZ is done by private businesses as is the case with the New Deal. Here, the question arises over whether private sector providers are more incentivised into simply placing people in jobs in order to meet their contractual targets without taking the needs of their clients – the unemployed – into consideration.

'Glasgow Works'

Established in 1994, **Glasgow Works** provides a local **intermediate labour market (ILM)** programme overseeing 13 projects with 500 participants per year. It provides supported employment initiatives to offer people who have been outside the labour market access to paid work experience. The Glasgow Works programme has acted as a model for other British cities to tackle worklessness through local programmes. One of the Glasgow Works schemes, the Glasgow City Centre Representatives (CCR) set up in 1995, placed 83 per cent of its trainees into a job in the first four years (Helms, forthcoming, 2007). Trainees provide a range of services as part of their job – acting as city wardens, including providing information for tourists, acting as intermediaries between city centre businesses and public agencies and taking part in environmental improvement services. Trainees are paid the national minimum wage (£5.35 per hour as of October 2006 for over 21s) and are employed for up to 26 weeks. They receive formal training in customer services skills and job-search as well as being provided with support to find full-time employment and a personal development allowance. While initially very successful, the scheme has come up against the limits that confront all ILM schemes in old industrial areas; the increasing difficulty over the longer term in recruiting suitable trainees and meeting its 55 per cent target for providing trainees with permanent jobs after the programme has finished.

There are also other drawbacks to ILMs revealed through the workings of the CCR scheme. As an ILM, the project used to employ staff for 52 weeks but can now only employ staff for up to 26 weeks, which provides little time to become professional and confident in their tasks. While this issue does not seem to be easily resolved, the impact on the regulation of the workforce of such initiatives is expressed in the assessment given by managers and supervisors, whose task ultimately is to place people into employment rather than provide meaningful training and skill acquisition. This, as expressed in the following quote, involves a much broader understanding of training and is about preparing unemployed local people to understand the demands of a changed economy.

> "The most important aspect of the job is getting people to understand that the days of [...] the ship yards, the steel industry, the whisky in the street, the days where welders were getting £15, £20 an hour [...] we can't do that anymore. Those jobs are away. They will never come back. [...] I've got friends, welders, they don't work now because they won't take a job that's less than £20 an hour. We've got to educate to the standard [...] to understand that coming into a job like this may only be £3, £4 an hour and it may be seen as a training course but it's to train people in different aspects of skills. So that they can be here and hopefully get into a job that they gonna get £5 or £6 or £7 an hour. Nowadays, £5, £6 or £7 an hour [...] it's a reasonable wage. That's what people have – we are giving transferable skills here. We're *educating* people to the fact that they hopefully will leave here and get a job like that. As soon as people realise what this job is about and how we can help people back into work [...]. That's the main aspect of this job" (Manager , City Centre Representatives, in Helms, 2007).

Glasgow's ILM projects are able to provide particular services within the local economy and, as such, are closely linked to the local labour market, its institutions and also its problems. This often leads to a higher success rate for participants being placed into unsupported employment, as well as higher rates for people still in employment after 13 weeks. This success rate is 62 per cent, which compares favourably to 18 per cent for the national programme, New Deal (Marshall *et al*, 2002). Yet as Marshall *et al* (2002) argue, the co-existence of national and local programmes for ILM in one locality, with the former increasingly incorporating compulsory elements of welfare-to-work policies, makes for conflict arising among participants not able to enter more successful localised ILMs, such as Glasgow Works. Added to this is the fact that the higher drop-out rates in Employment Zones means that these participants are more likely to remain unemployed.

These localised initiatives are supplemented by benefits provided to those who are working on low wages – notably through the Working Tax Credits (WTC) – that are, again, conditional upon participation in the labour market. While the National Minimum Wage is intended to provide a guarantee of a certain income, the comprehensive reworking of the benefits system towards WTC effectively subsidises cheap labour as low wages are supplemented by benefits. As such, it is in line with how New Labour sees work as the primary mechanism for providing social inclusion and access to welfare.

Conclusion

British social policy on work and worklessness has changed over the past 30 years, as have the approaches on how to address the problems of unemployment and worklessness. Definitions of work and worklessness have been subjected to various redefinitions, with the Job Seekers' Allowance being the most striking example. Unemployment and worklessness have risen sharply in the UK and most particularly in old-industrial regions and cities affected by large-scale deindustrialisation from the 1970s onwards. The jobs created through the growth of the new service-sectors industries have not alleviated the problem in these areas. Individual experiences of worklessness, such as its concentration in workless households, child poverty, long-term unemployment, incapacity benefits as well as its concentration in particular places, make clear the extent to which *worklessness is a social problem.*

Various programmes designed to tackle worklessness such as the New Deal, Employment Zones and other, more localised initiatives, focus largely on the labour supply by increasing the *employability* of the workless people who enter these programmes. This poses problems for the success of these programmes since the underlying social and structural problems are neglected. *Social inclusion* in contemporary British social policy is to be achieved mainly through employment. This policy focus not only applies to young people and the long-term unemployed, but increasingly to other marginalised groups like single mothers, people on incapacity benefits and ex-prisoners. This field of social policy also raises debates as to how social control is being exerted through labour market initiatives in relation to individuals' willingness to accept often poorly paid and **casualised work**. With the delivery of benefits becoming increasingly dependant upon individuals' willingness to participate in the labour market and often for low pay subsidised by WTC, social care, welfare and voluntary sector workers are more and more drawn into the management, delivery and contestations of the 'welfare-to-work model'.

The old-industrial regions of urban Scotland are seriously affected by worklessness. Economic restructuring has significantly affected the availability of employment, which raises questions over whether worklessness can indeed be addressed solely by supply-based approaches. While localised responses such as EZ or Glasgow Works do offer some flexibility and responsiveness, these are nonetheless limited by the focus merely on individuals' skills and willingness to take *any* job.

The continuing importance of the economy for social policy has been stressed throughout the chapter. Such understanding of training and the acquisition of new skills is critically discussed by Thompson (2004), who emphasises the highly personalised and often generic nature of 'soft' social skills increasingly seen as more important than technical skills in recruitment selection.

The current government assigns particular importance to being in employment as a means of social inclusion. To this end, numerous initiatives such as the New Deal and Employment Zones, alongside Working Tax Credits and other benefits, have been established to encourage, even to force, individuals to take up employment. Bailey (2006) discusses survey data that raises some doubt over the extent to which employment provides social inclusion. He concludes that "work brings some benefits in financial and social terms, but there remain very large numbers of in-work poor and excluded" (Bailey, 2006: 181). Such a conclusion should not come as a surprise when we consider that there currently co-exist relatively low unemployment rates, with much higher levels of poverty. This may be partly explained by the fact that the rise of employment in service sector industries often creates jobs with little in terms of employment security, career development and pay. This means that many workers remain in poverty (see Scott, **Chapter 5**).

A further problem is that any labour market initiatives will inevitably place in work first those unemployed who have the least difficulties in finding employment. This leads to fairly high success rates for initiatives in the early stages. However, the problem arises with the one-third of people on programmes who are difficult to place and face severe obstacles to finding suitable, if not 'good' employment. Here, the reliance on private sector providers can actually worsen the situation for those least employable and offer little other than the threat of both losing benefits and a welfare system that can act as a safety net (Jones and Gray, 2001).

It should be clear, then, that mandatory employment initiatives that focus on the individual characteristics of the unemployed merely contribute to a situation by which the essentially social problem of worklessness is defined largely in terms of individuals failing to compete successfully. From the evidence assessed above, such policies seem bound to fail.

Further Reading

Allen, J. and Massey, D. (eds.) (1988) *The Economy in Question*, London, Sage
Grint, K. (2005) *The sociology of work* (3rd Edition), Cambridge, Polity Press
Peck, J. (2001) *Workfare states*, New York, NY, Guilford
Toynbee, P. (2003) *Hard work: Life in low wage Britain*, London, Bloomsbury

Useful Websites

Department for Work and Pensions: www.dwp.gov.uk
International Labour Organisation (ILO): www.ilo.org
International Confederation of Free Trade Unions: http://www.icftu.org
Job Centre Plus: www.jobcentreplus.gov.uk
LabourNet UK: http://www.labournet.net
Social Exclusion Unit – Employment and Opportunity: http://www.socialexclusion
unit.gov.uk/page.asp?id=4
Scottish Low Pay Unit: http://www.slpu.org.uk

Bibliography

Allen, J. and Massey, D. (eds.) (1988) *The Economy in Question*, London, Sage
Andersen, J .G. and Halvorsen, K . (2002) 'Unemployment, welfare policies and citizenship', in Andersen, J .G. and Jensen, P . (eds.) *Changing labour markets, welfare policies and citizenship*, Bristol, Policy Press
Bailey, N. (2006) 'Does work pay? Employment, poverty and exclusion from social relations', in Pantazis, C ., Gordon , D . and Levitas, R . (eds.) (2006) *Poverty and social exclusion in Britain. The millennium survey*, Bristol, Policy Press
The Guardian (2005) 'No win situation', 29 October
Beatty, C ., Fothergill , S . and MacMillan, R . (2000) 'A Theory of Employment, Unemployment and Sickness', in *Regional Studies*, 34
Deery, S. and Kinnie, N. (eds.) (2004) *Human Resource Management and Call Centre Work*, Houndsmills, Palgrave
Dickens, R., Gregg, P. and Wandsworth, J. (eds.) (2003) *The labour market under New Labour: The state of working Britain*, Houndsmills, Palgrave
Faggio, G. and Nickell, S. (2003) 'The rise of incapacity benefits among adult men', in Dickens, R., Gregg, P. and Wandsworth, J. (eds.) (2003) *The labour market under New Labour: The state of working Britain*, Houndsmills, Palgrave
Fothergill, S . (2001) 'True scale of the regional problem in the UK', in *Regional Studies*, 35

Gallie, D ., White , M ., Cheng , Y . and Tomlinson, M . (1998) *Restructuring the employment relationship*, Oxford, Clarendon Press

Grint, K. (2005) *The sociology of work* (3rd Edition), Cambridge, Polity Press

Helms, G . (forthcoming, 2007) *Towards safe city centres? Remaking the spaces of an old-industrial city*, Aldershot, Ashgate

Jahoda, M., Lazarsfeld, P. and Zeisel, H. (1972) *Marienthal: The sociography of an unemployed community*, London, Tavistock Publications

Jones, M. and Gray, A. (2001) 'Social capital, or local workfarism? Reflections on Employment Zones', in *Local Economy*, 16

Levitas, R. (1998) *The inclusive society? Social exclusion and New Labour*, Hounsdmills, Macmillan

Marshall, B ., Boyes , L . and McCormick, J . (2002) *The full employment city*, Glasgow, Scottish Council Foundation

Mitchell, K., Marston, S. and Katz, C. (eds.) (2004) *Life's work: geographies of social reproduction*, Malden, MA, Blackwell

Mitchell, K., Marston, S. and Katz, C. (2004) 'Life's work: an introduction, review and critique', in Mitchell, K ., Marston , S . and Katz, C . (eds.) (2004) *Life's work: geographies of social reproduction*, Malden, MA, Blackwell

Nickell, S. (2004) 'Poverty and worklessness in Britain', in *Economic Journal*, 114

Office of National Statistics (2005) 'Incapacity Benefit and Severe Disablement Allowance', in *Quarterly Summary Statistics*, February 2005, London, Department of Work and Pensions

Pantazis, C., Gordon, D. and Levitas, R. (eds.) (2006) *Poverty and social exclusion in Britain. The millennium survey*, Bristol, Policy Press

Peck, J. (2001) *Workfare states*, New York, NY, Guilford

Ritzer, G. (1993) *The McDonaldization of society. An investigation into the changing character of contemporary social life*, Newbury Park, CA, Pine Forge Press

Sunley, P ., Martin , R . and Nativel, C . (2001) 'Mapping the New Deal: local disparities in the performance of Welfare-to-Work', in *Transactions of the Institute of British Geographers*, 26

Thompson, P., Van de Broek, D. and Callaghan, G. (2004) 'Keeping up appearances: Recruitment, skills and normative control in call centres', in Deery, S. and Kinnie, N. (eds.) (2004) *Human Resource Management and Call Centre Work*, Houndsmills, Palgrave

Tonge, J . (1999) 'New packaging, old deal? New Labour and employment policy innovation', in *Critical Social Policy*, 19

Toynbee, P. (2003) *Hard work: Life in low wage Britain*, London, Bloomsbury

Section 3:

Policy Areas

Chapter 7

Family Policy in Scotland

Jason Annetts

Introduction

Family policy incorporates an intricate and complex web of diverse government policies and legislation from benefits and tax rules to paternity leave that all have an affect on the family and family life. At times, the government may make explicit statements on family policy while at other times it may be implicit in the changes they are making. Since family policy covers so many aspects of government activity it can be difficult to define. Put most simply, family policy can be viewed as "everything that government does to and for the family" (Harding , 1996 : 206). This very wide definition necessarily would include almost everything done by the government, since most government activities affect the family in one way or another. Therefore, it is useful to distinguish as Kamerman and Kahn (cited in Harding, 1996) have between *three* different types of family policy. Kamerman and Kahn (cited in Harding, 1996: 206) distinguished between *explicit* family policy and *implicit* family policy, where the impact on the family is unintentional. *Explicit* family policy is then subdivided into policies that are "designed to achieve specified family goals" and those that, although they are designed to have an impact on the family, are not trying to achieve specific family goals.

In the past, family policy in Britain has been largely characterised as implicit (Harding, 1996; Centre for Research on Family and Relationships (CRFR) 2002 ; Wasoff and Cunningham -Burley, 2005) , wi th successive governments – especially Conservative – not believing that government should interfere in family life. However, since the New Labour election victory in 1997, the family has become subject to increased policy activity and both the UK government and the Scottish Executive have shown an increased willingness to intervene directly in family affairs. This can be seen in the Scottish Executive's early intervention and domestic violence strategies and its wide-ranging reform of family law to ensure that Scottish family law reflects the diversity of family forms (Wasoff and Hill, 2002). However, whilst the Scottish Executive is more willing to involve itself in family matters, the emphasis is on *supporting* families rather than telling families how to live. This was made clear in the recent Scottish Executive (2006) booklet, *Family Matter: Living together in Scotland*, which outlined the changes to Scottish family law following the passing of the Family Law (Scotland) Act 2006:

> "Where families are strong and working well, Scottish Ministers believe that the government should not get involved. Family life should, wherever possible, be a matter for the families themselves. They believe that the government should help families by supporting good values in family relationships (things like trust, tolerance and fairness), not tell people what to do or tell parents how to bring up their children" (Scottish Executive, 2006: 1).

Although we have seen considerable change with the shift to a more explicit family policy, the Scottish Executive, as with past UK governments, is unwilling to be seen to be interfering in the private affairs of families. Direct involvement in family life is largely restricted to those designated as 'problem families' by the criminal justice system and social services. Beyond these families, governments have believed that they should only have a supporting role, even if this is a more active supporting role today than with previous administrations.

Before going on to discuss family policy since devolution, this chapter will also consider the ways in which the family, both in Scotland and throughout the UK, has been transformed since the 1960s. The decline of the traditional 'nuclear' family, rising divorce and cohabitation rates and the liberalisation of the social norms governing sex and relationships, have forced the government to reconsider how they define 'the family' and how they should respond to these social changes. In particular, this chapter will discuss:

- The *different types* of family in Scotland, defining what is meant by the terms 'nuclear', 'extended', 'lone parent' and 'reconstituted' families and the concept of 'families of choice'.

- The *changing composition* of the family in Scotland and, particularly, the move towards smaller and childless households.

- What is meant by family policy and the difference between *implicit* and *explicit* family policy. This section will also discuss the shift to a more explicit family policy since the 1997 New Labour General Election victory.

- Family policy in Scotland since devolution, outlining the areas of family policy that are reserved for the UK government in Westminster and those areas that have been devolved to the Scottish Parliament. This section will also explore the continuity between UK and Scottish family policy and highlight *the few* areas of divergence.

Defining the Family

Nuclear and Extended Families

Although we all are familiar with the idea of the family, its diverse and changing form makes it difficult to define. In Western industrial society the family is often portrayed as consisting of parents and their biological children. This is normally referred to as the **nuclear** or **conjugal family**:

> "[A] small unit derived from the relationship between a man and a woman legally bound together through marriage as husband and wife. The nuclear family is created when a child is born to this couple. The unit shares a common residence and is intended by ties of affection, common identity and support" (Muncie and Sapsford, 1995: 10).

However, despite popular assumptions, the majority of families do *not* conform to this nuclear family stereotype and family policy has begun to recognise that in Scotland relatively few people live in such households. For example, there has been a shift to smaller households and a considerable rise in lone parent and single occupancy households. This can be contrasted with many ethnic minority families that often contain members of their extended kinship network. Before **industrialisation** the **extended family**, which included members of the extended kinship network such as grand-parents, uncles, aunts, and/or cousins, was most likely the typical family form. With industrialisation the nuclear family became the dominant configuration of the family being better suited to the needs of industrial society, although there has been some debate concerning whether the nuclear family was the *result* of industrialisation or whether the development of the nuclear family *encouraged* industrialisation (Laslett, 1977; Berger and Berger, 1983). It would be wrong, though, to consider the extended family as being of only historical importance. Numerous studies have illustrated the continued importance of extended kinship ties in our society. One such example was Young and Wilmott's (1961) classic study of working class families in Bethnal Green during the 1950s, which found numerous households contained three generations of kin organised around the relationship between mothers, daughters and grandchildren.

A more recent example drawn from research on minority ethnic communities demonstrates the continued importance of the extended family in these communities (Dallos and Sapsford, 1995). It should also be recognised that although the majority of us do not live with our extended families, this does not mean that the extended kinship network is of no importance in our lives. Technological advancement means that even if geographically separated the extended family can remain an essential support network (Finch and Mason, 1993).

Pause for thought
- How important is your extended family to you and what role, if any, do they play in your everyday life?
- Has there been any time or particular circumstance where they have had a greater involvement with you and your immediate family?

Lone Parent and Reconstituted Families

Lone parent families are becoming increasingly common both in Scotland and the rest of the UK and can be defined as comprising of:

> "One parent, frequently the mother, living alone with her children, with a greater proportion of responsibility for caring for children financially and emotionally" (Dallos and Sapsford, 1995: 128).

Ninety-one per cent of 'lone parent families' comprise a single mother and her children compared to just 9 per cent being headed by a lone father (Popay, Rimmer and Rossiter, 1983; Macionis and Plummer, 2002). Despite concerns about the sharp rise in the number of lone parent households, the majority of children continue to be raised in nuclear style families consisting of two adults and dependent children (Dallos and Sapsford, 1995). However, more often than not these are **reconstituted families** that include one of their biological parents, a step-parent as well as biological siblings, step-siblings and half-siblings.

Therefore, despite recent concerns about the family, it remains one of our most cherished institutions even if it has become increasingly diverse (*Social Trends*, 2002). It is often assumed that marriage and children are at the very heart of family, however, recent changes have questioned this belief. Although marriage remains very popular, the rise in cohabitation and divorce, the creation of reconstituted families and the increasing numbers of people choosing to live alone as well as the relaxation of social conventions or 'rules' governing family life, have all contributed to this increased family diversity in Scotland today. These changes necessarily have resulted in a reconsideration of what constitutes 'the family'. The Scottish Executive, having recognised that the legal definitions of the family were no longer relevant to modern Scottish society, instituted a wide ranging consultation on family law that led to the passing of the Family Law (Scotland) Act 2006. This Act extended some legal protections and rights to cohabiting couples that were in the past only available to those who were married. However, those that choose to cohabit still do not have the same rights as married couples or gay and lesbian couples who have registered their relationship through the civil partnership legislation enacted in 2004 (Scottish Executive, 2006). This reflects the government's continuing strong support for marriage and its belief that children are best raised in two-parent married families.

Co-habiting Families

Despite this support for traditional married relationships, a growing proportion of children are being raised in both lone parent families and families where the parents choose **cohabitation** over marriage. This has been illustrated by the growing number of children now being born to unmarried parents in Scotland, which rose from 31.2 per cent of children born in 1994 to 46.7 per cent of children in 2004 (General Register Office (GROS), 2004). Although this does not suggest that marriage is on the wane, it does imply that a significant minority of Scots no longer believe that marriage is a necessary precursor to having and raising children.

'Families of Choice'

There is also no compelling reason that families necessarily need to be based upon kinship ties. **'Families of choice'** describes unrelated individuals who have chosen to constitute themselves as family (Weston, 1991). The most obvious example would be gay male and lesbian couples, who have only recently had their relationships formally recognised, first through various legal rulings that extended the legal definition of the family to include same sex couples and then in 2004 through the Civil Partnership Act. The growing acceptance in society of gay male and lesbian partnerships have also been reflected in changes such as the repeal in Scotland in June 2000 of Section 2a (often referred to as Section 28), which had formerly prohibited the promotion of homosexuality in any school under local authority control.

Pause for thought
List the types of family units that you and your friends live in.

- What percentage of them live in a traditional nuclear family and what proportion live in other types of family unit?
- What do your findings tell you about the family?

The Family in Scotland

The Scottish family changed profoundly during the 20th century, becoming smaller and more diverse with a sharp rise in cohabitation and lone parent households. Although marriage remains very popular, witnessed by the fact that a majority of Scottish adults (56 per cent) are married, a further eight per cent are married but separated or divorced and 10 per cent are widowed, an increasing number of couples are now choosing *not* to marry (Scottish Household Survey (SHS), 2000). This increase in cohabitation, coupled with a rising divorce rate, has resulted in a growing number of Scottish children being raised by either lone parents or unmarried couples.

Declining Birth Rates

However, only a quarter of households today contain any dependent children under the age of 16, which is largely the outcome of our declining birth rate that has fallen from 35.1 births per thousand of the population between 1861-1865 (Devine, 2000) to 10.1 births per thousand in 2002 (GROS, Annual Review of Demographics, 200 2, www.gro-scotland.gov.uk). While in 1911 Scottish women had on average 5.8 children (Devine, 2000), by 2002 this had fallen to a low of 1.47 children, the lowest total fertility rate in the UK (Paterson *et al*, 2004). Since 2002, Scotland has experienced a slight rise in the total fertility rate to 1.62, however, this still falls far short of the necessary replacement rate of 2.1 (GROS, 2006). Despite the low birth rate in Scotland and after years of decline, Scotland's population is rising. In the year ending 30 June 2005, Scotland's population rose by 16 thousand to 5,094,800, the third year in a row that the population has increased. These small increases are largely due to migration to Scotland from elsewhere in the UK or European Union, however, the population is still projected to fall below 5 million by 2036 (GROS, 2006).

The Diminishing Size of Scottish Households

This decline in the Scottish total fertility rate has been mirrored by a substantial decrease in the size of both households and families in Scotland (see **Table 7.1**). During the 1960s the average household contained over three people ; this has now declined to just 2.2 people per household and is likely to dip below two by 2024 (GROS, 2006). Small households containing one or two adults now account for over 60 per cent of all households, whilst only 28 per cent of Scottish households now contain any dependent children under the age of 16. Although the percentage of households with two adults and children has consistently fallen over the past 25 years, the number of lone parent households has increased (see **Table 7.1**).

Table 7.1 Trends in Household Composition in Scotland 1981-2004

Percentages	1981	1991	1999	2000	2001	2002	2003	2004
1 adult: male	7	11	13	14	14	14	14	15
1 adult: female	15	18	19	19	19	19	19	19
1 adult, 1 child	1	3	3	4	3	4	4	4
1 adult, 2+ children	1	2	3	3	3	3	3	3
2+ adults, 1+ children	33	25	23	22	22	21	21	21
2 adults	28	30	29	29	30	30	30	30
3+ adults	14	11	10	10	9	10	10	9
Total (%)	100	100	100	100	100	100	100	100

(Source: General Register Office for Scotland Household Estimates and Projections, Table 5: Trends in Household Composition, Scotland, 1981-2004, www.gro-scotland.gov.uk.)

There is, however, considerable variation in Scotland, with cities like Dundee (22 per cent), Aberdeen (23 per cent) and Edinburgh (24 per cent) having a particularly low proportion of households with children compared to the Shetland Islands (36 per cent), which have the highest proportion of households with dependent children under the age of 16, followed closely by East Renfrewshire and West Lothian, both with 34 per cent (Scottish Household Survey, 2000). Of those households with dependent children, the majority only have one or two children and are classified as 'small family households' (Scottish Household Survey, 2002).

However, the figures in **Table 7.1** may disguise the actual number of dependent children still living with at least one of their parents, since it excludes children over the age of 16 who are still living at home and who may still be dependent on their parents for financial support. The figures from the 2002 Scottish Household Survey clearly illustrate that most young people aged 16-24 still live with their parents, with 60 per cent living in households described as being large family or large adult households (Paterson *et al*, 2004). The push in recent years to increase the level of young people in further and higher education has resulted in many more young people being financially dependent upon their parents well beyond the age of 16 and, therefore, while the proportion of households with children has declined, young people remain dependent upon their families for longer.

This trend to smaller households has been the outcome of far reaching social changes, including a significantly later age of first marriage, the high level of divorce and the overall decline in the number of Scots getting married every year. Not only do fewer and fewer households now contain children, but an increasing number of Scots are choosing, or being forced through separation and divorce, to live alone. In 2004, there were 765,000 single occupancy households, which accounts for just under 35 per cent of all households in Scotland. Lone females account for some 57 per cent of all single occupancy households. However, the number of lone women households is rising at a slower rate (from 15 per cent of all households in 1981 to 19 per cent in 2004) than single male households.

Traditionally, higher rates of single occupancy for older women are likely to be the outcome of the greater life expectancy of women where they outlive their partners. However, the massive increase in single occupancy households is largely due to the growing number of men who are living on their own, which has nearly doubled since 1981, rising from seven per cent of all households to 15 per cent of households in 2004 (GROS, Household Estimates and Projections, Table 5: Household Estimates for Scotland by Local Authority, 1991 to 2005, www.gro-scotland.gov.uk).

Rising Divorce Rates, Remarriage and Late Marriage

Part of the reason for this rise in single occupancy households may be the rising divorce rate in Scotland. In 2004, 11,227 divorces were granted in Scotland (General Register for Scotland statistics for Divorces, by marital status at time of marriage, Scotland, 1971 to 2004, www.gro-scotland.gov.uk). However, the extent to which these divorces help to explain the rise in single occupancy households is unclear. Nearly half of all women (aged 30-59) living on their own are either separated or divorced, whereas for men (aged 30-59) the majority have never been married (CRFR

Briefing Paper Number 20, 2005, www.crfr.ac.uk). This, however, may simply be the result of the growing number of people cohabiting and the rising age of first marriage.

The later age of marriage is one of the many structural changes that have resulted in smaller households and a growing number of single occupancy households. In recent years there has been a considerable decline in the number of people in Scotland getting married. In 1940, 53,522 Scots were married compared to just 30,367 in 2000 (GROS, Statistics for Marriages, 1855-2000, www.gro-scotland.gov.uk). This figure, however, does not reflect the true number of people living in Scotland getting married, but rather reflects Scotland's popularity as a marriage destination as nearly 30 per cent of those married in Scotland were *not* Scottish residents (CRFR, 2004).

Those who do get married do so at a significantly later age. The average age of those getting married has risen from 27.6 years for men and 25.3 years for women in 1981 to 36.3 years for men and 33.8 years for women in 2005. Although this rise is due partly to the number of remarriages following divorce, if remarriages are excluded the mean age only drops to 31.9 years for men and 29.9 years for women (GROS, Statistics for Marriages, Mean Age of Marriages, by Sex and Marital Status, Scotland, 1855-2005, www.gro-scotland.gov.uk).

Cohabitation

One of the major causes for the rising age of marriage in Scotland, a rate that had been fairly stable since the mid-16th century, is the increasing number of people who choose to live together before they get married. In the ten years between 1991 and 2001, the number of cohabiting couples nearly doubled from four per cent to seven per cent of households (CRFR, 2004). However, despite this rise, **cohabitation** tends to be a short-lived phase during which a couple decides whether to get married or go their separate ways. The reason for this may be related to the unwillingness of governments to extend the same rights, legal protection and privileges that are enjoyed by married couples to cohabiting couples, even though these were extended to same sex couples in 2004 through the civil partnership legislation. The government's justification for *not* extending civil partnerships to heterosexual couples was that unlike same sex couples, they have the right to get married. However, as noted earlier, the Family Law (Scotland) Act 2006 *does* extend certain rights to cohabiting couples, but they still do not have the same legal protections as married couples.

The levels of cohabitation differ widely across Scotland. The highest rates of cohabitation are to be found in the big cities of Aberdeen (10.35 per cent of all households) and Edinburgh (10.36 per cent), whereas the lowest cohabitation rates are in the deeply religious Western Isles (4.05 per cent). While there is not a strong relationship between class background and likelihood to cohabit, there does seem to be a relationship between age and religiosity and cohabitation. Those from younger age groups are more likely to cohabit than those from older age groups and the more religious the less likely people are to cohabit (Barlow, 2002). This rise in cohabitation rates has resulted in an increasing proportion of children being born to unmarried couples.

Historically, the levels of children being born outside of wedlock have been low in Scotland, although significant regional variations have existed, with both the northeast and southwest of Scotland having a much greater proportion of children being born to lone mothers or unmarried couples than elsewhere. This can be partly explained by the strength of the Scottish church and church discipline after the 16th century **Reformation**. While in the 19th century the number of children born out of wedlock increased, during the late Victorian period and early 20th century it began to decline, reaching a low of 4.2 per cent between 1956 and 1960 (GROS, 2004). However, from 1980 onwards the percentage of children born to unmarried couples began to substantially increase from 15.2 per cent of all births between 1981 and 1985 (GROS, 2000), to an all time high of 45.5 per cent of all births in 2003 (GROS, 2004).

As with the pattern of cohabitation, there are significant regional differences in the percentage of children born outside of marriage. In Dundee, for example, 59.4 per cent of all births were to unmarried couples compared to only 24.8 per cent of all births in the Western Isles and 23.6 per cent in East Renfrewshire. Interestingly, the two cities that have the highest rates of cohabitation have relatively low levels of birth outside of marriage; births outside of marriage account for 43.2 per cent of births in Aberdeen and only 38.1 per cent in Edinburgh.

Teenage Pregnancy

Age is closely related to the likelihood of children being born to unmarried parents. Therefore, it is not surprising that towns such as Dundee, with a very high rate of teenage pregnancy, also have a very high percentage of children being born to an unmarried couple. The younger a mother is, the greater the likelihood that she will not be married, with 95 per cent of teenage mothers in 1999 being unmarried compared to 72 per cent of mothers between the ages of 20-24, whereas only 23 per cent of mothers in the 30-34 age group were not married (GROS, 2000). In recent years there has been considerable concern about the number of teenage mothers.

Table 7.2 Teenage Pregnancy by Council Area 1991-2004[2]

Council Area[1]	1991/2	1999/0	2000/1	2001/2	2002/3	2003/4[p]
Scotland	50.1	44.7	44.0	43.1	42.1	42.4
Aberdeen City	59.2	48.5	49.3	44.5	50.3	52.5
Aberdeenshire	39.3	31.3	27.6	25.8	29.1	28.0
Angus	50.4	51.2	42.9	48.9	38.2	45.9
Argyll and Bute	42.8	33.6	26.7	31.7	30.1	32.2
Clackmannanshire	46.6	49.4	54.4	49.9	51.7	54.4
Dumfries and Galloway	47.1	45.7	47.3	44.9	43.5	41.7
Dundee City	66.9	63.5	61.9	58.5	61.4	64.4
East Ayrshire	62.3	51.7	48.9	48.0	43.5	43.2
East Dunbartonshire	21.2	19.9	28.1	22.3	20.5	23.5
East Lothian	45.4	41.9	36.4	47.4	36.3	39.7
East Renfrewshire	22.5	23.0	21.3	27.5	18.4	19.5
Edinburgh City	47.3	46.3	43.1	42.6	39.8	42.7
Eilean Siar	31.1	24.9	22.0	15.1	24.0	15.9
Falkirk	46.9	46.8	46.4	42.2	43.2	39.5
Fife	52.2	47.2	46.9	45.9	42.6	46.6
Glasgow City	65.7	53.8	54.3	52.1	52.4	50.4
Highland	44.4	47.3	46.7	42.7	38.3	42.5
Inverclyde	53.0	52.5	52.2	39.3	53.8	45.3
Midlothian	39.6	53.0	51.6	48.4	51.4	47.5
Moray	51.7	38.5	42.5	31.5	40.7	34.6
North Ayrshire	56.7	45.4	46.8	51.6	48.2	41.8
North Lanarkshire	50.0	42.3	46.4	46.9	44.9	44.1
Orkney Islands	40.2	24.3	17.1	14.5	39.9	29.3
Perth and Kinross	48.9	38.9	39.2	36.1	34.7	37.1
Renfrewshire	44.3	48.1	47.0	43.6	48.4	40.7
Scottish Borders	43.2	33.3	33.4	34.6	32.2	37.7
Shetland Islands	36.5	29.4	24.8	35.8	24.5	25.3
South Ayrshire	50.1	41.8	39.4	48.1	37.0	40.6
South Lanarkshire	41.6	36.6	35.6	36.7	33.2	37.3
Stirling	44.4	33.4	34.7	33.1	31.2	28.3
West Dunbartonshire	51.0	44.6	45.3	48.3	50.0	43.1
West Lothian	53.3	52.9	46.4	48.9	47.7	50.8

1 – Council areas came into being on April 1, 1996 following local government re-organisation. The 1991-1992 rates have been calculated using back mapped GRO population estimates.

2 – Rates per 1,000 women in each year.
p – Provisional.
(Source: Constructed from statistics available from ISD Scotland, www.isd.scotland.org.)

However, it should be remembered that the average age at which women are giving birth to their first child is actually rising and that births to teenagers form a very small percentage of total births. The number of teenage pregnancies actually peaked between 1971-75 when they accounted for 11.8 per cent and have since declined, accounting for only 7.7 per cent of mothers in 2005.

There has also been a sharp decline in the number of women between the ages of 20 and 25 giving birth, from a high in the early 1970s of 34.5 per cent of all births to just 18.7 per cent of all births in 2005 (GROS, Statistics for Live births, numbers and percentages, by age of mother and marital status of parents, Scotland, 1946-2005, www.gro-scotland.gov.uk).

Despite the declining rates of teenage pregnancy, Scotland has one of the highest levels of teenage pregnancy in Europe (Family Planning Association (FPA), 2005) and research suggests that teenagers who experience greater levels of social deprivation are most likely to become pregnant and are least likely to terminate the pregnancy (McLeod, 2001). There is also a wide variation in the rate of teenage pregnancy across Scotland. For example, Dundee City Council area has consistently had the highest level of teenage pregnancy in Scotland with a rate of 64.4 pregnancies per 1000 women in 2003/04, followed by Clackmannanshire with a rate of 54.4 (see **Table 7.2** above). These extremely high rates can be contrasted to the very low rate of teenage pregnancy in the Eilean Siar Council region of just 15.9 per 1000 women.

There has also been a worrying increase in the rates of teenage pregnancy in some areas such as Aberdeen and Dundee City Councils after many years of decline. In order to tackle this persistently high rate of teenage pregnancy, the Scottish Executive has emphasised the need for good sex and relationships education across both primary and secondary schools and recognises that the delivery of sex education in Scottish schools up to this point has been 'patchy' (Scottish Executive, 2000). Until recently the main focus has been on the delivery of sex education in secondary schools. However, there has been a growing realisation that sex and relationships education in primary schools is essential in order to enable young people to make positive and informed choices about sexual relationships and practices (Scottish Executive, 2000).

The widespread changes in family form and household composition have had a major impact on not just the number of households that contain dependent children, but the type of families in which those children live. Although the majority of dependent children still live in nuclear style family units consisting of two married adults (increasingly one of those adults will not be their biological parent), the number of those raised by cohabiting couples has more than doubled, rising from four per cent of children in 1991 to ten per cent in 2001. There has also been a substantial increase in the number of children being raised in lone parent households, rising from 19 per cent in 1991 to just under 25 per cent of all dependent children in 2005 (GROS, Household Estimates and Projections, Table 5: Household Estimates for Scotland by Local Authority, 1991 -2005, www.gro-scotland.gov.uk). Women head the overwhelming majority of lone parent families, with less than 10 per cent of them comprising a father and his children (Scottish Household Survey, 2002).

The rise in the proportion of lone parent households may partly explain the continued high rate of child poverty in Scotland. Although this rate has fallen in recent years (Scottish Executive Briefing Note Households Below Average Income, 2003/04 , www.scotland.gov.uk) children in Scottish society are still more likely than any other group to live in poverty and "remain poor for a longer period of time..." (Phillips, 2002: 97). While 25 per cent of all children in Scotland live in households with below 60 per cent of median income, the vast majority of these are children living in lone parent families. Forty seven per cent of all children living in lone parent households compared to just 16 per cent of children living in two parent families live in households with below 60 per cent median income. One of the major obstacles for lone parent families is the failure of successive governments to provide both well-funded and widely available childcare in Scotland (Scott, 2002). The difficulty lone parents have in finding good quality inexpensive childcare limits their ability to take advantage of further education and employment opportunities that could lift them out of poverty. While the government has, through its childcare strategy, tried to improve access to childcare, the evidence suggests that there are regional variations that mean some parents find it difficult to access childcare services.

> "However, the research suggests that local variations prevail and rural labour markets imply different demands being placed upon childcare services as a result of longer working days and the distances that must often be covered to access work and education" (McKendrick *et al*, 2003: 8).

Although the employment rate for lone parents in Scotland has dramatically increased from just 38 per cent of lone parents being in work in 1999 to 55 per cent in 2005, this is still considerably lower than many of our European partners (One Parent Families Scotland Factfile General statistics 2, www.opfs.org.uk; Scottish Executive, 2005). Reducing the material deprivation of children through encouraging lone parents back to work has been one of the central planks of New Labour's family policy. Initially, they sought to tackle the levels of child poverty through the introduction of their **'Sure Start'** programme and through the provision of additional resources for 'capital spending on early years' education in disadvantaged areas' (Scott, 2002). They also introduced a number of measures, such as the 'Working Families Tax Credit' in April 2000, which was then supplanted by the 'Child Tax Credit' in 2003, in order to ensure that parents returning to work did not experience an overall decline in household income through a loss of benefits. The purpose of this policy was "to make work pay and tackle child poverty in workless households through a single simplified payment for children" (Phillips, 2002: 100; see also Scott, **Chapter 5**).

Pause for thought
Examine **Tables 7.1** and **7.2** in the above section and summarise what they tell you about the composition of Scottish Households and teenage pregnancy in Scotland.

- In what way do you think this information would be useful to the Scottish Executive in the development of its family policy?

'Crisis' in the Family

The changing family patterns, a decline in **family values** and the growing numbers who cohabit rather than marry, for some commentators, amount to a 'crisis' in the family. This has been a recurring theme in media coverage, which has tended to view changes in the family structure, such as the rising proportion of lone parent families or divorce, in solely negative terms. These changes are normally contextualised by the media, politicians and other concerned citizens by reference to a 'golden past' where children were raised by their biological parents who remained married throughout their lives.

> "[S]ocial and political concern over the supposed decline of 'family values' is endemic; in every era comparisons are made with a 'golden' mythologized family of past times [...]. The current concerns of governments – for example, with increases in divorce, the growing number of unmarried mothers and the rise in the number of infirm elderly people needing some level of support – are themselves a result of changing social and economic circumstances in the contemporary period; changes in the ways in which households and kin units produce, consume and reproduce. The problems are novel ones which reflect far more than a putative decline in family solidarity or family values. They are

issues rooted in broader patterns of freedom and constraint experienced by individuals, and cannot be resolved by appeals to past family behaviour" (Allan, 1999: 3-4).

Whilst some commentators despair the decline of 'family values', others are concerned that the changing social organisation of family life raises questions concerning the continued relevance of the family and wonder whether it will be able to survive in its present form. Certainly, there is little doubt that recent changes in the economic and social organisation of Western society have increased the strain upon the family. This strain is the result of the changing labour market, the lack of emotional support available to the nuclear family due to a declining importance of wider kin support networks and the changes in the family form (Weeks, 1992).

However, simply because the family is changing does not mean that it is under imminent danger of disappearing. The institution of the family has, throughout history, demonstrated its resilience and although it is increasingly difficult to talk of 'the family' due to its diverse and changing nature, it remains extremely popular and is our primary source of "affection, security, intimacy, sexual love, parenthood" (Barrett and McIntosh, 1991 : 133). Whilst critics of the family, such as Barrett and McIntosh (1991), would prefer society to find better ways of meeting these needs, successive governments in both Westminster and Holyrood have actively promoted the family.

Family Policy in Scotland

As indicated in the introduction, family policy in the UK has been characterised as largely *implicit*, particularly during the 1980s. The Conservative administrations of both Thatcher and Major in Westminster – influenced by the **'New Right'** economic agenda (see Sweeney, **Chapter 2**) and the activities of Christian moral crusaders – saw the family as not only central to the rolling back of the welfare state, but as a panacea for almost every serious social problem (Abbott and Wallace, 1992; Dunphy, 2000). Promoting traditional 'family values' through pro-family policies was part of a 'New Right' anti-welfare agenda, which they hoped would enable the state to withdraw from the provision of social and welfare services (Abbott and Wallace, 1992). Both the Thatcher (1979-1990) and Major (1990-1997) administrations expected the family to increasingly shoulder the burden of welfare provision "particularly in relation to the 'dependent' population of children, people who are sick or have disabilities and older people" (Clarke and Langan, 1993: 65).

The New Labour government, following its election victory in 1997, has continued to stress the importance of both marriage and the family. For example, Jack Straw, the then Home Secretary, emphasised the importance of marriage for raising children and for 'New' Labour's family policy in July 1998 when he said:

> "That strengthening the institution of marriage as a basis for bringing up children was a cornerstone of Labour's family policy" (Straw, 1998, cited in Dunphy, 2000: 189).

However, the Home Office publication, *Supporting Families* (1998) and the publication by the Scottish Office (1999) of *Helping the Family in Scotland*, heralded the shift to a much more explicit family policy (cited in CRFR Research Briefing, Number 3, 2002, www.crfr.ac.uk).

The Labour-Liberal administration in Holyrood following devolution and the setting up of the Scottish Parliament in 1999, also emphasised the importance of marriage and the family for society. Even though the Scottish Executive was much quicker to repeal the notorious Section 2A of the Local Government Act 1986, which banned the promotion of homosexuality by local authorities, than its counterpart in Westminster, it continued to emphasise the importance of 'family values'. The Scottish Executive's guidance to the Directors of Education that "[p]upils should be encouraged to appreciate the value of stable family life, parental responsibility and family relationships in bringing up children and offering them security, stability and happiness" (Scottish Executive Circular, 2/2001, www.scotland.gov.uk) is a testament to this fact.

However, while both the Scottish Executive and the government in Westminster has strongly supported and promoted the family, clearly believing that by supporting the family they will strengthen society, they have recognised and accepted a diversity of family forms (CRFR Research Briefing, Number 3, 2002, www.crfr.ac.uk).

> "The orientation of the present Scottish and UK governments to defining 'the family' has a mix of normative and diversity-recognising strands, with a mix of universal and selective policies. There is promotion of marriage and two-parent households on the one hand, but also the acceptance and to some degree support of 'non-conventional households' on the other. New Labour claim to be developing a 'third way' more tolerant of the diversity of family life than previously and more focused on responsibilities as well as rights" (Wasoff and Hill, 2002: 173).

This greater acceptance of 'non-conventional households' is clearly illustrated by the 2004 Civil Partnership Legislation that allowed, for the first time, gay male and lesbian couples to register their partnership thereby receiving similar rights to married couples. Despite the criticism that this was a form of second class marriage for gay male and lesbian couples, who were still denied the right to marry (and that cohabiting heterosexual couples, who may not like the religious overtones associated with the institution of marriage, could not register their partnerships), it does reflect the willingness of the government to accept and support a diversity of family formations.

Since devolution, Scotland has been subject to the family policies of both the UK government and the recently established Scottish Executive. As part of the devolution settlement, certain areas of government have been devolved to the Scottish Parliament, which Wasoff and Hill (2002: 174) suggest "cluster around the social provision, and the socialisation and reproductive activities of family life" whereas reserved matters "are clustered around the productive and economic activities of families," for which only the UK government in Westminster can legislate (see **Table 7.3**).

Table 7.3 Family policy areas devolved to the Scottish Parliament and reserved to the UK Parliament

Devolved Family Policy Areas	Reserved Family Policy Areas
Family Law	Social Security
Child Care and the Personal Services for Children and Families	Taxation and Fiscal Policy
Some Policies on Health and Community Care	Employment and Economic Policy
Education	Immigration and Nationality
Transport	Equal Opportunities
Housing and the Environment	Abortion, Genetics and Surrogacy
Criminal Justice and other areas of Law	

(Source: CRFR Research briefing Number 3 February 2002, www.crfr.ac.uk)

The Scottish Executive's family policy is, therefore, restricted to areas such as family law, children and family services, health and personal care, education, housing and crime. These policies can be divided into those that are explicitly aimed at the family and those that have an indirect impact on the family (Wasoff and Hill, 2002). Policies that are explicitly aimed at the family would include the drive to reduce levels of social exclusion and to ensure that all children in Scotland were given the best possible start in life. An example of this policy is the Scottish Executive's **'early years' strategy'**, which incorporates the Sure Start programme, the Childcare Strategy for Scotland,

Pre-school education and the Health Improvement Fund (Wasoff *et al*, 2004). Other examples of policies that are directly aimed at the family would include the high profile campaign against domestic violence, the promotion of family friendly employment policies and the reform of Scottish family law to ensure that it reflects the diversity of Scottish families. These can be contrasted with policies that are not specifically aimed at the family but have an indirect effect, such as the provision of free personal care for the elderly (see Cavaye, **Chapter 11**) and public health campaigns.

Pause for thought

Make a list of all the different ways in which both the policies of the UK government and the Scottish Executive affect your family's life.

- Which of these policies would you categorise as 'explicit' and which are 'implicit'?

This shift to a more explicit family policy reflects a growing willingness of governments to intervene directly in family life. In the past, governments have generally been hesitant about intervening directly in families and although many areas of government policy clearly affected family life, direct involvement in families tended to be focused on 'problem' families and (despite the government's increasing willingness to support families in their child care duties and in the provision of personal care) it largely still does. Typically, such interventions occur when a family does not adequately care for its vulnerable members or in situations of domestic violence. The problem with this is that it "encourages a punitive preoccupation with family 'breakdown' and 'ineffective' parenting" (Wasoff and Dey, 2000: 70).

However, since the New Labour victory in 1997 there has also been a greater willingness for 'the state' to be involved in 'non-problem' families , for example, through its childcare support, an area that was before seen very much as part of the family's duties. While the New Labour government in Westminster and the Scottish Executive have not sought to usurp the family's role in looking after children, both have explicitly tried to support families in caring for their children. The Scottish Executive's 'early years' policy and its childcare strategy are good examples of its new willingness to intervene in family life, which has acted to blur the boundary between the *private sphere* of the family and the *public sphere* in which governments usually operate.

"The shifting boundary of responsibility for care between families and the state has been a strong theme of childcare policies since 1997, where the state has assumed a much greater role for the care and support of children and the boundary between state and family, or market or voluntary sector and family has not only moved but has become more permeable than it was under the previous Conservative government, which tended to the view that childcare was a family responsibility in which the state had little legitimate role" (Wasoff and Cunningham-Burley, 2005: 265).

Although in areas such as childcare provision, the involvement of the government has generally been well received, the government's increasingly interventionist approach to family policy has not always been successful or welcomed. For example, the attempt to make biological parents who do not live with their children more responsible for their care and financial support has been heavily criticised for its punitive nature, as has their **'welfare to work'** programme (Wasoff and Cunningham-Burley, 2005; see also Helms, **Chapter 6**).

The New Labour election victory in 1997 followed by devolution in Scotland in 1999, has resulted in a significant redrawing of the boundary between the state and the family. Although there has been an increased acceptance of a diversity of family forms, New Labour has been a staunch defender of the family and actively promoted two parent families. The shift to a more explicit and interventionist family policy has signalled the increased willingness of the government to involve itself in what was considered, by previous administrations, to be solely family matters.

Pause for thought

Discuss what the role of the state should be in family life.

- Should the government intervene directly in the family?
- If so, when is this appropriate?
- If not, what safeguards, protections and support are available for family members, including children?

Conclusion

Although the family continues to be one our most cherished institutions, far reaching changes to the family structure in Scotland have resulted in an increasing diversity of family forms. The continuing rise in the number of lone parent or reconstituted families, as well as families of choice, has resulted in a sharp decline in the traditional nuclear family. While the traditional nuclear family for many remains an ideal, few families actually conform to this configuration. Family policy in Scotland and the rest of the UK has had to recognise and take account of the increasing diversity of family forms and this has led to a more relaxed definition of the family and the acceptance of same sex partnerships. However, the primary focus of family policy and government intervention in family life has been, as in the past, on 'problem' families. In particular, the increasingly explicit and interventionist family policies of the UK government in Westminster and the Scottish Executive have been concerned with tackling issues of social exclusion and child poverty and have sought to encourage unemployed parents back into the workplace through targeted benefits.

Scottish family policy since devolution has closely followed the New Labour family policy agenda in Westminster. However, there have been areas of divergence, such as the issues of free personal care for the elderly and university tuition fees. In the future it is possible that the areas of divergence will grow, especially if a change in administration in either Westminster or Holyrood results in a situation where competing political parties with different family policy objectives are in power.

Further Reading

Centre for Research on Family and Relationships (CRFR) (2004) *Family formation and dissolution: Trends and attitudes among the Scottish population*, Centre for Research on Family and Relationships, Research Findings, No 43, 2004

McKie, L. and Cunningham-Burley, S. (eds.) (2005) *Families in Society: Boundaries and Relationships*, Bristol, The Policy Press

Wasoff, F. and Hill, M. (1992) 'Family Policy in Scotland', in *Social Policy and Society* 1(3)

Useful Websites

www.crfr.ac.uk: The Centre for Research on Family and Relationships based at Edinburgh University has links to a large number of research briefings and reports on the family and family policy in Scotland.

www.gro-scotland.gov.uk: The General Register for Scotland website contains is an excellent source of current statistics on the family and other areas of Scottish life.

www.isd.scotland.org: Contains a constantly updated wealth of health statistics.

www.opfs.org.uk: One Parent Families Scotland. Statistics and literature on one parent families in Scotland.

www.Scotland.gov.uk: The Scottish Executive website contains numerous reports and policy briefings on the family.

Bibliography

Abbot, P. and Wallace, C. (1992) *The Family and The New Right,* London, Pluto Press

Allan, G. (1999) *The Sociology of the Family: A Reader*, Oxford, Blackwell

Allen, I. and Bourke, S. (1998) *Teenage Mothers: Decisions and Outcomes*, Oxford, Policy Studies Institute

Barlow, A. (2002) 'Attitudes to Cohabitation and Marriage', in Curtice, J., McCrone, D., Park, A., Paterson, L. (eds.) (2002) *New Scotland, New* Society, Edinburgh, Polygon

Barrett, M. and McIntosh, M (1991) *The Anti-Social Family*, 2 nd Edition, London, Verso

Berger, B. and Berger, P.L. (1983) *The War over the Family: Capturing the Middle Ground*, London, Hutchinson

Bocock, R. and Thompson, K. (eds.) (1992) *Social and Cultural Forms of Modernity*, Cambridge, Polity Press

Brown, U., Scott, G., Mooney, G. and Duncan, B. (eds.) *Poverty in Scotland 2002: People Places and Policies*, Glasgow/London, CPAG/Scottish Poverty Information Unit

Clarke, J. and Langan, M. (1993) 'Restructuring Welfare: The British Welfare Regime in the 1980s', in Cochrane, A. and Clarke, J. (eds.) (1993) *Comparing Welfare States: Britain in International Context*, London, Sage in association with the Open University

Centre for Research on Families and Relationships (2002) *Research Briefing 3: Family Policy in Scotland*, Edinburgh, CRFR

CRFR (2004) *Family formation and dissolution: Trends and attitudes among the Scottish population*, Centre for Research on Family and Relationships, Research Findings, No. 43

Curtice, J., McCrone, D., Park, A. and Paterson, L. (eds.) (2002) *New Scotland, New Society?* Edinburgh, Polygon

Dallos, R. and Sapsford, R. (1995) 'Patterns of Diversity and Lived Realities', in Muncie, J. *et al* (eds.) (1995) *Understanding the Family*, London, Sage

Devine, T.M. (2000) *The Scottish Nation, 1700-2000*, Harmondsworth, Penguin

Dunphy, R. (2000) *Sexual Politics: An Introduction*, Edinburgh, Edinburgh University Press

Family Planning Association (FPA) (2005) *Factsheet: Teenage Pregnancies*, London, Family Planning Association

Finch, J. and Mason, J. (1993) *Negotiating Family Responsibilities*, London, Tavistock/Routledge

General Register Office for Scotland (GROS) (2000) *Annual Report 1999*, Edinburgh, General Register Office for Scotland

GROS (2003) *Marriages, mean age at marriage, by sex and marital status, Scotland, 1855 to 2002*, Edinburgh, General Register Office for Scotland

GROS (2004) *Population and Vital Events, Scotland*, Edinburgh, General Register Office for Scotland

GROS (2006) *Annual Report of the Registrar General of Birth, Deaths and Marriages for Scotland 2005*, Edinburgh, General Register Office for Scotland

Harding, L. (1996) *Family, State & Social Policy*, Houndsmills, MacMillan

ISD Scotland (1999) 'Teenage Pregnancy in Scotland 1989-1998', in *Information & Statistics Division; part of the Common Services Agency for the Scottish Health Service*, Health Briefing number 99/04, issued June 1999

Laslett, P. (1977) *Family Life and Illicit Love in Earlier Generations*, Cambridge, Cambridge University Press

Macionis, J. and Plummer, K. (2002) *Sociology: A Global Introduction.* 2nd Edition,

Essex, Pearson Education

McKendrick, J., Cunningham-Burley, S. and Backett-Milburn, K. (2003) *Life in Low Income Families in Scotland: Research Report*, Centre for Research on Families and Relationships, Edinburgh, University of Edinburgh/Scottish Executive

McKie, L. and Cunningham-Burley, S. (eds.) (2005) *Families in Society: Boundaries and Relationships*, Bristol, The Policy Press

McLeod, A. (2001) 'Changing patterns of teenage pregnancy: population based study of small areas', in *BMJ*, 323

Muncie, J. and Sapsford, R. (1995) 'Issues in the Study of "The Family", in Muncie, J. *et al* (eds.) (1995) *Understanding the Family*, London, Sage

Muncie, J. and Wetherell , M. (1995) 'Family Policy and Political Discourse', in Muncie, J. *et al* (eds.) *Understanding the Family*, London, Sage

Muncie, J. *et al* (eds.) *Understanding the Family*, London, Sage

Paterson, L., Bechhofer, F. and McCrone, D. (2004) *Living in Scotland: Social and Economic Change Since 1980*, Edinburgh, Edinburgh University Press

Phillips, D. (2002) 'Child Poverty in Scotland', in Brown, U., Scott, G., Mooney, G. and Duncan, B. (eds.) (2002) *Poverty in Scotland 2002: People Places and Policies*, Glasgow/London, CPAG/Scottish Poverty Information Unit

Popay, J. , Rimmer , L. and Rossiter , C. (1983) *One Parent Families: Parent , Children and Public Policy,* London, Study Commission on the Family

Scott, G. (2002) 'Social Policy and Family Poverty', in Brown, U. Scott, G. Mooney, G. Duncan, B. (eds.) (2002) *Poverty in Scotland 2002: People Places and Policies*, Glasgow/London, CPAG/Scottish Poverty Information Unit

Scottish Executive (2000) *Report on the Working Group on Sex Education in Scottish Schools*, June 2000, Edinburgh, Scottish Executive

Scottish Executive (2001) S*ocial Justice Annual Report Scotland*, Edinburgh, Scottish Executive

Scottish Executive (2005) *Annual Population Survey in Scotland 2005*, Edinburgh, Scottish Executive

Scottish Executive (2006) *Family Matters: Living Together in Scotland*, Edinburgh, Scottish Executive

Scottish Household Survey (SHS) (2000) *Scotland's People: Results from the 1999/2000*, Edinburgh, A Scottish Executive National Statistics Publication

SHS (2002) *Bulletin 7 – Life Cycles*, Edinburgh, Scottish Executive, A Scottish Executive National Statistics Publication

Social Trends (2002) *National Statistics United Kingdom No 32*, London, The Stationery Office

Wasoff, F. and Hill , M. (2002) 'Family Policy in Scotland', in *Social Policy and Society*, 1(3)

Wasoff, F. and Dey, I. (2000) *Family Policy*, Eastbourne, The Gildredge Press

Wasoff, F., MacIver, S., McGuckin, A., Morton, S., Cunningham-Burley, S., Hinds, K. and Given, L. (2004) *A Baseline Study of Outcome Indicators for Early Years Policies in Scotland: Final Report*, Edinburgh, Scottish Executive

Wasoff, F. and Cunningham-Burley, S. (2005) 'Perspectives on Social Policies and Families', in McKie, L. and Cunningham -Burley, S. (eds.) (2005) *Families in Society: Boundaries and Relationships*, Bristol, The Policy Press

Weeks, J. (1992) 'The Body and Sexuality', in Bocock, R. and Thompson, K. (eds.) (1992) *Social and Cultural Forms of Modernity*, Cambridge, Polity Press

Weston, K. (1991) *Families we choose: lesbian, gays and kinship*, New York, NY, Columbia University Press

Young, M. and Wilmott, P. (1961) *Family and Kinship in East London*, Harmondsworth, Penguin

Chapter 8

Children and Young People, Social Work and Scotland

Mo McPhail

Introduction

The focus of this chapter is on historical and critical perspectives of state intervention in the lives of children and young people, who are considered to be in need of care and protection and/or who commit offences in Scotland. The book wide themes of change and continuity, social division, the voices of service users and the care and control debate are explored through the following questions:

1. **Change and continuity:** How has the relationship between children, young people, their families and the Scottish state changed over time? What are the continuing themes?

2. **Social division:** Are certain groups of children and young people more likely to come to the attention of the social work system in Scotland? How does this affect their chances in life?

3. **Service user voices:** What shapes and influences the way society responds to children and young people in need of support over time and how far are the voices of children and young people heard in this?

4. **Care and control:** The current Scottish **Children's Hearing** system enjoys an international reputation. In terms of care and control of children and young people, how has this changed over time?

These issues and questions will be discussed, drawing on a thematic case study, commentary from professionals and relevant social policy literature.

Pause for thought

- Why study the past?
- What is the relevance of history to looking after children and young people today?

Students across health, social care and social sciences courses may wonder about the relevance of what has happened to children and young people in the past. There are many reasons why this is important:

1. To assess the significance of current issues in a wider historical context, learning from the mistakes and successes of the past.

2. To recognise continuing themes for children and young people and dimensions of both care and control in social policy.

3. To detect underlying assumptions about the nature of intervention in the lives of children and young people and how certain activities come to be defined as social problems and others not.

4. To develop critical skills of analysis in identifying a range of economic, political, social and ideological factors that shape polices, recognising that there are different views and interests at stake.

Scottish (and United Kingdom) child welfare policy over time will be considered with ongoing reference to a case study featuring a young man by the name of George, who lives in a major city in Scotland and has been in care for 15 years, since the age of two.

Box 9.1 Case Study: George's story

George is 17 and lives with his foster carer. He is keen to tell the story of his experience as a young person 'looked after' and 'accommodated' by the Scottish State.

George's parents have been unable to look after him since he was two years old because of their difficulties in relation to drugs and offending. He has maintained some contact with his mother. His experience of being 'looked after' is a mixed one.

He speaks warmly of the security and consistency of his current foster home, "She is *always* there for me." This has not always been his experience of local authority care. He remembers incidents of mistreatment with previous foster carers and harsh restraint in residential care. He feels that this and his mother's attempts to raise the alarm were "blanked". George thinks this was because his mother's views would be dismissed due to her drug use and her own record of parenting.

George has a history of offending behaviour and feels he needed social workers to really get to know him and help him manage his anger.

Was George's voice heard? He nearly explodes at this question. He is annoyed at the number of times he has heard the phrase, "We want to do what's in your best interests," and then feels that the opposite has happened. His view on Children's Rights Officers is that "they should be young people, who have been through what you have."

George's story raises a number of issues:

- How the state responds to children and young people who are both in need of care and protection and who offend.
- The impact of attitudes to parents who offend and use drugs.
- The reality of an approach that focuses on 'children's rights' and ensuring the voices of children and young people are heard effectively.

How have historical institutions like the parish, the church, charitable and voluntary organisations and latterly the state responded to these types of situations over time? *Three* periods in Scottish welfare policy for children and young people have been selected in particular to show continuities and changes in themes and issues over time. These three periods are:

1. From the **Scottish Poor Laws** to the mid-1960s, to illustrate the situation for children and young people before the introduction of a landmark piece of legislation, the Social Work (Scotland) Act 1968.

2. The period between the Social Work (Scotland) Act 1968 and the mid-1990s, which highlights forces and influences leading to another significant piece of social policy, the Children (Scotland) Act 1995.

3. From the mid-1990s to the current day. Reflecting on this period provides an opportunity to consider the impact of devolution and Scottish Executive policies on children and young people in the first decade of the 21st century.

These time periods cover vastly different lengths of time but all provide examples of the key drivers, influences and pressures for changes in social policy in this area of practice.

From the Scottish Poor Laws to the Late 1960s

Over this time frame there was a particularly slow and fragmented response to the welfare needs of children and young people from the harsh and stigmatising Poor Laws of the 1840s onwards. To a limited extent, by 1845, children and young people came to be regarded as eligible for some welfare provision in their own right. Changing economic factors, religious and social attitudes and developments in psychiatry all contributed to varying extents to the evolution of views about children and young people in need of state support and guidance.

Marshall (2001) traces the history of children's rights in Scotland since records were kept. She identifies both Celtic and Roman influences. Celtic influences appear to stem from practices where children were brought up in clans other than their own in order to encourage cross breeding and trade. The Roman influence is based on a **patriarchal** (male-dominated) system where authority rested with the male head of the extended family. There appeared to be a general reluctance to interfere with the authority of the father in the family. Children, like other dependents, were regarded as the property of their 'superiors' (Marshall, 2001: 13). From these early times there was clear evidence of the impact of social division on intervention in the welfare of children and young people. Marshall identifies a distinctive class bias in that the exercise of the law in relation to the upper and middle classes was more to do with administration of property rights. The focus of legal intervention with the poor was to do with the administration of the Poor Laws.

The Poor Laws

The central concern of the Poor Laws of 1838 and 1845 was to control and ultimately end vagrancy and begging, and enshrined the principles of the **'deserving'** and the **'un-deserving' poor** (see Law, **Chapter 3** and Scott, **Chapter 5**). These principles are based on the idea that some people's poverty results from their own actions or inactions and are therefore 'un-deserving' of aid, whereas those who find themselves impoverished due to forces beyond their control, are deserving of public assistance. The 1845 Act enabled children to be removed from the pauperising influence of their parents if they were classed as beggars – the undeserving poor. This legislation also enabled the provision of **poorhouses**, such as the Glasgow Barony Parish Poorhouse, described as a "capacious asylum for the children of poverty" (Higginbottom, 1995).

Tidsall (2003) notes that this legislation broke new ground in that the children of 'undeserving' parents were entitled to access to welfare in their own right. Parton (1985) also notes that with the onset of industrialisation, there was a greater distinction between what were considered to be public or private matters. The family, he argues, became seen as a psychological and economic unit and children a separate category, in need of separate treatment.

In 1868, The Poor Law Amendment Act introduced the offence of 'child neglect', where it became illegal for parents to fail to provide food, clothing or medical care for their child. The practice of the **'Boarding Out'** of children to relatives, friends or others who were prepared to take them in, had a long history and was often a preferred option to the poorhouse. This reflected an early belief in Scotland of the harmful effects of institutions on children. However, there was no state inspection of these placements on the grounds that this would be stigmatising for the children (Higginbottom, 1995).

Pause for thought

- What role did the charitable organisations play in children's welfare?

Prevention of Cruelty to Children

The influence of charitable organisations towards the end of the 19th Century was considerable and was driven by philanthropy and religious zeal. The creation of the Royal Scottish Society for the Prevention of Cruelty to Children (RSSPCC, now called Children First) is a powerful example of how the process of a personal tragedy – the ill-treatment of a child – became an issue of public concern and state intervention. This charitable organisation originated in the United States, through the actions of a church worker frustrated by the lack of legislation to prosecute adoptive parents who had brutally abused an eight year old child in their care. Eventually, a prosecution was secured through legislation designed to protect animals from cruelty. This led to a successful campaign to introduce legislation to protect children from cruelty, which resulted in the establishment of the Prevention of Cruelty to Children Act in the UK in 1889, regarded by some as the first children's charter. That same year, in Scotland, branches of the RSSPCC were established in Glasgow and Edinburgh (www.children1st.org.uk).

The main focus at that time was to rescue children who were living rough and begging, and to investigate alleged cases of child abuse and neglect. Other charitable organisations such as the Aberlour Orphanage, Barnardos, Quarriers, Dr. Guthrie's East of Scotland Children's Homes and National Children's Homes established children's homes to support homeless or orphaned children. The emphasis appeared to be on attending to the physical and moral welfare of children in their care, which possibly reflected social attitudes about the need to contain and control the children of the poor. It is noteworthy that the Aberlour Trust raised a special appeal during the depression in the 1930s to raise funds for the increased number of orphans.

Changing Attitudes to the Care and Control of Children and Young People

Changing beliefs and understandings about the nature of children, young people and crime are identified as key influences on welfare provision for children and young people during the late 19th and early 20th century (English, 1992). Previously, if children broke the law they were treated like adult criminals with no special protection against abuse or neglect. Victorian views of children were influenced by a desire to impose strict moral and religious codes. Partly too though, there was a shift towards a more **welfarist** ethos stemming from ideas developed in the field of psychiatry, with punishment (while never completely removed) coming to play a secondary role. A series of laws set up separate juvenile courts and special justices were trained to work with children and young people who offended. The age of criminal responsibility was even raised from 7 to 8!

Parton (1985) offers the more critical view, that Victorian society was as concerned about protecting society from potentially violent children as with child protection. The rise in charitable work also offered an opportunity for upper class women to "display the success of her husband publicly and to present herself as an idealised example of a wife and mother" (Parton, 1985: 29). The Children Act 1908 introduced the legitimisation of state intervention with families who did not co-operate with the charitable organisations. Parton (1991) identifies this as a significant shift from previous charitable work, which was based on the use of financial and material support as incentives to help poor families overcome their 'deficiencies'.

Impact of the Second World War and Introduction of the Welfare State on Welfare for Children and Young People

Atkinson and Gearing (1997) comment that the war-time evacuation of children and the resultant impact on families heralded significant changes both to children's services and to welfare services generally. According to Timmins, "[i]t threw people together, and forced one half of the country to see how the other half lived" (Timmins, 1996: 31). The conclusions drawn by Atkinson and Gearing are that the experience of evacuation increased public awareness of the existence of poverty in the UK, which helped to shift public attitudes, paving the way for the creation of the **welfare state**. This widespread experience also raised public awareness of the needs of children separated from their parents and heralded the gradual decline of large scale children's homes.

A range of factors in addition to the experiences of evacuation, including increased scrutiny of the family, the death of a child in foster care in England, and a series of committee reports, were catalysts for the introduction of the Children Act 1948. Children's Departments were established in Scotland, located in the local authority Education Department, thus representing a far greater role of the state in the lives of children for the prevention of neglect and to both provide and monitor substitute care.

Pause for thought
- How did the Welfare State benefit children and young people in particular?

This new legislation is set in the context of the introduction of the welfare state by the post-war Labour government. The welfare state was to be responsible for issues of health, education and income maintenance and the new Children's Departments were to deal with abandoned and destitute children. Significantly, the Poor Laws were abolished by the Public Assistance Act 1948, though many would argue that the associated stigma has lingered.

Focus on 'Juvenile Delinquency'

The term, **'juvenile delinquency'**, became a commonplace expression throughout the 1960s and 1970s and a series of government committees were set up to examine the 'problems of youth'. The application of the term juvenile delinquency is not a straightforward process and is the subject of much sociological debate. Cicourel (1976), for example, descr ibes the allocation of the term 'delinquent' to a young person as a complex set of interactions, based on responses to and meanings given to certain behaviours and attitudes by people, such as the police. He maintains that these perceptions and responses are strongly influenced by social class.

The idea that children who are in need of care and protection and children who offend have similar needs prevailed to a greater extent in Scotland than in the rest of the UK. The Children and Young Persons Act 1963 introduced duties on local authorities to divert young people away from crime by offering them guidance, assistance and advice. The matter was further pursued by the setting up of a government committee in 1964 – the Kilbrandon Committee – to consider the law in relation to juvenile delinquents and children in need of care and protection. Kilbrandon proposed a system of Hearings, where a panel of local people would consider the child or young person's needs, as an alternative to a juvenile court system. Children and young people would receive the care and control they needed, whatever route they came to the Hearing. The Sheriff Court would be responsible for proving whether the young person was guilty of an offence, or acknowledging his of her innocence if this was disputed. Notably, here, the child's welfare was to be the central consideration.

Kilbrandon's recommendations were generally accepted, though the 1966 White Paper expanded the proposals to introduce a comprehensive social work department, in addition to the **Children's Panels**. This also heralded a shift away from the local authority Education Department being the body responsible for child welfare.

Box 9.2 Case Study: George's story continued . . .

Let us return here to George. Consider the situation of George in this time period. As a young child in need of care and protection, what would be likely to have happened to him during this time?

Remember that the enduring legacies of the past, specifically the concept of 'deserving and undeserving poor' would have been prominent in this time period. There also appeared to be a distinction between the upper/middle classes and the poor in the operation of the law, with the focus on the latter on policies of deterrence and containment of poverty and homelessness. These harsh social attitudes would have implied that George's parents brought their trouble on themselves and were therefore 'undeserving'. A young child, like George in this situation, would probably have been boarded out. Alternatively, he might have been placed in one of the emerging charitable organisations for 'waifs and strays'.

The abolition of the Poor Laws in 1948 and the development of the welfare state meant that there was increased responsibility for the care and protection of children and young people by the state. From 1948 onwards, a child in George's situation would be increasingly likely to be placed in foster care as institutional care for children and young people became a less attractive option. As a young adult, George would have experienced the impact of a general liberalising of the treatment of young offenders throughout the first half of the 20th century, though he would have been dealt with by juvenile courts until 1968.

In sum then, factors influencing the development of the various policies for children and young people during this time frame include: religious, social, political, ideological, economic, medical, psychiatric and developing theories about juvenile delinquency. Very specific influences include the war time experiences of evacuation and the expansion of the welfare state in the post-1945 era.

The Social Work Scotland Act of 1968 to the Mid-1990s

This next section will consider influences and forces that shaped the introduction and content of the Social Work (Scotland) Act 1968 and subsequent developments. This legislation provided a firm basis for Scottish child welfare for almost 30 years, creating local government social work departments and the internationally renowned Children's Hearing system. Asquith and Stafford (1995) comment that the 1968 Act represents a shift in the public's perception about society's responsibility to children. The basis of intervention in the lives of children and young people and families was now held to be a welfare principle. Under the 1968 Act, the requirements of the new social work departments were to bring to the attention of the **Reporter to the Children's Hearings** circumstances indicating that a child may be in need of compulsory measures of care. This means decisions were required about whether the child should stay at home, receive foster care or residential care or be placed on a supervision order if a crime had been committed.

The local authorities were given a number of powers and duties to take action to protect a child from significant harm, including the removal of a child to a place of safety, the placing of a child under supervision either at home or away from home, or to provide cash or services in kind where otherwise it may prove necessary for them to be received into care. There was also provision to receive a young person into care on a voluntary basis. Contained in the 1968 Act was an important, if limited, recognition of the role of material factors such as poverty in the difficulties faced by many parents. The ethos of Children's Hearings is based on an holistic approach to treating the whole child and to promote family participation in the Hearing, though the degree of participation achieved is contested.

In relation to child protection issues, there was a concern about the balance between the rights of parents and the rights of children:

- Are the rights of the child to protection from abuse or neglect, for example, greater than the parents' right to continue to care for their child?

There was a lack of clarity on this issue. Asquith and Stafford (1995) comment that a further challenge was the consideration of issues of responsibility and punishment for criminal acts in relation to the welfare principle. Hill and Tisdall (1997) also recognise that treatment, as opposed to punishment, can be seen as a challenge to civil liberties and that Children's Hearings were seen as less able to deal with serial offending.

Child Protection in the 1970s and 1980s

In the introductory chapter in this book, there is reference to the processes involved when a particular issue comes to be regarded as a social problem. Parton (1985) provides a clear example of this when he explores the issue of child abuse. He outlines processes by which the issue was brought to public attention and the nature of the state intervention that followed. The dominant way of understanding this issue at the time was based on the **medical model** (see McCafferty, **Chapter 9**), a way of thinking about health and social care that emphasises individual and biological factors and underplays the social dimensions of a particular issue. Parton (1985) examines the assumptions and explanations underlying this with reference to a series of inquiries into the tragic deaths of or serious injury to children in both England and Scotland, which had considerable influence on child protection work. Parton's (1985) work on tracing the construction of child abuse as a social problem requiring state intervention is located in England. There was nonetheless a considerable impact on child protection policy and practice in Scotland.

Box 9.3 The issue of ill treatment of children as a 'social problem' in the making

Parton (1985) charts the construction of child abuse in the 1970s as a medico-social problem requiring state intervention and medical and social work solutions. He argues that the historic context of state interventions with children and young people up to that point had been largely about control of children, child rescue and containment of the poor.

However, in the 1940s some paediatric radiologists in the United States concluded that what had previously been considered brittle bones in babies, were now thought to be injuries inflicted by their carers. X-rays revealed that there was indeed a history of such injures to the children. Henry Kempe, an American paediatrician, introduced the label, **'The Battered Child Syndrome'** in 1962. The problem was seen as a medical issue, requiring a diagnosis and treatment for dysfunctional families. The issue was then taken up by the National Society for the Prevention of Cruelty to

---

Children (NSPCC) in the UK. Parton's (1985) argument was that the tragic death of a seven year old child, Maria Caldwell, at the hands of her step father in 1973 was the catalyst for a public outrage and draconian government responses. Social workers were blamed for the tragedy.

Parton (1985) claimed that the death of Maria Caldwell triggered a moral outrage because it occurred in a particular political, professional and social context. A group of powerful professionals took the issue up in order to focus public attention on child abuse. They organised a conference to publicise the issue professionally and politically. The media also picked up on these concerns and played a powerful role in publicising the issue, blaming social workers for the tragedy. The issue also resonated with the Conservative Secretary of State for Social Services at the time, Sir Keith Joseph, who had proclaimed strong right-wing views on the causes of poverty and the **'cycle of deprivation'**, which he defined thus:

"Deprived, inadequate parents pass on to their children the very habits and behaviours which cause their condition. Not given the skills, motivation or strength of character to change, the next generation reproduces the same failings" (Sir Keith Joseph, in Parton, 1985: 72).

An understanding of the social, economic and political context of the time is important here. High and increasing unemployment and governmental concerns about the cost of welfare provision and fears of escalation of violence were prominent issues of the day. This is consistent with the values and beliefs of the Conservative government of the time (see Sweeney, **Chapter 2** and McCafferty, **Chapter 9**). Parton (1985) argues that it was a combination of the above factors; the power of the medical profession to define the problem, the targeted focus of the NSPCC, the interest of powerful professionals and a 'fit' with dominant political ideas of the 'cycle of deprivation' and the role of the media, that led to this particular social reaction.

Parton (1985) goes on to argue that the social response to this case illustrates a shift in the nature of the relationship between the state and the family, where the state intervened more decisively when things began to go wrong for a particular family. Less weight than ever was given to structural, material and environmental factors in state responses. In a later publication (Parton, 1991), he describes the 1970s as a period where child abuse is seen as a **medico-social problem**, requiring medical and social work intervention. He contrasts this with a shift to a socio-legal process in the late 1980s, where the courts, police and lawyers become more involved as a result of particular child abuse inquiries. The Cleveland Inquiry in 1988 into the investigation of child sexual abuse was very significant in this shift. The main criticism stemmed from over-reaction to and over-reliance on medical evidence. This was in stark contrast to previous public criticism of social work of 'doing too little too late'. This was followed in 1991 by the Clyde Inquiry into the treatment of allegations of sexual abuse of nine children in Orkney (Asquith, 1993).

The lessons from these inquiries are considered by Asquith (1993), who acknowledges the very different policies between Scotland and England and Wales, but also recognises parallels raised by the Cleveland report and the report on the situation in Orkney. A common concern was the tension of achieving a balance between establishing legal grounds for removing children from their families on an urgent basis to protect them from harm, with safeguarding parental rights. A key recommendation of the Cleveland Report in England was to ensure that adequate legal powers are available where there is a child protection emergency, open to swift legal challenge by parents or carers. These and issues of the relationship between rights and responsibilities between children, parents and the state are addressed in the subsequent child care legislation for England and Wales, the Children Act 1989.

Pause for thought
- What other influences shaped the Children (Scotland) Act 1995?

Children (Scotland) Act 1995

In addition to the review of child care law and the report on family law by the Scottish Law Commission, other reports had a significant influence on the new child care legislation in Scotland. These included:

- **The Kearney Report** (1992), *Report of the Inquiry into Child Care Policies in Fife*: this highlighted the need to improve mutual respect and co-operation between a social work department and its related Children's Hearings service.

- **The Skinner Report** (1992), *Another Kind of Home: A Review of Residential Child Care*: this resulted from investigations into allegations of abuse in residential care and focused on improving the quality of good basic care, partnership with parents, rights and responsibilities for children and young people in care.

- The ratification of the **UN Convention of the Rights of the Child** by the

UK government (Newell, 1991). Although the UK government ratified the Convention, it had not enshrined it within a legal context. However, it does help establish nationally and internationally recognised standards, such as children being able to expect to be treated with humanity, dignity and respect.

Other key contextual factors that influenced the development of the new children's legislation are identified by Asquith and Stafford (1995). These included social and demographic changes in Scotland in the early 1990s, such as:

- Falling birth rates.

- Increase in divorce rates.

- An increase in the number of children living in poverty.

- High levels of poverty linked to a high number of lone parents, relatively high unemployment and low income.

Similarly, Kendrick and Hartnoll (1995) identify key social issues that impacted on the welfare of children and young people's welfare in Scotland at that time. These were:

- The increasing economic divide between the rich and the poor.
- Women's changing aspirations.
- Demographic changes.
- Increased diversity of family structure.

Kendrick and Hartnoll (1995) make some hard hitting points about the fact that it is children from the poorest families who come into care, making stark comparisons between the life chances of children living in poverty and children from financially secure families. Therefore, the impact of social division through economic disadvantage and impoverished life chances continues.

Box 9.4 Case Study: George's story – how would George experience social work services between 1968 and 1995?

The increasingly interventionist approach to child protection would have had considerable consequences for George and his family. Before the various inquiries into abuse of children and young people in residential care, there was less awareness of this form of abuse. George and his mother's attempts to raise the issue of abuse and mistreatment in care would be less likely to be heeded at that time. Theories of the cycle of deprivation advanced by Keith Joseph (Parton, 1985), would have shaped the responses to George and his parents, based on highly critical and judgemental views on individual causes and consequences of poverty.

With the introduction of the Children (Scotland) Act 1995, George would have come to the attention of the Reporter and referred to the Children's Hearing as in need of compulsory measures of care, both as a young child and later as a young person who had offended. It is not known if either of George's parents would have been able to attend the Hearings and how much of a say he would have had in the major decisions affecting his life.

The Mid-1990s to the Present Day

A great array of factors influenced and shaped the Children (Scotland) Act 1995, implemented from April 1996. A major theme was an attempt to clarify where justification for state intervention in family life exists and where it does not. The Act directs that children are not to be regarded as the property of their parents, rather that parents' rights are dependent on their ability to discharge their responsibilities to their children. The main themes of the Act are that children's welfare is paramount; there should be a **'no order' principle**, which means that no unnecessary orders should be made and that the child's view should be taken into account regarding all major life decisions affecting the child. Tidsall's (2003) criticisms of the Children Act 1995 include a concern that there would be a greater emphasis on the legal aspects of child protection at the expense of family support services, early intervention and preventative work. Definitions of 'children in need' were being applied differentially across Scotland and were interpreted and influenced according to the availability of resources.

In relation to issues of diversity, the 1995 Act also requires local authorities to have "regard to the child's religious persuasion, racial origin and cultural and linguistic background." This builds upon similar requirements of the (England and Wales) Children Act 1989. This was an important first legal recognition of the diversity of Scotland's children. A publication (The Scottish Office, 1998), *Valuing Diversity. Having Regard to the Racial, Religious, Cultural and Linguistic Needs of Scotland's Children*, was commissioned to consider this requirement, recognising that social work services historically reflect the white majority and the need to challenge this. The determination was expressed to make use of the legislation to ensure fair treatment of every child and a commitment to challenge racism wherever it exists. Tidsall (2001) further comments on issues of disability, race and gender in relation to the Children (Scotland) Act 1995. She argues that the greater potential in the legislation to assess and identify children with disabilities as 'children in need' is frustrated by insufficient resources. There is some sensitivity to race and ethnicity in the Act, but a virtual silence on issues of gender. The other area of discrimination highlighted is that of age discrimination. Tidsall is critical of an approach to children's rights that fails to address what she refers to as a potential assault on children legitimised as **'reasonable chastisement'**, arguing that a physical assault should be illegal, whatever the size or age of the person (Tidsall, 2001: 73).

The Impact of New Labour and Devolution on Children and Young People

The election of New Labour in 1997 heralded a major commitment to welfare reform, which has certainly been significant in terms of the volume of social policy for children and young people. Stewart (2004), however , comments that those aspects of social policy that relate directly to child poverty, such as social security, are still under the control of the Westminster Parliament, as referred to in earlier sections of this book. He cites the overwhelming impact of child poverty on Scottish children, but that this area is largely outside the remit of the Scottish Executive.

There has been a wealth of consultations, commitments and policies in relation to children and young people by the Scottish Executive, with a clear emphasis on health and welfare. Hendrick (quoted in Stewart, 2004) acknowledges this commitment to children and young people, though detects the Scottish Executive's reference to children as having greater emphasis on children as **'human capital'**, as 'investments in the future', rather than a focus on the child's current experience. Stewart (2004) also laments what he sees as a move away from a welfare approach to juvenile justice to a more punitive ethos with the introduction of **Anti Social Behaviour Orders (ASBOs)** for children under 16.

A review of the situation of children in Scotland, *For Scotland's Children* (Scottish Executive, 2001a), acknowledged that Scotland had one of the highest rates of child poverty in the developed world and that child welfare services were struggling to cope with demand. One recommendation was that there should be a statement of impact on children and young people across all policy areas and a Cabinet Sub-Committee be set up to monitor all new legislation.

Pause for thought
- What were the major Scottish Executive policy initiatives in relation to children and young people since 1999?

In the area of care and protection, there has been a raft of measures introduced. The Scottish Institute for Residential Child Care was introduced in 2001 to raise standards for children and young people in residential care, following the Kent Report, 1997. The Regulation of Care Act 2001 brought about the establishment of **National Care Standards**, standards for children and young people in residential care, outlining what each child should be able to expect from the beginning of their stay in residential care, to after care support. These are based on principles of dignity, privacy, choice, safety, realisation of potential and promotion of equality and diversity. A breach of these conditions could ultimately lead to the cancellation of the registration of the residential home. A colleague working in residential care identifies the principle of privacy as problematic for children and young people looked after by the state, that their lives are constantly lived 'under a microscope'.

The policy document, *The Same as You* (Scottish Executive, 2001b) was intended as a far-reaching review of services for people with learning disabilities. Each young person with a learning disability for example, would have a plan for their future. There have clearly been resources issues regarding the implementation of aspects of the review and there are particular challenges at the point at which a child with a learning disability interfaces with Adult Disability Services.

The Scottish Executive announced a three year child protection reform programme following the death of a three year old child, Kennedy MacFarlane, at the hands of her step father in Dumfries in May 2000. In 2002, The Child Protection and Audit Review reported, placing onus on local authorities to develop positive childhood initiatives based on a children's rights approach. The Framework for Standards in Child Protection programme was launched to deliver national standards in order to clarify what was expected from professionals responsible for the protection of children, rigorous inspection and a **Children's Charter**. The international charity, Save the Children, was involved in drawing up the charter, which was based on consultation with children and young people. The main conclusion of the review, *It's* *everybody's job to make sure I'm alright* (Scottish Executive, 2002), focused on the following:

- Effective identification of high risk situations.

- Methods of working, such as family group conferencing.

- Secondary prevention and community intervention programmes.

- Counselling.

- Proper consultation with and listening to children and young people.

- Effective inter-agency partnership work with parents and other family members.

The report recommends: a greater need to take account of disability; identifying insufficient training in child protection for children with disabilities; and variable practice across Scotland. There was an acknowledgement of the wider context of child protection, the shortage of skilled workers and the need to develop longer term social and economic interventions. A specific recommendation was the need for cultural change in relation to the vexed issue of 'reasonable chastisement' as a smokescreen for physical assault of children.

The introduction of **Children's Rights Officers** was a recommendation of the Kent Report, 1997, though there has been variable cover across the country. In 2003, legislation was enacted to establish a much welcomed **Children's Rights Commissioner** as a champion for children and young people, with particular reference to the UN Convention on the Rights of the Child. The tragic death of an 11 month old child, Caleb Ness (O'Brien, 2003), raised again issues of the balance between parents' rights to care for their child and the protection of the child. A further high profile case of abuse of people with learning disabilities in the Borders contributed to the call for a fundamental review of social work. *Changing Lives, Report of the 21st Century Social Work Review*, published early in 2006, makes strong recommendations on the role of social work, leadership and management in social work, capacity issues and a stronger culture of quality assurance and performance improvement in line with wider welfare reform.

A further report on an inspection into the protection of children in the Western Isles (Scottish Executive, 2005a), *An Inspection into the care and protection of children in Eilean Siar*, reinforces these issues and highlights how a range of professionals involved for over 10 years failed to protect three young girls who were emotionally, physically and sexually abused. Significant recommendations were made regarding fostering regulations, the need for independent advocacy and a multi-agency national resource to assist with complex child protection cases. The recent publication, *Getting It Right for Every Child* (Scottish Executive, 2005b), proposes a unified approach to children's services, with integrated assessment, a planning and recording framework and improvements to the Children's Hearing system. This is a challenging agenda in terms of implementation costs, multi-disciplinary training and support. Dedicated resources will be required to ensure that the recommendations regarding Children's Hearings can be fully implemented and issues of recruitment and retention of trained social workers addressed. Legislation is expected in 2006.

Developments in Juvenile Justice

In relation to juvenile justice in Scotland, the introduction of the Anti Social Behaviour (Scotland) Act 2004 seems to undermine the welfare approach of the Children's Hearing system, albeit there is a requirement for the Sheriff to consult a hearing before an ASBO can be attached to a child under 16. The NCH report (2004), *Where's Kilb randon now?* considered approaches to young people who offend in post devolution Scotland. The authors of the report argue against an over-reactive punitive approach to juvenile justice, citing negative experience south of the border, that "social justice and inclusion should not be replaced by social control and condemnation". The authors considered that a more punitive approach, such as court based action to combat anti-social behaviour is likely to increase re-offending and promote a greater identification with a criminal lifestyle. An effective argument is made in the report for the retention, adequate resourcing and improvements to the Children's Hearing system, further attention to the crisis in social work recruitment and retention and the report noted that:

> "The children most in need of good public services are the least likely to get them and the most likely to suffer poor health, poor education, bad housing and social circumstances" (NCH Scotland, 2004: 26).

Pause for thought
- How successful has the Scottish Executive been in improving the welfare of children and young people and addressing material/social class disadvantage following devolution in 1999?

There is no doubt that the Scottish Executive has made a commitment to improving the lives of Scotland's children and young people since the 'reconvening' of the devolved Scottish Parliament in 1999. It has not been possible to detail every relevant piece of policy and legislation during this period, but hopefully a flavour has been given and examples identified of factors and forces leading to specific cases of state intervention. A snapshot of the statistical picture of children and young people looked after by local authorities in March 2005 reveals a picture of continuing concern. Scottish Executive statistics of Children's Social Work Services show that there are over 12,000 children 'looked after' by local authorities in Scotland. Twenty nine per cent of these are in foster care and a further 13 per cent in residential care. There are 93 children and young people held across the five secure units in Scotland. Overall this is a four per cent increase in children and young people looked after by local authorities. In relation to child protection, whilst there is a *decrease* in the number of child protection case conferences, there is a substantial *increase* in the number of child protection referrals. Significantly, the increase in the number of children registered as 'in need' is based on the grounds of neglect.

There was also a slight increase in the numbers of black and minority ethnic children and young people who were looked after by the state during this period. A continuing concern is that there are insufficient numbers of qualified black and minority ethnic social workers to ensure appropriate preventative early intervention and access to social work services relevant to the needs of children and young people from a diverse range of cultural backgrounds. The child protection review, *'It's everyone's job to make sure I'm alright'* (Scottish Executive, 2002), highlighted that the needs of black and minority ethnic children and young people are less likely to be met because of either *under* or *over* intervention or *over* or *under* punitive approaches, based on racist stereotypes or assumptions.

Pause for thought
- What possible explanations may account for the increase in children and young people looked after by the state?

There is considerable concern over the numbers of children affected by parental drug abuse. One estimate in 2004 was that approximately 41,000 to 59,000 children in Scotland were affected by parental drug use. This represents four to six per cent of children under the age of 16 in Scotland. *Hidden Harm* (Scottish Executive, 2004) reflects the Scottish Executive's response to the Inquiry by the Advisory Council on the Misuse of Drugs. Although there is a growing recognition of this need, it is not yet matched with adequate community based resources. A key challenge is the continuing difficulty in the recruitment and retention of specialised child care social workers. Considerable efforts have been made by the Scottish Executive to attract and train increasing numbers of social workers, however the situation in 2005, according to Scottish Executive figures (July to October 2005) is that of the 536 vacancies, more than 50 per cent are in children's services. This is a cause for continuing concern, as the shortage of qualified and experienced social workers is cited as a contributing factor in child protection inquiries and difficulties identified in the implementation of recommendations of some Children's Hearings. Some services, such as **family group conferencing**, are still subject to short term funding and are not fully accessible across Scotland. One Children's Rights officer laments that only a small proportion of children and young people have any substantial contact with Children's Rights Officers.

The Continuing Theme of Poverty

A major recurring theme throughout the history of social policy is the overarching issue of the impact of child poverty and the increased likelihood that children and young people from poor backgrounds will come to the attention of the state social work departments. The report, commissioned by the Joseph Rowntree Foundation, *Monitoring Poverty and Social Exclusion in Scotland 2004* (Palmer, Carr and Kenway, 2004), noted that the percentage of children in low-income households was falling, but that there were actually mixed trends for children over the last five years. Stewart (2004) notes that both Westminster and Scottish governments are committed to abolishing poverty within 20 years and by 25 per cent in 2004. The Child Poverty Action Group (cpag.org.uk), a voluntary organisation that campaigns against child poverty, estimated in 2004 that about a third of Scotland's children live in poverty – about 300,000 children. Whilst they welcome the government's commitment to ending child poverty, concern remains over the unacceptably large number of children living in poverty and over the pace of change. They raise questions about New Labour's **'welfare to work'** approach and its relevance to Scotland, where 40 per cent of the poor are already in work (the **'working poor'**) and there is also a higher percentage of people in Scotland (compared to the rest of the UK) who are economically inactive due to sickness and disability (see Scott, **Chapter 5** and Helms, **Chapter 6**).

Progress has tended to be made among the groups of children who fall just below the poverty threshold and are therefore arguably the group easiest to pull out of poverty. The continuing challenge will be to address those groups where poverty is more entrenched (see Scott, **Chapter 5**). Child poverty matters because children who are poor have a greater chance of low birth weight, a greater chance of dying in infancy and overall face disadvantage in health and education. There have been some considered approaches to the welfare of children and young people in Scotland since devolution, but serious limitations exist on their effectiveness if the realities of the impact of child poverty are not fully addressed.

Box 9.5 Case Study: George's story – what has been the impact of the Children (Scotland) Act 1995 and the raft of Scottish Executive policies since devolution on children and young people like George?

George is cynical about whether his best interests have been met and whether the stream of social workers he has experienced in 15 years have actually had the power to help him in dealing with his response to situations beyond his control. The words of Tidsall seem particularly relevant here; in relation to young people it is social exclusion based on "socio-economic disadvantage that continues to have a stronger overall influence on differential life expectation, than any other factor" (Tidsall, 2001: 73).

In relation to the youth justice agenda, young people in similar situations to George are subject to Anti-Social Behaviour Orders. The welfare ethos of the Children's Hearing in Scotland is seriously threatened by an approach that undermines the principles that children and young people should receive the care and control they need, whichever route brought them to the Hearing, and that the child's welfare must be the central consideration.

Conclusion: Continuities and Changes

In this chapter we have explored Scottish society's response to the care and protection of children and young people from the Poor Laws of the 1800s through to the period following devolution from 1999 to 2006. Changes have reflected dominant political, economic, religious, social, medical, and wider European factors and influences.

Changing Lives, Report of the 21st Century Social Work Review (Scottish Executive, 2006) makes welcome recommendations about early intervention, prevention and support to children and families. Adequate funding for inter disciplinary training and further development of integrated social services is essential. The persistent difficulties of recruitment and retention of skilled staff in children's social work services must be further addressed, to enable workers to fully attend to the needs of children and young people in the most difficult circumstances. Successful short term funded projects, such as mentoring schemes and family group conferencing need to be available on a secure mainstream funding basis.

The pendulum swings between the emphasis on *care* and *control*. Over the last 500 years there has been a swing from regarding children as little adults requiring no special treatment, to the view that children's welfare is paramount – including the advocacy of children's rights, through to the potential demonisation of young people resulting from the introduction of Anti Social Behaviour Orders (ASBOs). Children and young people's voices are still very small and often not heard. There is great variation in practice, some quite tokenistic as George has experienced, and other pockets of good practice by, for example, organisations such as Who Cares.

A continuing theme is the impact of social division on the life chances of Scotland's children and young people stemming from the grinding impact of poverty and the broader pattern of inequality, disadvantage and exclusion. A continuing tendency is to hold individuals and families wholly responsibility for difficult circumstances in which they sometimes find themselves, rather than addressing the structural inequalities that underlie the chronic problems faced by many of Scotland's children. The continuing experiences of stigma and exclusion are reminiscent of notions of the deserving and undeserving poor. George and his parents experienced the insidious stigma and discrimination that still exists in social attitudes towards drug users, people who offend and their families. The life chances and quality of life of children and young people who are accommodated by the local authority continue to be significantly worse than their compatriots, particularly in the areas of health and education.

It is not surprising, then, that the words of Asquith and Stafford (1995) continue to resonate more than a decade later:

> "In short, the development of policies and practices that impact on families and children which ignore basic social inequalities in the distribution of wealth and life chances may offer little by the way of attempts to ameliorate the conditions in which many families find themselves" (Asquith and Stafford, 1995: 4).

Further Reading

Crimmens, P. and Milligan, I. (2005) *Facing Forward. Residential Care in the 21ˢᵗ Century*, Lyme Regis, Russell House Publishing

Scottish Executive (2006) *Where do we Go from Here?* Edinburgh, Stationary Office, www.scotland.gov.uk

Young Minds (2004) *Devolution. So far so Good?* London, Young Minds, www.youngminds.org.uk

Useful Websites

www.aberlour.org.uk: The Aberlour Orphanage
www.barnardos.org.uk: Barnardos
www.cpag.org.uk: Child Poverty Action Group
www.children1st.org.uk: Children First
www.fsu.org.uk: Family Service Units (now under the Family Welfare Association)
www.nch.org.uk: National Children's Home
www.savethechildren.org.uk: Save the Children
www.scotland.gov.uk: Scottish Executive

Bibliography

Asquith, S. (ed.) (1993) *Protecting Children. Cleveland to Orkney: More Lessons to Learn*, Children in Scotland, Edinburgh, SCAFA/NCB

Asquith, S. and Stafford, A. (1995) *Families and the Future*, Edinburgh, HMSO

Atkinson, D. and Gearing, B. (1997) *The Reflective Social Worker*, Milton Keynes, The Open University

Baillie, D., Cameron, C., Cull, L.A., Roche, J. and West, J. (2003) *Social Work and the Law in Scotland*, Houndsmills, Palgrave MacMillan

Chakrabarti, M. (2001) *Social Welfare, Scottish Perspective*, Aldershot, Ashgate Publishing Limited

Cicourel, A.V. (1976) *The Social Organisation of Justice*, London, Heinemann

Cleland, A. and Sutherland, E.E. (2001), *Children's Rights in Scotland*, Edinburgh, W. Green/Sweet & Maxwell

Clyde Report (1992) *Report into the Inquiry into the Removal of Children from Orkney in February 1991*, Edinburgh, HMSO

Crimmens, P. and Milligan, I. (2005) *Facing Forward. Residential Care in the 21ˢᵗ Century*, Lyme Regis, Russell House Publishing

English, J. (1992) *Social Services in Scotland*, Edinburgh, Scottish Academic Press

Fife Inquiry (1992) *The Report of the Inquiry into Child care Policies in Fife* (The Kilbrandon Report), Edinburgh, HMSO

Higginbottom, P. (1995) *The Workhouse in Scotland*, http//users.ox.ac.uk/~peter/workhouse/Scotland.shtm!

Hill, M. and Tidsall, K. (1997) *Children and Society*, London, Addison Wesley Longman Ltd

Kendrick, A. and Hartnoll, M. (1995) 'Introduction: Children and families', in Ridley, J. and Anderson, B. (eds.) (1995) *Directory of Social Work Research in Scotland 1995*, Dundee, SSRG Scottish Branch/Association of Directors of Social Work

Marshall, K. 'The History and Philosophy of Children's Rights in Scotland', in Cleland, A. and Sutherland, E.E. (eds.) (2001) *Children's Rights in Scotland*, Edinburgh, W. Green/Sweet & Maxwell

NCH Scotland (2004) *Where is Kilbrandon now? Report and Recommendations from the Inquiry*, Glasgow, NCH, ww.nch.org.uk/kilbrandonnow

Newell, P. (1991) *The UN Convention and Children's Rights in the UK*, London, National Children's Bureau

O'Brien, S. (2003) *Report of the Caleb Ness Inquiry*, Edinburgh, Edinburgh and the Lothian's Child Protection Committee

Palmer, G., Carr, J. and Kenway, P. (2004) *Monitoring Poverty and Social Exclusion in Scotland 2004*, York, Joseph Rowntree Foundation

Parton, N. (1985) *The Politics of Child Abuse*, Houndsmills, MacMillan Education

Parton, N. (1991) *Governing the Family. Child Care, Child protection and the State*, Houndsmills, MacMillan Education

Ridley, J. and Anderson, B. (eds.) *Directory of Social Work Research in Scotland 1995*, Dundee, SSRG Scottish Branch/Association of Directors of Social Work

Scottish Executive (2001a) *For Scotland's Children*, Edinburgh, Stationary Office

Scottish Executive (2001b) *The Same as You*, Edinburgh, Stationary Office

Scottish Executive (2002) *'It's everyone's job to make sure I'm alright' – Child Protection Audit and Review*, Edinburgh, Stationary Office

Scottish Executive (2004) *Hidden Harm. Scottish Response to the Report of the Inquiry by the Advisory Council on the Misuse of Drugs*, Edinburgh, Stationary Office

Scottish Executive (2005a) *An Inspection into the care and protection of children in Eilean Siar*, Edinburgh, Stationary Office

Scottish Executive (2005b) *Getting It Right for Every Child, Proposals for Action*, Edinburgh, Stationary Office

Scottish Executive (2006) *Changing Lives, Report of the 21st Century Social Work Review*, Edinburgh, Stationary Office

Scottish Executive (2006) *Where Do we Go from Here?* Edinburgh, Stationary Office, www.scotland.gov.uk

Skinner Report (1992) *Another Kind of Home: a Review of Residential Child Care*,

Edinburgh, HMSO

Stewart, J. (2004) *Taking Stock, Scottish Social Welfare after Devolution*, Bristol, Polity Press

Scottish Office (1998) *Valuing Diversity. Having Regard to the Racial, Religious, Cultural and Linguistic Needs of Scotland's Children*, Edinburgh, HMSO

Tidsall, E.K.M. (2001) 'Equal Opportunities? Race, Gender, Disability and Children', in Cleland, A. and Sutherland, E.E. (eds.) (2001) *Children's Rights in Scotland*, Edinburgh, W. Green/Sweet & Maxwell

Tidsall, E.K.M. (2003) 'Critical Perspectives on Welfare: The Example of Child Care Services', in Baillie, D., Cameron, C., Cull, L.A., Roche, J. and West, J. (eds.) (2003) *Social Work and the Law in Scotland*, Houndsmills, Palgrave Macmillan

Timmins, N. (1996) *The Five Giants. A Biography of the Welfare State*, London, Fontana Press

Young Minds (2004) *Devolution. So far so Good?* London, Young Minds, www.youngminds.org.uk

Chapter 9

Safe in their Hands? Understanding Health and Health Policy in the Devolved Scotland

Patricia McCafferty

Introduction

It seems that few topics have the ability to promote discussion and debate like 'health'. Similarly, the issue of 'health' evokes anxiety and even indignation. UK government policy on health has formed one of the defining features of hotly contested political debates and this has become increasingly so in recent decades. This is clearest when we look at the National Health Service (NHS), in particular, as it seems often to be used as something of a 'political football' even outside election times. So, we have become quite used to key politicians trying to convince us that, in the words of former Prime Minister, Margaret Thatcher, 'health' is 'safe in their hands' (BBC News Online, 2006). Indeed, there is a sense in which we are encouraged to think of 'success' or otherwise in managing the nation's 'health' and the health service as one of the most important indicators of a government's success overall. Therefore, how politicians have approached 'health' is key to our understanding of the issues around it and a discussion of this is central to the aim of this chapter.

What is Health?

Certain difficulties arise as we try to discuss, analyse and understand issues of 'health' and health policy. You are likely to have noticed the 'inverted commas' used around the word 'health' thus far. This is, in part, to introduce you to the notion that ideas of 'health' and what is 'healthy' are often contested. The meanings of such terms are never fixed in time nor universally agreed. A useful comparison here would be of the different views of what might constitute a 'healthy' bank balance or, more seriously perhaps, how we might assess the 'health' of the UK in relation to other countries or the varying health of regions within the UK.

Pause for thought

As you are probably aware, data on life expectancy is a key element of our understanding of health and is important in relation to the formulation of health policy. Indeed, much health policy in the UK and beyond is directed at improving life expectancy statistics. With this in mind, have a go at the following task.

- What is the current male life expectancy in:

  1. Iraq?
  2. 'The Calton' housing estate in Glasgow?
  3. The Gaza Strip?

(Answers can be found at the end of this chapter.)

The likelihood is that you found the answers here quite surprising to say the least. The point of this is to help to firm up your understanding of the context within which our discussion takes place, to alert you to the fact that, where this issue is concerned, our assumptions are often 'off the mark' and, of course, to hint at some of those 'local' distinctions that are considered in more detail below. Let us assume then that 'health' is a 'loaded' term that might need some unpacking! To assist in this process some important terms that we need to understand at the outset will be outlined.

Political developments in *two* key periods are the key to our understanding of current debates on health and health policy:

- The *first* of these concerns the decade or so following the so-called breakdown of the arrangements for health that were most closely associated with the *social democratic* **welfare state** (see Law, **Chapter 3** and Sweeney, **Chapter 2**). Important here is the flagship policy of 'care in the community' and the development of an 'internal market' within the NHS that represented a decisive break from the policies and ethos of social democracy. This shows how fluid notions of 'care' and 'control' can be. Also, the resultant impact of Conservative rule presents us all too readily with our first opportunity to explore social divisions and inequalities in health.

- The *second* key period followed the election of the 'New Labour' government in May 1997, which seemed to represent a decisive break with the Conservative/**New Right** rule of the previous 18 years. The current

Prime Minister, Tony Blair, has demanded that "we need a system designed not for yesterday, but today" (Blair, 1998, cited in Ferguson *et al*, 2002: 164). From our discussion of this period we can explore the key theme of 'continuity and change'. Key questions we need to ask here are 'what is new?' and 'what has changed?' in what have emerged as the apparent solutions to what is persistently portrayed as 'health in crisis'? In doing so, we will look at shifts in funding arrangements that strike at the very heart of another key question raised about modern healthcare, 'who pays?'

Paradoxically, it is often the case that those who experience the 'ill-effects' of health inequality are those in need of greater and more effective access to health services. This is clearly an important feature worthy of some attention and from our point of view a useful issue in terms of our exploration of 'inclusion and exclusion'. We can do this through considering questions like 'do the sick (always) get what they deserve?' Thus, we will look at patterns of health inequality and the social geography of health throughout that form a central feature of the experience of many Scottish people. As such, we will be using and developing our 'Calton' example as a critical illustration of such key features.

Two particular aspects of the Scottish context are important to our analysis:

- First, since devolution in July 1999, Scotland's health and health policy have been the responsibility of the Scottish Parliament in Edinburgh. This means that decisions are devolved to Members of the Scottish Parliament (MSPs) at Holyrood rather than MPs at Westminster, allowing for, in theory at least, the development of Scottish-specific health policy.

- Second, is what has been officially dubbed 'the Scottish Effect' (Scottish Executive, 2004). This, in turn, will act as a springboard for further discussion of our key theme of 'social division and differentiation'.

Therefore, the chapter generally presents us with an important opportunity to further unpack and engage effectively with our book-wide themes. Central to this is the need to be aware of the complex nature of what we understand as health and health related issues.

Understanding Health

The meanings of the concepts and terminology in the study of health and health policy are both **socially constructed** and contested. Just as the term 'healthy' is a loaded term, so is the term 'unhealthy'. This latter term carries with it notions of people being 'deserving' and 'undeserving' of healthcare. Let us turn our attention once again to comparisons of life expectancy between Iraq, the Gaza Strip and 'The Calton', Glasgow (see 'Pause for thought', below).

Pause for thought

Think again about those statistics that you were presented with comparing Calton in Glasgow, Iraq and the Gaza Strip.

- Why do you think life expectancy is at these levels?
- How might differences be accounted for?

Chances are your answers might be linked to specific behaviours. Here are some more statistics that might help you reach some preliminary conclusions:

- 52 per cent of Calton residents smoke compared with 25 per cent of Scotland's average population.
- Alcohol abuse admissions to hospital are way above the national average.

(Source: NHS Health Scotland, cited in *The Guardian*, 21st January 2006.)

This leads onto another key question about health that is worth raising here:

- Should people who smoke or drink have the same access to health care as people who do not have such 'risky' habits?

It would appear then that such startling figures for life expectancy are linked to some less than startling features of contemporary living in Scotland. Put simply, it seems as if we are dealing with problems that are readily associated with an apparent fondness for the legendary battered Mars Bar and rolls on sausage, washed down with Irn Bru or an infamous tonic wine, all consumed – of course – between puffs! Yet health is much more complex than this. Therefore, we should remain alert to the idea that the delivery of health services occurs in a context framed by dominant notions of who might deserve (or not) access to treatment. This is in itself further complicated by the fact that elements of **exclusion** and **marginalisation** are at play here too. For example, the spotlight on specific behaviours more often than not is fixed on the poor and deprived. Hence, drinking in particular communities is often constructed as more problematic than in others.

Next, it should be noted that ideas of 'risk' and what is 'risky' are not without their complications either. These are socially and culturally defined by and in the interests of more powerful social groups. Extreme examples of this are not that hard to find. Dangerous hobbies like skydiving or rock climbing are risky yet these are rarely, if ever, the focus of negative attention. Everyday activities for many, such as driving a car, can be risky too. Whilst public attention has been alerted to the environmental damage caused by car use, the activity itself is rarely criticised as risky in the sense that car drivers or accident victims are deemed to be *undeserving* of health care. Many people who engage in other so-called risky behaviours do not own or drive cars. In the Glasgow city area, for example, which covers 'the Calton', 56 per cent of households *did not* have a car in 2001 (Office of National Statistics, 2004). This does not seem to be the subject of public outcry nor targeted government initiatives so far. As a result, it is possible to argue that the health of already marginalised groups can be negatively affected by the actions of relatively advantaged groups. It seems that such 'unhealthy'/'risky'/'damaging' behaviour is not always a matter of concern.

Somewhat less controversial is the term **'life expectancy'**, introduced above. This is a measure of how long on average a person is expected to live at the time of their birth. There are *two* things worth noting in respect of this term:

1. It is used as a key indicator of the state of the nation's health.

2. There are clear differences in life expectancy both between *places* (as our Iraq versus Glasgow versus Gaza Strip example demonstrates) and, crucially, between the *sexes*, women in general outlive men often by quite a considerable number of years (Office of National Statistics, 2002).

Other key terms that are important to understand are **mortality** and **morbidity**. The former is relatively straightforward and means the death rates within a population. In this respect, infant mortality is often taken as a key marker (Smith and Goldblatt, 2004: 51). The latter is a little more complex as it means the incidence and prevalence of illness and disease within a population at a particular time (Wikipedia, 2006). Together these represent the key *measurement* of the health and well-being of different populations and groups at a given time. Indicators such as these are generally used by all commentators on health and health policy. However, it is important to understand different *models* of health and illness and these are often linked to different sociological and political perspectives.

Models of Health and Illness

The **'medical'** or **' biological' model** views the human body as something of a machine (Smith and Goldblatt, 2004). In this model there is a focus on illness, on symptom observation and scientific 'fixing' through the administering of pharmaceutical medicines. Basically, 'bad' behaviour leads to 'bad' health and the 'machine' breaks down. However, as you will see below, this can be problematic and offers no real explanation for the clustering of 'broken' people, particularly in areas of high material and economic deprivation. Clearly, the development of the inequalities that helped to characterise our experience of health in the last two decades alone suggests that a comprehensive understanding cannot be gained simply by focusing on faulty, poorly functioning 'machinery'. So, our second model – the **'social' model** – focuses on issues of environment and the susceptibility of particular groups to poor health based on other (i.e. non body-related) factors. It is this particular perspective that will help to frame what follows in the rest of this chapter.

'Safe in our Hands'? Health and Health Policy under the Conservatives

As highlighted at the outset of this chapter, health is an extremely sensitive issue in political terms. This is, of course, linked to the relatively high regard which the general public seem to have for institutions like the NHS and, especially, the ideals which underpinned its creation – despite the problems that beset the modern service. However, it is also connected to the many tensions brought about by apparently competing social and economic demands. Indeed, the NHS itself had a difficult 'birth' as a result of the initial hostility from the British Medical Association (BMA) to its creation. The cost of healthcare in the context of having to balance the nation's books has been a continual source of tension and controversy. In fact, the politician even now most closely associated with the creation of the NHS, Aneurin Bevan, resigned from the Labour government in 1951 over the introduction of prescription charges of one shilling (five pence), which was largely in response to the need to raise funds for the Korean War (1950-1953) (nhshistory.net, 2006).

However, it was in the 1970s that the issue of cost became a critical political focal point connected in part to the 1974 oil crisis. Wider economic problems in the UK, and difficulties in managing and financing the public sector generally, again brought questions about rising costs and economic efficiency of the health service to the fore. This coincided with a major political and ideological shift that threatened to undermine the very ethos and values that had brought us the NHS in the first place (see Sweeney, **Chapter 2** and Law, **Chapter 3**). Questions of financial boundaries soon became enmeshed with those of whether the public purse could, or even should, continue to strive to fund anything and everything that was medically possible.

At the same time, as the years of Labour's time in office drew to a close, another issue emerged that seemed to illustrate in sharp relief an apparent lack of success and ability in tackling continuing health problems and, crucially, the nature and contours of the features that underpinned this. Fundamentally, the "crude differences in mortality rates between various social classes," as Labour Secretary of State for Social Services, David Ennals, put it in 1977 (quoted in Townsend *et al*, 1992: 1), needed to be addressed and a Research Working Party, headed by the then President of the Royal College of Physicians, Sir Douglas Black, was set up to carry out this task. The challenge, however, "for the next ten or more years to try to narrow the gap in health standards between different social classes" (Ennals, 1977, in Townsend *et al*, 1992: 1) was one that was to be confronted by the Conservative government of Margaret Thatcher elected in May 1979.

The Black Report (1980)

Unsurprisingly perhaps, given the aims and, in particular, the values that came to characterise this administration as we progressed into the 1980s, the comprehensive yet highly controversial outcome of the Working Party's research – known as **The Black Report** (1980) – received a "frosty reception" (*The Lancet*, quoted in Townsend *et al*, 1992). Significantly, the report was clear that the relationship between class and ill-health was becoming more pronounced and yet, crucially, the underlying causes of health problems were related to issues out with the remit of the NHS. Additionally, the report noted that there was lower uptake of services among those marginalised groups most in need of help, further exasperating the social gulf that increasingly characterised experiences of the health services. Clearly, this is early confirmation that three decades on the NHS had seemingly failed to address problems of exclusion and disadvantage that it was in part set up to address.

The Black Report (1980) made 37 recommendations that were neither made widely known nor endorsed by the Thatcher government. These recommendations were framed by an underlying concern to address the health of the 'whole person'. Crucially, the Working Party concluded that the answer to health inequalities lay in "radically improving the material conditions of life of poorer groups" (quoted in Townsend *et al*, 1992: 2). This, of course, was unlikely to sit well with the newly elected government resolute in its endeavour to cut public spending and promote individual responsibility. Furthermore, its Secretary of State for Social Services, Patrick Jenkin, fundamentally rejected the Black Report's findings on the characteristically 'New Right' grounds of cost that "could be upwards of £2 billion a year...quite unrealistic in present or any foreseeable economic circumstances" (Jenkin, quoted in Townsend *et al*, 1992: 2).

Pause for thought

The Black Report helps to reiterate how ill-health is rarely a simple matter of 'broken' bodies.

Returning to our 'case study' of the Calton, note down any factors (other than those 'behavioural' ones noted already) that you think might result in low levels of male life expectancy.

Comparing Life Expectancy: Glasgow and Edinburgh

Poor housing, overcrowding and poverty might be some of the factors that you have come up with in the previous 'Pause for thought'. In the Calton, 44 per cent of people are on incapacity benefit, 37 per cent live in a workless household and 30 per cent of homes are occupied by a lone parent (*The Guardian*, 21 January 2006). This helps to highlight that the clustering of ill-health and early death is about more than differences of 'make up'. The physical concentration of social problems produces a concentration of health problems. Also, differences occur *within* countries as well as *between* them. So, in Scotland for example, there are stark differences between wealthy areas like Edinburgh city and Glasgow city, where male life expectancy in 2001 was 74 and 68, respectively (NHS/ISD Scotland, 2004). This latter statistic illustrates a further key point – differences can also be detected between neighbouring *communities*. The average Glasgow city figure is 14 years higher than the Calton area contained within its boundaries. Despite the fact that a few streets away from an area like the Calton there are shops selling designer labels like Versace (*The Guardian*, 21 January 2006), the Glasgow of the 21st Century can still 'boast' a figure of 40 per cent of its population living in poverty (*The Herald*, 1 July 2002).

Such complexity confirms again the need to proceed with caution when we make assumptions about national and even regional behaviour and its effects. This is clearly demonstrated in the important work carried out by Peter Townsend and his colleagues in the 1980s that sought to update evidence on the causes of health inequalities. *The Health Divide*, published in 1987 as a report for the Health Education Council, concluded that different lifestyles did *not* explain "most of the differences in health" (Whitehead, 1988: 296). Importantly, this report, alongside subsequent developments and contemporary evidence, demonstrates that nearly three decades since the original Working Party was commissioned, the system is still blighted by the persistent and pervasive structural inequalities that The Black Report comprehensively outlined.

Having focused so far on what was *not* implemented in policy terms by the Conservatives, let us now turn to flagship health policies that *were* put in place and briefly consider their impact. Surprisingly, in the light of the sort of evidence presented above, as well as mounting concerns regarding hospital waiting lists and staff morale (Corby and White, 1999), the 'defining moment' of the Conservative approach to health did not come until a decade and two further general elections had passed.

The NHS and Community Care Act 1990

The NHS and Community Care Act 1990 was clearly developed in keeping with concerns about the financial burden that the NHS represented for the Conservatives, alongside the promotion of the key 'New Right' values of individualism, individual responsibility and competition. It is not possible here to comprehensively outline the Act and the full impact of its provisions, so we will concentrate on *two* important features that had wide reaching implications in relation to the issues that we are discussing in this chapter.

First, was the consolidation of the Conservative's 'care in the community' thrust, which had gradually shifted the care of vulnerable people, like the elderly and people suffering from mental and emotional illnesses, away from the often virtual isolation of old style asylums and into regular housing schemes (see Cavaye, **Chapter 11**). Taken at face value, this seemed a welcome shift away from formal institutionalisation. However, the hoped for fully integrated care packages that were supposed to replace it rarely, if ever, materialised. Moreover, over time such policies have served to further marginalise already disadvantaged groups like people living in poverty, women and older people. Currently, for example, 12 per cent (600,000) of the population in Scotland are unpaid or informal carers, 62 per cent of them women, 26 per cent are retired and a further 25 per cent are economically inactive (Scottish Executive, 2002b). It would seem that in the long term, there has been a shift of the care 'burden' away from the state. Given the informal nature of this care, the *cost* of care has also shifted.

The second key element of the Act and its impact was the obligation to 'purchase' care and health services from 'outside' providers, which facilitated a growth in private sector provision of health and social services (Pollock, 2004/5). In terms of community care this actually meant that the large scale closure of hospitals and other institutions forced local authorities – to whom purchasing and funding of care was transferred – to 'buy in' services from the private sector. Where this really impacted, though, was in the NHS with the development of an 'internal' market of purchasing provision within newly created NHS Trusts. This replaced bulk-buying health authorities and GP fund-holders in charge of budgets to buy in diagnostic, palliative and acute health care. This **'marketisation'** of healthcare and its attendant **'managerialism'**, helped to ensure the uneven distribution of funding and a shift in resource allocation towards the private sector. As central to the Conservative's view of health service spending as proscriptive (anti-choice), wasteful and inefficient (Ferguson, 2005), ultimately this meant cuts in services overall, including a loss of hospital beds (Pollock, 2004/5). This brought about problems with NHS waiting lists, further exacerbating health inequalities and, as the 1990s wore on, questions were raised as to whether the NHS really was 'safe in their hands'.

New Labour – New Health Service?

At face value, at least, it was the provisions contained within the NHS and Community Care Act 1990 and the effects of it outlined above, that the New Labour government, elected in 1997, apparently sought to confront in its approach to health. The building of a 'new modern, dependable NHS' (Department of Health, 1997) was promised, by a government confident "that one of the main reasons people elected a new government on May 1st was their concern that the NHS was failing them and their families" (Blair, 1997b). Of course, from this historical vantage point it is possible for us make some tentative judgements about whether the distinction between the approaches of New Labour and the Conservatives is sharp.

First on the list of promises from New Labour were 'new hospitals' and "high quality care based on need, not ability to pay" (Blair, 1997b). Also, in language consistent with the terms and values of the 'Third Way' (see Sweeney, **Chapter 2**), New Labour's approach "combine[s] efficiency and quality with a belief in fairness and partnership [...] [related to] a changing world" and was based on the clear understanding that "the NHS need[s] to modernise in order to meet the demands of today's public" (Blair, 1997b). Effective funding would be tied to the responsibility to change within the service.

Next was the planned replacement of the internal market with "integrated care," saving "£1 billion" of red tape and bureaucratic costs (Blair, 1997b) and a commitment to put that money into frontline patient care. In addition, less than a year after the election of the first Labour government in more than eighteen years, the then Health Secretary, Frank Dobson, pronounced the Conservative's flagship 'care in the community' policy as an abject failure, announcing that it would be scrapped in favour of a return to '24-hour back-up' for both vulnerable and, from the government's viewpoint, 'dangerous' people (BBC News Online, 1998). Although there would be no return to costly institutional care in asylums, Dobson admitted that the proposed (partial) return to residential care would be expensive and was not going to be "so low that you could do it with a whip round" (Dobson, quoted in BBC News Online, 1998). The issue of funding was raised by mental health charities, clear that plans would need a "huge injection of resources" (SANE, cited in BBC News Online, 1998).

Clearly, it is not possible for us to explore in detail all of New Labour's health policies and how they affect us. However, taking a closer look at finance and funding strikes at the heart of the tensions that have beset the NHS since its inception. As you will see, it also helps to demonstrate a key area of some continuity with the previous Conservative era, despite the apparent dismantling of their regime that the New Labour approach outlined above seemingly suggests. Also, we should look briefly at the underlying ideas of such policy statements and examine some judgements that have been made about New Labour's success thus far. Again, we can make useful comparisons with the Conservative approach to health that voters on 1 May 1997 (and subsequently in June 2001 and again in May 2005) arguably roundly rejected.

Funding the NHS

Pause for thought
Clearly, modern, dependable health care comes at a price and NHS funding is the subject of much debate and controversy. Both main political parties seem to have struggled with financing the NHS.

- Note down the ways that *you* think this money should be raised.
- Should there be return to a system of paying 'up front' for health services?

To begin this process, let us consider your answers to the task in 'Pause for thought', above. One of the ways that money is currently raised is through direct taxation in the shape of National Insurance contributions and income tax that is levied on the general public. It is likely that, in line with the majority of your fellow citizens (Jowel *et al*, 2000), you have suggested the possibility of increasing the levels of this type of taxation in order to fund an improved NHS. This seems to make sense in that it is based on paying for services generally 'as you earn' and hence is (in part at least) based on the principle that those who can afford most pay most. It is certainly quite distinct from the option of paying 'up front' for services, though this is sometimes what people do in order to overcome problems of waiting lists and waiting times that, overall, were noted as having "barely changed" in the years between 1997 and 2001 (*The Times*, 2001, cited in nhshistory.net).

Public Private Partnerships (PPPs)

The key to official responses from the government lie in Tony Blair's earlier evocation of the notion of partnership generally (Blair 1994; 1997a; 1998) and in relation to the NHS (Blair, 1997b). This partnership, which was central to the Labour government's whole approach, was crucially between government and the private sector and was much like that of their Conservative predecessors though with distinct features. New Labour's new **Public Private Partnerships (PPPs)** replaced the Conservative's **Private Finance Initiative (PFI)**, but retained key elements of it. First, and crucially, this was couched in what would have previously been seen as familiar Conservative ideas. PPPs would act as a central mechanism through which private sector methods would be imported into a key public service in an effort to rid the NHS of the one-size-fits-all, heavy -handed, top -down approach that had apparently held it back for many decades (Blair, 1998). Additionally, PPPs took the involvement of the private sector further – into the building, managing and running of hospitals, for example – and offered business guarantees in relation to the ability to profit from areas hitherto protected from such activity. In effect, the cost of paying back what the private sector had 'invested' in the NHS and other public services over a thirty year period meant public taxation could now "ensur[e] a guaranteed income stream for private corporations" (Pollock *et al*, 2001). These partnerships have thus proved controversial and, some would say, costly. In Scotland, for example, the new Edinburgh Royal Infirmary, fully opened in 2003, was predicted to cost the taxpayer £990 million compared with the £180 million it would have cost had it been funded through the traditional method of up-front capital from taxation (Monbiot, 2000: 74).

Comparing New Labour and the Conservatives on Health Policy

The overall outcome of the policy thrust and the funding issues outlined above is demonstrated in sharp relief in our everyday experience of health. This was summed up in the first few pages of Derek Wanless' 2002 report for The Treasury into the long term future of health: "We have fallen behind other countries in health outcomes. We have achieved less because we have spent very much less and not spent it well" (Wanless, 2002: i-ii). Clearly, there are echoes here of the lack of improved outcomes that blighted the Conservatives of the 1980s and 1990s well into New Labour's term in office.

There are two further ways in which we are able to detect continuity between the Conservative and New Labour eras. The first relates to the position of workers at the front-line of delivering improvements in the context outlined above, who seem to bear the brunt of weaknesses just as much as they did under the Conservatives in relation to pay and conditions. In relation to those PPPs that are mentioned above, for example, some research has concluded that "there are serious grounds for concern that PPPs are contributing to greater income inequality [and] a deterioration of terms and conditions particularly among relatively low paid staff [...]" (Sanchdev, 2004: 6). Hence, fro m the point of view our understanding, we have both a lack of distinction from the Conservative years and the potential for the government's 'modernisation' and 'reform' programme, especially in relation to private sector involvement, to actually further promote exclusion and marginalisation. This has gone some way to allowing even a Labour politician to conclude that:

> "We need to bring about the complete separation of the NHS from the private sector for the sake of preserving and developing the system of collectivised health care that the vast majority of the British public remain deeply committed to" (David Hinchliffe, former Labour MP and Chair of the Health Select Committee, 2001: 5).

The issue of exclusion and marginalisation can be further explored with regard to a second parallel with the Conservative approach: the scape-goating of particular groups as a 'drain' on resources. One crucial example of this in practice is in the area of Incapacity Benefit. Although this is not a health-specific policy, it is certainly related.

New Labour have always shared with the Conservatives a concern to cut down on the costs of welfare, social and health services (Ferguson *et al*, 2002) and apparently improve spending efficiency, largely through restructuring key benefits. It is certainly the case that in the second and then the third term of office there has been an impetus to impose much tougher solutions in relation to the more than two million people on incapacity (long-term sickness) benefit, in particular (*The Guardian*, 2004). The aim was to cut the £8 million per year spent on this benefit by half (Ferguson *et al*, 2002). What is important from our point of view, however, is that this is not straightforwardly an attack on the sick but may be construed as a further attack on already disadvantaged communities like the Calton where, you will recall, 44 per cent of people are in receipt of this benefit, with a Glasgow-wide figure of over 17 per cent (Ferguson *et al*, 2002). Research has demonstrated the reliance on such a benefit in former industrial areas like South Wales, the North of England and, of course, the West of Scotland (McCormick, 2000).

All of this could be taken to be evidence that there is a sense in which the New Labour government has been carrying out the 'unfinished business' of **Thatcherism** and the New Right (see Sweeney, **Chapter 2** and Law, **Chapter 3**). In respect of health, then, the overall 'balance sheet' shows that in the final analysis the New Labour period has not been all that distinctive in relation to the sort of outcomes that we are examining. In the context of Scotland, however, approaches and outcomes *were* supposed to be distinctive and it is to this that we now briefly turn.

Devolved and Divided Scotland

As referred to in the introduction to this chapter, the health 'reforms' and policy initiatives that have been discussed or alluded to above came with a specific twist in Scotland. They were coupled with an apparent concern for, in the words of Scotland's (first) First Minister, Donald Dewar, "a fair and just settlement for Scotland" that would "strengthen democratic control and make the government more accountable to the people of Scotland" (Dewar, 1997, quoted in Chadwick and Heffernan, 2003: 181). In short, the responsibility for key policy areas was devolved to the Scottish Parliament and the Scottish Executive. Thus, we were promised 'Scottish solutions for Scottish problems' in some important spheres of Scottish social life, including health. This is particularly important since, as shown above, poor health and health problems can be clustered in particular geographical areas. Scotland is one such place as the discussion of Glasgow's Calton has clearly illustrated. Like the rest of the countries in the UK, it is important that we do not 'lump' all of Scotland together and assume uniformity. We do, however, need to explore Scotland as a valuable 'case study' in its own right as there *is* a 'Scottish effect' (Scottish Executive, 2004) that we should account for.

Two key points emerge from this:

- First, Scotland is divided in terms of health and health care and we can make useful comparisons between locations by using key indicators such as mortality and morbidity. You will remember that average life expectancy in Glasgow was 68 years. This is compared with rates of just over 76 for two more affluent areas that border the city; namely East Renfrewshire, which contains Newton Mearns, and East Dunbartonshire, which contains Bearsden (NHS/IDS, 2004). In terms of morbidity and the prevalence of disease, there is again a concentration of heart disease and cancer in the poorer areas. Hence, it is possible to argue that: "the unavoidable fact [is] that the poorest people living in the most disadvantaged circumstances suffer more avoidable illness and disability and premature mortality" (Blamey *et al*, 2002). It is worth reminding ourselves here that this is more than two and a half decades since the Black Report and that in a few short years the NHS will celebrate its sixtieth anniversary.

- The second important point is that the prevalence of these concentrations of poor or good health and the overall pattern and persistence of ill-health in Scotland compares unfavourably with other European countries, earning Scotland the title of the 'sick man' of Europe. For example, male deaths from cardiovascular disease and lung cancer are the highest in Europe and for women they are the highest in the world (Paterson *et al*, 2004). Moreover, the UK average male life expectancy is 77 (*Metro*, 11 November 2005), which is higher than the level in *any* of Scotland's regions, *including* the most affluent.

It is in this context that the apparent endeavour to create specifically Scottish solutions for what seem to be specifically Scottish problems takes place. These solutions, as noted above, are often focused on behavioural change and the promotion of cultural shifts.

One such policy comes in the form of key legislation that has been seen by some to represent Scotland as a pioneering and innovative beacon of health solutions in the UK context. One such example is the Smoking Health and Social Care (Scotland) Act 2005 or , as it is more familiarly known to us, 'the smoking ban'. This is a central, indeed perhaps *the* central piece of health legislation thus far in the life of the Scottish Parliament, as it makes smoking in public places illegal in an effort to overturn a situation that sees around 13 thousand deaths in Scotland each year from smoking related illnesses (Scottish Executive, 2005).

Pause for thought
- What do you think are the advantages and disadvantages of the 'smoking ban'?

Your answers to the above 'Pause for thought' are likely to be influenced by your own views on smoking and perhaps how it affects you personally. They may also be affected by our discussions so far and perhaps you are beginning to understand that a focus on behaviour and culture is only part of the story. We also need to look at 'structural' factors like the benefits system and employment, *neither* of which are the responsibility of the Scottish Parliament. Moreover, it has also been pointed out that "old style targeting of direct government spending to boost poorer regions is out of fashion" (*The Guardian*, 21 September 2004). It has been replaced by regional development through devolution (with little evidence of success thus far) (*The Guardian*, 21 September 2004) and the promotion of an entrepreneurial spirit to bring about social justice (McCafferty, 2004).

In Scotland, we have devolution alongside division and debates about the causes and solutions to what seem like our particular problems. Although it has not been possible to go into the issues in detail, there are concerns regarding the 'downgrading' of services due to health board restructuring, waiting lists (*The Scotsman*, 11 March 2006) and, of course, finance and private sector involvement. In this context we have the key questions raised about 'who pays?' and 'do the sick get what they deserve?', which are mirrored in the cultural/structural tension highlighted in this chapter (and, indeed, throughout this Book). It does seem, however, that we are presented at all too regular intervals with plenty of evidence that after seven years of devolution there is still much work to be done in relation to the overall 'health' of Scotland. The experience of the residents of the Calton is certainly a clear, if unwelcome, illustration of this.

Conclusion

This chapter has tried to ensure that in order to fully understand health and health policy you are left in no doubt that this is a highly complex and much debated issue. It is clear that, when dealing with health, we must leave our assumptions behind in order to recognise that health is about more than 'faulty people' and 'faulty bodies'. Local, regional and national differences in health and the clustering of ill-health, alert us to the contention that susceptibility to death and disease cannot simply be explained by behaviour. Social and economic structures matter, too!

Political structures are also important and the 'politics of health' has long since involved managing the tensions between 'new' and already existing priorities, particularly in relation to finance and the balance between public and private involvement and its impact.

The development of apparently localised political solutions has also been an important element of our story and we need to be aware of the 'Scottish Effect' and some of the efforts that have been made to try to address it. It has not been possible to cover all of these, but what have been highlighted are some important developments and some of the key ideas underpinning them.

Clearly, it is important that we are aware of the different facets of health, healthcare, health policy and, of course, health inequalities, as we try to understand policy and what helps to frame it, both as practitioners and as 'service users'. Certainly, as comprehensive an understanding as possible can be achieved by those who seek to explore the complexities of health in the contemporary context as we concern ourselves with building the foundations for moving 'towards a healthier Scotland'.

Further Reading

Mooney, G. and Scott, G. (eds.) (2005) *Exploring Social Policy in the 'New' Scotland*, Bristol, Policy Press

Stewart, J. (2004) *Taking Stock: Scottish Social Welfare after Devolution*, Bristol, Policy Press

Timmins, N. (2001) *The Five Giants: a Biography of the Welfare State*, London, Harper-Collins

Useful Websites

NHS History: www.nhshistory.net

Health Scotland: www.healthscotland.com

Wikipedia: http://en.wikipedia.org/wiki/Wikipedia (Online dictionary)

Bibliography

BBC News Online (1998) 'Care in the Community to be scrapped', 17 January, http://news.bbc.co.uk/1/hi/uk/48168.stm (accessed on 25 November 2005)

BBC News Online (2006) *Thatcher's Famous Speeches*, http://news.bbc.co.uk/1/hi/uk_politics/1888158.stm, (accessed on 17 January 2006)

Blair, T. (1994) *Socialism*, London, Fabian Society

Blair, T. (1997a) 'Foreword', in *New Labour: Because Britain Deserves Better*, General Election Manifesto, London, Labour Party

Blair (1997b) 'Foreword', in Department of Health (1997) *The New NHS. Modern. Dependable* (White Paper), London, HMSO

Blair, T. (1998) *The Third Way – New Politics for the New Century*, Fabian Pamphlet 588, London, Fabian Society

Blamey, A., Hanlon, P., Judge, K. and Murie, J. (eds.) (2002) *Health Inequalities in the New Scotland*, Glasgow, NHS Scotland/Health Promotion Policy Unit/Public Health Institute

Heffernan, R. and Chadwick, A. (2003) 'The New Labour Phenomenon', in Heffernan, R. and Chadwick, A. (eds.) (2003) *The New Labour Reader*, Cambridge, Polity Press

Heffernan, R. and Chadwick, A. (eds.) (2003) *The New Labour Reader*, Cambridge, Polity Press

Corby, S. and White, G. (1999) *Employee Relations in the Public Sector: Themes and Issues*, London, Routledge

Department of Health (1997) *The New NHS. Modern. Dependable* (White Paper),

London, HMSO

Ferguson, I., Lavalette, M. and Mooney, G. (2002) *Rethinking Welfare: A Critical Perspective*, London, Sage

Ferguson I. (2005) 'Social Work and Social Policy in the "new" Scotland ', in Mooney, G. and Scott, G. (eds.) (2005) *Exploring Social Policy in the 'New' Scotland*, Bristol, Policy Press

Guardian, The (2004) 'Fewer carrots, more of the stick', 12 September

Guardian, The (2006) 'In Iraq, life expectancy is 67. Minutes from Glasgow city centre, it's 54', 21 January

Herald, The (2002) 'Revealed: the yawning gap between rich and poor', 1 July

Hinchliffe, D. (2001) 'Foreword', in Pollock, A., Shaoul, J., Rowland, D. and Player, S. (2001) 'Public Services and the Private Sector: A Response to the IPPR', in *Catalyst*, November 2001, http://www.catalyst-trust.co.uk/paper1 (accessed on 8 March 2002)

Hinchliffe, S. and Woodward, K. (eds.) (2004) *The Natural and the Social: Uncertainty, Risk and Social Change*, London/Milton Keynes, Open University/Routledge

Jowel, R. *et al* (2000) *British Social Attitudes 17th Report*, London, Sage

McCafferty, P. (2004) *Working the Third Way: New Labour, Employment Relations, and Scottish Devolution*, unpublished PhD thesis, Glasgow, University of Glasgow

McCormick, J. (2000) 'On the Sick: Incapacity and Inclusion', *Scottish Council Foundation*, Paper 17 (extracts), www.scottishpolicynet.org.uk/sccf/publications/ paper17 /chapter1.shtm (accessed on 27 October 2001)

Metro (2005) 'Why Scots mean won't reach 70', 11 November

Monbiot, G. (2000) *Captive State: The Corporate Take Over of Britain*, Houndsmills, Macmillan

Mooney, G. and Scott, G. (eds.) (2005) *Exploring Social Policy in the 'New' Scotland*, Bristol, Policy Press

New Policy Institute/Joseph Rowntree Foundation (2004) *Monitoring Poverty and Social Exclusion in Scotland 2004*, York, Joseph Rowntree Foundation

NHS/ISD Scotland (2004) *Healthy Life Expectancy*, www.isdscotland.org/isd/ files/HLE_report_2004.pdf (accessed on 24 January 2006)

NHS History (2006) 'Short NHS History', www.nhshistory.net/short_history.htm (accessed on 13 January 2006)

NHS History (2006) 'NHS Policy', www.nhshistory.net/policy.htm (accessed on 13 January 2006)

Office of National Statistics (2002) *Health Statistics Quarterly*, Issue 13, London, HMSO

Office of National Statistics (2004) *Social Trends 34*, www.statistics.gov.uk /STATBASE.ssdataset.asp?vlnk=7239 (accessed on 31 October 2005)

Paterson, L., Bechhofer, F. and McCrone, D. (2004) *Living in Scotland: Social and Economic Change since 1980*, Edinburgh, Edinburgh University Press

Pollock, A. (1994/5) 'The Creeping Privatisation of Community Care', *Health Matters*, Issue 20, Winter 1994/5

Pollock, A., Shaoul, J., Rowland, D. and Player, S. (2001a) 'Public Services and the Private Sector: A Response to the IPPR', *Catalyst*, November 2001, http://www.catalyst-trust.co.uk/paper1 (accessed on 8 March 2002)

Rivett, G. C. (1998) *From Cradle to Grave: Fifty years of the NHS*, London, Kings Fund

Sanchdev, S. (2004) 'Paying the Cost? Public Private Partnerships and the Public Sector Workforce', in *Catalyst*, http://www.catalystforum.org.uk/pdf/ppp.pdf (accessed on 17 March 2005)

The Scotsman (2006) 'Health Service waiting times "conning" public', 11 March

Scottish Executive (2002a) New Rights Scotland's Carers, *Press Release*, 30 August, http://www.scotland.gov.uk/News/Releases/2002/08/2151 (accessed on 20 January 2006)

Scottish Executive (2002b) 'Ministers welcome PPP inquiry outcome', *Press Release*, 2 October

Scottish Executive (2004) *Health in Scotland 2004*, Edinburgh, The Stationary Office

Scottish Executive (2005) *Building Health Service Fit for the Future*, Edinburgh, The Stationary Office

Scottish Executive (2006) 'Celebrating a new smoke-free Scotland', Advertisement (various newspapers)

Socialist Worker (2002) 'More than an echo of Thatcher', 18 May

Smith, B. and Goldblatt, D. (2004) 'Whose Health is it anyway?' in Hinchcliffe, S. and Woodward, K. (eds.) (2004) *The Natural and the Social: Uncertainty, Risk and Social Change*, London/Milton Keynes, Open University/Routledge

Stewart, J. (2004) *Taking Stock: Scottish Social Welfare after Devolution*, Bristol, Policy Press

Tannahill, C. (2005) 'Health and Health Policy', in Mooney, G. and Scott, G. (eds.) (2005) *Exploring Social Policy in the 'New' Scotland*, Bristol, Policy Press

Timmins, N. (2001) *The Five Giants: a Biography of the Welfare State*, London, Harper-Collins

Townsend, P., Whitehead, M. and Davidson, N. (eds.) (1992) *Inequalities in Health: the Black Report and the Health Divide*, Harmonsworth, Penguin

Wanless, D (2002) *Securing our Future Health: Taking a Long Term View*, London, HM Treasury

Whitehead, M. (1988) 'The Health Divide', in Townsend, P., Whitehead, M. and Davidson, N. (1992) (eds.) *Inequalities in Health: the Black Report and the Health Divide*, Harmonsworth, Penguin

Answers to 'Pause for thought'

Pause for thought

- What is the current male life expectancy in:

    1. Iraq?
    2. 'The Calton' housing estate in Glasgow?
    3. The Gaza Strip?

1. Iraq = 67 years. 2. Glasgow's Calton = 54 years. Gaza Strip = 70.5 years.

(Source: *The Guardian*, 21st January, 2006.)

Chapter 10

Learning Disability in 21st Century Scotland

Sue Dumbleton

Introduction

This chapter is about people living in 21st century Scotland who have a learning disability. The chapter will be of particular interest to people who work in learning disability services and those who want to gain a better understanding of the effects of learning disability.

It will also be useful to social care workers not working directly with people who have a learning disability, because although people who have a learning disability tend to be marginalised as a social group, according to Scottish Executive (2000) figures more than one in 50 of the Scottish population has a learning disability. This means that most people know someone in their family, community , school or neighbourhood who has a learning disability.

The chapter attempts to illustrate the central themes of the book using aspects of the lives of some people who have a learning disability. Fictitious case studies involving 'Gordon', 'Sheila' and 'Sophie' are used to illustrate some of the changes in social policy which affect people who have a learning disability.

These cases studies begin on the following page.

Three Case Studies

Box 10.1 Case Study 1: Gordon

Gordon was born in 1915. By the time he was 6 years old it was clear that he was not developing as quickly as his four siblings and his three year old sister was able to do more for herself than Gordon. He had severe epilepsy, often having 10 or 12 seizures each day. He did not attend school, having been judged unable to benefit from education so he was at home all day with his mother and young sister.

Gordon's father had been killed in the last months of World War 1 and his mother struggled to bring up her family on her small income. He needed constant supervision and care to ensure that he did not hurt himself during his seizures or in any other way. His understanding of danger was limited and he tended to run out of the house if left alone.

In 1921 Gordon, who had been classified as an 'imbecile', was taken from his home to an institution for the education of imbecile children that had opened in the previous century. Ten years later, at the age of 16, Gordon was transferred to a newly opened institution for adults with a mental deficiency living in a villa built to house fifty people.

Gordon remained in this institution until 1985 when, at the age of 60, he moved to a recently opened supported hostel for people with a learning disability. He remained there for five years until his health began to fail and he was re-admitted to the institution where he died three years later.

In total Gordon had spent 67 years of his life in institutional care.

Box 10.2 Case Study 2: Sheila

Sheila was born in 1963. Sheila has Down Syndrome, which was diagnosed immediately after birth. Shortly after she was born Sheila's mother was advised to have the baby admitted to institutional care as it was almost certain that she would need care for the rest of her life. It was explained to Sheila's mother that as the baby was a 'mongol' she would not be able to walk, speak or recognise other people and that she would be happier in a special environment.

Sheila's mother was not convinced by this though and decided to take Sheila home to care for her herself. There was little support available to Sheila's mother, but she managed by herself, with help from her family, to look after Sheila until it was time for her to go to school when she was aged 5, in 1968.

However, Sheila was classified as 'mentally handicapped' and 'ineducable and untrainable' and therefore not eligible to go to school. Instead, she went to a Junior Occupation Centre until she reached the age of 16 when she transferred to the occupation centre for adults, which was within the same building.

Sheila's mother had contact with some other parents who were campaigning for more and better services for their mentally handicapped children and together they set up a special club that their children could attend to meet friends and have some leisure time together.

During this time, Sheila's mother often needed a break from caring. Occasionally, her GP would arrange for Sheila to be admitted to the children's ward of the local hospital for a week or fortnight.

In 1990, Sheila moved to live in a 'group home' with three other people from the occupation centre, which had been re-named as a day centre. The group home was staffed by several people, all working shifts.

In 2001, Sheila's day centre closed and she began a new programme of supported day time activities such as swimming, shopping and attending the local further education college.

In 2004, when Sheila was aged 41 she began to show signs of ill health and was eventually diagnosed as having dementia. Her illness progressed rapidly and before long it became clear that she could not remain in the group home. At the age of 43 Sheila was admitted to a care home which specialised in dementia care. All the other residents were aged over 70.

Box 10.3 Case Study 3: Sophie

Sophie was born in 1982. By the time she was three there was sufficient concern about her development that she was referred to the local psychological services for assessment. Following this assessment it was decided that Sophie had 'special educational needs'. A Record of Needs was opened for Sophie and she was allocated a place at a special school where her needs could be met.

Sophie lived at home, with occasional respite with another family recruited through a social work department scheme to provide family based respite care for disabled children and their families.

When Sophie left school in 1997 it was assumed that she would go to the local further education college to continue her general education. Sophie is keen to have a job and volunteers at a local charity shop one day per week. She has some supported leisure time, but her days can be quite empty and lonely. Sophie lives in her own tenancy, with support from one of a team of support workers.

In themselves, the people in these three case studies are not so very different from each other. All have what would currently be called a learning disability. However, the policy responses to them, the language used to describe them and the services available to them do differ and have differed over time. Contemporary approaches to people who have a learning disability are concerned with supporting choice, respecting dignity, promoting independence (for example, Sophie's living arrangements in her own home) and other core skills of contemporary social care work. These approaches are applied to people with learning disabilities because learning disability is a 'social problem' and current policy towards learning disability dictates that these are the best solutions to this problem.

This is not to say that individual people who have a learning disability are problematic but that society sees them, as a social group, as presenting problems for the rest of that society. The problems, for example, of where people who have a learning disability should live, how they should be treated and how they should spend their time, have been addressed in a variety of ways over the centuries. Our own society's attempts to address this social problem are only the latest of many and are based on the beliefs and values of 21st century Scotland. Most of the structures to address the social problem, such as day centres or group homes, have been inherited from the late 20th century – and these solutions are often based on earlier values and beliefs that might have come from the 19th century, or even earlier than that.

Social problems are defined or constructed by powerful groups in society whose power gives them a louder or more authoritative voice than that of most individuals. It is only when problems are recognised as requiring public action that social policy is made. The 'problem' of learning disability has not always been recognised as a public or social concern. Private troubles can often become social problems, not least with regard to the social problem of learning disability. Some powerful voices belong to the professionals who work with people who have a learning disability – doctors, teachers and social workers. More recently, people who have a learning disability themselves and their family carers have attempted to have their voices heard. Listening to the voices of these groups can help us to understand why social policy develops at particular times and in particular ways.

The Same As You? (2000)

An important current policy document in relation to people who have a learning disability is the Scottish Executive report *The Same As You?*, published in 2000. This report makes 29 recommendations about the ways in which services should be provided. The recommendations are underpinned by the principle that people who have a learning disability have the same human rights and needs as anyone else and are entitled to be included in society, for example, living in ordinary homes rather than hospitals or hostels. This point of view is widely accepted in 21st century Scotland, but is not uncontested – and in many cases provision has not yet caught up with the policy. For example, *The Same As You?* says that local authorities need to develop a range of employment opportunities for people who have a learning disability, yet Sophie's days are rather empty and lonely. Sheila is being cared for in a care home for older people, though *The Same As You?* states that there should be mainstream services for people who have both a learning disability and dementia.

Other aspects of policy and the law, for example, the Children (Scotland) Act 1995, the Human Rights Act 1998, the Adults with Incapacity (Scotland) Act 2000, the Mental Health Care and Treatment Act 2003, the Regulation of Care (Scotland) Act 2001 and many more affect the lives of people who have a learning disability. These separate pieces of policy and legislation do not always work together in a consistent way, so that the rights conferred by one might be restricted by another. For example, the rights conferred by the Human Rights Act 1998 can be suspended by the terms of mental health legislation. Or the needs and wishes of an individual who has a learning disability can be at variance with the needs and wishes of his or her family carer. If the person who has a learning disability has a guardian in terms of the Adults with Incapacity (Scotland) Act 2000, the decisions made by the guardian may be the ones that stand, even if the person who has the learning disability disagrees with them.

Why Words Matter

The words used to describe people are important because they carry meanings and values. Sometimes the language that was used in the past grates on 21st century ears. The words used to describe people who have a learning disability have changed over the period that this chapter considers and reflect changes in social values and social policy. Currently, the favoured term is 'people who have a learning disability' but some of the terms from the past are familiar. Terms such as 'idiot', 'moron', 'imbecile' and 'feeble minded' were in use in the late 19th and early-mid 20th centuries. The term 'mental handicap', used in Scottish educational legislation and practice, emerged in the 1960s and 1970s as the favoured term in health and social work in the UK. In the 1980s came another change – the 'mentally handicapped' became 'mentally handicapped *people*'. Later in the 1980s 'mentally handicapped people' became '*people with* a mental handicap'.

The term 'learning disability' does not lend itself to straightforward definition, partly because, like so many other aspects of social policy, definitions vary according to time, place and social context. Atkinson and Walmsley (1999: 204) note that, "prior to the mid-19th century there were no consistently used definitions or diagnoses of learning disability" and since then society's view of what learning disability is has changed, in some respects, along with the words used to describe it and the possible solutions to the social problems it poses. The Scottish Executive document, *The Same As You?* (2000: 3), proposes the following definition and, as it reflects current understanding of learning disability in Scotland, it will be used for the purposes of this chapter:

- "People with leaning disabilities have a significant, lifelong condition that started before adulthood, that affected their development and which means that they need help to:

  o Understand information
  o Learn skills; and
  o Cope independently."

Without insight into the social influences that have shaped them, definitions in themselves have limited value. This is one of the important aspects of social policy that this chapter will consider. All social care provision is driven by policy and policy itself is driven by the cultural and historical values of the society from which it derives. For example, Scottish Executive figures (2000) indicate that there are

120,000 people who have a learning disability living in Scotland. However, there can never be a precise calculation of this number, because of the way in which people are defined, or define themselves, as having a learning disability changes.

Key Themes of this Chapter

Throughout the chapter the following *four* key themes of the book will be addressed:

1. **Social division and differentiation:** Solutions to the social problem of learning disability tend, currently, to be called *services*. Services are, or are not, provided by professional 'gatekeepers', such as social care workers, doctors, teachers, educational psychologists, who decide whether or not an individual has 'the problem' and how it should be 'solved'. Professionals who provide services for people who have a learning disability might call this process 'assessment'.

   As Egan (2003: 8) puts it:

   > "The state uses labels as a means of identifying people believed to be in need of specialised support or supervision. Depending on the policies followed and the ways they are implemented this can be beneficial to those labelled, but it also tends to result in social exclusion and stigma."

   Any discussion of learning disability has to address not only 'sameness' (implied by *The Same As You?*), but also the ways in which people with disabilities differ from most other people. *Difference* in itself is not negative, but as Ryan and Thomas (1980: 13) note, difference is not usually viewed positively:

   > "The assertion of differences between people is seldom neutral, it almost always implies some sort of social distance or distinction. The differences between mentally handicapped people and others have mostly been seen negatively, making them a problem to themselves and others."

   The social view of difference and the ways in which policy addresses difference, are topics to be considered by this chapter.

2. **Inclusion and exclusion:** Current trends (Scottish Executive, 2000) favour the inclusion of people who have a learning disability in all aspects of their communities. Despite this, many people with learning disabilities receive services that segregate them from mainstream society. These can be in education (special schools or units), in leisure (special clubs or sports

activities), in housing (hostels or group homes), transport (special buses) or any other aspect of service provision. The provision of special services such as these is not in itself negative, but it does run counter to current social policy. Moreover, Stalker *et al* (1999) report an overall picture of social isolation amongst people who have a learning disability. The lack of paid employment opportunities and the difficulties in negotiating the benefits system identified by the Scottish Executive (2000) increase the social exclusion of learning disabled people. Social policies, in other words, can *minimise* or *emphasise* inclusion and exclusion.

3. **Care and control:** This theme runs through the chapter and indeed through any history of people who have a learning disability. It is not possible to separate the two since care always involves some measure of control. Control is not always an overt aim as in, for example, the early philanthropic, educational concern for children with a learning disability. Control was, however, at the very least a 'by-product' as these institutions removed 'troublesome' children from wider society. This was replaced in the late 19th century and for the first half of the 20th century, with more explicit aims to control and eventually led to the incarceration of thousands of people and to a widespread and not altogether forgotten view that people who have a learning disability are a danger to society.

4. **Continuity and change:** Having a learning disability is not a socially valued attribute and it never has been in Scottish society. Although the ways in which services are provided to people who have a learning disability have changed, these changes are not always as great as we might suppose. Change comes about when social attitudes, context and values change, but continuity is assured because attitudes and values are usually slow to change and are in any case informed by beliefs from the past. However, change *does* take place. For example, current service user and advocacy movements give a voice to people who have a learning disability in a way that would have been unimaginable 100 years ago.

Messages from the Past and the Present

In order to understand the contemporary position of people who have a learning disability in Scottish society it is necessary to look to the past, because *continuity* is as much an aspect of the lives of people who have a learning disability as is *change*. This chapter is not a comprehensive history of learning disability in Scotland, but an attempt to examine the key themes of the book through the social problem of learning disability. It is easy to read history from the perspective of the present and to make unfavourable comparisons between an unenlightened past and an enlightened present. This is not intended here. Societies and their responses to social problems change, but sometimes not as much as we might think. There are many echoes of the past in the ways in which current Scottish society views people who have a learning disability, as well as some distinctively new approaches. Past approaches may have been appropriate in their time and our 'new' approaches will seem outdated as circumstances change.

From Family Responsibility to 'Social Problem'

Although, we can guess, there have been people with a learning disability in Scotland for as long as Scottish society has existed, this chapter will deal only with the situation from the 19th century onwards tracing varying social responses. In the early years of the 19th century, learning disability was not seen as a 'social' problem. The organisation of society meant that most activity took place in the home. People worked in and around their homes and such education as was provided (for most people) came largely from the family. So, responses to people who had a learning disability were private, located in the home. They were responses that did not come to public attention; for example, people who had a learning disability were supported by the family, in the family home, as Ingham (2002: 10) suggests:

> "Recent research in the UK strongly suggests that, until the twentieth century, care for the mass of people now labelled as having a learning disability was left to the family, supplemented by various types of outdoor relief or workhouse provision."

One possible explanation for this is that, in the early 19th century, work increasingly moved from the home, a private space, to factories, which were public spaces. While production had largely centred on the home, families had to make the most of the abilities of all members. Family members who had a learning disability had to contribute, even at a reduced rate of efficiency. However, as production moved to the factory, it was not in factory owners' interests to employ people who could not work as fast, or as effectively, as most. People who had previously worked at home and could provide care for those family members who had a learning disability were now employed in factories and unable to provide such care. With a changing social context for work, learning disability started to be seen as a problem affecting more people than the immediate family. It became a 'public' problem. A public solution to the problem, in the form of institutional care, began to take shape.

The Scottish Poor Law Act 1845 established a Central Board of Supervision to regulate a new form of poor relief that could be given in cash or in kind, or through a poorhouse, set up to shelter the sick or destitute. About 70 poorhouses were eventually established across Scotland. The 1881 Census shows that many 'idiots' and 'imbeciles' were to be found in poorhouses, along with other people classified as 'lunatic', 'deaf and dumb', 'blind' (Census UK). As in the factory, though, these were not the people for whom the poorhouse was designed and their presence made its operation more difficult.

The first institution for mentally disabled children in Scotland, Baldovan Asylum, near Dundee, opened in 1856 with overtly educational aims. Prior to the introduction of **'universal' education** most children who had a learning disability would not have attended school, for the same reasons that adults who had a learning disability would not have required public care. They would have stayed at home, undertaken such work as they could and simply would not have come to public attention as a social problem.

However, once most children were going to school, after the Education (Scotland) Act 1872 established 'universal' education for children aged 5-13, children who had a learning disability became visible in the education system. The social problem of these children came to the attention of teachers – a very powerful social group. 'Feeble minded' children prevented the smooth running of schools, in much the same way that adults who had a learning disability prevented the smooth running of the poorhouse. Class sizes were much larger than those today and children were more regimented in the classroom. Children who could not follow instructions, or understand the teaching that was offered, would have posed a problem to both teachers and other pupils. A solution to the problem had to be found. In the interests of all, doctors and teachers decided that those 'feeble minded' children who were deemed able to benefit from schooling should be accommodated in special classes. The introduction of 'special' education heralded another system that, in part, endures to the present.

Pause for thought
- To what extent do you think that the interests of 'feeble minded' children were considered in this decision?
- Whose voices were most powerful in introducing and sustaining this system?

'Special Education'

Some children with the greatest difficulties were taken to 'colonies', such as the Scottish National Institution for Education of Imbecile Children, which opened in Larbert in 1862 (Hutchieson, 2005). These institutions offered control, physical care and some limited training. Children with less severe difficulties might also be found in colonies, and were often taught simple work skills that could be put to use within the colony. Those deemed feeble minded would remain at home and attend separate 'special' education, struggle to get by in mainstream schools or be permanently excluded from school.

As an 'imbecile', Gordon (see **Box 10.1 Case Study 1**) was taken away from home to institutional education and then institutional care. However, many learning disabled children and adults did not enter institutional care, but stayed at home cared for by family members. Then, as now, people with learning disabilities lived in a range of settings. The apparent discontinuity between institutionalisation *then* and community care *now* is exaggerated, for there have always been learning disabled people living in the community.

Although the 1872 Act established 'universal' education, children who posed a problem in the classroom may well not have received an education. It is only since the implementation of the Education (Scotland) (Mentally Handicapped Children) Act 1974 that children with the highest support needs have been recognised as 'educable'. This is why Sheila (**see Box 10.2 Case Study 2**) did not go to school, though if she had been born a few years later she would have. Sheila's disability did not change but the policy context did. This is a good example of how social policy affects lives and **life chances**.

In 21st century Scotland there is a presumption of inclusion in mainstream schools, as evidenced by Standards in Scotland's Schools etc Act 2000 (Scottish Parliament, 2000). This contrasts sharply with educational provision in the distant and more recent past. The move to 'inclusive' education can be traced to the 1978 Warnock Report (DES, 1978), which led to the Education (Scotland) Act 1980 (as amended) and to a more 'integrated' system of education. However, simply being physically present in a mainstream education setting does not guarantee inclusion. In relation to disabled students in further education colleges, for example, Riddell *et al* (2001) found that they "may be in the same building as mainstream students but have "virtually nothing" to do with them."

Pause for thought
- To what extent is this (above paragraph) a feature of further education colleges?
- Should attempts be made to change this situation? If so, what might they be?

'Care' and 'Control'

Gordon was born at a time of considerable social change in relation to people who had a learning disability. By the end of the 19th century there was growing public concern about the social 'problem' of learning disability. People with a learning disability were seen as presenting an increasing burden on society. Some prominent doctors (though by no means all) proposed that not only were human characteristics, including learning disability, inherited, but that the problems of early 20th century British society were concentrated in learning disabled people.

Doctors tend to have powerful voices and these voices contributed to the development of a new social movement. An organisation called The Eugenics Education Society was founded in 1907 (Jones, 1986). It was mainly supported by professional people and some well known public figures and it campaigned for the better protection of society from the genetic influence of people who had a learning disability. Pressure from such powerful voices led to the establishment of the Royal Commission on the Care and Control of the Feebleminded, which reported in 1908, seven years before Gordon was born.

Although the overt influence of the eugenics movement in Britain waned from the 1930s, particularly after what was learned of Nazi eugenics policies, there are continuities in relation to people who have a learning disability. People who have a learning disability have a greater than average chance of being denied the right to life because the Abortion Act 1967 permits the termination of pregnancy if there is a substantial risk that if the child were born it would be 'seriously handicapped' and antenatal screening can detect such conditions as Down Syndrome. In 1990, the time limit on abortion was lowered from 28 to 24 weeks of a pregnancy (Human Fertilisation and Embryology Act 1990), except when the foetus is presumed to be 'seriously handicapped'. In this case, termination can take place up to the end of the pregnancy. Where the foetus is not presumed to be disabled, termination is allowed only until the 24th week of pregnancy. It is Scottish Executive policy that all women be offered a foetal anomaly scan at 18-20 weeks of pregnancy (European Commission, 2005). When a foetal abnormality is detected, the pregnant woman is routinely offered a termination of the pregnancy.

Pause for thought
- Does this social policy have resonance with the eugenics policies of the past?
- Given the social and political values of contemporary Scotland, is this policy likely to change?
- Which social group has the most powerful voice in retaining or abolishing this policy?

The 1908 Royal Commission report led to an important piece of legislation that, nearly 100 years later, has many echoes, or continuities, for people who have a learning disability in Scotland. The Mental Deficiency and Lunacy (Scotland) Act 1913 gave statutory recognition to the distinction between mental illness and mental handicap and required District Boards of Control to provide institutions for the mentally handicapped separate from the asylums, which were now to concentrate on the treatment of the mentally ill. The Act formally recognised the category of 'feeble minded' persons who required " care, supervision and *control* for their own protection or *for the protection of others*" (this author's emphasis).

This is an example of the overt control exerted over people who had a learning disability. While care was also offered, there was a clear focus on protecting wider society from the negative influence of people deemed to require care and control. Although not causing the immediate incarceration of all people who had a learning disability, the 1913 Act gave considerable impetus to the development of *institutional* care and control.

By the 1930s, the institutionalisation of people with a learning disability in Scotland had grown apace. In 1924, the Edinburgh District Board of Control opened an institution at Gogarburn House to provide specialised care for 24 women – rising by 1948 to 540 patients (Ingham, 2002:4). This was seen as a "satisfactory, efficient and economical means of *solving the problems* associated with mental deficiency" (this author's emphasis) (General Board of Control for Scotland, 1925).

In 1931, the Colony at Larbert (later the Royal Scottish National Hospital) opened with five villas, each housing 50 people. The year 1936 saw the opening of Lennox Castle Hospital – with 1,200 beds the largest mental deficiency hospital in Britain. By the early 1970s, the number of beds had risen to 1,620, thereafter falling until the hospital was closed in 2002 (Greater Glasgow NHS Board Archive).

Box 10.4 Classification

Gordon was classified as an *imbecile*. Classification was an important aspect of the 1913 Act. This classification of people is a good example of social division and **differentiation**. There were *four* types (or grades) of defective under the Act:

- **Idiots:** The most severely disabled.
- **Imbeciles:** Less severely affected than idiots but people who, like Gordon, needed support.
- **Feeble-minded people:** Both adults and children.
- **Moral defectives:** People who, from an early age, displayed "some permanent mental defect coupled with strong vicious or criminal propensities on which punishment had little or no effect." Many women who became pregnant outwith marriage were classified as moral defectives too.

Although these terms are not used to describe or classify people who have a learning disability today they remain in common usage. **Classification** influenced all aspects of the remainder of the person's life. This is what happened to Gordon. Classification in other forms persists and services are, or are not, provided on the basis of this classification.

Many people working in learning disability services today will know men or women who lived in one of the learning disability hospitals. Some were established shortly after the 1913 Act. Others, such as Lynebank in Dunfermline and Craig Phadrig in Inverness, were built and opened as late as the 1960s. Life in some of the hospitals has been chronicled. For some excellent and moving accounts of living in a long stay hospital and personal views of the extent to which people with a learning disability themselves benefited from the 1913 Act, see Hutton (2002), Mitchell (1997) Ingham (2002).

Pause for thought
- What were conditions like in these hospitals?
- Why would these conditions now be considered inappropriate for people who have a learning disability?
- There have been many policy changes since 1913 – is there also continuity?

Post-war Developments in Learning Disability Legislation

The Second World War and its immediate aftermath saw the development of a considerable amount of social legislation. Reform of education and health services were of particular note as they had most to do with learning disability. The establishment in 1948 of the National Health Service (NHS) was mainly concerned with groups other than the learning disabled, though some legislative changes applied to them. For example, the report of the Dunlop Committee (1958), led to the Mental Health (Scotland) Act 1960. The 1960 Act sought to ensure that people with mental disorders were not automatically subject to legal controls and to protect the rights of those who were detained against their will. It thus enabled the discharge from hospital of people detained under the 1913 Act, which was the beginning of what came to be called **'community care'**. Slowly, and often through the campaigning of voluntary organisations, the rights of the mentally handicapped, as people who had a leaning disability were then called, began to come to public attention.

The development of new services for children with learning disabilities are often led by parents, as was the case for Sheila in **Case Study 2**. One example is the provision of short breaks, or respite services. In 1955, the newly formed Scottish Association of Parents of Handicapped Children (now Enable) opened the first day care centre for children who had a learning disability and in 1956 opened a respite holiday home (Enable, 2004). Early respite services for the families of learning disabled children were often provided through short term admission to hospital, which remained the case until Oswin (1984) did much to shift respite care away from hospitals to, for example, family based or more homely residential care.

The gradual closure of learning disability hospitals was given impetus in the early 1990s with the introduction of the NHS and Community Care Act 1990. This and subsequent legislation, such as the Community Care and Health (Scotland) Act 2002, has emphasised the current policy that people with learning disabilities should live in the community, rather than in long stay hospitals – for example Sophie from **Case Study 3**. The general influences on the 1990 Act have been rehearsed by Patricia McCafferty in **Chapter 9** and by Joyce Cavaye in **Chapter 11**, but what of the influences specific to people who have a learning disability?

The conditions in which people who had a learning disability were incarcerated in some hospitals had been the subject of inquiry in England and Wales from 1967-1972, e.g. the Ely Hospital Enquiry (DHSS, 1969). The publication in 1967 of *Sans Everything, a case to answer*, a collection of articles edited by Barbara Robb, brought worrying circumstances to light. The collection dealt with the condition of elderly residents in institutions and included accounts of individual cases of ill-treatment in institutional care. Public opinion, again a powerful voice, began to turn against the long stay institution. Hospitals were increasingly criticised for their failure to provide opportunities for personal development, which was an important aspect of life in the 1960s and 1970s.

Pause for thought
- Why were the voices of people who have a learning disability themselves starting to be heard?
- Why in the late 20th century when they had been silenced before?

The 'Social Model' and 'Normalisation'

The Social Model

The 1960s and 1970s were a time of campaigning against oppression. Women, Black people and gay and lesbian people found a powerful voice to challenge the discrimination that they experienced and some social changes, such as the Sex Discrimination Act 1975 and the Race Relations Act 1976, resulted. The idea of human rights extending to previously marginalised groups in society was becoming accepted. Some disabled people, too, began to identify themselves as an oppressed group in society and campaigned strongly, though some would say not yet successfully, for the full rights of citizenship (Union of Physically Impaired Against Segregation, 1976; Oliver, 1990). This movement gave rise to the social model of disability, which claims that it is not individual impairment that disables people but the *reaction of society* to that impairment. For example, if someone who is a wheelchair user were to live in a completely accessible environment where it was possible to go anywhere in a wheelchair, would s/he be disabled? People who subscribe to the **'social model'** claim that s/he would not and that people are disabled by society's physical and attitudinal barriers rather than by, for example, individual difficulty in walking. The social model led to a relative decline in the power of doctors and other medical experts to define disability and propose solutions to the social problems it posed. The voices of disabled people themselves became more powerful as did those of, among others, social care workers whose careers depended upon the provision of social services to meet disabled peoples' assessed needs.

Normalisation

In relation to learning disability, the **'normalisation'** movement became the dominant voice. Originating in Scandinavia (Nirje, 1969), developed in North America (Wolfensberger, 1972) and taken up in Britain (O'Brien, 1989) with enthusiasm, the principles of normalisation were based on **labelling theory**, which proposed that the 'labels' given to people affected both their own and others' perceptions of them. The labels attached to learning disabled people were negative and, consequently, people with learning difficulties were devalued by society and developed **stigmatised** identities. Wolfensberger (1972) in particular proposed that, to reverse the negative effects of labelling, services should promote more positive, or 'valued' ways of living. One example is the promotion of friendships between learning disabled and non-disabled people, which is informed by the assumption that the non-disabled person's more highly valued status would 'rub off' on the person with the learning disability. The principles of normalisation have been subject to sustained criticism in the past two decades (Culham and Nind, 2003; Chappell, 1997; Ward, 1992), but their legacy in learning disability services remains.

One of the criticisms of the normalisation movement is that it devalues learning disabled people because of their learning disability. In contrast to physically disabled people, or Black, gay or lesbian people who embraced and celebrated difference, learning disabled people's differences were assumed to be negative, both by themselves and by others. Some critics argue that implicit in the principles of normalisation is a belief that learning disabled people themselves have to change in order to fit in to society. This runs counter to the social model of disability, which demands that society changes to accommodate difference and not the other way around. This view has, more recently, been challenged. For example, it is now acknowledged that some people who have a learning disability need personal assistance to engage in aspects of ordinary life, even though most people do not need such assistance. It is not unusual to see a person who has a learning disability speaking in public, supported by someone who does not have a learning disability. An organisational instance of this is the self advocacy movement, People First, which is run by and for people who have a learning disability and supported by non-learning disabled allies or employees.

The citizen and self advocacy movements (Gray and Jackson, 2002) also led to attitudinal and policy changes where people with learning disabilities are seen, in policy terms, as having the same human rights and needs as others in society. Change, however, is gradual. For example, supporters of the social model of disability might say that it is teachers, schools and colleges that require a Co-ordinated Support Plan in terms of the Education (Additional Support for Learning) (Scotland) Act 2004, rather than 'categories' of children.

Who benefits from this perspective? Certainly from personal accounts (Atkinson and Williams, 1990; Ingham, 2002), we know that many people who have a learning disability lead more fulfilling and happier lives outwith the confines of long stay hospitals. The growth of the self advocacy movement has led to a stronger and more powerful voice for some individuals with learning disabilities as well as for learning disabled people as a social group. Yet not all individuals have benefited and accounts of isolation, boredom, poverty, exploitation and lack of respect still feature in the current literature in relation to learning disability (Stalker *et al*, 1999; Scottish Executive, 2000). The rise of the social model of disability has led to *waning power* for the medical profession in the lives of people with a learning disability, but to *increased power* for social care workers to assess and provide service, or not, on the basis of that assessment. The rise of the consumerist approach (discussed in McCafferty, **Chapter 9** and Cavaye, **Chapter 11** in relation to the community care reforms of the 1980s and 1990s) to social work services and the legal requirement to consult service users about the services that are provided means that the views of learning disabled people are sought in ways that would have been unimaginable in 1913. However, the extent to which these voices are heard and acted on by policy makers remains unclear.

Given the stated wish of people who have a learning disability in contemporary Scotland to live, work in and enjoy the facilities of ordinary Scottish society (Scottish Executive, 2000) it would be perverse to suggest that social policy should take a different approach. Social policy and its implementation do not always benefit people in the ways they might expect, though. Policy recognition of identified difficulties does not guarantee that a person who has a learning disability will have control over his or her life. For example, the aim of the Scottish Executive (2000) is to close all long stay hospitals (the institutions created by the 1913 Act) by 2005, yet in 2003 some 800 people were still living in learning disability hospitals in Scotland (Whoriskey, 2003). While people who have a learning disability state that they do not want to live in hospitals, but want to enjoy the full range of housing options available to others (Scottish Executive, 2000), this is not yet a reality for many. People who have a learning disability live in hospitals, hostels, group homes, their own homes – with or without support, with parents, in homes arranged through adult placement or supported lodging schemes and in communities such as those run by the Camphill Movement (Scottish Executive, 1999). Even when they do live in 'ordinary' homes the lives of people who have a learning disability are far from ordinary in the sense that most of us would understand (Simons, 1995), because of the ways in which services are, or are not, provided.

Social differentiation need not have a negative outcome, but for people who have a learning disability it often does. Having a learning disability tends not to be highly valued in contemporary Scottish society – or indeed in most cultural and historical contexts – and many people who have a learning disability experience prejudice. For example, a report by Enable (1999) states that 65 per cent of respondents had experienced bullying because they have a learning disability, 38 per cent of them regularly. Learning disabled people from minority ethnic communities report that services do not meet their linguistic needs (Stalker, 1999).

The Children (Scotland) Act 1995 makes specific reference to children "with, or affected by, disability " defining them (s93 (4) (a)) as "children in need." Local authorities are required (s23 (1)) to design services to minimise the effects of disability on a child and to give disabled children "the opportunity to lead lives which are as normal as possible." This can only happen, though, through assessment and service provision, which is itself an example of social division and differentiation. The very services designed to minimise difference can be obtrusive and stigmatising, since most children do not receive such services. Most children, for example, do not need to be formally assessed to go to an after school club, but a child who has a learning disability and who requires additional support to attend will almost certainly have some kind of assessment. The attempt to provide an 'ordinary' experience provokes an extraordinary response in the form of an assessment and 'special' provision. Such provision often has positive outcomes but it does differentiate some children from the majority. This echoes Egan's (2003) view of the ways in which even positive interventions can stigmatise and exclude.

In contemporary Scotland, adulthood is often marked by the capacity to choose and create a personal lifestyle and identity. Of course, everyone's identity and lifestyle is to a greater or lesser extent constrained by factors such as social class, geography and gender, but people who have a learning disability are likely to be more constrained than average. Public recognition of this has come from the Scottish Executive (2000, recommendations 3 and 26) with the statement that "everyone with a learning disability who wants to should be able to have a 'personal life plan'."

The purpose of a personal life plan is to enable someone who has a learning disability to develop a fulfilling life and is a process of planning and discussion that involves the person who has a learning disability him or herself and any other important people of his or her choosing.

Having a personal life plan, however, will not be a guarantee of a fulfilling life because people who have a learning disability are more dependent than most on services determined by changing social policy. Their voices, though arguably more powerful than in the past, are less powerful than those of teachers, doctors and social care workers. As Stalker (2002: 3) notes, "anecdotally it seems that, as yet, few of these (plans) have been developed [...]."

Conclusion

The key themes of this book – social division and differentiation, inclusion and exclusion, care and control and continuity and change are well illustrated by an examination of historical and contemporary social policy in relation to people who have a learning disability.

While it is arguable that the position of people who have a learning disability in contemporary Scotland is 'better' than, for example, in 1930, this is because the policies that result in contemporary services are a product of current values and thinking. These are the values that tend to be promoted, for example, through the professional education of service providers and so come to be seen as 'common sense'. A child who has a learning disability born in 2006 will, as s/he grows up, experience some different approaches, supports and services to Gordon, Sheila or Sophie, but in other respects will, we can suppose from the study of social policy, also experience some continuity. The differences will arise from the prevailing social values and beliefs of the time and the continuity from the legacy of the past, which will inform some of those beliefs. We can guess that, in the future, people who have a learning disability will continue to be identified as presenting a social problem. There will be new 'solutions' to that 'problem' but they are likely, as in contemporary Scotland, to have echoes of past 'solutions'.

Internet Resources

Census UK: www.censusuk.co.uk
British Institute of Learning Disabilities: www.bild.org.uk
Scottish Consortium for Learning Disability: www.scld.org.uk

Bibliography

Abbot, P. and Sapsford, R. (1987) *Community Care for Mentally Handicapped Children*, Milton Keynes, The Open University

Anderson, N. and Langa, A. (1997) 'The development of institutional care for 'idiots' and 'imbeciles' in Scotland', in *History of Psychiatry*, June 8 (30, Part 2)

Atkinson, D. and Walmsley, J. (1999) 'Using Autobiographical Approaches with People with Learning Difficulties', in *Disability and Society*, Vol. 14, No. 2

Atkinson, D. and Williams, F. (1990) *Know Me As I Am*, Sevenoaks, Hodder and Stoughton Educational

Barton, L. and Oliver, M. (eds.) (1997) *Disability Studies: Past Present and Future*, Leeds, The Disability Press

Brown, H. and Smith, H. (eds.) (1992) *Normalisation: A Reader for the Nineties*, London, Tavistock/Routledge

Census UK, http://www.censusuk.co.uk/1881new.htm (accessed on 29 October 2005)

Chappell, A.L. (1997) 'From Normalisation to Where?', in Barton, L. and Oliver, M. (eds.) (1997) *Disability Studies: Past Present and Future*, Leeds, The Disability Press

Culham, A. and Nind, M. (2003) 'Deconstructing normalisation: clearing the way for inclusion', in *Journal of Intellectual and Developmental Disability*, Volume 28, Number 1

Department of Education and Science (DES) (1978) *Committee of Enquiry into the Education of Handicapped Children and Young People* (The Warnock Report), London, HMSO

Department of Health and Social Security (DHSS) (1969) *Report of the Committee of Enquiry into Allegations of Ill-treatment of Patients and other Irregularities at the Ely Hospital, Cardiff*, Cmd. 3975, HMSO, March 1969

Disability Rights Commission (2002) *Disability in Scotland*, Edinburgh, Disability Rights Commission

Egan, M. (2003) *Presentation for Scottish Health History: International Contexts, Contemporary Perspectives Colloquium*, Glasgow, University of Glasgow

Enable (1999) *Stop It! Bullying and Harassment of People with Learning Disabilities*, Glasgow, Enable

Enable (2004) *Far Beyond Our Dreams*, Glasgow, Enable

European Commission (2005) *Prenatal Screening Policies in Europe*, Newtownabbey, EUROCAT Central Registry

General Board of Control for Scotland (1925) *Eleventh Annual Report*, Edinburgh, HMSO

Gray, B. and Jackson, R. (2002) *Advocacy and Learning Disability*, London, Jessica Kinglsey Publishers

Hutchieson, I. (2005) 'Voices from the past: early institutional experience of children with disabilities – the case of Scotland', in *Paediatric Rehabilitation*, January, 8 (1)

Hutton, G . (2002) *Royal Scottish National Hospital – 140 Years*, Falkirk, Forth Valley Primary Care NHS Trust

Ingham, N. (ed.) (2002) *Gogarburn Lives*, Edinburgh, The Living Memory Association

Jones, G . (1986) *Social Hygiene in Twentieth Century Britain*, Beckenham, Croom Helm

Kurgel, R. and Wolfensberger, W. (eds.) (1969) *Changing Patterns in Residential Services for the Mentally Retarded*, Washington, DC, The President's Committee on Mental Retardation

Mitchell, H . (1997) 'Sporting Institutions: Football, Masculinity and Community Identity at Lennox Castle Hospital', in *The Journal of the Oral History Society*, Volume 25, Numbers 1-2

Nirje, B. (1969) 'The Normalization Principle and its Human Management Implications', in Kurgel, R. and Wolfensberger, W. (eds.) (1969) *Changing Patterns in Residential Services for the Mentally Retarded*, Washington, DC, The President's Committee on Mental Retardation

O'Brien, J . (1989) *What's Worth Working For? Leadership for Better Quality Human Services*, Georgia, Responsive Systems Associates

Oliver, M. (1990) *The Politics of Disablement*, Houndsmills, Macmillan

Oswin, M. (1984) *They Keep Going Away*, London, King's Fund/Open University Press

Parliament (1995) *Children (Scotland) Act 1995*, Edinburgh, HMSO

Parliament (1998) *Human Rights Act 1998*, London, HMSO

Parliament (1913) *Mental Deficiency and Lunacy (Scotland) Act 1913*, Edinburgh, HMSO

Riddell, S., Baron, S. and Wilson, A. (2001) *The learning society and people with learning difficulties*, Bristol, The Policy Press

Robb, B. (1967) *Sans Everything, a case to answer*, London, Nelson

Ryan, J. and Thomas, F. (1980) *The Politics of Mental Handicap*, Harmondsworth, Penguin

Scottish Executive (1999) *The View from Arthurs Seat*, Bristol, Norah Fry Research Centre

Scottish Executive (2000) *The Same As You? A review of services for people with learning disabilities*, Edinburgh, HMSO

Scottish Executive Education Department (2003) *Summary Handout on the Additional Support for Learning Bill*, Edinburgh, HMSO

Scottish Parliament (2000) *Adults with Incapacity (Scotland) Act 2000*, Edinburgh, HMSO

Scottish Parliament (2003) *Mental Health Care and Treatment (Scotland) Act 2003*, Edinburgh, HMSO

Scottish Parliament (2000) *Standards in Scotland's Schools etc. Act 2000*, Edinburgh: The Stationery Office

Simons, K . (1995) *My Home My Life*, Bristol, Values into Action/Norah Fry Research Centre

Stalker, K . *et al* (1999) *If You Don't Ask You Don't Get Review of Services for People with Learning Disabilities: The Views of People who use Services and their Carers*, Edinburgh, Scottish Executive

Stalker, K. (2002) *Young disabled people moving into adulthood in Scotland*, York, Joseph Rowntree Foundation

Union of Physically Impaired Against Segregation (1976) *Fundamental Principles of Disability*, London, UPIAS

Ward, L. (1992) 'Foreword', in Brown, H. and Smith, H. (eds.) (1992) *Normalisation: A Reader for the Nineties*, London, Tavistock/Routledge

Whoriskey, M . (2003) 'Progress with Learning Disability Hospital Closures in Scotland', in *Tizard Learning Disability Review*, Vol. 8, Issue 1

Wolfensberger, W . (1972) *The Principle of Normalization in Human Services*, Toronto, National Institute of Mental Retardation

Chapter 11

The Care of Older People in Scotland

Joyce Cavaye

Introduction

This chapter explores the care of older people and highlights differences in policy and practice between Scotland and England. In recent years governments have paid increasing attention to the care of older people. New policies and standards have been developed despite concerns about escalating costs of care for the increasing numbers of older people. Since devolution, policy in Scotland in relation to older people has become increasingly divergent. Controversial policies that are now enshrined in legislation include free personal care for older people and rights for unpaid family carers.

The care of older people is important not least because one day we will all be considered old, but also because they are the highest users of health and social care services. For students of health and social welfare this chapter is essential reading because it provides up to date information about legislation, policy and practice in the care of older people. Reading this chapter will increase your knowledge and understanding of the political and legislative context within which you may come to work.

The chapter considers the following issues:

- Perceptions of old age.
- The changing structure of Scotland's population.
- Gerontological theories of ageing.
- Health of older people, with a focus on dementia.
- Policy and legislation governing the provision of care services.
- Provision of care services by informal carers, statutory, voluntary and private providers.

The book wide themes underpinning this chapter are:

- Social divisions.
- Inclusion and exclusion.
- Continuity and change.

Whilst policy is driven by the concept of inclusion, the chapter highlights how the exclusion of older people is shaped by cultural perceptions, **ageism** and frailty. Older people do not encounter inequalities for the first time when they retire. On the contrary, the inequalities experienced during their earlier life are continued into old age. The case studies in this chapter are drawn from the authors' empirical research and from personal experience as a practitioner.

How Old is 'Older'? Perceptions of Age

Growing older is often viewed as being a 'problem'. Ageing or growing old is associated with negative images and ideas. There are more stereotypes about the physical and mental abilities of older people than there are about the abilities of people in any other age group. Some stereotypes depict older people as slow in their thinking and movements; as living in the past and unable to change; and as cranky, sickly and lacking in social value (Atcheley, 2001). A number of expressions have been used to describe 'people who are older', for example, the elderly, the aged, pensioners or geriatrics. More derogatory terms also used to describe older people include 'wrinklies', 'old biddies', and 'old fogies' (Featherstone and Hepworth, 1993: 308). That older people use such self-depreciating phrases as "I'm having a senior moment" and "it must be my age" when they forget something or make a mistake, helps to sustain and promote these negative stereotypes.

Pause for thought
- What images do the words 'old age' conjure up in your mind?

Older people dislike being called 'old dears', 'the elderly' or 'geriatrics'. A European survey of people aged 60 years and over revealed that one third preferred to be called 'older people' and one third 'senior citizens', whilst others preferred to be called 'retired' (Walker, 1993). The term 'older people' has increasingly been used over the last decade and is now accepted as the politically correct term.

So, who exactly do we mean by 'older people'? Whilst there is no agreed definition, one commonly used for older people is those over retirement age. This is because retirement tends to mark a watershed in people's lives, although this will mean different things for different people depending on their individual circumstances.

The notion of retirement as a particular phase of life is a **social construction** (see Mooney, Sweeney and Law, **Chapter 1** and Sweeney, **Chapter 2**). It is also a good example of how policy and attitudes towards older people change over time. Retirement is usually measured by the age at which a person is eligible for a state pension. This is currently 65 years for men and 60 years for women. However, the age at which people can retire has changed over time and is likely to do so again in the near future. The Pensions Act 1995 increased the state pension age for women to 65 years, a change that is to be phased in between 2010 and 2020 (Department of Social Security, 1994). Before the development of the welfare state there was no such thing as 'retirement' as people went on working for as long as they were physically capable. If they continued in paid employment then their status remained that of a worker. When pensions were first introduced in 1908 they were payable only to men aged 70 years and above. This was reduced to 65 in 1925 and has remained so ever since. Pensions for women were not introduced until 1948. Nowadays, many men and women are not in work as they approach their 65th birthday, but with recent alterations in employment law this may change with more workers being encouraged to work beyond retirement age.

Pause for thought

For women not in the labour market and people who may be self employed the concept of retirement is not entirely satisfactory.

• Why do you think this might be?

Older people are in fact simply people of either one or two generations who have lived to a certain age. The term refers to everyone within a very wide age band, from 50 or 60 to 100 years or more, irrespective of whether they are fit, ill, working, retired, rich, poor, white, black, male or female. They are not a **deviant** group or some special section of the population. They are ordinary people who happen to have reached a particular age. Yet few people would attribute the same characteristics to a 30 year old as they would to a 60 year old. Why then should those in their sixties and their nineties be constructed as one homogenous group with similar needs, desires and attributes, such as social class and sexuality? Surely it is only reasonable to expect that older peoples' contribution to society, their demands and expectations will be as varied as the rest of the population.

Pause for thought
- Can you think of examples of people in their 20s or 30s who you might describe as 'old' because of their behaviour, attitude and thoughts?

Ageism

Ageism is defined as prejudice and discrimination against people on the basis of age. Ageism is a social problem that particularly excludes and **stigmatises** older people. The term was introduced in the 1970s to describe how myths and misconceptions about older people produce age-based discrimination. Just as sexism and racism perpetuate stereotyping and discrimination against women and ethnic minorities, ageism perpetuates stereotyping of older people and age-based discrimination (Bytheway, 2000).

Box 12.1 Examples of Ageism

1. Being refused interest-free credit, a new credit card or car insurance because of age.
2. An organisation's attitude to older people resulting in a lower quality of service.
3. Age limits on benefits such as Disability Living Allowance.
4. A doctor deciding not to refer you to a consultant because you are 'too old'.
5. Losing a job because of your age.

(Age Concern, 2004)

A recent study by Age Concern (2004) found that ageism was the most widespread type of discrimination with almost 30 per cent of people reporting it. As many as 29 per cent said that they had been treated unfairly because of age, compared to 24 per cent who cited gender, the next most prevalent form of discrimination. Ageism remains high throughout the life course and, from the age of 55 onwards, people were nearly twice as likely to have experienced age-related prejudice as any other form. At the moment older people have no legal protection against ageism. However, new legislation outlawing age discrimination in the workplace will be introduced in October 2006 (Department of Work and Pensions, 2005). The Employment Equality (Age) Regulations 2006 will mean that older workers will have the same employment rights as younger workers. If people want to work past the usual retirement age of 65 they will be able to ask their employer who must consider their request seriously. By allowing people to work past retirement age, this new legislation aims to be inclusive and seeks to encourage the independence of older people. Unlike other forms of discrimination, ageism is often complex and subtle but has the potential to affect us all.

To understand the negative image of old age we need to consider why youth is so highly valued. Two phrases that sum up the association between youth, attractiveness and age in relation to women are 'growing old gracefully' and 'mutton dressed as lamb'. These phrases make assumptions about age and appropriate actions, behaviours and appearances. Mutton is older and tougher meat in comparison to youthful tender lamb (Fairhurst, 1998).

Pause for thought
- Can you think of any similar descriptions of older men dressing in an 'inappropriate' manner?

The Changing Structure of Scotland's Population

This section looks at the increasing number of older people living in Scotland and how this is increasing in size as a proportion of the population. This change has serious implications for the provision of welfare services.

One of the most significant features of contemporary society is a general increase in the population over pensionable age. This marked growth in the proportion of older people means that living to old age is a common experience and death before old age is the exception. The trend towards an ageing population is accelerating and is often referred to as the **'demographic time bomb'**.

In 1911, people over 65 formed 5.2 per cent of the population. By 1996, this had increased to 15.7 per cent and by 1997 it was 18.11 per cent. The most recent population projections for Scotland estimate how the age structure of the population is expected to change in the next 25 years (see **Table 12.1**).

The total population of Scotland is currently 4.9 million. Older people comprise one fifth of the population. This means that there are approximately one million older people living in Scotland. Of these, one in three lives alone and 4.9 per cent live in communal establishments such as care homes or long-stay hospitals. Of those aged over 85 years, 21.9 per cent stay in communal establishments.

The over 80s are the most rapidly growing age group. Women live longer than men on average and therefore single and widowed women form a large proportion of the older population. More than three quarters (77 per cent) of pensioners living alone are women. What these figures illustrate is that more and more people are surviving 'early old age' and living to be 'very old'.

Table 12.1 Population projections for Scotland: 2004 – 2019 (Percentage of the population)				
	Projections			
	2004	**2009**	**2014**	**2019**
Children under 16	18.8	17.8	17.3	17.2
Working ages 16-64/59*	62.8	62.8	64.9	60.4
Pensionable ages 65/60 and over*	18.5	19.5	17.9	22.5
65/60 – 74	11.4	12.0	9.9	14.0
75 – 84	5.5	5.6	5.9	6.2
85 and over	1.6	1.9	2.1	2.3

*Pensionable age is currently 65 years for men and 60 years for women until 2010; between 2010 and 2020 pensionable age for women increases to 65 years and the figures take account of that. (Source: General Register for Scotland, 2005 (www.scrol.gov.uk).)

Ways of Thinking about Older People: Theories of Gerontology

This section looks at the various theories used in **gerontology** – the study of ageing. Gerontologists use a number of theories to study the process of growing old. Theories are sets of ideas or beliefs. They are important because they are concerned with trying to *explain* rather than simply *describe* social events (see Sweeney, **Chapter 2** and Law and Law, **Chapter 4**).

In order to explain the problems associated with growing old, gerontology has traditionally focused on the **medical model** of health, which tends to portray older people 'as a social problem'. The medical model regards ageing as an inevitable biological process whereby the body grows, matures and then physically deteriorates. By focusing on physical deterioration, this approach emphasises the decline and loss of mental and physical abilities. Widely accepted by the medical profession, the dominance of this model has led to a tendency amongst doctors to view health problems associated with old age as being inevitable and therefore not worth treating (Bond *et al*, 1999).

The medical model of ageing has been challenged by social gerontologists who use a number of theories to study the *social* rather than the *biological* context of ageing. Social, cultural, economic and environmental factors all play a role in shaping the experience of old age.

Disengagement Theory

Disengagement theory (Cumming and Hendry, 1961) suggests that as people reach old age they gradually remove themselves from participating in society. People disengage in terms of their social contacts, roles and responsibilities. Disengagement has been likened to a leaf or piece of fruit withering in that the process is one of very gradual loss. The process of disengagement probably begins in mid-life when changes in perception occur. These changes draw attention to the value of life and people start to feel that there is 'no time for all I must or want to do'. As a result, people reduce their attachments to people, groups, material possessions and ideas.

Some people may also select and allocate time to activities that they see as important, such as spending more time with their family or visiting foreign places. This change in perception can include a change in attitude towards work and career, whereby older people might become less motivated, less interested in promotion and achieving targets. This process prepares the older person and society in general for the ultimate disengagement in terms of incapacity or death.

Pause for thought
- Can you think of some people who have changed their attitude to work, their activities and ambitions as they grew older?

Disengagement is said to be an inevitable and mutually satisfying process that allows individuals to prepare in advance for the ultimate disengagement of death. The theory claims that as death is inevitable, society and the older person prepare, so that when it comes the individual has divested him/herself of life's functions and associations and is ready for it. An example of disengagement is retirement from the paid work force when individuals cease to be essential to the functioning of society. On this basis their death does not result in any significant disruption since older people have ceased to be part of the work force.

A number of problems with this perspective have been highlighted. Bond *et al* (1999) argue that this theory is based on an assumption that disengagement is a natural and inevitable occurrence. They point out that many older people may still be actively engaged in society, while for others old age is part of a lifelong experience of non-engagement and social isolation. Disengagement theory also fails to explore how access to financial resources and the social circumstances in which people live can influence how people adjust to old age. The final criticism that can be made of disengagement theory is its failure to appreciate that certain social practices (such as enforced retirement from the workforce) and cultural values (ageism) combine to ensure that disengagement actually does become the experience of many older people.

Activity or Role Theory

Activity or **role theory** as it is sometimes called was developed as a response to disengagement theory (Parsons, 1961). According to Parsons (1961), it is the loss of the work role that causes men in particular to experience uncertainty about their social identity. Once they retire, they are no longer engaged in an activity that is culturally defined as purposeful and they also discover that the ties they have to the wider community are weakened. Disengagement theorists see this role loss as something to be positively welcomed by older people, as it reduces demands on their time and energy. However, activity or role theory focuses on role stability and continuity as being necessary to ensure a successful transition into old age.

Activity theory asserts that the majority of older people have a natural inclination to continue to pursue an active social life and maintain links with the wider community (Havinghurst, 1963). Activity theory assumes that role loss leads to a reduction in self-esteem and low morale. Consequently, successful ageing depends on maintaining a high level of activity by ensuring that some roles are preserved and any which are lost are replaced. In the interest of psychological and social well-being, retired people should be encouraged to take up activities commensurate with their age, health and personality that promote continued social involvement.

These theories have important implications for the social inclusion of older people. By encouraging older people to relinquish some of their roles and responsibilities, disengagement theory promotes age isolation and social exclusion. On the other hand, activity theory supports integration and social inclusion. It suggests that new roles need to be adopted to prevent disengagement leading to social isolation and exclusion.

Structured Dependency Theory

This theory centres on the social creation of **structured dependency** (Townsend, 1981; Walker, 1981). According to the structured dependency argument:

- Older people are constructed, or perceived, as being dependent on the state.

- There is a structural relationship between older people and the rest of society.

- It is the state and society who construct the institutions and rules within which old age and the experience of ageing is defined.

A primary cause of older people's dependence is that they are excluded from the paid work force through enforced retirement at a particular age and as a result have restricted access to a wide range of resources such as income. The potential effects of retirement are poverty, inequality and a reduction in social relationships (Bond *et al*, 1999). Thus, many of the experiences affecting older people come about from structural causes such as a particular division of labour and inequality, rather than as a natural result of the ageing process.

In other words, the state and society create the framework of institutions and rules, such as retirement, pensions and the benefits system, within which the problems of older people emerge or are indeed 'manufactured'. Thus, in the everyday management of the economy and welfare systems, the position of older people is subtly shaped and changed. Older people are one of the groups who are at greatest risk of poverty because of their dependence largely on welfare benefits. They do not encounter inequalities for the first time when they retire. On the contrary, they carry into old age the inequalities of health, wealth and income experienced during their earlier life.

Pause for thought

As you can see there are a number of competing theories of old age.

- Which of them do you find most useful in explaining the experiences of older people?

Health and Wellbeing in Later Life

This section provides a picture of the health and wellbeing of older people and highlights the health inequalities they experience. It will focus particularly on **dementia** because it is more prevalent amongst older people.

The physical changes that come with age are varied and do not necessarily develop at the same time in each older person. Many people think that there is nothing that can be done for older people who are unwell since it is assumed that the person's condition is simply due to his or her age. In fact, older people who experience illness tend to suffer from treatable conditions of one sort or another.

Health problems which affect older people are often strikingly similar to those in other age groups, with *four* important distinctions:

1. Many conditions are more common in old age, e.g. cancer, arthritis, cataracts and dementia.

2. Some conditions predominantly affect older people, e.g. strokes.

3. Several acute conditions such as the super-bug MRSA (methicillin-resistant Staphylococcus aureus) and other infections carry much greater hazards for older people.

4. Often older people experience several conditions at the same time, thereby amplifying their disability.

According to Raab and MacDonald (2004), the *four* most commonly reported causes of illness and disability in older people are:

1. Mobility problems with legs and feet.

2. Heart and circulatory problems.
3. Chest and respiratory problems.
4. Eye complaints.

Older people experiencing health problems do not always seek the help that they need, and when they do, their problems may be dismissed as insignificant or inevitable. This suggests that there are sets of essentially ageist values that perpetuate the notion that older people's needs are of less importance than those of younger people. Whilst there is no evidence of systematic discrimination against older people, research has found that there is a tendency to support the care of younger people rather than those who are nearing the end of their lives, to whom services were rationed (Langan, 1998; Busfield, 2000).

According to Langan (1998), there are *five* main methods of rationing:

1. **Delay**: Services are rationed by the appointment system and delays in seeing specialists.

2. **Dilution of services**: Refers to the provision of some forms of services but not necessarily the most effective and the most expensive forms.

3. **Denial of services**: Some treatments are simply not available through certain health authorities. Age is often a significant factor in determining access to some surgical procedures.

4. **Deterrence:** A cost may be attached to some treatments or services and that may deter people from using them.

5. **Exclusion:** This refers to the power of clinicians to determine who is in need of treatment and the type of treatment to be used.

The health needs of older people are similar to those of the population in general, so it should be difficult to discriminate purely on the grounds of age. Age discrimination, however , can work to the advantage of older people. They have recently been offered free flu vaccinations on the basis of increased risk, while those not deemed to be at risk have to pay for this treatment.

In general, the quality of life for the majority of older people living independently is not greatly influenced by the rationing of health care. Rather it is influenced by very basic factors, such as the availability of heated homes, the ability to walk, to use transport, to move around the home safely and to have support from and contact with other people. For many older people isolation, poverty, bereavement and declining health are all part of the experience of later life, all of which can have an impact on mental health and wellbeing.

Dementia

The most common mental health condition affecting older people is **dementia**. Dementia is not in fact a 'modern' disease. As a condition it has been described for many hundreds of years. However, its prevalence is increasing and it can also affect younger people.

Dementia currently affects 62,000 people in Scotland, of which 1,600 are under the age of 65 years. One in 20 people over the age of 65 years and one in five (20 per cent) over the age of 80 suffer from some form of dementia. Overall, 66 per cent of sufferers are female (Alzheimer's Scotland (www.alzscot.org.uk), 2005). As people are now living longer, the number of people with dementia is expected to increase steadily over the next 20 years: it is estimated that by 2016 there will be about 71,000 and by 2026 there will 84,300 people with dementia in Scotland (General Registrar's of Scotland, 2005).

What is Meant by Dementia?

Dementia is the name given to a range of progressive brain disorders. There are nearly 100 different types of dementia, the most common of which is Alzheimer's disease. Other forms of dementia include vascular dementia, mild cognitive impairment (MCI), Pick's disease and dementia with Lewes bodies. Rarer forms include Creutzfeldt-Jacobs disease (CJD), Korsakoff's syndrome and supranuclear palsy (Sutcliffe, 2001).

The Disease Process

The main feature of dementia is a loss of brain cells. The loss of a few brain cells makes no real difference to our ability to function. However, in dementia the loss of brain cells increases to such an extent that it can have a catastrophic effect on the individual. People are often not diagnosed with dementia until their symptoms begin to affect the quality of their lives and their ability to carry out everyday activities.

Alzheimer's disease begins gradually with minor changes in the individual's abilities or behaviour. Common early signs might be loss of short term memory so recent events or conversations may be forgotten about; there may be slight confusion and the repeating of questions and phrases. The individual may also find it harder to make decisions, may lose interest in other people or activities and develop a readiness to blame others for 'stealing' items s/he ha s mislaid. As the disease progresses the changes become more marked. The individual may become increasingly forgetful, fail to recognise people, become easily upset, angry or aggressive owing to frustration and the perception that 'something is wrong'. Other symptoms may include wandering off and becoming lost, mixing up day and night and being confused about time, 'inappropriate' behaviour such as going outside in nightclothes, putting themselves and others at risk by forgetting to switch off cookers or fires and so on. The person will then need more help to manage the activities of daily living and might need frequent reminders or help to eat, wash, dress and use the toilet.

By the later stages of Alzheimer's, people will gradually have become totally dependent on others for care. Memory loss may be almost complete, with the person being unable to recognise family members, famil iar objects or surroundings. They will have lost weight and have become increasingly frail and may no longer be able to walk, eventually becoming confined to a wheelchair or bed. Other symptoms of this final stage of the disease include difficulty in eating and swallowing, loss of speech and incontinence.

There is no single cause of dementia. Researchers believe that many factors work together and lead to the onset of the disease (Sutcliffe, 2001). The main risk factor for dementia is age and if we consider possible treatments for this condition we find that there is the potential for discrimination against older people. Whilst there is presently no cure for dementia, there are a number of drug treatments that can alleviate the symptoms and slow down the disease process. Until recently many health authorities had a policy of *not* prescribing these drugs. Their decision was made on the basis of cost and uncertainty about the effectiveness of the treatment. In 2002, a new drug was licensed for use in the UK, but it is not yet widely available through the NHS. The majority of the health authorities who do fund drugs for Alzheimer's restrict their use to specialists, which effectively rations its use.

The majority of people with dementia are cared for by their partners or other family members, who may themselves be old, in poor health or have other work or family commitments. Therefore, an increasing number of sufferers need help from health and social care services. Community care is the key policy under which services for all older people, with or without dementia, are provided.

Provision of Care: Policy and Legislation

This section outlines the main policies and legislation that shape the delivery of community care in Scotland. It outlines key policies and legislation, such as community care, free personal and nursing care, the Griffiths Report (1988), the NHS and Community Care Act 1990 and the Community Care and Health (Scotland) Act 2002.

Community Care is the main policy that directs the provision of care for older people in Scotland. The main aim of community care policy has always been to maintain individuals in their own homes or in small homes in the community wherever possible, rather than provide care in long stay institutions. It was believed that not only was this the best option from a humanitarian and moral perspective, but it was also a less expensive form of care.

Community Care is not a new idea. As a policy it has been around since the early 1950s and supported by successive UK governments. Despite this support, the number of in-patients in large institutions continued to increase and very little changed until the 1980s when again there was increasing criticism about the quality of long term care. There was also concern about the experiences of people leaving institutional care and being left to fend for themselves in the community. In 1986, the Audit Commission report, *Making a Reality of Community Care*, highlighted the slow progress being made to promote care in the community. This report was a catalyst for the Griffiths Report (1988) and subsequent legislation.

The Griffiths Report (1988)

Sir Roy Griffiths, the then chairman of Sainsburys, was asked by Prime Minister Margaret Thatcher to examine the entire system of community care. His report, *Community Care: Agenda for Action* (Department of Health, 1988), prompted the subsequent 1990 NHS and Community Care Act. Griffiths believed that many of the problems facing the welfare state were caused by a lack of strong effective leadership and management and that community care was not working because no one wanted to accept the responsibility for it. He referred to community care as being 'everybody's distant cousin but nobody's baby'. Griffiths intended his plan to sort out the mess in 'no-man's land', that grey area lying between health and social services, which included the long term care of dependent groups such as older people. The Griffiths Report made six key recommendations, elements which were included in the 1990 NHS and Community Care Act.

The NHS and Community Care Act 1990

The NHS and Community Care Act 1990 was the first major reform of the NHS since its inception in 1948. Based on the two white papers, *Working for Patients* (1989) and *Caring for People* (1991), this was the first legislation to try to bridge the gap between health boards and local authority social services.

This legislation was influenced by the **New Right** ideology (see Sweeney, **Chapter 2**), which believed that because the state funded, provided and purchased care for the population, the welfare system was inefficient and bureaucratic. As we have already seen in **Chapters 2** and **4**, the New Right believed that efficient and good quality services could be achieved by a **'mixed economy of care'**. In order to achieve this, local authorities had to allow care to be delivered by a variety of providers, including organisations from the independent sector.

Under this Act, social work departments were given the responsibility for community care for older people. Because they had to purchase services on behalf of their clients from other organisations, social work departments became 'enablers' rather than 'providers' of services. This situation was referred to as a 'quasi' or artificial market. Services were to be provided on the basis of what the older person needed rather than being determined by what was actually available. These needs were ascertained by means of a community care assessment. Home care, day and respite services were to be developed to enable people to live in their own homes wherever possible. This legislation was also the first time that the needs of carers had been taken into account.

This legislation marked a watershed in the development of health and social care services. Not only did it make radical changes to the way services were organised with the introduction of the **'quasi-market'** and mixed economy of care (see Sweeney, **Chapter 2**, Law, **Chapter 3** and Law and Law, **Chapter 4**), but it redefined the boundaries between health and social care. It placed the responsibility for community care with social services, where previously this had been provided by the NHS. Services provided by the NHS are free, whereas those provided by social services are **'means tested'** and only free to those on a low income.

Joint Future Agenda

Since devolution in 1999, there has been a determined move to deliver more integrated health and social care services for older people in Scotland. This is being driven by the Joint Future Unit set up by the Scottish Executive in 2000 to monitor and evaluate the implementation of the Joint Future Agenda (www.scotland.gov.uk/jfa).

The aim of the Joint Future Agenda (JFA) is to provide better and more integrated community care services. This is to be achieved by developing joint working relationships between local authorities, health boards and a range of other voluntary and independent organisations. Joint working is not a new idea, having been a recommendation in the Griffiths Report (1988), but different professions and organisations had difficulty working together and this had prevented the delivery of 'seamless services' as envisaged by Griffiths. The development of joint working is made possible by joint financial arrangements whereby local authorities and health boards are jointly responsible for the cost of particular services, for example, aids and equipment. Thus, since 2002, all community care services for older people in Scotland are jointly funded and provided by the local authority and health board working in partnership.

JFA also aims to prevent hospital admissions and facilitate early discharges of older people and thus prevent **'bed blocking'**. These objectives are to be achieved though:

1. Single Shared Assessment.
2. Intensive Home Support Services.
3. Rapid Response Services.
4. More short breaks or respite.
5. Joint Equipment and Adaptation Service.
6. Joint Resourcing and Joint Management for health, housing and social work.

Many large local authorities and health boards have now established joint occupational therapy services for aids and equipment and have integrated health and social care rapid response and intensive home support teams. Others are currently putting in place systems for sharing information across health and social work. All potential service developments are now planned within the context of the Joint Future Agenda.

Regulation of Care (Scotland) Act 2001

The main aim of the Regulation of Care (Scotland) Act 2001 is to improve standards of social care services. The new Act means that far more care services and people who work in them will come under scrutiny and should conform to established standards. Failure of a care service or an individual to comply with the Act and associated regulations may mean they are de-registered and, therefore, unable to continue providing care services.

The Act created *two* new bodies that work closely together:

1.   The Scottish Commission for the Regulation of Care (Care Commission).
2.   The Scottish Social Services Council (SSSC).

The Care Commission's main function is to register and inspect all care services. In doing this they must take account of the National Care Standards for particular services, such as those for care homes and home support services. The SSSC is responsible for maintaining a register of social workers and other persons employed to provide a care service. The respective English equivalents of the Care Commission and the SSSC are the Commission of Social Care Inspection and the Social Services Council.

Community Care and Health Act 2002

In relation to the long term care of older people, the Community Care and Health Act 2002 introduced *two* important changes. The first change was the introduction of Free Personal Care for older people. Issues about long term care came to a head following the report in 1999 of the Royal Commission on Long Term Care (The Sutherland Report), *With Respect to Old Age: Long Term Care – Rights and Responsibilities*. The Commission had looked at options for a sustainable system of funding of long term care for older people in the UK. It considered the provision of care both in the people's own homes and in other settings. It recommended that personal care, not including 'board and lodging' costs, should be free in all settings and not, as before, to only the relatively poorest older people living at home or those in hospital. The UK government refused to accept this recommendation, arguing that given the increasing numbers of older people requiring care, it would be too expensive to implement. The Scottish Executive also refused, but eventually succumbed to political pressure to implement the policy of Free Personal and Nursing Care for Older People. This policy is unique to Scotland.

Free Personal and Nursing Care

The definition of personal care contained in the Community Care and Health Act 2002 is mainly based on the one used by the Royal Commission on Long Term Care, except that it takes account of the needs arising from cognitive impairment and behavioural problems as well as physical frailty. It also places importance on counselling and psychological support, particularly for people with dementia. Thus, the definition of personal care used in Scotland differs from that used by social services in England and Wales. The definition of personal care is used as a basis for

Community Care Assessments. It essentially describes the range of tasks that might be undertaken by home carers employed by the statutory care sector. It also reflects accurately the range of care activities undertaken by informal carers.

Personal care is defined in terms of *seven* dimensions:

1. **Personal Hygiene:** bathing, showering, hair washing, shaving, oral hygiene, nail care.

2. **Personal Assistance:** assistance with dressing, surgical appliances, prostheses, mechanical and manual aids, assistance to go to and get up from bed.

3. **Continence Management:** toileting, catheter care, skin care, incontinence laundry and bed changing.

4. **Food and Diet:** assistance with eating, special diets, managing different types of meal service and food preparation.

5. **Problems of Immobility:** dealing with the consequences of not being able to move.

6. **Simple Treatments:** assistance with medication, eye drops, application of creams and lotions, simple dressings and oxygen therapy.

Rights for Carers

The second change introduced by the Community Care and Health Act 2002 was the creation of new rights for informal or unpaid carers. The intention is to provide carers with adequate support services to ensure the continuation of care giving in the community. This is discussed in more detail in the following section on the provision of care.

Mental Health (Care and Treatment) (Scotland) Act 2003

This major piece of legislation came into force at the beginning of October 2005. It is an important piece of legislation because it increases the rights and protection of people with mental disorders, many of whom are older people. The Act places additional duties on local authorities to provide care and support services for people with 'mental disorders' – a term that encompasses mental illness, learning disability and personality disorder. The Act introduced changes needed to develop community based mental health services, involvement of services users and carers in decisions concerning treatment and respect for the human rights of people with mental health problems. The provisions of this new Act are intended to ensure that care and compulsory measures of detention can be used only when there is a significant risk to the safety or welfare of the patient or other persons.

Direct Payments

Direct payments enable individuals to direct and manage the care they receive. A direct payment is money paid by a local authority social work department directly to a person whom it has assessed as needing community care. The council makes the payment instead of arranging services. This helps increase the flexibility, choice and control older people have over their lives, so that they can live more independently. Older people can decide to become responsible for buying some or all of the care that they need. Direct payments can be used to buy services from an agency, a private or voluntary organisation or local authority, or to employ staff such as a personal assistant.

Although local authorities have a duty to provide direct payments, some have been very slow to do so and older people are wary about purchasing services from private agencies. From February 2004 to March 2005, only about 500 older people in Scotland received direct payments (Scottish Executive, 2005). This figure is very low compared to the level of uptake in England, where this method of providing services was introduced as an experiment ten years ago and has become increasingly popular.

Provision of Care: the Care Journey

This section uses case studies to explore how care is provided and by whom. It will begin by discussing informal care and will also consider the care services available from the statutory, voluntary and private sectors.

The majority of older people lead independent lives without the need for help and support from others. Older people who report that they need help or care are in the minority. For the 75-84 age group, only 17 per cent of men and 23 per cent of women said they needed care. Even amongst women over the age of 85, when people are most likely to be dependent, only 47 per cent said they needed care (Scottish Household Survey, 2003, cited in Raab and MacDonald, 2004). Nonetheless, the likelihood of needing care increases with age and infirmity.

257

In Scotland, local authorities remain the biggest providers of care services; they solely provide 70 per cent of home care services, with 30 per cent solely provided by private and voluntary organisations. The remainder is provided by a combination of local authority and the private and voluntary sectors (www.scotland.gov.uk/stats/ccare.asp). This contrasts with England where the private and voluntary sectors provide 54 per cent of home care services.

Informal Care

The vast majority of older people are cared for by their families. This type of care is sometimes referred to as 'informal' or 'family' care. The term currently used by the Scottish Executive and service providers and suggested by family carers themselves is 'unpaid care'. These terms are used to distinguish the care given by family members from that provided by care workers who are employed and, therefore, paid to provide a service.

The role of informal carers in the delivery of community care is paramount and Scotland is in many ways leading the UK in supporting carers. Formal recognition of carers was enshrined in the NHS and Community Care Act 1990 and the Carers (Recognition and Services) Act 1995. A continued commitment to carers was made by the Scottish Executive's (1999) *Strategy for Carers in Scotland*. This policy committed extra funding for social work departments to develop information, support and short break services for carers. The Community Care and Health (Scotland) Act 2002 also contained important sections relating to informal carers. Under this legislation carers are regarded as 'partners' in the provision of care. They have a right to an assessment of their needs and any services provided as a result are seen as part of the overall care package to older people and carers are not charged for them. This differs from English legislation where services are provided to the carer, who is seen by local authorities as the client and who may be charged for any service provided. A recent report on the future of informal unpaid care in Scotland reaffirms the Scottish Executive's commitment to support and provide training for carers (Scottish Executive, 2006)

What is Informal or Unpaid Care?

Informal care can be thought of as a relationship between two people; one a care *giver* and the other a care *recipient*. The care may be on a 24 hour basis and may or may not take place in the home of the carer. This kind of care is usually provided 'free of charge'. This is what makes informal care qualitatively different to the 'formal' care provided by paid carers employed by welfare agencies such as social work departments. One is a business arrangement and one is not. For every paid carer there are five unpaid carers (Scottish Executive, 2006). The exact value of caring to the economy is a contested question, but one recent report estimates that unpaid care saves the Scottish taxpayer £4.3 billion a year (Lothian Anti-Poverty Alliance, 2004, cited in Scottish Executive, 2006).

Who Provides Informal Care?

Box 12.1 Case Study: Mrs Thomson

Mrs Thomson's father, Mr Mack, was found lying unconscious in the street and admitted to hospital. Until this emergency admission he had lived quite independently in his own home. Mrs Thomson, a 44 year old carer, explains how she became her father's carer and what she has to do for him:

"My dad was brought home from hospital on the understanding that he wouldn't last 6 weeks. That was four years ago. He used to be about 11 stones and when I got him out of hospital he was only 6 stones and when I took him back for a check up he was 8 stones. He just got better and better and after eight weeks the hospital staff said 'don't bring him back.' But he still wasn't able to look after himself so he just stayed here with us... I do everything for my dad. Everything! When he came out at first I thought, 'how am I going to manage?' He'll be embarrassed. I'll be embarrassed. But I get him up, shower him, toilet him, dress him, cut his hair, see to his catheter, everything ... because he can't do it himself. He doesn't want home carers or social workers coming in to help because he doesn't like anyone else washing him, he says that they don't clean him right. It's not easy. I get myself up to high doh about my dad. Sometimes I shout at him. He can be difficult and very moody. He can lose his temper easily. I find that he's far more pleasant with everybody else than he is with me. I get all the grumps and moans and the bad moods and the tempers... But I know that he used to worry that he would end his days in an old folk's home and I suppose I have kept him from that. When it comes to the crunch and it's time to say farewell, I'll be able to put my head on the pillow that night and know I've done my best" (in Statham, 2003).

- Mrs Thomson says, 'I do everything for my dad'. Take a few minutes to list the activities that you think she might have to undertake when looking after him.

- Now put yourself into the role of care manager. You are responsible for identifying the needs of your client. *Who* would you consider to be your client – Mrs Thompson or her father Mr Mack?

Reading the section on informal care will help you answer this.

According to recent statistics there are estimated to be about 668,200 informal carers in Scotland, of whom approximately three quarters are looking after older people (Raab and MacDonald, 2004). Around 50 per cent of carers are looking after someone over the age of 75. This means that one in eight people provide informal care at any one time, and 503,000 of those are providing care to people living outside their own homes (Community Care Statistics (www.scotland.gov.uk/stats/ccare.asp), 2004). A carer may be female, male, a wife, a mother, a husband, brother, sister, cousin or even a friend or neighbour. Sixty per cent of carers are women (Carers UK, 2002). In Scotland, the 50-65 year old age group are the most likely to be providing care. People often have no choice in whether they want to become a carer or not.

Once an older person in hospital is deemed by the doctor to be fit and a discharge date determined, a community care assessment is carried out and follow-on arrangements are put in place. The usual period for local discharge planning is six weeks. For most people, the necessary care support and accommodation arrangements are put in place in the community without delay and patients like Mrs Thomson's father (see **Box 12.1**, above) experience a safe and appropriate discharge from hospital.

Delayed Discharges

However, not all older people are so fortunate in having a relative who is willing and able to look after them. In the case of Ethel (see **Box 12.2**), no one was able to take her home and she remained in hospital until other arrangements could be made. This situation is referred to as a 'delayed discharge', and because Ethel was occupying a bed when she was deemed fit for discharge she was labelled as a 'bed blocker'. In other words, she was occupying a bed that was needed for another patient but she could not be discharged until appropriate care arrangements had been put in place.

In July 2005, a total of 1465 older people in Scotland were ready for discharge from hospital, 15 of these people had been ready for a year or more (ISD Scotland, 2005). The reasons for delay include:

1. Awaiting a community care assessment.
2. Awaiting funding for a care home.
3. Awaiting a place in a care home or specialist residential facility.
4. Awaiting a healthcare assessment or treatment.
5. Other legal or financial issues.
6. Patient exercising their statutory right of choice.

Box 12.2 Case Study: Ethel

One evening Ethel tripped over a rug in her hallway and banged her head on the corner of a table. In great pain and unable to walk properly Ethel managed to phone her GPs surgery for help. The doctor dressed the wound on Ethel's forehead but felt her condition was not serious enough to warrant sending her to hospital. Instead he arranged for the *Rapid Response* service to visit her that evening and the following morning. After spending two days in her bed, Ethel was still unable to walk and she was sent to the local hospital for an x-ray, which showed that she had broken her hip and required surgery.

After six weeks in hospital plans were being made to discharge 90 year old Ethel as she was considered fit to go home. However, her wound was infected with MRSA and she was having difficulty walking again. There was concern that she might not be able to look after herself now as she had also become very forgetful and rather confused.

Ethel's only daughter lived 300 miles away and because of her own poor health was unable to care for her mother. Because her bed was needed for another patient, arrangements were made for Ethel to go home under the care of the *Intensive Home Support Team*. The team visited Ethel four times a day to help her with all the activities of daily living. They got her up in the morning and helped her back to bed in the evening. The community nurse came in every day to dress her wound and to make sure she was taking her medicines (Statham, 2003).

Rapid Response Services

Rapid Response Services were established under the Joint Future Agenda in order to prevent unnecessary admissions to hospital. For an older person who has fallen at night and is at risk of hospital admission, it means a rapid service provided at home to prevent unnecessary admission. This could mean a care worker or a community health care assistant going into her home within an hour of the telephone call, to spend the rest of the night with her until home care and other services are arranged to support her at home, where older people want to stay. In Ethel's case, however, she eventually had to be admitted because of her broken hip (see **Box 12.2**, above).

Intensive Home Support

Intensive Home Support services were also developed under the Joint Future Agenda. The aim of this service is to facilitate early discharge from hospital and so prevent 'bed blocking'. The Intensive Home Support team is a multi-disciplinary team comprising community nurses, care assistants, social workers and occupational therapists. They provide whatever level of care is required to maintain an older person in her/his own home. This service can last for a number of weeks until the patient makes a complete or partial recovery and the level of support can be safely reduced. For someone like Ethel in hospital, it means that a higher level of service and rehabilitation can be provided in her own home rather than in hospital or having to go into a nursing home. This means that Ethel, living on her own, was not discharged to a cold, dark home but received intensive home care to help her regain her ability to cook, wash and dress, maintain her independence and dignity (see **Box 12.2**, above).

Home Care Services

Intensive Home Support is usually withdrawn once the older person is settled at home and routine home care services have been arranged. Home care services can be funded and arranged privately by the older person and her/his family, or they can be commissioned by the local authority on behalf of the older person. In some areas this service can be provided directly by local authority home care staff or bought from a voluntary or private organisation. Home care services entail a paid carer going into the home of the older person and providing whatever care is required, whether that is personal care or simply help with domestic chores. Home care services can also be enhanced by other support services, such as **Meals on Wheels**. These services are not free, they are means-tested. Older people are subjected to a financial assessment and charged according to their level of disposable income. The local authorities providing the services submit a monthly account to the older person.

Box 12.3 Case Study: Mrs Thomson continued . . .

Mrs Thomson found caring for her father stressful and very tiring and she was eventually treated for depression. When she felt that she could no longer manage to look after him on her own, she approached her GP for help. Her GP made a referral to the social work department and a social worker made contact with Mrs Thomson to arrange an *assessment* of her and her father's needs. On completion of the assessments, the social worker discussed with Mrs Thomson and her father how their needs could be met.

Mrs Thomson needed emotional and physical support. Her father needed personal care and interaction with other people. Services such as *day care* and *short breaks* were thought suitable for meeting these needs and were subsequently arranged. Day care was provided three days a week and a two week short break arranged for the following month. Whilst her father was initially reluctant to attend the day care centre, after a week or two he looked forward to meeting up with the new friends he had made there. Mrs Thomson found having more time to herself enabled her to continue looking after her father and the short break allowed her and her husband to take a well earned holiday knowing that her father was being cared for in her absence (Statham, 2003).

Single Shared Assessment (SSA)

Single Shared Assessments are at the heart of community care policy for older people. The aim of single shared assessment is to end the practice of multiple assessments by a range of different professionals such as social workers, occupational therapists and community nurses. This means that an older person will have one visit from a professional such as a community nurse, to carry out a community care assessment. The information gathered by the nurse is recorded on a duplicate form and shared with other professionals in the community care team. A copy of the assessment is also left with the older person or her/his carer.

Day Care Services

Day Care Services are provided in a centre to which older people are brought together for social activities. It provides brief periods of care from which older people return to their own homes. Older people may attend the day care centre every day or just two or three times a week. Some day care centres that cater specifically for people with dementia are open seven days a week. Day care is also a place where people's health can be monitored and potential problems dealt with promptly. These centres are provided by a range of service providers and may be located in local hospitals, community centres or on private premises.

Short Break Services

These services are sometimes referred to as **respite care**. Short breaks and respite care involve an older person being temporarily separated from their carer (if they have one). A key feature of this service is that the break should be a positive experience in order to improve the quality of life for the older person. Breaks or respite care can be provided in a variety of settings such as a hospital unit, a care home, a guest house or purpose built unit. These facilities may be close to the older person's home or further away. These services may be provided by the local authority or through individual arrangements paid for by 'direct payments'.

Care Homes

> **Box 12.4 Case Study: Ethel continued . . .**
>
> Since Ethel had been discharged from hospital her physical condition improved but she was becoming increasingly confused. Sometimes she thought her home carer was her daughter but when her daughter came to visit, Ethel didn't recognise her. She had also taken to wandering out of the house during the night dressed in her nightclothes and on occasions had almost caused a fire by leaving pans on the cooker. Thanks to an efficient smoke detector and a watchful neighbour, relatively little damage had been done. In consultation with Ethel, her daughter, the GP and community nurse, the social worker arranged for admission to a care home. Initially this was for a six week assessment period after which a decision would be made as to whether Ethel would stay in the care home or return to her own home. There was a marked improvement in Ethel's physical and mental health after six weeks in the home and her daughter was happy for her mother to remain there (Statham, 2003).

Care homes provide permanent or occasional periods of care for older people who can no longer live, or have difficulty living, in their own homes. In 2005, there were 969 care homes in Scotland providing places to 33,716 older people. Of these, 186 were in the statutory sector, 638 in the private sector and 145 in the voluntary sector (Community Care Statistics, www.scotland.gov.uk/stats/ccare.asp, 2006).

Long term care for older people has been transferred out of the free-at-the point-of-use health service and into that of the means-tested social care sector. As a result, older people are increasingly being required to use their savings and the value of their homes to fund long term care. The introduction of free personal and nursing care has somewhat eased this situation for many older people. For those who cannot afford to pay for long term care in a home, the cost is met by the local social work department.

For many older people care homes are associated with loss of liberty and autonomy, stigma and poor quality care and are often viewed as places of 'last resort'. Concern about the adequacy of care homes has brought about the establishment of Care Standards and the Care Commission, both of which aim to improve and maintain high standards of care. Since 2002, all care homes are regulated by the Care Commission. Previously, private nursing homes were regulated by health boards and residential homes by local authorities.

The Mixed Economy of Welfare

Providing care which meets the complex needs of older people can be challenging for local authority social work departments which have to co-ordinate a mixture of provision for their clients through a number of providers. This is what is known as the mixed economy of care. The following case study illustrates how the mixed economy operates, i.e. services from the statutory, voluntary, private and informal sectors come together to provide support for older people.

Box 12.4 Case Study: Mr Roberts

Mr Roberts is 87 years old and lives on his own in a Church of Scotland sheltered housing complex where a warden is available if required. He attends a lunch club run by Age Concern in his local church hall. He pays for a local authority home carer to come for four hours a week to clean his flat and shop for him. Any other help with financial and business matters is provided by his 60 year old son who visits twice a week. Every four months he goes into a private care home for a fortnight's respite care (short break). His situation is monitored and future needs discussed with his care manager.

Who is providing care for Mr Roberts?

- Statutory sector: home carer, care management and assessment of needs.
- Voluntary sector: Age Concern lunch club, sheltered housing.
- Private sector: care home.
- Informal sector: son's visits.

Conclusion

This chapter has highlighted themes of social division, inclusion and exclusion, change and continuity. Social divisions and exclusion are created by labelling persons over a certain age as being 'old people' and by enforced retirement at a particular age. By encouraging older people to lead full and active lives, policy is trying to be inclusive, but poor health, limited mobility and dependence on state benefits also encourage the exclusion of older people.

There have been attempts to reduce social divisions and exclusion by changing the ways in which older people are perceived and treated. This has entailed changes to legislation that will remove age discrimination in the workplace and enforced retirement at a particular age. Other changes have seen a move towards promoting the independence of older people by providing Direct Payments and more integrated health and social care services. Despite these changes there are elements of continuity in the care of older people. For example, the majority of care for older people continues to be provided by informal carers. Older people also continue to be subjected to ageism. These themes underpin attempts by policymakers and organisations such as Age Concern to promote a positive image of old age as a period of new opportunities. Despite this, old age and the process of growing older continues to be perceived as problematic.

Care for older people is a key responsibility for statutory health and social care services. The care of older people is important because they are major users of health and social care services. Scotland has about one million people aged 65 years and over. Over the coming decades the number of older people in the population will continue to increase. Although poor health is not an inevitable consequence of ageing, older people do experience relatively high levels of longstanding illness and disability. Their use of certain forms of services, particularly emergency hospital in-patient care, has increased substantially in recent years and has encouraged recent changes to health and social care policy.

Key Points

1. People are living longer.

2. The number of older people as a proportion of the population is increasing.

3. Ageism refers to negative attitudes about the ageing process and older people.

4. Older people are the highest users of health and social care services.

5. Certain health conditions such as dementia are more prevalent amongst older people.

6. Older people do not always enjoy the same access to health care as other sections of the population.

7. The majority of care for older people is provided by the family.

8. Welfare services are provided by the informal, statutory , voluntary , and private sectors.

Further Resources

MacDonald, C. (2004) *Older People and Community Care in Scotland: A Review of Recent Research*, Edinburgh, Scottish Executive Central Research Unit
Scottish Executive (2006) *The Future of Unpaid Care in Scotland*, Edinburgh, Scottish Executive

Useful Websites

Age Concern Scotland: www.ageconcernscotland.org.uk
Alzheimer's Scotland: www.alzscot.org.uk
Carers Scotland: www.carerscotland.org.uk
Scottish Executive: www.scotland.gov.uk/Topics/People/older-people, including Community Care Statistics available at: www.scotland.gov.uk/stats/ccare.asp

Bibliography

Age Concern (2004) *How Ageist is Britain?*, www.ageconcern.org.uk/AgeConcern/Documents (accessed 26 March 2006), London, Age Concern
Atcheley, R. (2001) *Continuity and Adaption in Old Age*, Baltimore, MD, John Hopkins Press
Audit Commission (1986) *Making a Reality of Community Care*, PSI, London
Bond, J., Coleman, P. and Peace, S. (eds.) (1999) *Ageing and Society: An Introduction to Social Gerontology* (2nd Edition), London, Sage
Busfield, J. (2000) *Health and Health Care in Modern Britain*, Oxford, Oxford University Press
Bytheway, W. (2000) *Ageism*, Milton Keynes, Open University Press
Carers UK (2002) *Without Us? Calculating the value of carers support*, London, Carers UK
Cumming, E. and Hendry, W. (1961) *Growing Old: The Process of Disengagement*, New York, NY, Basic Books
Department of Health (1991) *Caring for People*, London, HMSO
Department of Health (1988) *Community Care: Agenda for Action* (The Griffiths Report), London, HMSO
Department of Health (1989) *Working for Patients*, London, HMSO
Department of Social Security (1994) *Security, Equality and Choice: the future for pensions*, London, HMSO
Department of Work and Pensions (2005) *Discrimination at Work*, www.direct.gov.uk/Employment/Employees/DiscriminationatWork (accessed on 26

March 2006)

Fairhurst, E. (1998) ''Growing old gracefully' as opposed to 'mutton dressed as lamb': the social construction of recognising older women', in Nettleton, S . and Watson, J. (eds.) (1998) *The Body in Everyday Life*, London, Routledge

Featherstone, M. and Hepworth, M. (1993) 'Images of ageing', in Bond, J., Coleman, P. and Peace, S. (eds.) (1999) *Ageing and Society: An Introduction to Social Gerontology* (2nd Edition), London, Sage

Fulton, M. (2003) *Personal communication about older people as volunteers in charity shops*, Glasgow, Cancer Research

Havinghurst, R. (1963) 'Flexibility and the social roles of the retired', in *American Journal of Sociology*, 59

ISD Scotland (2005) *Local Authority Partner Information on Patients Ready for Discharge in NHS Scotland* (figures from July 2005 census), Edinburgh, NHS National Services

Langan, M. (1998) 'Rationing health care', in Langan, M. (ed .) (1998) *Welfare: Needs, Rights and Risks*, London, Routledge/Open University Press

Langan, M. (ed.) (1998) *Welfare: Needs, Rights and Risks*, London, Routledge/Open University Press

MacDonald, C. (2004) *Older People and Community Care in Scotland: A Review of Recent Research*, Edinburgh, Scottish Executive Central Research Unit

MacDonald, C. (1999) *Support at Home: Views of Older people about their Needs and Access to Services*, Edinburgh, Scottish Executive Central Research Unit

McGinley, A. (2001) *"You can take him home now" – Carers experiences of hospital discharge*, Supplementary Report for Scotland, Carers National Association, Scotland and Crossroads Scotland

Nettleton, S. and Watson, J. (eds.) (1998) *The Body in Everyday Life*, London, Routledge

Parsons, T. (1961) *The Social System,* London, Collier-MacMillan

Raab, G. and MacDonald, C. (2004) *Older People in Scotland: Results from the Scottish Household Survey 1999-2002,* Edinburgh, Scottish Executive Social Research Unit

Scottish Executive (2001) *Fair Care for Older People,* Edinburgh, Stationary Office

Scottish Executive (1999) *Strategy for Carers in Scotland*, Edinburgh , Stationary Office

Scottish

Scottish Executive (2005) *Statistics Release, Direct Payments Scotland*, Edinburgh, Stationary Office

Scottish Executive (2006) *The Future of Unpaid Care in Scotland,* Edinburgh, Stationary Office

Scottish Executive Health Department (2005) *The Health and Wellbeing of Older People in Scotland*, Edinburgh, Stationary Office

Statham, J. (2003) *A Day at a Time: a study of unsupported carers of older people,* unpublished PhD thesis, Glasgow, University of Glasgow

Sutcliffe, D. (2001) *Introducing Dementia: the essential facts and issues of care*, London, Age Concern

Sutherland Report (1999) *With Respect to Old Age: Long Term Care – Rights and Responsibilities*, Report by the Royal Commission on Long Term Care, London, The Stationary Office

Townsend, P. (1981) 'The structured dependency of the elderly: a creation of social policy in the twentieth century', in *Ageing and Society*, 1

Walker, A. (1993) *Age and Attitudes: main results from a Eurobarometer survey*, Brussels, Commission of the European Communities

Walker, A. (1981) 'Towards a political economy of old age', in *Ageing and Society*, 1

Internet Resources

Alzheimer's Scotland (2004) statistics available at: www.alzscot.org.uk/info.sts (accessed on 8 October 2005)

Community Care and Health (Scotland) Act 2001 available at: www.scotland.gov.uk/health/ltc/legislation.asp (accessed on 14 October 2005)

Community Care Statistics available at: www.scotland,gov.uk/stats/ccare.asp (accessed on 1 October 2006)

Employment Equality (Age) Regulations 2006, an outline and main points is available at: www.ageconcern.org.uk/AgeConcern/Documents/IS17Age DiscriminationMar06

General Registers of Scotland, SCROL Scottish Census Results on Line, available at: www.scrol.gov.uk/scrol/common/home.jsp (accessed on 15 October 2005)

ISD Scotland, *The Strategy for Carers in Scotland*, available at: www.scotland.gov.uk/library2/doc10/carerstrategy.asp (accessed on 26 March 2006)

Chapter 12

Policies for the City and Community in the Devolved Scotland

Gerry Mooney

Introduction

In many of the chapters in this collection, the 'city' and 'community' provide the backdrop for a wide range of the issues that are discussed. From the examination of poverty through to the analysis of trends in crimes, health policies and their impacts, employment policy and so on, community and city are often a crucial, though not always acknowledged, part of the context in which these policies and issues are discussed. This is not to say that such issues *only* matter in urban areas or in Scotland's large towns and cities, but to suggest that they frequently take on a particular importance and resonance in cities. Cities are, of course, places full of policy interventions and applications. Health policy, housing and employment policies, transport, criminal justice, social care, drugs policies and so on are all part and parcel of the urban fabric – as they often are too in rural areas. In addition, though, specifically urban policies are developed to address a particular 'urban' issue that is defined as problematic in some way. While 'community policies' (and policies that make appeals to 'community') feature across the entire length and breadth of contemporary Scotland, these too often take on a particular resonance and importance in urban areas. Appeals to 'community' have been an important part of social policy, in its widest sense, throughout the post-1945 era. Arguably, these have been revitalised by New Labour across the UK since 1997, in particular in relation to policies for cities and urban areas, but also with respect to housing policy, criminal justice and crime reduction strategies, among others.

At first glance it may seem rather odd to have a chapter devoted to the 'city' and 'community' policies in a book that is primarily concerned with health, social care and social policy in contemporary Scotland. However, we do not have to look far to uncover just some of the many ways in which concerns with cities and communities overlap and inter-relate with many of the other policies that are explored in the different chapters that comprise this book. There are other important reasons why it was decided to have a chapter on the themes of community and city:

1. Scotland is a highly urbanised country with over 60 per cent of the population living in large towns, cities and in built-up areas in 2001 (2001 Census).

2. A concern with 'urban' and/or 'community' problems ' has long been a feature of social and public policy in Scotland and this has taken on a renewed status following devolution in 1999. Since 1999, 'urban problems' have come to be reconstructed and redefined in terms of the contribution that cities can make to economic growth in Scotland. In the 2003 **'Partnership Agreement'** between the Coalition Partners, Scottish New Labour and the Scottish Liberal Democrats, for instance, there is an explicit role for each city in this respect (Scottish Executive, 2003). Addressing the 'problems' of socially excluded communities is also a stated goal of the Scottish Executive.

3. While (as we will see) it is difficult to define 'urban policy' in any narrow way, since 1997 under New Labour across the entire UK, urban policy has been revitalised with explicit social and economic objectives that connect with other key areas of New Labour policy making, for instance, social inclusion and crime reduction policies. In exploring urban policy, therefore, we are also able to gain different insights into the rationales and workings of other types of social policies.

4. In different ways, 'Community' has re-emerged as a key dimension both in terms of political debate and in terms of policy making, not only but not least in the urban context.

The discussion in this chapter is wide ranging. From the outset the chapter considers some of the difficulties in defining urban policy and questions the notion of 'urban problems'. This critical approach also features in the exploration of 'community' and the different ways that this is now re-appearing across a wide range of government policies. As with urban problems, the notion of community is widely used but even more difficult to define. The chapter concludes by arguing that any discussion of the problems affecting Scotland's cities must be located in the context of a discussion of wider social divisions and inequalities in Scottish society, issues that are picked up in a number of other chapters in this Book.

This chapter links, then, with several of the Book wide themes identified in **Chapter 1**:

1. **Social Divisions and Differentiation.**
2. **Social Inclusion and Exclusion.**

3. **Continuity and Change.**

In particular, we are concerned to uncover some of the ways in which 'community' continues to be a recurring theme of social policies – while acknowledging that the degree and significance attached to this may change over time. Importantly, we also relate the discussion here to the overall thrust of this Book, which is concerned with the different dimensions of social and economic inequality in contemporary Scotland.

The 'Scottish' 'Urban Problem'

The idea that there is an 'urban problem' in Scotland is not a new one, but what is meant by this?

Pause for thought
- Do you feel that there is an 'urban problem' in Scotland today?
- What do you feel are the key dimensions of this?

In beginning to develop a response to this deceptively simple question, it is important to understand from the outset that for much of the past century and a half – and certainly since the latter decades of the nineteenth century – 'urban problems' in Scotland's cities have been a notable concern of politicians and policy makers, even if the term 'urban problem' itself (at least in the way it is generally understood today) really only emerges in the 1960s and 1970s (Pacione, 1997). Many of the 'problems' that became only too evident in the second half of the 20th century, for example, slum housing, severe overcrowding, pollution, congestion, high mortality rates, industrial decline and so on, are predominantly the legacies of massive and rapid urbanisation and industrialisation in the 19th and early 20th centuries . Addressing the social consequences of deindustrialisation, poor housing and urban poverty, etc., was a key goal of the post-1945 **welfare state** and in particular the employment and housing policies pursued by successive post-war governments. While rarely 'badged' as 'urban' in this period, nonetheless the economic and social policies pursued by government had a strongly urban slant or bias.

While to different degrees of intensity and geographical spread, the problems highlighted above were arguably a feature of most, if not all, of Scotland's main cities and towns. There was also an uneven geographical pattern of growth and decline across urban Scotland.

Pause for thought
- In what ways have the fortunes of separate Scottish cities differed in the post-1945 period?

Uneven Development

In the 1970s, for example, the expansion and economic growth of Aberdeen on the back of the discovery of North Sea oil was in marked contrast to the declining fortunes of many of the 'older' industrial towns on Clydeside, where **'deindustrialisation'** (that is large-scale industrial and manufacturing decline) had reached a new level and perhaps more notably in contrast with Dundee, where the jute industry in particular had been in long-term decay. The collapse of employment in towns such as Greenock and Motherwell, reliant on what increasingly came to be termed 'older industries' was in marked contrast to East Kilbride, which had been successful in securing investment (often from American companies) in 'newer' industries and services.

This uneven development, by which is meant the differential patterns of growth and decline over time and between different parts of Scotland, has re-emerged in a new form in the early 2000s. The re-establishment of a Scottish Parliament based in Edinburgh has, along with new waves of investment in banking and related services, provided a notable boost for much of the economy of Edinburgh and the Lothians. On a much smaller scale such growth is also evident in Perth and Inverness and to some extent in the Stirling area. In contrast, the fortunes of Aberdeen have taken a down-turn as North Sea oil exploration activity and revenues decline while in towns such as Clydebank and Coatbridge among others, the industries on which they were built in the later 19th and 20th centuries have largely declined if not completely collapsed (see also the discussion by Helms, **Chapter 6**).

This is memorably captured in The Proclaimers' highly poignant song from the late 1980s, *Letter from America*, which tells of a Scotland ravaged by industrial decline, increasingly abandoned by large multinational companies: 'Bathgate no more, Linwood no more, Methil no more, Irvine no more … ' However, *Letter from America* also captures another dimension of such uneven development in that many of those newer industries that were attracted to Scotland in the post-1945 era (in places such as Linwood, Bathgate and Irvine) have themselves now largely collapsed with overseas companies now looking to cheaper areas elsewhere in the world to pursue profits.

Alongside and interconnected with these industrial changes and changes in work and unemployment, are shifts in Scotland's population. Glasgow's population has been in long term decline and more recently cities such as Dundee and Aberdeen have also experienced a reduction in population. Edinburgh's population has grown slightly while the growing demand for housing in areas such as East and West Lothian reflects on Edinburgh's economic growth. The Stirling-Falkirk, Perth and Inverness areas have also experienced a growing demand for housing, also on the back of increased economic growth and activity in these areas.

Through all of this then, we can identify a pattern of continual change in the urban landscape of Scottish society over the past 100 years and more. The legacies of the past continue to be notable features of this landscape, however, reflected in the swathes of now unused 'brown' land that once accommodated heavy industries. Transport infrastructure, particularly the railways, is predominantly a late nineteenth century legacy. Large council estates on the edges of the main cities, for instance, Wester Hailes in Edinburgh, Whitfield in Dundee and Easterhouse and Pollok in Glasgow, represent arguably failed attempts to provide housing for those needing new homes following slum clearance in the post-1945 period. 'New Towns' such as East Kilbride, Glenrothes and Cumbernauld bear the hallmarks of previous attempts to 'modernise' and rejuvenate both the Scottish economy and urban areas in the 1960s and 1970s (Levitt, 1997; Roberts, 2004). Across the entire landscape, in every major town and city across Scotland, we can see the enduring legacies of these previous efforts to 'do something' about 'urban problems' or the problems 'of' the cities (see www.bestlaidschemes.com).

Glasgow – Urban Problems in Scotland's Biggest City

Throughout all of this there is a notable constant. Although deliberately avoiding mentioning this thus far, perhaps this is now the most appropriate place to highlight this point. In all the discussions of 'urban problems', industrial decline, poverty, deprivation, crime, ill-health, slum housing, unemployment and so on, one place, one city stands out as the focus for much of the political debate and for the policies that often result – Glasgow. Without wishing to minimise the problems that have long featured in other Scottish towns and in acknowledging that at times many of the disadvantaged populations of these places have felt neglected by the continuing focus on Glasgow, nonetheless there is a considerable amount of evidence, much of it built up over the past 40 to 50 years, to support the argument that the focus on Glasgow is not without some justification. Report after report after investigation after investigation have confirmed, re -confirmed and re-stated time after time the 'problems' 'of' or 'in' Glasgow (and its surrounding areas) as being among the most acute in Western Europe (Damer, 1989; Mooney and Danson, 1997; Mooney and Johnstone, 2000; Pacione, 1995; 1997).

While over the period 1995 to 2005 the Glasgow economy shows some signs of growth, particularly in the proportion of the working age population who are in employment, this remains well below that of many other areas of Scotland and indeed of the UK (Turok and Bailey, 2004; Turok *et al*, 2004). In 2005, Glasgow had 17.9 per cent of its working age population on sickness benefits – the largest absolute number of any British local authority (Beatty *et al*, 2002; OECD, 2002 ; see also Helms, **Chapter 6**). (The high proportions of working age people on sickness benefit in many British towns and cities has led to the government in 2005-2006 introducing policies which mean that those who currently receive them will be subject to increasing scrutiny.)

A focus on employment trends alone fails to tell us much about the quality of the work that is being provided, how well paid it is or perhaps more correctly how low paid and '(in)secure' it might be. It also tells us little about the wider problems of poverty and disadvantage, now largely re-badged as 'social exclusion' (see Scott, **Chapter 5**). Social exclusion and poverty are Scotland-wide issues affecting people in every village, town and city, whether in urban or rural areas. However, the extent of the social problems that continue to characterise much of Glasgow in the first decade of the 21st century was evidenced, once again, in the Scottish Executive's *Scottish Index of Multiple Deprivation* published in 2004 (Dorling and Thomas, 2004; Kenway *et al*, 2002) . The City of Glasgow, with 11.4 per cent of the population of Scotland, had 51.1 per cent of its population living in the most deprived 10 per cent of zones. All other local authority districts had less than their proportionate share of deprivation (Scottish Executive, 2004c; Johnstone and McWilliams, 2005; McWilliams, Johnstone and Mooney, 2004).

Reflecting on the question posed at the outset then, it is already clear that 'urban problems' are not evenly spread among Scotland's towns and cities. Importantly, further, it would be mistaken to ignore the fact that Glasgow has high levels of wealth and prosperity. Or more correctly, some sections of its population are very wealthy and there are, of course, areas within the city that do not fall into the most deprived or deprived categories. Conversely, in Edinburgh, it would similarly be mistaken to suggest that economic growth and prosperity are widely and evenly distributed throughout the city. Cities across the world today are places of enormous wealth and prosperity – and also places of immense poverty. As such, they are characterised by social inequalities and social divisions on a massive scale. There is, in other words, a gulf, or growing polarisation, between those groups and places in the city that are '*doing well*' and those people and areas that are impoverished and forced to live in increasingly harsh conditions (Davis, 2006). While it would be a serious mistake to suggest that the levels of **polarisation** – both geographically and socially – are as great in Scotland's cities as they are in many of the larger urban areas of the 'third world', nonetheless it is important to grasp that the divisions and inequalities *within* Scotland's cities, that is *intra*-urban inequalities, are greater than any inequality *between* them, otherwise known as *inter*-urban differences.

Urban Problems – Shared by all?

What this is immediately highlighting, therefore, is that urban problems are not problems for all groups within the city. Are they, then, justifiably called 'urban problems'? Might it not be more adequate then to understand such problems and issues as more to do with class, gender and other social divisions and inequalities rather than as peculiarly urban problems? There has been a long debate on such matters that need not sidetrack us here (Atkinson and Moon, 1994; Cochrane, 2006). However, it is important to grasp that there is *no* shared understanding of what constitutes an 'urban problem' and, indeed, attempting to arrive at an all-encompassing definition may be a pointless exercise. Instead, more critically thinking academics and researchers, as well as successive generations of community activists and those who work in delivering urban and community policies on the 'frontline', have argued that it is more helpful to understand *why* it is that certain things – behaviours, processes, etc. – come to be defined as 'problems', *and by whom!* In this respect, urban poverty is a problem for marginalised and disadvantaged groups living in cities, but it is rarely a problem for the wealthy (other than in any fears they may have about crime and 'disorder' that may be threatened by the disadvantaged). Large suburban shopping centres and the supermarkets and property developers that push for their construction, are rarely viewed by policy markers as a 'problem', but there is considerable evidence that such developments increase road congestion and pollution, 'squeeze-out' smaller 'local' shops and businesses and are often inaccessible to many poorer people who do not have access to a car (Crichton, 2006; New Economics Foundation, 2003).

As the discussion moves to focus on the ways in which urban and community policies are being framed by New Labour and the Scottish Executive, it is important that you take with you this understanding of the complex difficulties that emerge in defining urban problems and policies, likewise with the notion of 'community', of 'regeneration', 'partnership' and so on. Ambiguities and disputes over definition and meaning abound here. These are all 'slippery' terms, contested and used in different ways by politicians, academics and activists. However, as you read through the sections that follow, in building on these critical insights you can begin to make sense of the ways in which at different times (and here we return to some of the themes raised by Mooney, Sweeney and Law, **Chapter 1** and to the ideas of C.

Wright Mills) 'personal troubles' come to be constructed as 'public issues' (Mills, 1959: 7-9), that is 'social problems' that require intervention by the government through policy.

Policies for urban areas and for deprived communities are often couched in terms that speak of the 'problems' *of* such places in ways that imply that their populations might be responsible in some way for these. This is all too often an integral element of how such problems are constructed. That is, the way in which an issue comes to be defined as problematic will be reflected in any of the policies that result. We can all, then, identify a range of 'problems' that have to be tackled. What is crucial, though, is that we understand that these might not be specifically 'urban' or community based.

New Labour's 'Urban Renaissance' and the 'Rediscovery' of 'Community'

Today cities are at the centre of the UK economy and society and increasingly UK politics, albeit devolved politics. New Labour has highlighted the 'regeneration' of cities – an 'urban renaissance' – as a key part of their project to 'modernise' Britain (Atkinson and Helms, 2007; Imrie and Raco, 2003; Johnstone and Whitehead, 2004). After years of comparative neglect under the Conservatives, New Labour was quick to re-centre cities in its political ambitions. The re-focus on cities forms part of a more general appeal to a new vision of a 'modern' and competitive Britain. New Labour's vision of an 'urban renaissance' in Scotland, as elsewhere in the UK, is largely founded on the argument that through economic growth the entire country will benefit. Social policies, here urban policies, should be about helping to provide the right conditions for capital investment and for the generation of wealth. While the urban policies of Labour and Conservative governments in the 1970s, 1980s and 1990s largely saw cities in terms of large-scale 'urban problems', under New Labour in the late 1990s and early 2000s cities (and their populations) are now to be understood as under-used resources that can be utilised in the project of securing an economically competitive Britain. Poverty, crime, poor housing and other social 'disorders' are now viewed as barriers to such competitiveness and economic growth. According to this line of thinking, policies *should* be targeted to remove such barriers to prosperity.

In this we can identify an important change under New Labour with the policies being pursued by previous governments in relation to cities. However, as you will have uncovered elsewhere in this Book, alongside *change* there is also important *continuity* with the past, here in relation to another key dimension of government policies, the appeal of 'community' and 'community' policies. New Labour inherited from the Conservatives an approach to urban regeneration that was based on competition (not least between cities through place marketing strategies, for instance, *Glasgow's Miles Better*, European City of Culture awards and other 'flagship' events (Garcia, 2005; Mooney, 2004) and growing consumption – and an increasingly free hand for the market in urban planning and 'regeneration' (at least in England if arguably less so in Scotland, though in 2006 there are some signs of a change in policy). To this 'mix', New Labour added 'community'. Communities, based on local neighbourhoods, represent for New Labour the key building blocks of **social order**, crime prevention and community. This is also to play an important role in neighbourhood regeneration and in managing the delivery of public services in local areas, for instance, in relation to social housing (that is, housing provided by organisations set up to manage housing stock transferred out of local authority control, such as the Glasgow Housing Agency). Community 'partnership' and communities 'working in partnership' with a range of other government bodies and organisations have become oft-repeated statements in policy documents and political rhetoric (we will return to this below in relation to Community Planning).

Partnership working, community regeneration and so on are – as ever – ambiguous and flexible ideas. However, you should not underestimate the importance they play in securing public support for a range of policies. In critically unpacking such terms, we can also develop a better understanding of different areas of government policy as well as gaining insights into the underlying assumption upon which such policies are based. Community 'self-management' and community 'responsibility' have emerged in the early 2000s as key buzzwords in the trendy language that often accompanies community, urban and city policy statements. 'Community safety', **Community Service Orders** and other local based 'solutions' to problems of crime and disorder are increasingly key components of criminal justice policies (see Munro and Nicholson, **Chapter 14**). These are central to New Labour/Scottish Executive overall 'social' goals. Behind this lies a vision of well ordered and law abiding communities actively involved in the pursuit of the public good.

The Ambiguous Notion of 'Community'

We are still left, however, with an issue that has long plagued discussions of community – that the notion of 'community' itself is highly ambiguous, giving rise to many different definitions. The label 'community' has been applied to a wide and diverse range of policy initiatives and strategies, from 'community policing' through to 'community charge', 'community safety', 'community planning' and 'community care'. Although it is typically seen in a positive light, community is an 'essentially contested concept' where the same word can take on different political meanings.

Pause for thought
- What does the notion or idea of community mean to you?

Invariably, community is viewed as a 'good thing', something that we should pursue. Certainly, the idea of community as a socially purposeful and beneficial set of relationships characterises much of New Labour and Scottish Executive policy making, that is at least when 'good' communities are being considered, not the socially excluded, 'disorderly' and 'disorganised' communities that are frequently the target of government policy interventions. Community is all too often taken to imply or suggest a relatively homogenous group of people in a particular place. The image of 'the village community' often comes to mind in people's descriptions of community. However, this has been repeatedly shown to be problematic on a number of different levels. Communities, here understood in terms of a defined geographical locality, are also places of inequality, of difference and of social division. They are not 'free' from the effects of class, gender, race, age and other forms of social differentiation (see Law and Law, **Chapter 4**).

Think for a minute about the much heralded community care policies pursued by the Conservatives when in government during the 1980s and 1990s and now an important component of 'care' policies in the devolved Scotland (see Cavaye, **Chapter 11**). We probably all share a belief that for many of those requiring care, long-term stays in run-down hospitals and other institutions is not the answer. By comparison, care in the community is to be welcomed as long as it is properly funded and supported by the state. However, just who or what is the 'community' that will be doing the caring? For many commentators, community care is largely unpaid care provided by women in their own or other people's homes.

There are other limitations with seeing community as a 'bounded' place. Community as a sense of belonging, of 'something' that can bring us feelings of purpose and security need not be geographically bounded. Different groups of people may identify with others who live in other parts of the world. This might be especially so among recent migrants or those who share particular religious beliefs, though this is not necessarily always the case. The spread of the internet has for some commentators given rise to what have been termed 'e-communities', or otherwise enabled people in different countries to form strong relationships.

While the dominant sense of community is without doubt that it is something positive and to be welcomed, full of 'good things' such as togetherness, social cohesion, belonging, security, caring and mutual support, other views point to a more 'negative' side of community – as parochial, inward -looking, invasive , all too concerned with boundaries between *us*, who belong and *them*, the 'outsiders'.

Despite an increasing awareness that community can have a 'downside', nonetheless the view and understanding of community that tends to dominate is one that celebrates 'the upside'. This is rarely more apparent than when a 'loss of community' is being mourned. The 'community lost' story is not new, but tends to re-occur in discussions of community in the context of wider concerns about society and its direction. Here, the sense of a loss of community is used to capture wider fears about a range of social issues and processes, from globalisation and economic change to the collapse of 'older' forms of work (and workplaces) (see Helms, **Chapter 6**), of fears about crime and 'social disorder' (see Munro and Nicholson, **Chapter 14**), of family 'breakdown' (see Annetts, **Chapter 7**) and so on (Delanty, 2003). This idea of a loss of community/community lost story is frequently used to capture and portray a sense of 'a world that has changed beyond all recognition', where 'traditional' patterns of work, home life, etc., have been undermined. What this tells us, then, is that all too often community is invoked, highlighted at the very time in which it has been seen as declining and disappearing (Lee and Newby, 1983). Thus, in the 1950s and 1960s, amidst the large-scale urban and industrial change that was such a notable feature of the UK urban landscape at the time, a widely held view was that new towns and large peripheral housing estates 'lacked' the community 'spirit' that was seen to have been such a vivid feature of life among the tenements and other overcrowded slum areas. This idea in part fuelled the great wave of sociological investigations of community life in towns and cities across the UK in the late 1950s and 1960s with researchers keen to show that community life continued to be a feature in the many different worlds and urban villages that comprise Britain's cities (Bell and Newby, 1971; Young and Willmott, 1957; Dench, Gavron and Young, 2006).

As we move now to explore some of the different ways in which policies for cities and communities have been developed in Scotland following devolution, it is hoped that you will continue to adopt this questioning and sceptical understanding of ideas such as community, while at the same time acknowledging the continuing significance of such an idea in social policy making.

City and Community in the Devolved Scotland: Exploring the Approach of the Scottish Executive

To develop an informed understanding of the Scottish Executive's policies for urban areas and towards disadvantaged areas in particular, we must locate these initially within the overall policy objectives of the Scottish Executive. In short, these revolve around the twin themes of *competition* and *cohesion*. In the discussion above you will have noted that at a UK-wide level New Labour has the pursuit of economic competitiveness as its primary objective. 'Cohesion', which yet again is one of those unfortunate but oft used terms that defy clear definition, is generally taken (in Scotland, at least) to encompass those wider social issues, including poverty and social exclusion, ill-health, low educational attainment, crime and disorder, low skills levels, unemployment, 'worklessness' and so on, that are seen as undermining the drive for competitiveness (see Helms, **Chapter 6**).

The Cities Review (2002)

In 2001, the Scottish Executive launched a review of Scotland's cities (Peel and Lloyd, 2005). The *Review of Scotland's Cities* (Scottish Executive, 2002d) was initially a short-term appraisal of the state of Scotland's cities, following on from the work of the Urban Task Force in England (chaired by architect Richard Rogers, which was established in 1997 and reported in 1999 (Urban Task Force, 1999)). This provided the basis for the much publicised '**urban renaissance**' agenda in England. By comparison the 'Cities Review' in Scotland was a much more modest affair that did not secure much publicity. However, following the publication of the Cities Review and in line with other studies and reports, notably '*Building Better Cities*' (Scottish Executive, 2002b; 2002c), Scotland's cities were increasingly identified as key contributors to economic growth and as playing a central role in national prosperity (Scottish Executive 2004a; 2004d; 2001). Echoing arguments and ideas that are being repeated elsewhere in the Western world, the Scottish Executive saw Scotland's cities as offering opportunities for increased tourist, consumer and commercial activities – as well as providing the cultural and social infrastructures that would attract up and coming entrepreneurs and those engaged in 'leading-edge', 'information' centred and 'creative industries'. All of which were identified as *key* to Scotland's economic future.

The Cities Review, apart from establishing a relatively modest £90 million 'growth fund' for Scotland's cities over a three-year period, almost of half of which was earmarked for Glasgow, has not led to the development of a specifically urban policy in Scotland. It does, however, reflect and indicate the renewed political interest in cities as evidenced by other policy measures and reports produced by the Scottish Executive. Arguably, it also contributed to providing the basis for the emergence of a new way of thinking about the futures of Scotland's cities, as major 'players' in 'growing' the Scottish economy:

"City policies are not simply about redistributing resources from successful to less successful places, rather, city, or place, policy is also essential in dealing with market and policy failures that limit productivity growth. City policies have to be creative as well as redistributive and they have national as well as local benefits. They support local change, creativity and adjustment which are all essential to wider national progress" (Scottish Executive, 2002d: 274).

In other ways the Cities Review also carried ideas that were much less novel in that there was a key role assigned, as in previous policies, to local communities in enabling area-regeneration in urban settings.

Regeneration and Competitiveness

In 2006, the Scottish Executive announced a 'new' approach to area 'regeneration' in its policy statement, *People and Place: Regeneration Policy Statement* (Scottish Executive, 2006). Again, though, we can see the continuity with 'older' approaches. This new approach had as twin goals an increase in private sector investment in urban areas that would also be used to help 'transform' some of the country's most deprived areas. Here we can see some of the ways in which the over-riding New Labour and Scottish Executive emphasis on wealth creation and entrepreneurial activity is now informing large swathes of policy making in the devolved Scotland. In the first edition of the Scottish Executive's key economic policy document, *A Smart Successful Scotland* (Scottish Executive, 2001; see also the second edition, 2004a) and in a range of other policy reports and announcements, these neo-liberal ideas are all too evident with an increasing emphasis placed on the role of the private sector (see Sweeney, **Chapter 2** and Law, **Chapter 3**). What is being argued now, representing an important shift on the policies pursued by the Conservatives, is that economic growth is central to the regeneration of deprived and disadvantaged communities. In turn, these communities can contribute to the health of the Scottish economy by enhancing its competitiveness. In other ways these policies continue with the approach of the Conservatives, albeit at a much greater level, in seeing in the market and in economic growth the salvation for all communities across Scotland.

In the 1960s and 1970s, urban regeneration and economic development policies were largely out of step and viewed as predominantly separate policy making areas. From 2003 and following the second Scottish Parliament elections, such thinking is now considered as old fashioned and unable to address the social and economic needs of contemporary Scotland – now refashioned as *competitiveness* and *cohesion*. Increasingly, 'social objectives' such as area/community regeneration and tackling unemployment, low skills and educational attainment as well as morbidity and mortality (see McCafferty, **Chapter 9**) are seen as vital if the overall economic objective is to be attained.

It is evident here that the development of the Scottish Executive's thinking around area-based and urban regeneration is very much in tune with other areas of New Labour social and economic policy making.

Pause for thought
- What do you feel might be the limitations of such an approach to urban regeneration?

What stands out is the primacy accorded to economic growth and wealth creation. Where the 'social' is introduced, for instance in relation to **social exclusion**, this is largely because it is seen to limit economic objectives. Social exclusion, to put it another way, 'matters' *primarily* because it undermines competitiveness. There is vagueness in the terms that are used and in the objectives that are identified in policy reports and announcements in relation to regeneration (though this can be said to be true of much urban and community rhetoric since the 1960s!). It is not at all clear how cities will contribute to economic growth. More importantly, it is far from evident that such a strategy will benefit all those living in cities, never mind in Scotland in general. The focus is very much on building the right conditions for entrepreneurial and creative activities to take place, which is supporting those who are already wealthy in the pursuit of more wealth. Such ideas seem to echo the **Thatcherite** 'trickle down' approach to urban renewal, whereby economic prosperity for the few would eventually filter 'down' to the more disadvantaged. That there has never been any evidence that 'trickle down' actually exists beyond liberal economic textbooks has not prevented it from becoming almost 'common sense' among politicians and policy-makers.

From SIPs to Community Planning

Social Inclusion Partnerships (SIPs)

With the election of New Labour in 1997 came a UK-wide commitment to tackling poverty, now largely understood as social exclusion (Levitas, 2005). In Scotland, then Secretary of State and subsequently (the first) First Minister, Donald Dewar, made repeated statements confirming the commitment of the Scottish Office and subsequently following devolution in 1999 the Scottish Executive, to tackling social exclusion (see Scott, **Chapter 5**). In addition to New Labour's national social inclusion policies built around the new deal for employment, area-based exclusion would be tackled through a particular programme, the **Social Inclusion Partnerships (SIPs)** (Johnstone and McWilliams, 2005; McWilliams, Johnstone and Mooney, 2004; Roberts, 2004).

SIPs would replace *two* Conservative strategies, *New Life for Urban Scotland* (launched in 1988) and the 1996 *Programme for Partnership*, though there were to be strong continuities with them. SIPs were to be both area-based (both urban and rural) and 'thematic', that is focusing on particular issues such as problems facing young people and 'improving health' also featured strongly. The main task falling to SIPs, as in many previous generations of area-based policies, was to focus on those 'most in need' while improving the coordination and delivery of services to the most disadvantaged groups and areas, identifying and filling any gaps in service provision.

SIPs were also charged with continuing other aspects of Conservative and previous area-based programmes in the renewed emphasis on 'partnership working' and on the role accorded to community 'involvement' and 'participation'. In this thinking, 'communities' would work alongside statutory government bodies and other agencies involved in the delivery of public services, as well as the voluntary and **'third sector'** organisations to achieve improvements in service delivery and impact.

Partnership Working

Partnership working and the involvement of a community in identifying local needs and service requirements can be potentially beneficial. Regeneration and other programmes can be 'tailored' to addressing the particular issues that are of concern in an area. However, while 'partnership working' sounds ideal in theory, in practice it amounted to little, either under the 'New Life' programme or with the SIPs. Further, the idea that the different partners have equal status or power is, of course, wishful thinking at its best . A further limitation of such an approach that has frequently been identified by researchers and community activists revolves around the idea that 'the community' is actively involved in the decision making. Some members of a community might come to be involved in such partnership working, but these will rarely represent everyone or all interests in a particular area. Such criticism is therefore targeted against the idea that communities have a homogenous set of interests.

While this 'return' to community involvement has been widely criticised as little more than rhetoric, and for what some researchers claim is an over-emphasis on local based 'solutions' to much wider social problems and inequalities (Alcock, 2004; Atkinson, 2003; North, 2003), it continues to be a significant aspect of Scottish

Executive policy-making. This is reflected in the development of a strategy that has come to replace SIPs – 'Community Planning'.

Pause for thought
- What do you feel are the advantages and disadvantages of 'partnership working'?

Community Planning

In the mid-2000s, **Community Planning (CP)** forms an important part of the Scottish Executive's overall programme of public sector 'reform' (Lloyd and Illsley, 2004). However, while the idea of community planning has been in development in the Scottish Office/Executive since the mid-1990s, it was the publication in 2002 of *Better Communities in Scotland: Closing the Opportunity Gap* (Scottish Executive, 2002a) that marked a new phase of policy making and the proposals that were to emerge in this report were subsequently enacted under the Local Government in Scotland Act 2003. This Act obliged local authorities across Scotland to actively consult with residents and communities about local service priorities and service delivery. 'Partnership working' was now re-established as a key element in Scottish Executive policy-making for disadvantaged areas in particular, echoing the *New Life for Urban Scotland* programme of the late 1980s and early 1990s. The **Community Planning Partnership (CPP)** Framework, as it became known, reflected a further focus on service implementation and 'integration', particularly in deprived areas. SIPs were seen to have 'failed' in this regard. CPPs were to link local and national priorities more effectively and this is reflected in the production of **Regeneration Outcome Agreements** by each CPP. These would in turn be used to secure funding from the Scottish Executive.

CPPs involved local authority and other local agencies together with voluntary and private sector interests along with "the community" in producing a "shared vision for promoting the well-being of their area" (www.scotland.gov.uk/topics/CP). This implies that a consensus can be arrived at in terms of what might be the 'best' policies and most *appropriate* forms of delivery in a particular community. Once again, however, critics of this CP approach argue that this model fails to comprehend that there are different interests with vastly different powers that make partnership working idealistic at best. CP *appears* to bring the community right to the very heart of policy making, delivery and implementation. Alternatively, it can be seen simply as a means by which local protest is neutralised, with community activists becoming incorporated into management activities. Thus, the idea of CP as an exercise in local democratic accountability is seen by many to be wanting, with 'real' power residing in the hands of government and private interests.

Goodbye to the Council House? Social Housing Policy in the Devolved Scotland

As with its policies for an urban 'renaissance' and community regeneration, in the field of 'social' housing, the Scottish Executive has promised to bring about a 'transformation' in the lives of tenants. The key vehicle for achieving this is **housing stock transfer** involving the wholesale restructuring of social housing and the provision of 'new' forms of housing management. Throughout all of this the key notion is 'choice'. Across Scotland – and elsewhere in the UK – much effort has been expended by government in 'pushing' the idea of stock transfer. For New Labour, the restructuring of council housing is not simply a 'bricks and mortar' strategy, but is founded on the promotion of choice and the transformation of the council tenant from someone who is 'dependent' on the state (local council) to provide their housing requirements to an 'active consumer' of rented housing. Here, the tenant will be a person who can exercise judgement in the choice of landlord or provider and who will want a greater say in the management of their housing.

The social housing that New Labour inherited in 1997 was characterised by long term decline, reflected in a massive backlog of repairs, the product of decades of underinvestment. **'Right to Buy'**, as is now well known, removed much of the better quality stock from the pool of housing available leaving behind housing that was generally of a poorer standard. The Scottish Federation of Housing Associations (SFHA) estimated that in 2000 some 66,000 homes in Scotland, including over 23,000 in Glasgow alone, fell below (the largely outdated) 'tolerable standard' classification, while over 530,000 homes (25 per cent of all homes in Scotland) suffered from dampness of varying types (see www.sfha.co.uk). It was estimated that the cost of repairing and bringing Scottish council housing up to standard was in excess of £2 billion.

The social housing policies pursued by the Conservatives during the 1980s and 1990s had other effects: the social profile of council housing had become more narrowly based and increasingly associated with housing for the poorest and most marginalised groups. In Scotland, the greater size of the state-housing sector, reflecting the important role that council housing has played in the housing of the population for much of the past century, meant that trends towards the **residualisation** (that is it becomes housing of the last resort) of council housing were perhaps slower than in other parts of Britain. Nonetheless, residualisation has become a major issue in Scotland with council housing now accommodating a higher proportion of marginalised households.

Reflecting the different histories of housing provision between Scotland and the rest of the UK, and the greater proportion of housing in the social sector, housing policy in Scotland has long been under the jurisdiction of the Scottish Office and is now a devolved power of the Scottish Parliament in Edinburgh. That is, with the exception of housing benefit that remains, somewhat controversially, a reserved power of Westminster. From 1997, it was clear that New Labour in Scotland, like its counterparts in other areas of the UK, was content to follow the Conservatives by continuing with right to buy and the promotion of owner occupation. However, the **'demunicipalisation'** of council housing through stock transfer was to take on a new significance. While varieties of stock transfer had been a feature of state housing for over a decade, it was to reach unparalleled proportions under Labour.

One of the clearest signs of this willingness to continue with much of Conservative policy was the Scottish Office's 1999 **Green Paper** *Investing in Modernisation: An Agenda for Scotland's Housing*. Produced only two months before the first Scottish Parliament Elections, it set the scene for the transfer policies that were to unfold during the first few years of the reconvened Scottish Parliament by proposing to move beyond "the 'municipal paternalism', which resulted in large single tenure estates" (Scottish Office, 1999: para. 7), by targeting the bureaucracy and inefficiency of local authority landlords. In addition, the Green Paper identified a lack of 'social balance' as a major problem of state housing and made an implicit attack on the 'dependency' of council tenants. As in England, Scotland's councils were to become *enablers* not *providers* of social housing. One notable outcome of New Labour's thinking was the establishment of the New Housing Partnership initiative. Here, additional housing resources would be made available to those local authorities that were developing proposals for social housing that would not be owned in the future by local authorities. Thus, there was an implicit drive towards demunicipalisation and stock transfer to other non-statutory agencies such as housing associations and other 'Registered Social Landlords' (RSLs).

When the Scottish Parliament first met in the summer of 1999, stock transfer had already been identified as a key component of the reform of Scotland's council housing sector under devolution. One of the most important aspects of this new policy was the emphasis on **'community ownership'**. As the then Minister for Communities, Wendy Alexander, claimed:

> "[T]here is now a growing recognition that direct community ownership of homes has the potential to bring benefits in empowerment, management and financing. In the future we believe that tenants in the non-market sector should

increasingly have choices about how their homes are owned and managed. Within that broad set of possibilities we see benefits stemming from ownership of housing by local communities where it represents best value and commands the support of tenants" (Minister for Communities, 2000).

From the early days of the new Scottish Parliament, then, stock transfer has been promoted as the *only* option available to regenerate the council housing sector in Scotland and following the second Scottish Parliament elections in May 2003, the Labour-Liberal Democrat coalition has in its 'Partnership Agreement' confirmed pre-election proposals to transfer a further 70,000 homes out of local authority ownership by 2006 (Scottish Executive, 2003). The notion of community ownership and the idea that tenants would be in control were to become pivotal claims in the political controversy that was soon to ensue, not least over the plans for the stock transfer of Glasgow's entire stock from the control of Glasgow City Council to the newly established Glasgow Housing Agency (Gibb, 2003; Daly *et al*, 2005).

Housing stock transfer has come to be established as the key policy for social housing both in the devolved Scotland and in England and Wales (Stirling and Smith, 2003). While it has now been implemented in some authority areas such as Glasgow, in others, notably Edinburgh, tenants have voted to reject stock transfer. Housing policy remains a highly controversial dimension of social policy in Scotland today, not least because it is now 'joined-up' with other controversial areas of government policy making in relation to the 'modernisation' and 'reform' of public services, which for many critics and commentators amounts to little more than privatisation (Defend Council Housing, 2003; Mooney and Poole, 2005). In all of this, New Labour is working to create a new relationship between the individual, community and state in which state provision is increasingly seen as *provision of last resort*. In this new world, 'consumer choice' and 'individual responsibility' has taken on a new significance and arguably it is this thinking more than any other that has come to be the dominant influence on social policy making under New Labour.

Conclusion

There is much for you to reflect on at the end of this chapter. A range of policy approaches have been highlighted, some of these explored in more depth than others. Instead of getting over-focused on a particular policy, more importantly perhaps is that you take away with you from this chapter a healthy scepticism about some of the language, rhetoric and terminology that tends to over-dominate the discussions of the issues that we have been concerned with. Much of the terminology used, as we have seen, is highly vague and ambiguous. Terms such as 'community' and 'regeneration' are also heavily value-laden, conveying as they do other meanings and understandings and prescriptions of 'what is to be done' about cities and poorer communities. This chapter has avoided the 'something must be done' type of approach. More important is a focus on why it is that over time it tends to be the same groups of people in the same kinds of poorer and disadvantaged places who come to be **labelled** as a 'problem' in some way, which can then lead to a range of policy measures that reinforce this problematising. This is not to claim that there are no problems that affect many of the populations in the areas identified – or across large parts of urban Scotland. It is more to argue, returning to the central themes of this Book, that such problems are *less* to do with these particular groups and the communities and localities in which they live and more to do with the divided and highly unequal nature of contemporary Scottish society.

As we have seen, there have been significant changes in urban and community policies over recent decades. There are also important continuities with the past through a range of enduring legacies of previous efforts to promote 'partnership', community 'engagement' and so on. Area-based policies, that is targeting particular deprived localities for specific policy measures and a concern with improving the 'coordination' and 'management' of service delivery, also remain significant goals of urban and community policy. Another constant, though one that it is all too often ignored is that such policies and the ideas that give rise to them occur not in a vacuum, but in the context of growing social inequality and a deepening polarisation between rich and poor in Scottish society. It is the failure, or perhaps more correctly, the *unwillingness* to address this that is the most significant factor that limits any effectiveness of urban and community policies.

Further Reading

In this chapter are referenced a range of sources that you might want to follow up if you have a particular interest in this field. There are a wide range of resources using different forms of media on the general themes of urban problems, social and economic change in cities, on community and on policies for urban areas and disadvantaged communities. For more discussion of key aspects of New Labour's 'urban renaissance' strategy, which is largely England-centred, look at Rob Imrie and Mike Raco's edited collection, *Urban Renaissance? New Labour, Community and Urban Policy* (The Policy Press, 2003). In relation to Scottish Cities, there is no one book that covers all Scottish urban areas in any comprehensive way. Another edited collection with a Scottish focus and which touches on many of the issues highlighted in this chapter is *Divided Scotland? The Nature, Causes and Consequences of Economic Disparities within Scotland* (Gower, 2004). Edited by Newlands, Danson and McCarthy, this contains a wealth of empirical information and other sources that you may wish to follow up. An interesting web source is Best Laid Schemes (www.bestlaidschemes.com), which contains film footage from the Scottish Film Archive on different aspects of urban and industrial change in post-1945 Scotland.

All Scottish Executive reports can be accessed at www.scotland.gov.uk, while Communities Scotland (www.communitiesscotland.gov.uk) contains additional materials on community and housing policies in contemporary Scotland. Finally, there are a multitude of academic journals devoted to studies of the city and community, drawing on social policy, human geography, economics, sociology, cultural studies and more. Key titles here include *Urban Studies, Local Economy, City, Cities, International Journal of Urban and Regional Research* and *Policy and Politics* (this is not a complete list by any means!).

Useful Websites

Best Laid Schemes: www.bestlaidschemes.com
Community Planning Partnerships (CCPs): www.scotland.gov.uk/topics/CP
Communities Scotland: www.communitiesscotland.gov.uk
Scottish Executive: www.scotland.gov.uk
Scottish Federation of Housing Associations (SFHA): www.sfha.co.uk

Bibliography

Alcock, P. (2004) 'Participation or Pathology: Contradictory Tensions in Area-Based Policy', in *Social Policy and Society*, 3 (2)

Atkinson, R . (2003) 'Addressing Urban Social Exclusion through Community Involvement in Urban Regeneration', in Imrie, R. and Raco, M. (eds.) (2003) *Urban Renaissance?* Bristol, The Policy Press

Atkinson, R. and Helms, G. (eds.) (2007) *Securing an Urban Renaissance: Crime, Community and British Urban Policy*, Bristol, The Policy Press

Atkinson, R. and Moon, G. (1994) *Urban Policy in Britain*, Houndsmills, Palgrave MacMillan

Beatty, C ., Fothergill , S ., Gore , T . and Hamilton, A . (2002) *The Real Level of Unemployment*, Sheffield, Sheffield Hallam University Centre for Regional Economic and Social Research

Bell, C. and Newby, H. (1971) *Community Studies*, London, Allen and Unwin

Boddy, M. and Parkinson, M. (eds.) (2004) *City Matters: Competitiveness, Cohesion and Urban Governance*, Bristol, The Policy Press

Cochrane, A . (2006) *Understanding Urban Policy: A Critical Approach*, Oxford , Blackwell

Crichton, T . (2006) 'The town that was eaten by Tesco', in *The Sunday Herald*, March 19

Daly, G., Mooney, G., Poole, L. and Davis, H. (2005) 'Housing Stock Transfer in Birmingham and Glasgow: The Contrasting Experiences of Two UK Cities', in *European Journal of Housing Policy*, 5 (3)

Damer, S. (1989) *Glasgow: Going for a Song*, London, Lawrence and Wishart

Davis, M. (2006) *Planet of Slums*, London, Verso

Defend Council Housing (2003) *The Case for Council Housing* (Second Edition), London, DCH, www.defendcouncilhousing.org.uk

Delanty, G. (2003) *Community*, London, Routledge

Dench, G., Gavron, K. and Young, M. (2006) *The New East End*, London , Profile Books

Dorling, D. and Thomas, B. (2004) *People and Places: A Census Atlas of Britain*, Bristol, The Policy Press

Garcia, B . (2005) 'Deconstructing the City of Culture: The Long-Term Cultural Legacies of Glasgow, 1990', in *Urban Studies*, 42(5/6)

Gibb, K . (2003) 'Transferring Glasgow's Council Housing: Financial, Urban and Housing Implications', *European Journal of Housing Policy*, 3(1)

Imrie, R. and Raco, M. (eds.) (2003) *Urban Renaissance? New Labour, Community and Urban Policy*, Bristol, The Policy Press

Jewson, N. and MacGregor, S. (eds.) (1997) *Transforming cities*, London, Routledge

Johnstone, C. and McWilliams, C . (2005) 'Urban Policy and the City in the 'New' Scotland', in Mooney, G. and Scott, G. (eds.) (2005) *Exploring Social Policy in the*

'New' Scotland, Bristol, The Policy Press

Johnstone, C. and Whitehead, M. (2004) *New Horizons in British Urban Policy: Perspectives on New Labour's Urban Renaissance*, Aldershot, Ashgate

Kenway, P., Mohibur, R. and Palmar, G. (2002) *Monitoring Poverty and Social Exclusion in Scotland*, York, Joseph Rowntree Foundation

Lee, D. and Newby, H. (1983) *The Problem of Sociology*, London, Hutchinson

Levitt, I. (1997) 'New Towns, New Scotland, New Ideology, 1937 -57', in *The Scottish Historical Review*, 76 (2)

Levitas, R. (2005) *The Inclusive Society? Social Exclusion and New Labour* (Second Edition), Houndsmills, Palgrave MacMillan

Lloyd, M.G. and Illsley, B. (2004) 'Community Planning in Scotland: Prospects and Potential for Local Governance?', in Newlands, D., Danson, M. and McCarthy, J. (eds.) (2004) *Divided Scotland? The Nature, Causes and Consequences of Economic Disparities within Scotland*, Aldershot, Gower

McWilliams, C., Johnstone, C. and Mooney, G. (2004) 'Urban Policy in the 'New' Scotland: the Role of Social Inclusion Partnerships', in *Space and Polity*, 8(3)

Mills, C.W. (1959) *The Sociological Imagination*, Oxford, Oxford University Press

Minister for Communities (2000) *Memorandum to the Social Inclusion, Housing and Voluntary Committee Report on Stock Transfers*, Edinburgh, Scottish Executive

Mooney, G. (2004) 'Cultural Policy as Urban Transformation? Critical Reflections on Glasgow, European City of Culture 1990', in *Local Economy*, 19(4)

Mooney, G. and Danson, M. (1997) 'Beyond "culture city": Glasgow as a "dual city"', in Jewson, N. and MacGregor, S. (eds.) (1997) *Transforming cities*, London, Routledge

Mooney, G. and Johnstone, C. (2000) 'Scotland Divided: Poverty, Inequality and Scottish Parliament', in *Critical Social Policy*, 63

Mooney, G. and Poole, L. (2005) 'Marginalised Voices: Resisting the Privatisation of Council Housing in Glasgow', in *Local Economy*, 20 (1)

Mooney, G. and Scott, G. (eds.) (2005) *Exploring Social Policy in the 'New' Scotland*, Bristol, The Policy Press

New Economics Foundation (2003) *Ghost Town Britain*, London, New Economics Foundation

Newlands, D., Danson, M. and McCarthy, J. (eds.) (2004) *Divided Scotland? The Nature, Causes and Consequences of Economic Disparities within Scotland*, Aldershot, Gower

North, P. (2003) 'Communities at the Heart? Community Action and Urban Policy in the UK', in Imrie, R. and Raco, M. (eds.) *Urban Renaissance?* Bristol, The Policy Press

Organisation for Economic Cooperation and Development (OECD) (2002) *Glasgow: Lessons for Innovation and Implementation*, Paris, OECD

Pacione, M. (1995) *Glasgow: The Socio-Spatial Development of the City*, London, Wiley

Pacione, M. (ed.) (1997) *Britain's Cities: Geographies of Division in Urban Britain*, London, Routledge

Peel, D. and Lloyd, G. (2005) 'City-Visions: Visioning and Delivering Scotland's Economic Future', in *Local Economy*, 20 (1)

Rees, G. and Lambert, J. (1985) *Cities in crisis*, London, Hodder Arnold

Roberts, P. (2004) 'Urban Regeneration in Scotland: Context, Contributions and Choices for the Future', in Newlands, D., Danson, M. and McCarthy, J. (eds.) (2004) *Divided Scotland? The Nature, Causes and Consequences of Economic Disparities within Scotland*, Aldershot, Gower

Scottish Executive (2001) *A Smart Successful Scotland*, Edinburgh, Scottish Executive

Scottish Executive (2002a) *Better Communities in Scotland: Closing the Opportunity Gap*, Edinburgh, Scottish Executive

Scottish Executive (2002b) *Building Better Cities: Guidance and Next Steps*, Edinburgh, Scottish Executive

Scottish Executive (2002c) *Building Better Cities: A Policy Statement*, Edinburgh, Scottish Executive

Scottish Executive (2002d) *Review of Scotland's cities: The Analysis*, Edinburgh, Scottish Executive

Scottish Executive (2003) *A Partnership for a Better Scotland: Partnership Agreement between the Scottish Labour Party and Scottish Liberal Democrats*, Edinburgh, Scottish Executive

Scottish Executive (2004a) *A Smart, Successful Scotland*, Edinburgh, Scottish Executive

Scottish Executive (2004b) *Closing the Opportunity Gap*, Edinburgh, Scottish Executive, www.scotland.gov.uk/closingtheopportunitygap

Scottish Executive (2004c) *Scottish Index of Multiple Deprivation: Summary Technical Report*, Edinburgh, Scottish Executive

Scottish Executive (2004d) *The Framework for Economic Development in Scotland*, Edinburgh, Scottish Executive

Scottish Executive (2006) *People and Place: Regeneration Policy Statement*, Edinburgh, Scottish Executive

Scottish Office (1999) *Investing in Modernisation: An Agenda for Scotland's Housing*, Edinburgh, The Scottish Office

Stirling, T. and Smith, R. (2003) 'A Matter of Choice? Policy Divergence in Access to Social Housing Post-Devolution', in *Housing Studies*, 18 (2)

Turok, I. and Bailey, N. (2004) 'Glasgow's Recent Trajectory: Partial Recovery and it's Consequences', in Newlands, D., Danson, M. and McCarthy, J. (eds.) (2004) *Divided Scotland? The Nature, Causes and Consequences of Economic Disparities within Scotland*, Aldershot, Gower

Turok, I., Bailey, N., Atkinson, R., Bramley, G., Docherty, I., Gibb, K., Goodlad, R., Hastings, A., Kintrea, K., Kirk, K., Leibovitz, J., Lever, B., Morgan, J. and Paddison,

R. (2004) 'Sources of City Prosperity and Cohesion: the Case of Glasgow and Edinburgh', in Boddy, M. and Parkinson, M. (eds.) (2004) *City Matters: Competitiveness, Cohesion and Urban Governance*, Bristol, The Policy Press

Urban Task Force (1999) *Towards an Urban Renaissance: report of the Urban Task Force – Executive Summary*, London, Urban Task Force

Young, M. and Willmott, P. (1957) *Family and Kinship in East London*, London, Penguin

Chapter 13

Scottish Education in the 21st Century : a Story of Tradition, Myth, Conflict and Progress

Colin Clark

> "The highest result of education is tolerance" Helen Keller (1880-1968).

> "Education is the ability to listen to almost anything without losing your temper or your self-confidence" Robert Frost (1874-1963).

Introduction

In the introduction to his historical tour of Scottish education in the 20th c entury, Lindsay Paterson (2003a: 1), Professor of Educational Policy at the University of Edinburgh, quotes from the Advisory Council on Education in Scotland, where the Council outlines what the purpose of schooling is. It is a passage written in 1947 that is worth repeating here as it succinctly draws together some of the key themes that will be covered in this chapter, such as 'continuity and change', 'social divisions and differentiation' and 'social justice and social inclusion'.

> "The good school is to be assessed not by any tale of examination successes, however impressive, but by the extent to which it has filled the years of youth with security, graciousness and ordered freedom" (quoted in Paterson, 2003a: 1).

Pause for thought
Read the above statement from the Advisory Council back to yourself.

- Before reading this author's interpretation below of what this means, what do *you* think the Advisory Council means?

There are some parts of this statement that are worth underlining in this introduction. The first thing that stands out is the statement on examinations. In the current era of league tables, parental 'choice' and creeping private sector involvement in state education, this is something that would be seen as rather controversial. In 1947, exams or 'performance' were clearly *not* being viewed as the 'bottom line' by the Advisory Council. Examination results give you an *impression* of what a school is like but they are not, on their own, indicators of 'the good school'.

What about 'security'? This is the second thing that demands some comment. The Advisory Council, it seems, was concerned that the state education system should fulfil a 'duty of care' towards its pupils, as we would refer to it today. Schools, or other educational institutions, should be places where students can feel safe and learn in an environment that offers comfort, stability and peace of mind. Without such security the learning process can be a troubled, interrupted state of affairs.

What did the Advisory Council have in mind when it mentioned 'graciousness'? Clearly, this reflects the notion that a moral education should also be part of the school curriculum, usually through religious instruction and the example being set by teaching staff. Today, **'citizenship'** has become another means of imparting 'graciousness' to pupils (Maitles and Gilchrist, 2005).

The fourth element to this short statement from the Advisory Council is probably the most interesting of all for our purposes in this chapter: the idea of 'ordered freedom'. On first glance it seems like a contradiction in terms, an oxymoron. Behind this statement lies the belief that democracy – in education, in life – needs its structures of support and is, in the final analysis, a delicate 'balancing act' between a need for *control* (order) and a need for *care* (democracy). It is argued that the **socialisation** that occurs in the playground and the classroom reaps its rewards when young adults leave 'real education' for the 'real world'; 'ordered freedom' is accepted as the state of being and that which encourages and brings about the 'good society', as discussed by the late J.K. Galbraith (1996). For Galbraith (1996), the 'good society' is one that should not be attached to any dogmatic ideologies and it should actively encourage economic growth, whilst offering full social protection for the young, old, disabled and the environment. It is also a society that places great importance on **universal access** to education.

So, what has changed since 1947? Over fifty years have passed since the words quoted above were written down by the Advisory Council, yet it appears that very similar concerns are being echoed today. The terminology and structures might have changed, slightly, but fundamentally education in Scotland still has these four core issues at its heart: exams, safety, values and democracy. This is not to say everything remains the same, far from it – since devolution in 1999 many significant changes regarding policy and practice in different educational settings have been noted in Scotland. For example, in her chapter for *Exploring Social Policy in the 'New'*

Scotland, Margaret Arnott (2005: 239) usefully highlights some of the main educational developments at secondary school level, in particular, whilst also acknowledging that the most public and visible shift in education policy has been regarding the decision "that Scottish university students studying in Scotland would not have to pay tuition fees while studying, but instead make a contribution after they start earning."

We can see that many new issues have appeared on the policy horizon in Scotland that did not feature in either 1947 or, indeed, 1999. To be sure, *two* of the key debates this chapter will examine, in the form of Scottish 'real life' case studies, will attempt to illustrate some of the (political) complexities of education in Scotland and how an agenda for the future is being shaped by forces both within government and education departments as well as by outside agencies and organisations, not least parents and pupils themselves.

To be clear, this chapter is set out into *four* main sections:

- **Section 1** will give a brief overview of the history and current structure of various education systems in Scotland. As is common in other texts, we will examine the 1870s and 1940s as representing key watershed moments in Scottish educational policy development (Paterson, 2003a), whilst reviews of current structures focus on post-devolution initiatives (Bryce and Humes, 2003).

- **Section 2** will look closely and critically at the *five* National Priorities in education and how they are shaping the policy agenda and experiences within different educational institutions across Scotland. This commentary will link into later discussions, for example, 'Excellent, Ambitious Schools' and how the Scottish Executive views the future of education in Scotland. The *five* National Priorities in Education are:

  1. Achievement and attainment.
  2. A framework for learning, inclusion and equality.
  3. Inclusion and equality.
  4. Values and citizenship.
  5. Learning for life.

- **Section 3** recognises that there are many areas of debate and controversy within education. Alongside the NHS, education is one of the most politicised areas of public policy in Scotland and indeed, across Britain. Although there are many examples we could point to, for the purposes of this chapter we will look at *two* issues that are of current concern – one involving school closures and the creation of so-called 'under 12 campuses' in Glasgow; the other involving the increasing number of parents who are not 'staying local' and are instead opting to send their children to schools outside their immediate communities. Both these case studies show us the social and political side to educational policy and practice – something that has always been evident in the history of state involvement in education policy (Anderson, 1983).

- **Section 4** offers some speculative comment, with the help of the Scottish Executive Education Department and HM Inspectorate of Education, on what the future might hold regarding some of the latest developments in education policy in Scotland, particularly looking to the five National Priorities and the creation of 'ambitious, excellent schools' in Scotland for the 21st Century.

All four of these sections, to different degrees, attempt to link in with some of the major themes with which this Book engages. With regard to education, the key themes that will be discussed in this chapter are:

1. **Continuity and change:** We will examine in what ways educational policy has changed throughout history and the ways in which policies and debates have the remarkable capacity to stay on the agenda for a number of years, even though the terms of reference and policy language might change. It is argued in this chapter that some key themes are as relevant today as they were back in the late 19th and early 20th centuries.

2. **Social division and differentiation:** It seems to be the case that the educational playing field is not always level and some people (parents and pupils) have more 'choice' than others. *Who* and *what* you are still seems to determine (to some extent) *how* you fare in the classroom. Whether this is concerned with gender, ethnicity or disability – or any other of the major social divisions for that matter – the education system can sometimes deal you an unfair hand and unequal **'life chances'**. What systems can the education system put in place to try and minimise such **differentiation**?

3. **Social justice and social inclusion:** Education policies can be, despite what was said above, a great equaliser. Schools and other providers of education and learning/training services can empower pupils and students and open up many doors of opportunity. For this reason, it is common for policies to do with social justice and social inclusion to include measures that look to education. The two case studies in this chapter illustrate some of the (political) dynamics of social justice and how social inclusion, more often

than not, needs to be fought over and led from the 'bottom-up' rather than imposed from above.

In addition to thinking about these three key themes it would be very helpful, as you read through this chapter, to try to keep these *five* key questions in your mind. They are particularly relevant when reading the case study materials:

1. What is 'social' about education in Scotland?

2. What are the connections between education and the 'social problems' that appear to exist in contemporary Scottish society?

3. What are the differences between general education and 'academic' education?

4. In what ways can education promote social justice and social inclusion across Scotland?

5. To what extent do systems of education 'care' or 'control' those individuals who are part of education systems – both student and teacher?

Pause for thought
When you finish reading this chapter you should come back to these five key questions and try to jot down some brief answers to them.

Having covered what this chapter aims to do we now move on to give a brief overview of the history and current structure of education in Scotland. This section will lead us into subsequent discussions regarding the current five National Priorities that the Scottish Executive (2004a) is leading on and its plans for 'ambitious, excellent schools' as we move towards 2007.

Section 1: Education in Scotland: an Overview

This section is split into *two* distinct sub-sections – the first will briefly examine the historical 'traditions and myths' of Scottish education and the second will review the contemporary set-up of the *four* key sectors in Scottish education – primary schooling, secondary schooling, further education colleges and higher education institutions. Some comment will also be made on other important areas, such as pre-school provision and special needs education (now packaged under the heading 'additional learning support').

An Historical Overview of the Education System in Scotland

For the purposes of this chapter and restrictions of space, we shall look very briefly and selectively at the historical dimension. The focus here is with the systems in place at the time of writing and how the different elements fit together to give us a Scottish 'education system'. To be clear, this chapter is *not* just about schools; education can be viewed much more broadly than this as will be shown throughout the chapter.

If we had to pick a year to begin with then that year would probably have to be 1872, which was when elementary schooling in Scotland was made a statutory concern. From this year onwards, parents were legally obliged to send their children to school. As Anderson (2003: 223) has noted, the 1872 Act "established common standards and filled the gaps which the voluntary system had been unable to reach." Growth and expansion since that time progressed year on year and the Education (Scotland) Act 1918 represented a key legislative moment and, with the benefit of hindsight, this Act is now considered to be "the key legislative measure in Scottish education" during the 20ᵗʰ century (Paterson, 2003a: 2). The Advisory Council was an important body in terms of taking new ideas forward during the 20ᵗʰ century and examples are plentiful, but *three* impor tant ones were: the introduction of a comprehensive secondary school system; the internal, teacher -assessed, leaving certificates upon completion of secondary education; and what today would be called a focus on 'child-centred' education – then talked about in terms of a 'social education' that focused on the linkages between the nature and growth of the individual pupil and his or her connection to wider society (Paterson, 2003a).

More broadly, especially after the 1940s, Paterson (2003a) has noted that *three* main changes were evident in Scottish education:

1. Expansion – increasing access – across all sectors of education: primary schooling, secondary schooling, further education colleges and higher education.

2. Less differentiation within and between the different sectors of education.

3. Improved responses to the individual needs of the student.

All three of these social changes are connected to what is often discussed in the literature as the 'tradition' (or sometimes the 'myth') of 'liberal opportunity' within Scottish education (McPherson and Raab, 1988). In essence, this debate is one about how 'democratic' educational opportunity can truly be. It is asking that most fundamental of questions: 'what is education for?' Is it about preparing people for work or is it something more than this? It is apparent that these are questions with many different answers; education policy has swung from ideological pillar to pragmatic post with the coming and going of successive governments.

Pause for thought

- How would you answer the question, 'what is education for'?

Think about your own experiences of education here (and not just school!) and what has led you to read this book.

- Are you reading this as part of a course?
- Are you taking the course to try to get a better job?

It is a difficult question to fully answer to everyone's satisfaction. What is more easily stated is the fact that the history of education in Scotland is a story of how some ideas have taken root and become the norm whilst other proposals never even left the ground. It was between 1872 and 1901 that education dominated the political agenda and progress was seismic; whether you chose to look at the primary, secondary, further education or higher education sectors. These three decades contained a huge number of reforms across all four sectors that were to have a lasting impact during the next five decades or so (Anderson, 1983). Between 1940 and 2000 it was the three changes – or rather *transformations* – noted above by Paterson (2003a) that called the shots, especially from the 1960s onwards when education was systematically opened up to increasing numbers of students from different social and class backgrounds and embraced progressive *ideas*, as well as *ideals*.

An Overview of the Education System in Scotland Today

As noted above, it is still the case that educational provision in Scotland is concentrated within *four* main sectors: primary schooling, secondary schooling, further education colleges and higher education institutions. However, it is important to acknowledge, especially since 1997 and the beginnings of the New Labour project, that pre-school nursery education has also become a very significant sector, especially when linked to wider social policy questions regarding high-quality childcare and getting parents back into work (Mooney and McCafferty, 2005). In Scotland, most pupils will begin their school-based education at primary school, at the age of four or five and then move onto secondary school at the age of 11 or 12. Pupils receive education that is suitable to their age, ability and skills. The 'exit points' between 16 and 18 see many pupils leaving to enter into some form of post-school educational provision – usually at college or university. The latest figures from the Scottish Executive (National Statistics) (2005) report that:

> "The proportion of young people entering full-time further or higher education has risen slightly from 50 per cent in 2003/04 to 52 per cent in 2004/05. This can be attributed to a 2 percentage point increase in those going on to full-time higher education."

We should proceed by briefly reviewing each of the main sectors and their contemporary 'standing' in Scotland.

Pre-school

The provision of high-quality and affordable pre-school provision has been a core feature of New Labour welfare policy and some successes have been noted, especially in after-school clubs in places such as Enfield (Walker, 2005). In Scotland, the expansion of nursery care has matched, unsurprisingly, statistics indicating that more women of working age in Scotland are working outside the home than ever before. In 2002, the figure stood at 75 per cent (Graham and Boyle, 2003). Despite some progress there are still at least *three* key issues that need to be addressed regarding childcare in Scotland:

1. The quality of childcare can be variable.
2. The costs can be high and out of the reach of many parents.
3. Childcare is often not readily accessible in many communities in Scotland.

It is also important to note that nursery workers in Scotland have been taking industrial action regarding pay and conditions, illustrating wider issues with New Labour approaches to the 'management' and control of the public sector workforce (Mooney and McCafferty, 2005).

Primary School

The main changes at primary level are largely driven by demographic factors. Indeed, later in this chapter you will read about how Glasgow City Council is attempting to deal with this issue via its 'under-12 campuses' project. In just over two decades – 1980 to 2000 – Scotland 'lost' about 200 primary schools. Despite this there are still around 430,000 primary school pupils in Scotland (Paterson, 2003b) although warnings are continually being heard regarding the **'demographic timebomb'** in Scotland and the impact this will have on schools (*The Scotsman*, 2005). Such closures have been brought about by school registers falling and shifts in the population from rural to urban areas. Other closures have been the result of policy; not least measures in the Education (Scotland) Act 1980 that saw 'parental choice' come to the frontline with parents being able to choose the school their child would attend. Again, later in the chapter, you will read about a contemporary example of this practice regarding **'placing requests'** in Scotland and the impact it can have on both – perceived – 'popular' schools and 'unpopular' schools. Thus, the main challenges at the primary level are still connected to demographic factors but certain policy measures, such as placing requests, have added new unintended pressures to the system.

Secondary School

At the secondary level, as Paterson (2003b) notes, a strange contradictory trend has been apparent for some years now. Whilst secondary schools suffer from the same demographic trends that are impacting on primary school provision – simply put, fewer young people coming through the school-gates every year – they also benefit from the fact that more and more school children are staying on past the age of 16 and opting to complete 5ᵗʰ and 6ᵗʰ year. We might ask here, however, if this is less through 'choice' than the absence of viable options such as apprenticeships, well paid jobs and so on. The number of secondary pupils has been around the 330,000 mark for a few years now (Paterson, 2003b). Particular secondary schools, just like some primary schools, have also faced problems due to the placing request scheme. Requests are lower at the secondary level but often this is simply because in many local communities there is no other option at close quarters, with just one school serving the needs of the immediate area. The main challenges at secondary level are concerned with the 'staying-on' rates and schools ensuring they can provide for 5ᵗʰ and 6ᵗʰ year students whilst keeping a close eye on the numbers entering the school at S1 level.

Pause for thought
- Why do you think more secondary-age pupils are staying on to 5ᵗʰ and 6ᵗʰ year?
- Is it because school education is valued more nowadays or is it because there is a lack of other options for those wishing to leave earlier*?*

Post-school

For those leaving school, many students now go into further education (FE) or higher education (HE). As mentioned above, the latest figures indicate a rate of 52 per cent of school-leavers who go into either further or higher education (Scottish Executive National Statistics, 2005). Further education tends to be characterised as 'vocational' in nature and many students are in fact not school leavers but people returning to college to undertake part-time study on courses that either relate to their current occupation or might allow them to change jobs in the future. Some students are also unemployed and a further education course is seen as a route back into work. Current numbers stand at around 450,000 (Paterson, 2003b).

The higher education sector has grown very rapidly in the last two decades or so. According to Universities Scotland (2006), "[i]n Scotland as a whole, 27 per cent of the population of working age (18-64) have been to university. The UK average is only 24 percent and in England and Wales it is 23 per cent." There were some 263,000 students undertaking higher education courses in Scotland in 2000 (Paterson, 2003b).

The main factors behind the expansion have been economic, political and cultural. On the economic and political side, New Labour has been at pains to expand the HE sector and reach the target of 50 per cent participation rates of those aged 18-30 across the UK (DfES, 2003). This is largely driven by trying to ensure Britain remains competitive in world trade by having a skilled and educated workforce (Blair, 2006). On the cultural side, another change has been the number of women entering higher education. Women are now much more likely to be undergraduate and postgraduate students than men (according to Universities Scotland, 2006, some "59 per cent of the UK undergraduates studying in Scotland are women"). This is a major social change, especially when you compare the situation of working class women in education today with the situation that existed in Victorian times (McDermid, 2005) or even in the 1950s and early 1960s. The main challenges in higher education are largely concerned with changing funding structures and issues such as student retention; that is, trying to ensure 'drop-out' rates remain as low as possible and completion rates increase.

Pause for thought
- How can we best explain the massive rise in the number of young people attending university?
- Do you think that attending university is still a 'middle-class' privilege?

As well as these main sectors it is important to recognise other important sectors, such as different forms of community education and special education. The vast majority of these providers are state-based, governed by locally elected education authorities, of which there are currently 32. There are contributions made from the private and voluntary sectors in Scotland as well, especially in the pre-school sector.

An important factor to mention in the context of education in Scotland is religion (Finn, 2003). Schools linked to particular religions were incorporated into the public sector during the 1920s and they continue to be bound by the same rules and regulations on funding and governance that apply to non-religious (non-denominational) schools. The vast majority of denominational schools in both the primary and secondary sectors are Roman Catholic, although there is a Jewish school and an Episcopal Church school in Scotland. It is worth noting in this discussion that Scotland's only Muslim school, the independent Imam Muhammad Zakariya School in Dundee, is due to close soon, voluntarily, following an inspection report that highlighted poor standards. The closure is being regarded by the Campaign for Muslim Schools, which is attempting to make Willowbank Primary in Glasgow Scotland's first state-funded Muslim school, as a signal that the case for Muslim schooling has merits and would be meeting a demand and a need from this religious community. According to spokesperson Osama Saeed:

> "Catholic schools were brought into the state sector to ensure the quality of education that was provided in them [...]. We've had numerous teachers say to us they would be ready to teach in a Muslim school, but only if it had the safeguard of being within the state sector [...]. It's high time for this demand to be met" (Quoted on BBC News, 24 January 2006).

With regard to funding, further education colleges are 'incorporated bodies' that are funded by the recently created Scottish Funding Council (SFC) and other sources such as student fees and various private sources. Higher education institutions – universities, mainly – are also largely funded by the Scottish Funding Council but receive additional contributions from student fees, research grants and related sources. In total, the Scottish Funding Council distributes about £1.5 billion in funding for teaching, learning and res earch in Scottish colleges and universities every year (Scottish Funding Council, 2006).

Educational Inequalities in Scotland

Any review of the current 'state of play' in Scottish education would not be complete without some brief comment on the various inequalities that exist in the sector. It is the case that there are a number of challenges that face different sections and members of the community in accessing and receiving a fair, non -discriminatory education. In her contribution to the Scottish 2001 Social Justice Annual Report, Croxford (2001) suggested that:

> "The two main sources of inequality in *attainment* (authors' emphasis) are socio-economic differences in family background and social segregation between schools. Other sources of inequality include sex (gender), disability and ethnicity [...]."

In highlighting 'family background' and 'social segregation', in particular, Croxford (2001) is suggesting here that social class is a major factor in determining who does well at school (see Law and Law, **Chapter 4**). Such structural inequalities in attainment can be severe and raise difficult questions for social justice and social inclusion strategies being implemented by the Scottish Executive. Performance at school, often termed as **'educational attainment'**, can determine and shape pupils' post-school opportunities, or 'life chances' and it has been shown that unemployment is much more likely to affect those pupils who have left school with no or few qualifications (Palmer, Carr and Kenway, 2005). Whilst it is true that general levels of attainment are increasing year on year – including those who face disadvantage and inequality – the *gap* between the (educational) rich and (educational) poor remains as wide as ever and it seems to be the case that structural inequalities are actually reinforced, rather than challenged by, experiences of schooling (Babb, 2005).

However, policy and practice has not stood still on this issue and some recent measures have targeted the obstacles to achievement faced by disadvantaged youngsters. Croxford (2003) provides the example of the ScotXed initiative to produce more consistent and credible data when it comes to assessing how ethnicity and educational inequalities are connected. However, these policies compete with other policies and practices in the New Labour education 'market place', such as setting by ability and league-table inspired competition between schools, that merely reinforce structural social inequalities. It is worth noting that in 2005, the Child

Poverty Action Group in Scotland (2005: 4) launched a manifesto entitled 'Ten steps to a society free of child poverty' and one of the ten steps refers to educational inequalities, stating that the government must "[e]nsure all children have full access to requirements – meals, uniforms and activities – of their education." It is clear from the research evidence that this goal, to date, has yet to be achieved.

It is evident that social class and educational attainment are heavily linked, but educational inequalities are wider than this and are mentioned regularly in social research that examines the three major social divisions of gender, ethnicity and disability. As Tom Bryce and Walter Humes (2003: 13) have put it in their introduction to *Scottish Education: Post-devolution* (2ⁿᵈ Edition):

> "Educational systems are challenged by the particular difficulties and needs of varied groups of pupils and different systems respond in different ways [...] not all pupils find school satisfactory [...]."

Whilst space does not allow a detailed discussion of each social division, a few of the key elements should be mentioned in the context of this chapter. The common thread that appears to connect *all three* divisions appears to be experiences of *discrimination and exclusion* within mainstream schooling. Various studies and reports that have examined the complex relationships between education and gender (Croxford, Tinklin, Ducklin and Frame, 2001), ethnicity (SEED, 2003) and disability (Goodlad and Riddell, 2005) have all concluded that these major social divisions can have an impact on how pupils experience school and this, in turn, can affect their grades and performance more generally.

However, the debates are never straight-forward or clear-cut and are rarely static. If we take gender as an example, it is clear that not so long ago all the debates regarding gender and education were concerned with the performance, position and sex-stereotyping of girls and young women. Today, the main concerns appear to be connected to the position of boys and young men and their relatively weak performance in school – although this focus does not mean that the problems endured by girls and young women can now be ignored (Riddell, 2003). This transformation in terms of the focus of the gender debate in education is illustrative of how wider debates concerning social divisions and education can twist and turn depending on the political climate and other social changes across society.

Pause for thought
- How do different social divisions impact on someone's education?
- Can you think of any other social divisions, apart from gender, ethnicity and disability, which might potentially impact on how people experience the education system?
- In what ways can social divisions be addressed to try and ensure that the education 'playing-field' is more level?

One of the most important 'levers' for changing the education system, to make it more equal and fair for all pupils, is the teachers. One way of ensuring that teaching staff are up to the challenges, after qualification, is by a systematic approach to teacher-training. The national CPD framework is something that must be mentioned in closing this section.

The National CPD framework

An important element to consider in relation to education in Scotland is the role played by Continuing Professional Development (CPD). The Standards in Scotland's Schools etc Act 2000 made statutory provision for the General Teaching Council for Scotland (GTC) to look at the 'career development' possibilities of those under its charge. Following the **McCrone Report** and the agreement that followed (Purdon, 2003) 'professional development' within the teaching profession in Scotland was on the political agenda. At its simplest, CPD opportunities allow teachers to keep 'up to speed' with the latest skills and knowledge that are required to keep pace with the fast-changing educational environment and social world we live in. It is apparent that to teach at the highest level requires teachers to have access to CPD opportunities to enable them to learn new skills, or update existing skills, that allow them to support pupils and maintain best standards and practice. The Scottish Executive has worked with various 'stakeholders', including local authorities, teacher organisations, GTC Scotland, etc., to develop what is often referred to as a 'national framework for CPD'. This national CPD framework involves many different elements, but at its heart are *three* central components:

1. Addressing the development needs of the teaching profession.
2. Allowing teaching staff to maximise their strengths.
3. Having the skills and knowledge to deliver 'excellence in education'.

In essence then, the CPD framework is a package of accepted standards and procedures that cover initial teacher education, the induction process, the Chartered Teacher and Headship programmes (see below), in addition to all on-going staff development work and reviews. An important role in all this is played, as indicated above, by The General Teaching Council for Scotland. The GTC is responsible for accrediting and approving all Chartered Teaching programmes and modules, for managing claims submitted under the Accreditation of Prior Learning (APL) and, third, provid ing a 'tracking system' to ensure teacher progress is effectively monitored in meeting the required standard.

Two important elements in the above paragraph need to picked up and discussed, namely the Chartered Teacher and Headship programmes. 'Chartered Teacher' is a relatively new grade within the profession that was introduced via the agreement, *A Teaching Profession for the 21st Century* (SEED, 2001), and this in turn led to *The Standard for Chartered Teacher* (SEED, 2002) which has *four* key components to it, including values, knowledge, attributes and action. The aims of programmes leading to the award of 'Chartered Teacher' revolve around the following *three* things:

1. Enabling participants to enhance practical classroom skills.

2. Allowing teachers to develop their role as a classroom practitioner.

3. To provide expertise and support to fellow teachers in matters of classroom practice.

The achievement of these aims is via a combination of work-based learning and academic work, with a strong vocational leaning.

With regard to Headship, the 'Standard' was introduced in 1998 to give a framework for a training programme for those seeking to become effective headteachers. The *three* elements identified as supporting school leadership and management are: professional values, management functions and professional abilities. Through the Standard programme, prospective headteachers are able to demonstrate their understanding of the principles of educational management and improve and demonstrate their professional competence in senior management roles. In June 2005, the Scottish Executive published a Consultation Paper on revising the Standard for Headship entitled *Ambitious, Excellent Schools: standard for Headship* (SEED, 2005a) and a further document entitled *Ambitious, Excellent Schools: leadership* (SEED, 2005b). These will be discussed in Section 4.

Section 2: The Five National Priorities in Scottish Education

The 'National Priorities in Education' were approved by the Scottish Parliament on 19 December 2000. The Education (National Priorities) (Scotland) Order 2000 set out these priorities and defined them under *five* key headings (as discussed below). The National Priorities created a new statutory framework for school education and it requires all local authorities and schools to plan, monitor and report on improvements in education. It has been argued by John MacBeath (2003: 811) that National Priorities:

> "Has provided an opportunity to pursue a growth strategy [...]. It has promised to give equal status to the key areas of attainment, citizenship, inclusion and to consult as widely as possible in taking this vision forward."

Clearly, this is not just about 'education'; the five National Priorities have much wider social and economic interests and concerns. Likewise, Kay Livingston (2003: 971) has referred to the five National Priorities as offering a "rich diet of educational experiences." The five priority areas are:

1. **Achievement and attainment:** As the heading would suggest, this is principally about 'raising standards' in educational attainment for all pupils in schools, with an emphasis on **'core skills'** such as literacy and numeracy. In short, this is about raising grades and improving exam results.

2. **Framework for learning, inclusion and equality:** This measure is concerned with trying to support teaching staff and allowing them to develop new skills for the classroom (as discussed above, in relation to CPD opportunities for staff). From the pupil perspective, this priority is to do with self-discipline and standards of behaviour in school. Connected to this are wider issues regarding the environment of the school; making it conducive to learning and teaching (for example, supporting projects to 'makeover' school buildings and develop new infrastructure – e.g. new teaching rooms such as ITC suites).

3. **Inclusion and equality:** The third priority is a very important one in the context of this chapter (and book) in that the Scottish Parliament recognised that the school experience was not one without its problems or social inequalities. This measure attempts to 'level the (educational) playing field' as much as possible and ensure that equality is promoted at every stage of the school experience. The two main groups that have 'gained' from this priority are those pupils who have a disability or special educational needs, as well as those pupils for whom Gaelic and other languages are their mother

tongues or an important part of their everyday, cultural life.

4. **Values and citizenship:** Like priority three, this is an important measure with regard to this chapter and book. This priority is an explicit statement on the place of school in relation to the 'learning' and demonstration of citizenship and its position and importance in a democratic society. It aims to show pupils, in conjunction with parents, the connections and interdependencies between the individual, family, neighbourhood, community and society. It is the recognition that we are 'social beings'.

5. **Learning for life:** The final priority acknowledges the fact that education occurs long after we leave the school gates for the last time. This measure is aimed at giving pupils and students the skills, attitudes and confidence to be able to adapt to a fast-moving society and promote creativity, ambition and confidence.

Pause for thought

Read back over these 'five national priorities'.

- What themes and issues connect them together? (Bear in mind the general themes of the book here).
- Can you think of anything else that should be a 'national priority' when it comes to education?

According to Gordon Jeyes (2003: 173), the National Priorities were "generally welcomed" (by whom he does not say) and viewed as a "reasonable attempt to begin discussion of the definition of education beyond a narrow attainment agenda." Of course, as Jeyes (2003) acknowledges, the matter of setting National Priorities is much easier than the messy and costly task of transforming them into concrete outcomes and targets. Indeed, this issue is picked up by David Hartley (2003) in his discussion of connections between education and the economy in Scotland. It is a lengthy but important quotation and needs to be read in conjunction with the fifth National Priority of 'learning for life':

> "All this (the fifth priority) portends some difficulties for government. The emphasis has recently been on standards, and on more whole-class approaches to teaching. The fostering of creativity and emotional literacy, however, requires a pedagogy – a more expensive pedagogy – which has more of the characteristics of child-centred education. Even if government recognises the performative and instrumental effects of child-centred education (that is,

creativity is good for the economy), it may nevertheless decide not to fund it, because it would require pressure on the public purse" (Hartley, 2003: 291).

In the context of the five priorities it is probably useful to outline briefly the new 'additional support' mechanisms. On 14 November 2005, the Education (Additional Support for Learning) (Scotland) Act came into force and changed the way in which children and young people's educational support is identified, planned and recorded. The key changes included:

- Replacing Special Educational Needs (SEN) with what is now termed 'additional support needs'.

- The introduction of new duties on education authorities and other agencies.

- Measures to improve integrated working.

- Greater rights for parents and young people along with provisions for avoiding and resolving disputes and the introduction of the co-ordinated support plan (CSP).

In the main, the key word here is 'partnership' – the main aim is to try to get all those parties who have an interest in additional support for learning to work together more effectively (Children in Scotland, 2005). It is important to note that the term 'additional support needs' has a far broader definition than SEN and refers to *any* barrier to learning. A child or young person will have additional support needs if they require extra time and attention in order to 'benefit from school education'. The introduction of the duty on authorities to identify and make 'adequate and efficient' provision for all individuals with additional support needs gives far greater legal rights to such children and young people. This also applies to far more children and young people, including many who did not fall within the SEN system but do have additional support needs as defined by the new law (for example, groups in society who may face what is termed **'interrupted learning'**, such as nomadic Gypsies and Travellers or Fairground Travellers (Jordan, 2001). There are new duties on agencies other than education and this should help to ensure that where support is needed from health, social work and others, this is delivered and co-ordinated. 'Partnership in working' is the key to the new Act.

As we have seen, the National Priorities are helping to shape the educational future of Scotland, but what of current debates and controversies? In the three-part Channel 4 TV series *School Rules* (1997), Ian Hislop argued that the history of education in Britain has been one governed by controversy and a series of political machinations that have ensured the education system would never *just* be about education. The next section provides evidence for this argument and shows that education is bound up with larger questions of democracy, community, social class and power – all themes that are reflected directly and indirectly in this chapter and throughout the book.

Section 3: Areas of Debate – Two Contemporary Case Studies

In this section, two different case studies will be discussed. Both are contemporary examples of areas of debate and controversy within the provision of school education in Scotland. Through these case studies we can see elements of the main themes of this chapter and indeed the Book itself 'coming to life'. The first case study connects with wider debates on 'continuity and change' as well as aspects of 'care and control', whilst the second case study raises specific questions about the ways in which 'social divisions and differentiation' and 'social inclusion/exclusion' can best be tackled. Above all else, both case studies have something important to say about the (emotional) place and (physical) location of schools within local communities – the relative importance of places of learning as cementing social relations within that immediate environment.

Case Study 1: What Happens when your Local School is Threatened with Closure?

A recent issue in Glasgow throws up a number of questions about the role that schools play in local communities. Glasgow has recently launched a city-wide plan that will see the creation of what is termed 'under-12 campuses'. The Council Leader, Steven Purcell, has called the reforms 'wholesale' rather than 'piecemeal' and he is not wrong. The ambitious and far-reaching plan aims to merge about 70 primary schools and nurseries into 21 'campuses' – most of which are new-buildings designed and built by the Council. The logic behind the plans mainly revolves around falling school rolls in Glasgow that are leaving some schools, it is said, half-empty – a result of both birth-rate decline and also parents moving their children outside Glasgow City for their education.

This 'campus' plan has caused much controversy as some parents feel their views have not been heard on the matter. A lack of consultation has been a constant feature of the responses to the plans, as argued by those local communities that will be most affected by the changes. Easterhouse, one of the most socially disadvantaged housing schemes in Europe, is looking at a proposed school reorganisation that will close down ten primary schools and four nurseries and replace them with three 'campuses'. Likewise, in the affluent West End of the city, parents are also reacting against the plans and more than 800 objections were received over one proposal. Organised resistance to the plans has been forthcoming and a campaign group – Save Our Schools (SOS) campaign – has started and protests are happening across the city including weekend occupations, for example, at Carnwadric primary school in Thornliebank (*The Evening Times*, 31 January 2006).

The Carnwadric parent protest has caught the eye's of the national press and in a recent feature in *The Guardian* (21 March 2006) a parent, Lynne Wright, was quoted as saying:

> "We are going to keep protesting until someone from the education department comes to talk to us [...] this is basically a solid building. It needs refurbishment, because it hasn't been maintained for years. But it's on a great site, near the shops, near the park. We think someone has their eyes on this land [...]."

What has been interesting here is the response of the City Council to challenges by parents. The protests have largely been categorised as being 'reactionary' and 'anti-change' in nature, followed by statements about how parents and children will 'change their minds' when the new schools – or rather 'campuses' – are up and running (Kemp, 2006). The only formal political opposition to the plans has come from a councillor from the Scottish Socialist Party, Keith Baldassara, who has asked questions about the lack of effective consultation on the plan and a general lack of knowledge about what is involved in such a 'wholesale' project.

One of the main debating points has been surrounding class sizes. In some of the schools being targeted for closure, such as Blairtummock primary school in Easterhouse, class sizes are around the 20 mark. It is envisaged that the new campuses will generally involve class sizes going up to nearer the mid-30s range. This is one reason why some parents are unhappy about the plan. Another reason behind the protests is connected to the distances that some pupils will now need to travel to attend their local school and accompanying concerns about safety, for example, the closure of Provanhill Primary School will entail over 100 children having to negotiate a long route to school that local people consider to be far from safe for adults to travel.

The campaign intensified in February 2006 when Save Our School campaigners took their protests to Holyrood and submitted a 2000 signature petition demanding that the First Minister hold an inquiry into the Glasgow City Council plans (*The Evening Times*, 22 February 2006). The protest was timed to coincide with the stage one debate of the new Scottish Schools (Parental Involvement) Bill. At the time of writing protests are ongoing and support appears to be growing. Indeed, the SOS campaign even includes backing from the world famous psychic, Uri Geller!

At the beginning of this chapter the connection between education and democracy was raised. For those parents who have children who will potentially be affected by the 'campus' plans it seems to be the case that democracy is *absent* in this instance. The consultation sessions have been few and far between and Shona Graham, a parent and activist in Provanhall, had this to say on the matter:

> "We understand that education is expensive [...] we know what money means (here). But we don't want campuses. We can do without state-of-the-art facilities. *What we need is functional primary school buildings that are close to our communities* (this authors' emphasis) (quoted in Kemp, 2006: 5)."

This final sentence of Shona Graham is very telling; what is valued more is a school having a closeness and connection to the local community rather than pupils having access to new buildings and facilities that are removed and emotionally and geographically disconnected from the local area.

Pause for thought

After reading the case study, why not try writing some answers down to the following three questions?

1. What does this case study tell us about how Glasgow City Council is approaching the management of schools in its area? Is it a simple case of trying to manage rising costs?
2. What do you think about the response from local parents? Do their views count at all?
3. How important are schools to the community you live in? What would happen if the school in your local area was threatened with closure?

The second case study is a rather different debate – almost the polar opposite in fact – and the main theme explored here is concerned with issues of social inclusion/exclusion. What happens when your local school is not good enough and you want to send your children to another school outside your local area?

Case Study 2: What Happens when the Local School just isn't Good Enough?

Since the 1980s, parents have had the right to send their children to schools outside their local catchment area and there seems to be an increasing trend towards many parents acting on this right. Figures published in March 2006 by the Scottish Executive indicate that across Scotland nearly a quarter of parents now decide to send their children to a school that is not their local primary school – "23 per cent of the 52,000 pupils who entered P1 in 2004-05 were the subject of placing requests by their families" (Denholm, 2006: 9). Over 30,000 queries were made at primary and secondary level during 2004-05 and the vast majority of such requests were granted – 85 per cent in 2004-05 (Scottish Executive, 2006).

These figures raise a whole range of questions and issues about the place of schools in the local community, especially when seen in light of developments in Glasgow, as discussed in Case Study 1. What leads parents to seek a placing request? What circumstances would lead to a situation whereby the local school is not considered to be the 'natural' choice? Why is there, in effect, a lack of confidence in the local school to deliver a quality education? One explanation, offered by the Scottish National Party (SNP), is concerned with a rise in staff shortages at certain schools, although the Scottish Executive deny this and point to recent increases in the number of teachers working in Scotland, especially those recruited from England and elsewhere (Denholm, 2006).

However, according to *The Scotsman* (22 March 2006), 26.2 per cent of all *unsuccessful* placing requests were the result of a lack of staff at the school being approached by parents – an increase of more than 8 per cent when compared to figures from 2003-4. A critical factor appears to be parents being generally 'unhappy' with (i.e. lacking confidence in) the local school and seeing a neighbouring school as a better 'choice' for their son or daughter and offering a better standard of education. Is this a case of the 'grass being greener'? This certainly appears to be the case in Edinburgh, which has the highest number of placing requests in Scotland. Indeed, the situation in Edinburgh is causing real concern: according to a report in the *Evening News* (21 March 2006) falling numbers of young families in the city has led to predictions that Edinburgh will potentially be left with 27 empty primary schools by 2013. These figures are even more worrying given the fact that some schools are so popular in Edinburgh that they have to turn applicants away, such as James Gillespies in Marchmont, whilst other schools are half full and numbers keep falling.

Eleanor Coner of the Scottish Parent Teacher Council, in response to the placing request figures, suggested that preferences can be expressed, but many parents simply need to give their local schools 'a chance' (quoted in Denholm, 2006: 9):

> "If parents hear that the school down the road has a far better reputation then they tend to put in placing requests [...].There is room for parental choice, but we would encourage parents to think very carefully about putting their children

in the local school and helping to improve their local school rather than sending them elsewhere."

When looking at refusals, another key reason for a placement request being turned down seems to revolve around accommodation constraints – that is, schools not being physically capable of taking more pupils: this was the reason given in 39 per cent of cases at primary level and 49 per cent at secondary level (Scottish Executive, 2006).

This trend is one that needs careful attention, particularly when viewed in the context of the proposed changes in Glasgow. Placing requests – i.e. parental 'choice'– fit in with wider shifts in welfare where the market and privatisation have impacted heavily on those families who have slightly less choice than everyone else because of social divisions and inequalities (Arnott, 2005). It seems evident from Case Study 1 in Glasgow, that having a local school in the local community is seen as a vital and valued resource in helping to sustain and develop that community, in effect keeping it alive much like the role that a Post Office or a pub can play in a rural village. The two case studies, when placed side-by-side are a tale of two extremes – some parents fighting hard to keep their children's education local whilst other parents are placing requests to have their children educated outside their local community.

How can we explain this fundamental difference? Reasons of space mean that a full analysis cannot be given, but a social-scientific analysis would suggest that at the root of all this lie wider questions about class, power and politics. It connects to wider questions and debates about social divisions and social inclusion/exclusion in society – in the former case study it is largely working class communities who are campaigning to save their local schools (and, to some extent, their communities), whilst in the latter case study it is mainly the aspiring middle classes who are submitting placing requests for their children to, as they see it, 'trade-up' and attend schools outside their immediate locale. This is a kind of 'spatial apartheid' that renders questions of 'choice' as meaningless for those parents who are, in fact, trying to enact a New Labour obsession: the search for socially cohesive and 'just' communities that are part of the 'good society'. In closing this section, it is worth bearing in mind that one of the five National Priorities is explicitly concerned with 'inclusion and equality': to what extent do these case studies bear testament to that objective being pursued and met?

319

Pause for thought

After reading the case study, why not try writing down some answers to the following three questions?

1. How can we best try to understand the sudden and rapid rise in placing requests? What do you think is the main reason?
2. Should parents have the right to 'choose' the school for their children – even if the school is some distance from where the children live?
3. Do you think the rise in placing requests is leading us to a situation of a 'two-tier' state school system? (In the same way it is often argued that we have a 'two-tier' health system.)

Section 4: Looking to the Future?

Walter Humes and Tom Bryce (2003), in the closing chapter of their epic and definitive edited collection on *Scottish Education*, consider the future of education in Scotland:

*   What schools might look like in the future.

*   The kinds of teachers that will work in them.

*   Areas where more thinking and research is required and what the Scottish political context might throw up for reforms in education.

It is a twelve page review of some of the 'blue-sky' thinking that has taken place in recent years of where education policies might take us in Scotland. There are some truly wonderful and frightening ideas contained in this chapter, from further, determined measures to promote social justice and social inclusion within education systems, to the spectre of privatisation and a potential 'teacher exodus = education meltdown' scenario (Humes and Bryce, 2003).

However, since that speculative chapter was published in 2003, significant policy measures have occurred that have moved the debate even further on. For example, in 2004 the Scottish Executive published a blueprint for the future of Scottish education that built upon the earlier five National Priorities. In publishing *Ambitious, excellent schools: our agenda for action* (Scottish Executive, 2004a) and *A Curriculum for*

Excellence – the curriculum review group (Scottish Executive, 2004b), the foundations were put down for changes, it was hoped, that would take Scottish education truly into the 21st century.

With regard to 'ambitious, excellent schools', Peter Peacock, Minister for Education, and Euan Robson, Deputy Minister for Education, state in the foreword to the document that:

> "Ambitious, Excellent Schools sets out our agenda for the most comprehensive programme of modernisation for a generation or more. It ranges across actions to heighten expectations, to give freedom for teachers and schools, greater choice and opportunity for pupils and better support for learning and to create tougher, intelligent accountabilities."

At the heart of the project, alongside the *Curriculum for Excellence*, are *twelve* key action points to improve Scottish schools. These 12 measures are themselves part of a wider process of reform that builds on the 'national debate', started in March 2002, which fit together to 'modernise' the education sector. Principally aimed at secondary schools the reforms include:

1. The creation of the 'Excellence Standard' for top performing schools.

2. A new curriculum for 3-18 with an emphasis on 'choice', literacy and numeracy and extended time for pupils to study Highers.

3. A review of the Standard Grade system with an aim to try and simplify the exam structure (a decision will be made about their future by 2007).

4. Gifted pupils will be allowed to sit exams earlier if they are capable.

5. Greater linkages between primary and secondary schools, for example, allowing primary teachers to work in secondary schools to help with the transition between P7 and S1.

6. A new 'Leadership Academy' for headteachers.

7. A 'Schools of Ambition Programme' for schools needing to improve performance (some £8 million a year is being invested in the Programme and the Leadership Academy).

8. Extending devolved school management so that headteachers have more money to spend at their discretion, three year budgets to better plan change

and a greater say over staffing structures.

9. New 'Skills for Work' courses and qualifications to enhance vocational choices.

10. More international comparisons between Scotland's education performance and that of other countries.

11. A new Survey of Achievement to monitor school performance.

12. A new round of local authority inspections to ensure schools and headteachers are performing to expectations.

These plans are nothing if not bold and ambitious. The timescale is short and a lot is invested by the Scottish Executive in the plans being rolled out on time. Other agencies and actors are also throwing up interesting proposals too, however. For example, on 21 February 2006 a report was published by HM Inspectorate of Education (HMIe) entitled *Improving Scottish Education* (HMI e, 2006). This latest thorough review by HMIe, which provides a classic example of 'partnership working', suggests a number of areas that the different sectors of the Scottish education system need to address and improve upon, cutting right across proposals thrown up by both *Ambitious, excellent schools* and *A Curriculum for Excellence*. The HMIe report also highlights a number of areas of best practice. It is evident from this report that a key issue in improving Scottish education across the four main sectors, aside from important questions about funding mechanisms and structures, are staffing matters. This is not just connected to concerns over leadership, where the focus usually is, but actually common concerns across *all* staff; accepting advice and recognising that change is needed are vital elements in improving standards, along with working in a collaborative manner to achieve success for both staff and students/learners. In short, HMI e call s for 'fresh insight' as a means of effecting positive change.

Much of the HMIe report links into the 'Ambitious, Excellent Schools' project and the report identifies a number of strengths in Scottish education alongside areas that require improvement. One important aspect raised by HMIe is that measures of attainment need to include broader achievements than currently recognised, shifting away from the "general education = academic education" ethos that pervades Scotland, as Paterson (2003a: 3) has argued.

> ***Pause for thought***
> * Do you think the above 12 key action points will lead to significant and sustained progress in Scottish secondary schools?
> * Which individual points do you think are the most important? In other words, if you had to rank them in terms of importance, what order would you put them in?

Conclusion

This chapter has attempted to give an impression of the main issues and debates in 21st century Scottish education. In doing this, the chapter has embraced a number of the key themes that the book, more generally, is trying to engage with in a critical manner. In particular, the theme of 'continuity and change' has featured quite prominently, especially in relation to what has happened within the structures and practices of the Scottish education system since 1872 and the Act that made elementary schooling in Scotland a statutory concern. It was noted that many things are still as relevant today as they were back in the 19th century.

Similarly, the theme of 'social divisions and differentiation' has been apparent throughout this chapter but has, perhaps, best been illustrated via the two contemporary case studies that looked at the role schools play within local communities, as well as in the section dealing with educational inequalities (which also raises wider issues connected with how the Scottish Executive is trying to promote social justice and social inclusion via different education policy initiatives in Scotland). However, it is apparent that this chapter has had to cover much ground in a relatively 'compact and bijou' way, this being especially true in the brief historical review that explained how we have arrived at where we are now. This was followed by a more contemporary account of the nature and organisation of the Scottish education system across the four main sectors. It was noted that although much progress has been made, many challenges still face those delivering and accessing education in Scotland.

A lot of attention was given to the five National Priorities as this is a major lever that is guiding the current direction of Scottish education, especially in taking us beyond 'attainment-only' agendas and into the realm of changes demanded by the needs of those pushing forward, for example, citizenship and **lifelong learning** projects. CPD and additional learning support measures were looked at in some detail and these again are fitting in with the shift towards models that push to the foreground debates

323

on inclusion and social justice in education settings. In an attempt to 'bring to life' some of the debates, two up-to-date case studies were discussed. One concerned the creation of 'under-12 campuses' in Glasgow and the resulting school closures in various parts of the city. The other was a broader case study that examined what impact placing requests are having on schools across Scotland and some of the issues this throws up in terms of social inclusion/exclusion and social mobility.

As to the future, it was noted that the Scottish Executive's 'vision' of transforming Scottish education by 2007 is not without its issues; 'ambitious, excellent schools' will come with a hefty price tag and much political ground to manoeuvre. In all, this chapter has reviewed some of the main issues that are on the Scottish political agenda regarding education and where this agenda will take us as we move further into the 21st century. To close, it is evident from this chapter that Scottish education *does* tell a complicated and shifting story of 'tradition, myth, conflict and progress'; a story that in many ways will never reach 'the end', not least because of the political storms education can raise amongst parents, teachers, pupils and politicians. As was noted earlier in the chapter, education is *rarely* just about education.

Further Reading

Bryce, T.G.K. and Humes, W.M. (eds.) (2003) *Scottish Education: Post-devolution*, Second Edition, Edinburgh, Edinburgh University Press
Paterson, L. (2003) *Scottish Education in the Twentieth Century*, Edinburgh, Edinburgh University Press

Useful Websites

There are a range of excellent resources on the internet concerning education in Scotland. A few of the essential websites are listed below:

BBC – Education in Scotland: http://www.bbc.co.uk/scotland/education/information/webLinks.shtml
General Teaching Council for Scotland (GTC Scotland): http://www.gtcs.org.uk/
HM Inspectorate of Education (HMIe): http://www.hmie.gov.uk/
Learning and Teaching Scotland (LTScotland): http://www.ltscotland.org.uk/
National Debate on Education: http://www.scotland.gov.uk/education/nd homepage.htm
National Priorities: http://www.nationalpriorities.org.uk/index.html
Scottish Executive Education Department (SEED) : http://www.scotland.gov.uk/About/DepArtments/ED
Scottish Executive – education statistics: http://www.scotland.gov.uk/Topics/Statistics/15568/2299
Scottish Funding Council (SFC): http://www.sfc.ac.uk/
Scottish Parent Teacher Council (SPTC): http://www.sptc.info/
Scottish Qualifications Authority (SQA): http://www.sqa.org.uk/
Scottish Schools Online: http: //www.scottishschoolsonline.gov.uk/index.asp
SKILL – National Bureau for Students with a Disability: http://www.skill.org.uk/Scotland/Links.asp
Youth Link: http://www.youthlink.co.uk/
Young Scot: http://www.youngscot.org/

Bibliography

Anderson, R. (1983) *Education and opportunity in Victorian Scotland: schools and Universities*, Oxford, Oxford University Press

Anderson, R. (2003) 'The History of Scottish Education, pre-1980', in Bryce, T.G.K. and Humes, W.M. (eds.) (2003) *Scottish Education: Post-devolution*, Second Edition, Edinburgh, Edinburgh University Press

Arnott, M. (2005) 'Devolution, territorial politics and the politics of education', in Mooney, G. and Scott, G . (eds.) (2005) *Exploring Social Policy in the 'New' Scotland*, Bristol, The Policy Press

Babb, P. (2005) 'A summary of *Focus on Social Inequalities*', London, Office for National Statistics, http://www.statistics.gov.uk/articles/nojournal/FOSIsummary article.pdf (accessed on 19 April 2006)

BBC News (2006) 'Independent Muslim school to shut', 24 January 2006, http: //news.bbc.co.uk/1/hi/scotland/4643080.stm (accessed 16 February 2006)

Blair, T. (2006) 'Parents and children first: Tony Blair defends his school reforms', in *Progress Magazine* (March/April 2006), http://www.progressives.org.uk/ magazine/Default.asp?action=magazine&articleid=984 (accessed on 26 March 2006)

Bryce, T.G.K. and Humes, W.M. (eds.) (2003) *Scottish Education: Post-devolution*, Second Edition, Edinburgh, Edinburgh University Press

Child Poverty Action Group (2005) *Ten steps to a society free of child poverty*, Glasgow, CPAG, http://www.cpag.org.uk/scotland/CPAG-Scot-Manifestocot-2005.pdf (accessed on 19 April 2006)

Children in Scotland (2005) *Education (Additional Support for Learning) (Scotland) Act implementation*, Briefing Note, Edinburgh, Children in Scotland, http:// childpolicyinfo.ChildReninscotland.org.uk/index/news-app?story=4137 (accessed on 24 March 2006)

Croxford, L. , Tinklin , T. , Ducklin , A. and Frame, B. (2001) *Gender and pupil performance, Interchange 70*, Edinburgh, Scottish Executive, http:// www.scotland.gov.uk/library3/Education/ic70-01.asp (accessed on 18 April 2006)

Croxford, L. (2001) *Social Justice Annual Report Scotland 2001: socio-economic inequalities and educational attainment in Scotland*, Edinburgh, Scottish Executive, http: //www.scotland.gov.uk/library3/social/sjar-39.asp (accessed 18 April 2006)

Crowford, L. (2003) *Measuring performance – tackling inequalities?* Edinburgh , CES Briefings, http://www.ces.ed.ac.uk/PDF per cent20Files/Brief026.pdf (accessed on 18 April, 2006)

Denholm, A. (2006) 'Parents shun local schools and ask for move', in *The Herald*, 22 March 22, p.9

Department for Education and Skills (2003) *The Future of Higher Education* (White Paper) CM5735, London, DfES, http://www.dfes.gov.uk/hegateway/strategy/ hestrategy/ (accessed on 22 March 2006)

Evening Times, The (2006) 'Angry Mums' save our school sit-in', 31 January , http:

//www.eveningtimes.co.uk/hi/news/5048424.html (accessed on 14 February 2006)

Evening News (2006) 'Black marks for schools choice', 21 March, http://news.scotsman.com/education.cfm?id=445102006 (accessed on 22 March 2006)

Finn, G.P.T. (2003) ''Sectarianism': a challenge for Scottish Education', in Bryce, T.G.K. and Humes, W.M. (eds.) (2003) *Scottish Education: Post-devolution*, Second Edition, Edinburgh, Edinburgh University Press

Galbraith, J. K. (1996) *The Good Society: the humane agenda*, London, Sinclair - Stevenson

Goodlad, R. and Riddell, S. (2005) 'Social justice and disabled people: principles and challenges', in *Social Policy and Society*, 4(1)

Graham, E. and Boyle, P. (2003) 'Low fertility in Scotland: a wider perspective', in *Scotland's Population 2002: The Registrar General's annual review of demographic trends*, Edinburgh, General Register Office for Scotland (Chapter 3), http://www.gro-scotland.gov.uk/statistics/library/annrep/02annual-report/02annual-report-chapter3.html (accessed on 17 February 2006)

Hartley, D. (2003) 'Education and the Scottish economy', in Bryce, T.G.K. and Humes, W.M. (eds.) (2003) *Scottish Education: Post-devolution*, Second Edition, Edinburgh, Edinburgh University Press

Humes, W.M. and Bryce, T.G. K. (2003) 'The Future of Scottish Education', in Bryce, T.G.K. and Humes, W.M. (eds.) (2003) *Scottish Education: Post-devolution*, Second Edition, Edinburgh, Edinburgh University Press

Her Majesty's Inspector of Education (HMIe) (2006) *Improving Scottish Education – a report by HMIe on inspection and review 2002-2005*, Livingston, HMIe, http://www.hmie.gov.uk/ise/ (accessed on 24 March 2006)

Jeyes, G. (2003) 'The Local Governance of education: an operational perspective', in Bryce, T.G.K. and Humes, W.M. (eds.) (2003) *Scottish Education: Post-devolution*, Second Edition, Edinburgh, Edinburgh University Press

Jordan, E. (2001) 'Interrupted learning: the Traveller paradigm. Support for learning', in *British Journal of Learning Support*, 16(3)

Kemp, J. (2006) 'Fourteen into three won't go', in *The Guardian* (Education supplement), 21 March, p.5

Livingston, K. (2003) 'The European dimension', in Bryce, T.G.K. and Humes, W.M. (eds.) (2003) *Scottish Education: Post-devolution*, Second Edition, Edinburgh, Edinburgh University Press

MacBeath, J. (2003) 'School effectiveness, improvement and self -evaluation', in Bryce, T.G.K. and Humes, W.M. (eds.) (2003) *Scottish Education: Post-devolution*, Second Edition, Edinburgh, Edinburgh University Press

McDermid, J. (2005) *The schooling of working class girls in Victorian Scotland*, London, Taylor and Francis

McPherson, A. and Raab, C. D. (1988) *Governing education: a sociology of policy since 1945*, Edinburgh, Edinburgh University Press

Maitles, H. and Gilchrist, I. (2005) ''We're citizens now!' The development of positive values through a democratic approach to learning', in *Journal for Critical Education Policy Studies*, 3(1), http://www.jceps.com/index.php?pageID=article&articleID=45 (accessed on 25 March 2006)

Mooney, G. and McCafferty, P. (2005) 'Only looking after the weans? The Scottish nursery nurses' strike, 2004', in *Critical Social Policy*, 25(2)

Palmer, G., Carr, J., Kenway, P. (2005) *Monitoring poverty and social exclusion in Scotland, 2005*, York, JRF/NPI, http://www.jrf.org.uk/knowledge/findings/socialpolicy/0585.asp (accessed on 19 April 2006)

Paterson, L. (2003a) *Scottish Education in the Twentieth Century*, Edinburgh, Edinburgh University Press

Paterson, L. (2003b) 'Educational provision: an overview', in Bryce, T.G.K. and Humes, W.M. (eds.) (2003) *Scottish Education: Post-devolution*, Second Edition, Edinburgh, Edinburgh University Press

Purdon, A. (2003) 'The Professional development of teachers', in Bryce, T.G.K. and Humes, W.M. (eds.) (2003) *Scottish Education: Post-devolution*, Second Edition, Edinburgh, Edinburgh University Press

Riddell, S. (2003) 'Gender and Scottish education', in Bryce, T.G.K. and Humes, W.M. (eds.) (2003) *Scottish Education: Post-devolution*, Second Edition, Edinburgh, Edinburgh University Press

Scottish Executive (2004a) *Ambitious, excellent schools – our agenda for action*, Edinburgh, Scottish Executive, http://www.scotland.gov.uk/library5/education/aesaa-00.asp (accessed on 15 March 2006)

Scottish Executive (2004b) *A curriculum for excellence – the curriculum review group*, Edinburgh, Scottish Executive, http://www.scotland.gov.uk/library5/education/cerv-00.asp (accessed on 15 March 2006)

Scottish Executive (2006) *Placing requests by parents to local authorities that a child be placed in a specified school*, Edinburgh, Scottish Executive National Statistics Publication, http://www.scotland.gov.uk/Publications/2006/03/21112305/0 (accessed on 24 March 2006)

Scottish Executive Education Department (SEED) (2001) *A Teaching profession for the 21ˢᵗ Century: agreement reached following recommendations made in the McCrone report*, Edinburgh, Scottish Executive Education Department, http://www.scotland.gov.uk/library3/education/tp21a-00.asp (accessed on 17 February 2006)

Scottish Executive Education Department (2002) *Standard for Charter Teacher*, Edinburgh, Scottish Executive Education Department, http://www.scotland.gov.uk/library5/education/sfct-00.asp (accessed on 17 February 2006)

Scottish Executive Education Department (2003) *Educating for Race Equality – a toolkit for Scottish Teachers*, Edinburgh: Scottish Executive, http://www.antiracisttoolkit.org.uk/ (accessed on 18 April 2006)

Scottish Executive Education Department (2005a) *Ambitious, excellent schools: standard for headship? A consultation paper*, Edinburgh, Scottish Executive

Education Department, http://www.scotland.gov.uk/Publications/ 2005/06/17104149 /41509 (accessed on 19 February 2006)

Scottish Executive Education Department (2005b) *Ambitious, excellent schools – leadership? A discussion paper*, Edinburgh, Scottish Executive Education Department, http://www.scotland.gov.uk/Publications/2005/06/17104251/42534 (accessed on 19 February 2006)

Scottish Executive (National Statistics) (2005) *Destinations of leavers from Scottish schools, 2004-05* (statistics publication notice, education series), Edinburgh, Scottish Executive (Statistics Publication Notice), http://www.scotland.gov.uk/Publications/ 2005/12/06133725/37257 (accessed on 26 March 2006)

Scottish Funding Council (2006) 'Home page', http://www.sfc.ac.uk/ (accessed on 21 February 2006)

Scotsman, The (2005) 'Scotland's demographic timebomb', 20 October, http://news. scotsman.com/latest.cfm?id=2116812005 (accessed on 15 April 2006)

Universities Scotland (2006) 'Facts and figures: students and social inclusion', Edinburgh, Universities Scotland, http://www.universities-scotland.ac.uk/ (accessed on 15 March 2006)

Walker, D. (2005) 'Parents see improvements begin', *The Guardian*, 31 March, http: //society.guardian.co.uk/labourpublicservices/story/0,,1448951,00.html (accessed on 18 March 2006)

Chapter 14

Crime and Criminal Justice in Scotland

Mary Munro and Jan Nicholson

Introduction

Crime has increasingly become a major focus of everyday life. It is a dominant element of all news sources and we absorb it with a mix of fear and fascination. For example, we watch crime shows on TV and in the cinema and consume 'true crime' books for entertainment. At the same time there is now a growing concern with a rising 'fear of crime' and this has shaped crime policy in recent years.

A significant part of 'street' crime is clearly associated with social division and inequality. The courts are filled daily with people who are already marginalised or excluded, for example, people involved in drugs or prostitution. Often crime, and the way we respond to it, is just another stage in the continuum of **social exclusion**.

There also seem to be confusing and contradictory messages coming from the authorities about how best to deal with offenders, with the emphasis on care and control shifting as politicians focus on crime as a critical feature in major election campaigns, and parties compete to be thought of as 'tough' on crime.

This chapter aims to do the following:

1. Introduce you to some of the key ideas in modern criminology.

2. Give you information about the 'criminal justice system' in Scotland.

3. Encourage you to explore the themes of inequality and welfare in relation to thinking about victims *and* prisoners in Scotland.

What is Crime?

Most people would assume that a crime is committed when someone breaks the criminal law and that this simple legal definition is obvious and sufficient (Croall, 2003: 269). Such a view implies an acceptance of the idea that criminal law encapsulates society's formal rules against the "violation of core social or individual interests or shared values" (Lacey, 2002: 268).

One problem with this approach is that it underplays the importance of inequalities in power and class bias in the formation of criminal law across history. Sellin (1938, cited in Coleman and Norris, 2000), for example, recognised that criminal law was more likely to protect the values of the powerful rather than uphold the moral values of the population at large. Sutherland's investigations in the United States in the 1930s showed that **'white collar crime'** was more likely to be subject to 'regulation' than 'legislation', leaving the criminal justice system to focus on the less powerful, poorer sections of society (Sutherland, 1940).

Pause for thought
Murder and theft may be considered inherently (morally) wrong and have been recognised as crimes for centuries.

- Consider how social attitudes have changed in relation to the following:

    - Smoking in a pub.
    - Drinking and driving.
    - Domestic violence.
    - Homosexuality.
    - Using cannabis.
    - Prostitution.
    - 'Anti-social behaviour'.

- How have these changes been reflected in the law?

Another problem is that what is viewed as **'criminal'** or **'deviant'** changes over time and differs between cultures. For example, in recent years in Scotland the following behaviour has become defined as criminal:

- Smoking in an enclosed, public space.
- Sectarian harassment.

- Racial harassment.
- Using a mobile phone when driving.

Current laws on rape, homosexuality, abortion and drug use are quite different from the laws in the recent past. The criminal law is, therefore, constantly evolving to define certain acts or types of behaviour as criminal in response to political, economic, technological or social change.

How do We Know about Crime?

Crime and the Media

Most of us have little direct or protracted contact with crime and criminals. What we 'know' is often based on the messages we get from mass media and an impression of what is going on in our local area. This knowledge is not necessarily a true picture of crime, but leaves us with a range of ideas that are distorted. One such 'fallacy' is that crime is exciting and dramatic. The need to sell newspapers or hook an audience into a crime series on TV requires journalists and writers to emphasise the dramatic, the serious and the violent. In reality, most crime, such as breaches of the peace, road traffic offences, shoplifting, vandalism or theft, is mundane, relatively trivial and non-violent (Felson, 2002). Such dramatisation of the seriousness of overall crime can create **'moral panics'**, which feed into *fear* of crime amongst the public.

Another key source of information about crime comes from political rhetoric. Crime, and how to deal with it, is often presented as a key social concern – a problem that political parties promise to tackle. In the heat of debate it is often overlooked that, for most crimes, levels are stable or falling.

Official Sources of Information about Crime

Statistical records are routinely compiled by police and criminal justice agencies, such as courts, prisons and social work services and are collated by government statistical departments. These are published annually by the Home Office (England and Wales) and by the Scottish Executive for Scotland and are available on-line (see Bibliography). For example, if you want to know how many crimes were reported to the police in any year in Scotland you will find the information in the 'Recorded Crime' statistics. If you want to research facts about the imprisonment of women in Scotland you could consult the 'Prison Statistics'.

Large scale **Victim Surveys** are usually commissioned by the government from academic teams or market research companies. These include the:

- British Crime Survey (BCS).
- Scottish Crime Survey (SCS).
- National Household Survey on Victimisation and Fear of Crime.

Statistical evidence is very useful as a starting point in learning about crime, crime enforcement and people who commit crimes. However, there are limits to the information it conveys. **Official statistics** do *not* reflect the actual extent of crime and criminals. They can only measure crimes *reported* to and *recorded* by the police and then processed by the criminal justice agencies. They do not provide any information on crimes that go unreported, undetected or reported to other enforcement bodies such as the Ministry of Defence Police. Changes in recorded crimes may reflect police-targeting – such as during the seasonal drink drive campaigns – rather than the 'real' occurrence of such offences.

Victim surveys are designed to build a picture of the national experience of being a victim of crime by asking a representative sample of householders about crimes committed against them in the year in question. This cannot be a complete picture because not all crimes are included in the surveys (sexual crimes, for example). Similarly, the **'victimisation'** of young people or dependent elderly relatives will be less likely to be picked up. Furthermore, people are not always aware that they have been victimised by, say , losses from a pension fund, or health damage from environmental crimes. Even if they are aware of having suffered harm or loss they may not think of it as a 'crime'. There is also the obvious problem of *reliability* – is the respondent telling the truth, or remembering accurately?

A comparison of the victim surveys and the recorded crime statistics indicates the extent of crime that is not reported to the police. For some offences, such as theft of a motor vehicle, there is a close match (estimated at 97 per cent in Scotland in 2002). For others, such as household theft, there may be clear differences (only 16 per cent of these offences were reported in Scotland in 2002) (Scottish Executive, 2004b).

What are the Causes of Crime?

A wide range of theories has been advanced to explain crime. These ideas can be divided into those that focus on some characteristic of the individual offender and those that are more concerned with wider social explanations. Most controversial are the possibilities presented by some scientists researching a genetic or inherited link to criminal or deviant behaviour. A brief review of the range of ideas follows.

Something 'Criminal' about the Offender

One of the earliest criminologists was the Italian doctor, Cesare Lombroso (1835-1909). He considered that criminals had distinctive and recognisable physical characteristics. His **biological** studies were flawed, but very influential insofar as they contributed to common assumptions about 'criminals' as somehow *different* from 'normal' people. Another example of this approach was research into the supposed association between male body shape and criminality proposed in the 1940s by the American psychologist, William Sheldon (1898-1977). More recently, psychologists such as Eysenck (1916-1997) have explored the relationship between **psychological traits**, such as introversion and extroversion, and crime. A range of studies has also attempted to highlight a **genetic** link to crime, but while it may be possible to identify genetic links to a greater risk of displaying some types of behaviour, such as violence, the effects of life experiences and social factors cannot be eliminated (Coleman and Norris, 2000).

It's More about 'Society'

At roughly the same time that Lombroso was developing his ideas about the physical abnormality of criminals, the French sociologist, Emilé Durkheim (1858-1917), was arguing that crime was a normal feature of every society. He suggested that crime was useful, necessary and **functional** for society because reactions to it reinforce moral standards and shared values. Some people turn to crime as a response to the dislocating pressures of rapid social change. Robert Merton (1968) further developed this theme in the United States in the 1930s. He argued that crime arose where there was a strain between dominant social goals – such as financial success represented by the 'American Dream' – and the means of attaining them. Some people who were excluded from the legitimate means to achieve such goals might, he argued, resort to alternative criminal means or alternative lifestyles to do so.

Sociologists working in Chicago and other American cities in the mid-20th century then took up ideas about alternative 'opportunity structures'. They observed how young people exposed to a neighbourhood criminal culture might become drawn into crime. **Subcultural theory** describes delinquency, especially street gangs, as a means by which working class boys deal with their failure to succeed in conventional terms.

A completely different way of thinking about crime is associated with the work of the American sociologist, Howard Becker (1963). Based on his observations of the jazz and drugs scene in Chicago in the 1950s, he argued that those labelled as deviant and treated as such by criminal justice agencies, will take on the identity imparted by that label. **Labelling theorists** argue that categorising someone a 'criminal' or an 'offender' reinforces that identity and, consequentially, for a range of reasons, makes it more difficult to escape crime. This remains a useful way of thinking about the further marginalisation of 'criminals' and the related problems of trying to reduce re-offending.

Control theorists, such as Hirschi (1969), take another perspective. Instead of asking 'why do *some people* commit crime?' they suggest that the more fruitful question is, 'why do *most people not* commit crime? Hirschi's (1969) analysis of this question points to the formal and informal social controls that prevent most of us from behaving in a criminal way.

More recently, **realist** writers explored the link between crime and social inequality, deprivation and exclusion. The policy conclusions drawn from these analyses differ depending on the political perspective adopted (see Sweeney, **Chapter 2**). In the United States in particular, **'right realism'** is associated with anti-**welfarist** arguments supporting punitive interventions. **'Left realism'** is associated with the work of Jock Young (1992) and other British criminologists who emphasise the importance of **relative deprivation** as a cause of crime.

Much of this theoretical work has historically ignored women. Feminist criminologists reacted to such 'gender blind' assumptions by seeking to 'establish a fully sociological analysis of female crime and delinquency' (Bilton *et al*, 1996) and to expose the sexist treatment of women in the criminal justice system, both as offenders and victims, especially of domestic and sexual abuse.

Pause for thought
- What are your ideas about why people commit crime?

For example, you may consider that everyone is able to make the same choice about breaking the law, or you may consider that for some people there are circumstances that make it more likely or understandable.

- Do you think that 'criminals' are different in some way from 'normal' people?
- Which (if any) of the above theories might best explain:

  a) Female offending?
  b) White collar crime?

What do we Know about Crime?

The Geography of Crime

Studies in environmental criminology have highlighted correlations with crime and areas characterised by inadequate housing, high rates of poverty and ill health and those that generally attract a transient population. New crime mapping and combinatory database technologies are able to show patterns and concentrations of crime victimisation in particular areas. Later in this chapter we will look at how Scottish prisoners tend to have addresses in the most disadvantaged wards in the country.

Gender and Crime

Gender is *the* single most significant factor in crime and yet it continues to be the least explored. Statistics show that men commit far more crime than women and much more serious and violent crime. In Scotland in 2003, just 16 per cent of all convictions were of women. Men outnumber women in all categories of crime except those relating to prostitution (Scottish Executive, 2005c).

Criminologists have tried to understand what it is about women that might explain their lower rates of criminality. However, more recently, the problem has been turned on its head. Heidensohn (2002) has suggested that perhaps the most interesting question is not to ask 'what makes women's crime rates so low, but why are men's so high?'

Class and Crime: Street Crime versus Suite (or 'Suit') Crime

Our perception of crime is dominated by 'street crime', such as robbery, violence or burglary. Stories of the activities of, often young, male 'yobs' or 'neds' fill the news and are regularly linked by journalists to notions of 'evil'. These are certainly the crimes that are most likely to attract the attention of the police and the criminal justice system.

Criminologists use the term 'white collar crime' to cover offending by people in the course of their occupation (e.g. petty pilfering of stationery), or offending by firms and businesses (**'corporate crime'**). Corporate criminal activities may include fraud, forms of illegal trading, breaches of health and safety regulations, or environmental violations. The sums involved in fraud can be very considerable and, in total, may exceed the value of goods shoplifted or stolen by 'normal' criminals. However, such activities are often difficult to detect and when exposed do not necessarily result in prosecution. A study by the accountants, KPMG, found that in a sample of 100 major frauds committed by employees against the company in which they worked, no action was taken in nearly 20 per cent of cases, probably for fear of damaging the reputation of the firm (KPMG, 2004). Similarly, although HM Revenue and Customs reserves the right to take a criminal prosecution, it tends only to investigate serious fraud as a civil procedure, with the primary objective of negotiating the payment of the sum owed and a penalty.

Media coverage of these issues rarely hits the front page unless there is a crash, or a disaster of some kind with immediate loss of life. This contributes to a distortion in general awareness of the prevalence and seriousness of such crimes and a failure to recognise that the criminal justice system may be applied to such violations, including the most serious cases of corporate killing. Nonetheless, such an approach is possible and appropriate. For example, a recent report, prepared for the Scottish Executive by the Expert Working Group on Corporate Homicide, both defines what a law of corporate homicide might look like and how the array of criminal penalties including fines, probation and community service might be applied to companies or their directors (Scottish Executive, 2005b). (Up to date information on this issue can be found on www.cjscotland.org.uk.)

Age and Crime

The peak age for both female and male convictions in Scotland was 20 in 2003 (Scottish Executive, 2005c). Young people between 17 and 21 are more likely to be convicted in any year than any other age groups. However, the latest statistics show that there has been a steady overall fall during the last ten years in the proportion of young people in these age groups who are convicted.

Much youth offending is relatively trivial and can be related to life styles that present the context for crime, such as spending time outside the home with friends on the street, drinking, experimenting with drugs and clubbing. These factors are also the reason why young people are more likely than older people to become *victims* of crime, especially violence.

Most people grow out of offending by their early to mid twenties as they develop commitments and responsibilities. An alternative reading of the drop in convictions at this age is that it is easier for adults to hide their criminal activity than it is for 'kids' on the street.

Scottish Criminal Justice

In the first part of this chapter we looked at how it is important to think carefully about the meaning of 'crime', how we know what we know about crime and what research suggests might explain patterns of offending in our society.

In this second part of the chapter we will start by considering the 'criminal justice system' in order to understand how the official response to the crime problem is organised. By paying attention to this we do not mean to imply that the way that crime can be tackled and prevented is the exclusive responsibility of official agencies. Indeed, 'criminal justice has a very narrow, albeit important, role to play in creating and nurturing a safe and just society' (Coyle, 2003).

We will then look at examples of *two* important current criminal justice issues and will explore how these may be understood in terms of the themes of this book. This will take the following form:

- First, we will consider imprisonment in Scotland and see how the by now familiar constellations of exclusion, poverty, physical and mental ill health and inequality are mirrored in the prisoner population.

- Second, we will focus on emerging concerns about victims of crime and recent developments that attempt to address the longstanding neglect of their needs.

The Criminal Justice System: is it a 'System' at all?

Jack McConnell, as First Minister, told his audience at a lecture organised by APEX Scotland in 2003, "Scotland's criminal justice system has a long and proud history" (McConnell, 2003). The phrase, 'criminal justice system', is so commonly used both by people working within it and those commenting, often critically, from the outside, that we take it for granted. However, what does it mean and to what extent may it be said that there is a system at all?

The phrase 'criminal justice system' is usually assumed to include all those official agencies with responsibilities for the administration of aspects of the criminal law:

- Police.

- Procurators fiscal.

- Courts.

- Prisons.

- Local authority criminal justice social work teams.

- Private contractors who undertake work such as prisoner escort or electronic monitoring.

- Voluntary organisations that offer programmes and services to help offenders or their families.

However, the use of the word 'system' implies a deliberate and co-ordinated grouping of organisations with shared aims and an integrated approach to achieving them. There is little sense in which this is the case in Scotland. Instead, the term has the effect of hiding real complexities such as distinctive histories, working cultures and organisational aims.

Nonetheless, all these agencies in whole or in part, directly or indirectly are financed by public funds. The Scottish Executive, therefore, has a key role setting broad strategies within which these agencies work. The Scottish Parliament is the setting in which changes to the system that require legislation are debated and may pass into law.

We have noted that it is wrong to think of the 'criminal justice system' as being anything other than convenient shorthand to describe a complex set of institutions. We will now map these out in more detail.

The Scottish Executive

The Justice Department, headed by the Minister for Justice, is the executive department of the Scottish Executive with responsibility for criminal justice. In addition, there are two law officers who have ministerial status, who are members of the Scottish cabinet and who appear in Parliament to answer questions on justice matters. These are the **Lord Advocate**, who heads the **Crown Office** and **Procurator Fiscal Service** (see below), and the **Solicitor-General**, both of whom are senior lawyers rather than elected politicians.

Currently, the strategic political agenda is contained in the 'Partnership Agreement' drawn up by Labour and the Liberal Democrats following the 2003 Scottish

Parliamentary election (Scottish Executive, 2003). Cathy Jamieson, the Minister for Justice, has described this programme as being an ambitious long-term strategy of 'end-to-end' reform (Jamieson, 2006).

Typically, the path to reform begins with a Scottish Executive consultation document to which interested parties and members of the public are invited to respond. These responses are then analysed and a report published. The contents of the subsequent Bill introduced to Parliament may take these submissions into account.

Pause for thought

Go to the Scottish Executive website consultations page and browse through until you find a consultation that interests you.

- Why not send in your views?
- In the case of closed or archived consultations, what might you have wanted to say and how does this compare with the actual submissions?

(You might have to do some more searches on the website to find these: http://www.scotland.gov.uk/Consultations/Current.)

The Scottish Parliament

Scotland retained its separate system of criminal law throughout the period of direct government from London – from 1707 until the sitting of the reconvened Scottish Parliament in 1999. However, because Scottish legislation had to compete for time with the rest of business at Westminster, criminal justice reforms were long overdue by time the Holyrood Parliament began work. The power to legislate on criminal justice was devolved to the Scottish Parliament by the Scotland Act 1998. An example of an exception to this general rule is drugs legislation, which remains reserved to Westminster.

Between 1999 and mid-2006 the Scottish Parliament passed 14 Acts that deal directly with changes to criminal law and procedure. At the time of writing, another five **Bills** are in progress, covering matters such as the reform of custodial sentencing law, legal aid and the work of Scottish District Courts.

Legislation may be introduced into the Scottish Parliament in three main ways: by the Scottish Executive, by a Parliamentary Committee, or by an individual MSP.

There are two **Parliamentary Justice Committees**, both of which have responsibility for criminal matters (and **civil justice**, such as family law reform). It is part of their role to submit reports to the Scottish Parliament on proposals for legislation and these may be based on evidence gathered in a variety of ways, including interviewing witnesses. You are recommended to explore how this works by referring to the Scottish Parliament's website: http://www.scottish.parliament.uk.

The Police in Scotland

Policing is divided between eight separate territorial police forces. These range in size from the largest, Strathclyde, which is responsible for nearly half the Scottish population, to the smallest, Dumfries and Galloway, which is responsible for just under 150,000 people. Additionally, Common Police Services provide national support such as police training, criminal records, information strategies and tackling drug crime (through the specialist **Scottish Crime and Drug Enforcement Agency (SCDEA)**).

Another key organisation is the Association of Chief Police Officers Scotland (ACPOS). Through ACPOS, senior police officers meet to identify and support national level strategies and to convey collective views about police matters. Founded in 1870 as an informal association, it has now become a key player in an emerging debate between police professionals and the Scottish Executive as to the future management of Scottish policing.

It is the Chief Constable of each police force who carries personal and independent responsibility for operational matters. However, as Donnelly and Scott (2005) point out, "in practice there has always been considerable ambiguity surrounding police independence" and that since devolution there has been a "tendency to centralisation" and national level political control.

The Police, Public Order and Criminal Justice (Scotland) Act 2006 has made important changes to the present system. These include the establishment of a Police Complaints Commissioner and the creation of a national Police Service Authority to take over the specialist functions of the Common Police Services. The SCDEA (formerly the **Scottish Drug Enforcement Agency (SDEA)**) will be maintained by this new national authority, working to a strategic framework provided by the Scottish Executive and linking to the new **UK Serious Organised Crime Agency**.

The police in Scotland were allocated £938.9 million from public funds in 2004-5. Of that, 51 per cent is paid directly by the Scottish Executive and the remainder contributed by local authorities. There were also additional sums relating to capital expenditure and specific projects amounting to £153 million (HMCIC, 2005).

Crown Office and Procurator Fiscal Service (COPFS)

The Crown Office and Procurator Fiscal Service prosecutes all crime in Scotland and has other functions, such as the investigation of sudden deaths. It is a Procurator Fiscal rather than the police who decides if a case should proceed to prosecution and that decision is made taking the public interest into account. The Procurator Fiscal also has powers to impose fines, give a warning, refer an accused for specialist help and also refer the case for mediation, rather than proceed to court.

Courts

Criminal cases in Scotland are allocated to courts according to the seriousness of the offence. Many of the least serious, or **'summary cases'**, are heard by lay people, unqualified in law, at the **District Courts** run by local councils. Most of the rest go to the **Sheriff Courts** and the most serious, such as murder, to the **High Court of Justiciary**. At the time of writing, legislation is progressing through the Scottish Parliament to reform the District Courts system, improving training and accountability for magistrates and removing administrative responsibility from councils to the Scottish Court Service.

Prisons in Scotland

Prisons in Scotland are run by the Scottish Prison Service (SPS), an executive agency of the Scottish Executive.

The Minister for Justice is accountable to the Scottish Parliament for the work of the SPS at a strategic level: for example, strategic criminal justice policies impacting on imprisonment and setting the level of public funding for the Service. The SPS Chief Executive is directly responsible to the Scottish Parliament and Scottish Ministers for the management, planning and operation of the Service and for giving advice to politicians about policy relating to prisons (Scottish Prison Service, 2005b).

The SPS costs over £320 million a year to run 18 prison establishments (three of which are young offender institutions) across Scotland. The average annual revenue cost of a prisoner place is about £30,000 (Scottish Prison Service, 2005a).

Adult Criminal Justice in the Community

Unlike in the rest of the UK, there has been no Probation Service in Scotland since 1969, when local authority social work teams absorbed work with adult offenders in the community. Money for working with offenders had to be found from within social work budgets in competition with other, perhaps more clearly 'deserving' groups, such as children or the elderly.

From 1991, funding for criminal justice work was 'ring-fenced', allowing the development of specialist criminal justice social work teams to carry out legal responsibilities to work with offenders in the community and in prison. These include the provision of **social enquiry reports** for the criminal courts, supervising community orders such as probation, community service, restriction of liberty and drug testing and treatment orders. Criminal justice social workers are also responsible for the supervision of ex-prisoners released on parole or life licence.

The Scottish Executive's criminal justice social work budget doubled from £44 million in 2000-2001 to £88 million in 2005-2006 (Scottish Executive, 2004a). A typical probation order costs £1,173; a community service order costs about £1,499 (Scottish Executive, 2005d).

Voluntary organisations also play an important role in the development and provision of a range of services directed at offenders. For example, Sacro has a network of supported accommodation projects and runs a range of programmes designed to address specific problems, such as domestic abuse, alcohol abuse and sexual offending. Sacro has also been a pioneer in developing restorative justice initiatives in Scotland (see below). The work of APEX is focused on enhancing the employability of people with criminal convictions and the addictions charity, Phoenix House, provides addiction casework services within prisons.

The Scottish Executive contributes to the support of these organisations largely by contracting with them for the provision of programmes.

Imprisonment in Scotland

In the previous section we looked at some of the component parts of the Scottish 'criminal justice system'. The emerging picture, especially since devolution, is of change driven largely by a newly invigorated political agenda.

This section looks in more detail at *two* key issues in contemporary criminal justice:

1. The imprisonment of offenders in Scotland.
2. New approaches to meeting the needs of victims.

Prison Rates in Scotland

Today, across nearly a century of reform and innovation in the penal system, we are still grappling with the problem of what to do with people who offend. Although a minority of people who appear before the courts are sent to prison (13 per cent of all penalties in 2003), this is double the proportion imprisoned twenty years ago (Scottish Executive, 2005 c). Most adults (71 per cent) in the prison system are serving short sentences of less than three months (Scottish Executive, 2005c). It is generally acknowledged that 'prison works' for most people – not to 'rehabilitate' them – but only in the limited sense that the offender is removed temporarily from the community.

The number of people in prisons in Scotland is at record levels. In 2004/5, the average daily prison population was 6779 and by October 2006 there were consistently over 7100 people incarcerated. There are not enough prison spaces to accommodate all prisoners adequately and the resulting overcrowding severely undermines any attempt to engage in constructive work with them. Andrew McLellan (HMCIP, 2005), HM Chief Inspector of Prisons for Scotland (HMCIP), describes the impact of overcrowding in HMP Aberdeen in his annual report as follows:

> "It is difficult for those who have not been inside a prison to understand why overcrowding is so damaging [. . .] This can mean that prisoners [. . .] will be sharing cells designed for one person, with scarcely enough room to move about, with a person who has not been chosen, who may not be known, and who may have histories of behaviour or of medical conditions unknown to the other prisoner or indeed to staff. The impossibility of even the best members of staff having time to deal properly with the needs of individual prisoners; the impossibility of the best safety assessments being carried out on those new prisoners who might harm themselves; the impossibility of providing enough useful work, or programmes to address offending behaviour, or education to meet the needs of these very high prisoner numbers: it is not that these things are difficult: they are impossible. The prison has a laundry, a kitchen, a gym, a visit room, a health centre designed for half the number of prisoners who are there and who need to be dealt with" (HMCIP, 2005).

Many countries, but by no means all, have experienced rising levels of imprisonment over the last twenty or so years. In the case of the United States, there was a sharp rise from a rate of around 176 per 100,000 people before 1980 to 726 in 2004 (the highest in the world). Imprisonment rates for England and Wales (142 per 100,000 in 2004), and in Scotland (135 in 2005), are amongst the highest in Europe. In contrast, countries in northern Europe of similar population size to Scotland, such as Denmark (70) and Ireland (85) have significantly lower rates of imprisonment. It should be noted that there is no clear link between *crime* rates and imprisonment and it is difficult to sustain the argument that crime rates can be reduced substantially by locking more people up (Garside, 2005).

Tombs (2004) studied Scottish official statistics across the decade 1993-2002 and identified the following interplay of factors to explain much of the rise in the prison population in Scotland:

- First, as we have noted, there has been an increase in the proportion of people being sentenced to prison. This has occurred in both the High and Sheriff Courts, and is particularly noticeable amongst offenders convicted of shoplifting and 'other theft'.

- Second, there is a trend towards longer prison sentences over this period, especially for women prisoners.

- Other factors include more people awaiting trial in prison rather than on bail in the community; an increase in the number of offenders convicted of serious violence including murder; an increase in drugs convictions coupled with higher possible prison terms for these; and technical changes in release arrangements.

Tombs (2004) also interviewed sheriffs to understand what was happening. Most agreed that sentencing had become harsher. This could partly be explained by changes in the law and patterns of serious offending, but also because the "climate of political, media and public opinion had become more severe."

People who become prisoners in Scotland are typically from the poorest areas in the country, young and male. Roger Houchin (2005), a former governor of HMP Barlinnie, followed up the postcodes of everyone in prison on 30 June 2003 and found that the average imprisonment rate for 23 year old men from the 27 most deprived wards in Scotland was a strikingly high 3427 per 100,000 (compared with the overall rate of 135 noted above). Moreover, half the prisoners came from 155 wards that contain just fewer than 18 per cent of the Scottish population.

He goes on to make the challenging observation that "it is not simply that the most deprived are most at the risk of imprisonment, it is that at all levels of prosperity, the probability of imprisonment increases with increasing deprivation" so that "the risk of imprisonment is as much a correlate of social deprivation as are poverty, chronic unemployment or poor life expectancy" (Houchin, 2005).

These parameters of social disadvantage and distress, including drug addiction and psychiatric illness, were also exposed in a 1998 study of women prisoners at HMP Cornton Vale (Loucks, 1998, cited in Social Work Services and Prisons Inspectorates for Scotland, 1998).

Responses to Prison Overcrowding

One answer to prison overcrowding, inadequate accommodation in existing prisons and the projected increase in prisoner numbers is to build more prisons at considerable cost. As we have already seen, imprisonment is in any case an 'expensive option' and rates of reconviction are high, especially for young men (Scottish Executive, 2004 c; 2004d). Another answer is to reduce the number of people going into prison in the first place, especially on short sentences. New community sentences, such as **restriction of liberty orders**, are designed to do this. There is also an increasing recognition that a penal system designed for men is not necessarily appropriate for women offenders. For example, the 218 Project (http://www.218.org.uk/index.htm) was opened in Glasgow in 2004 to offer holistic services to women whose offending is related to substance misuse.

In 2004, the Scottish Executive consulted on proposals for a single corrections agency through which there would be a 'seamless management' of offenders, in an attempt to reduce re-offending by people who had been through the prison system (Scottish Executive, 2004b). This idea would have meant the merger of prisons and criminal justice social work and was rejected by most people and organisations that responded to the consultation (Scottish Executive, 2004c).

A revised approach embodied in the Management of Offenders (Scotland) Act 2005, set up liaison structures known as 'criminal justice authorities' (CJAs). For the first time the Prison Service and criminal justice social work teams are obliged by law to co-operate in producing and then delivering community offender services plans developed by the local CJA. The new structure is aimed at improving communications, integrating working arrangements and enhancing the effectiveness of the work with offenders across official agencies and with voluntary organisations. As such, it is hoped to achieve the benefits of closer working without the risks of a 'shotgun wedding' between reluctant partners. The new Authorities will be operational by 2007. However, the term 'management of offenders' has been criticised on the grounds that such impersonal language de-personalises the very human problems that people who commit crimes present and puts undue emphasis on control rather than helping individuals to stop offending (McNeill, 2006).

It remains to be seen what impact these new arrangements will have on the effectiveness of work with offenders. However, Houchin (2005), in evidence to the Justice 2 Committee, doubted that we can solve the problems of offending "by structurally altering how we deliver justice." Echoing Coyle's (2003) aforementioned view about the limited role of the criminal justice system in effecting change, he stressed to the Committee that "the problem can be solved only by social policy and by addressing the problems in those communities" (Justice 2 Committee, 2005).

Pause for thought

Taking into account what you have read above, as well as any opinions you might have on crime, think about the following questions:

- What do you think should be done with people who offend?
- Why do you think Scotland has a higher rate of imprisonment than many other European countries?

Being a Victim of Crime in Scotland

Many criminologists only began to think about issues to do with victims of crime towards the end of the last century. The change came about in part thanks to the influence of organisations such as Victim Support and also surveys that set out to compare the extent of people's experiences of crime with police recorded crime statistics. These crime surveys revealed that much crime and victimisation was not reported to the police. Another important development was the adoption of the *Declaration of Basic Principles of Justice for Victims of Crime and Abuse of Power* by the United Nations in November 1985, which set out an influential framework for constructing victim policies (UNHCR, 1985).

Just as the risk of being caught up in the criminal justice system as an offender is highest for people from poorer areas, the likelihood of being a victim of crime, or worrying about it, is higher for people from poorer areas than elsewhere. Residents of the 15 per cent most deprived wards in Scotland were found to be at greater risk of being a victim of household crime (such as theft) and personal crime (such as assault) than elsewhere in Scotland. Unsurprisingly, these residents worried more about being broken into or of being robbed or assaulted and were less likely to feel safe when out alone at night or at home than others in the rest of the country (Scottish Executive, 2004b).

As a result of the focus on the offender, criminal justice agencies have been guilty of marginalising and, in some cases, ignoring the needs of victims and their families. Many people who are victims of crime need support to deal with the emotional, financial and, possibly, health consequences. Beyond that, the experience of being caught up in a court case, whether or not the matter goes to trial and witness evidence needs to be given, can of itself be stressful and, for some, just as bad if not worse than the original crime (**'secondary victimisation'**). It has been a common experience that victims have not been kept informed of what is happening with 'their' crime and 'their' offender and then find out the result of the case from the local newspaper. There is also the worry about meeting the offender (if known to them) unexpectedly after the court case, or after his or her release from prison.

In 2001, the Scottish Executive launched its *Scottish Strategy for Victims* in order to "place the needs of victims right at the heart of our criminal justice system" (Scottish Executive, 2001). It is a reflection of the extent to which victims' needs were *not* being taken into account that the strategy was obliged to note the importance of the victim and their need for practical and emotional support, including the right to know what was happening in 'their' case (Scottish Executive, 2001).

The practical outcomes arising from this declaration have included more funding for Victim Support and other voluntary agencies, such as those working with victims of domestic abuse; changes in legislation and practice to increase protection for victims and witnesses, such as children, who are especially vulnerable in court; and the provision of more and better information for victims about their cases and legal procedures generally through the new Victim Information and Advice Service.

Other innovations include a pilot scheme in which victims could supply a statement to court setting out how the crime had affected them; and a notification scheme, whereby victims of certain serious offences are warned of the offender's release from prison. Procurators Fiscal may also inform the victim of the reason for a decision not to proceed with a case in some circumstances. New national standards to be met by those working with victims were published in 2005 and, in effect, re-iterate the basic principles in practical terms (Scottish Executive, 2005e).

'Restorative justice' is an approach to meeting the needs of *both* victims *and* offenders that, through the careful use of third party contact and possible face to face meetings, aims to resolve matters arising from the offence. This may benefit the victim by allaying fears and 'humanising' the offender. It may help offenders by confronting them with the impact of what they did and obliging them to take responsibility and apologise for what happened. Restorative justice schemes are limited to youth offender projects in Scotland at present. More information on restorative justice can be obtained at: http://www.restorativejusticescotland.org.uk.

Criminals and Victims: a Summary

In this section we have seen how – although only a minority of people convicted in Scotland are sentenced to custody – harsher sentencing has contributed to an unprecedented increase in the number of people sent to prison. A disproportionate number of these people are young men from the poorest communities. Looked at from this perspective we can see that something other than individual 'badness' must be going on to cause their offending. This is not to say that in any individual case the penalty is not in some way deserved, rather that explanations and remedies for such gross discrepancies should be sought at the social, economic, political and cultural, rather than individual level. Redesigning the way in which agencies in the criminal justice system work together may help, but in the long term, offending needs to be addressed by policies aimed at society and communities rather than the individual.

We have also noted how the welfare needs of victims of crime, many of whom live in Scotland's poorest communities or who have particular vulnerabilities, have been ignored or mistreated by the court process and how this is being addressed.

Conclusion

In comparison with the rest of the UK, Scotland's justice system prior to devolution was insulated from some of the more control and punishment orientated rhetoric in relation to responses to crime. It has been argued elsewhere that Scotland's approach to crime has been more 'welfarist' than punitive and that recent political initiatives are in tension with an essentially welfarist culture. However, in relation to adult offenders (as opposed to 'children in trouble') the picture sketched here would suggest that there are longstanding, class-biased continuities in the punitiveness of the criminal justice system.

To sum up, this chapter has looked at some ideas about what crime is and how it may be explained. We have looked at information about crime and also key features such as place, class, gender and age. We then reviewed the complexities of some agencies within the criminal justice 'system' in order to understand how this 'system' works in Scotland and the extent of current changes, especially since devolution. Our study of imprisonment and then victims' services offered a reminder of the substantial inequalities exposed by these issues.

Further Resources

Coleman, C. and Norris, C. (2000) *Introducing Criminology*, Cullompton, Willan Publishing

Hale, C., Hayward, K., Wahidin, A. and Wincup, A. (2005) *Criminology*, Oxford, Oxford University Press

Jones, S. (2005) *Criminology* (3rd Edition), Oxford, Oxford University Press

Useful Websites

218 Project: http://www.218.org.uk/index.htm (This offers holistic services to women whose offending is related to substance misuse.)

APEX Scotland: www.apexscotland.org.uk/

Association of Chief Police Officers Scotland (ACPOS): www.scottish.police.uk/main/acpos/acpos.htm

British Crime Survey (BCS): www.homeoffice.gov.uk/rds/bcs1.html

CjScotland: www.cjscotland.org.uk (This is a useful source of links to information about Scottish criminal justice. It also contains a daily log of news stories about criminal justice in the Scottish digital media.)

Crown Office and Procurator Fiscal Service: www.crownoffice.gov.uk/

Home Office: www.homeoffice.gov.uk/

Howard League: http://www.howardleaguescotland.org.uk/ (Organisation advocating penal reform.)

Restorative Justice in Scotland: http://www.restorativejusticescotland.org.uk

SACRO: www.sacro.org.uk/

Scottish Consortium on Crime and Criminal Justice: http://www.scccj.org.uk/

Scottish Crime Survey (SCS): www.esds.ac.uk/government/scs/

Scottish Drug Enforcement Agency (SDEA)/Scottish Crime and Drug Enforcement Agency (SCDEA): www.sdea.police.uk/

Scottish Executive: www.scotland.gov.uk/

Scottish Parliament: www.scottish.parliament.uk/

Scottish Prisons Service: www.sps.gov.uk/

UK Serious Organised Crime Agency: www.soca.gov.uk/

UNHCR: http://www.unhchr.ch/html/menu3/b/h_comp49.htm (*Declaration of Basic Principles of Justice for Victims of Crime and Abuse of Power.*)

Bibliography

Becker, H. (1963) *Outsiders: Studies in the Study of Deviance*, New York, NY, Free Press

Bilton, T., Bonnett, K., Jones, P., Skinner, D., Stanworth, M. and Webster, A. (1996) *Introductory Sociology* (3rd Edition), London, MacMillan

Coleman, C. and Norris, C. (2000) *Introducing Criminology*, Cullompton, Willan Publishing

Coyle, A. (2003) *Joining up criminal justice services: Scotland in an international context* (a speech to an ADSW conference, Dunblane, 20 November), http://www.adsw.org.uk/criminal.cfm (accessed on 21 January 2006)

Croall, H. (2003) 'Crime and Deviance', in Sweeney, T., Lewis, J. and Etherington, N. (eds.) (2003) *Sociology and Scotland: An Introduction*, Paisley, Unity Publications Ltd

Donnelly, D. and Scott, K. (eds.) (2005) *Policing in Scotland*, Cullompton, Willan Publishing

Felson, M. (2002) *Crime and Every Day Life*, London, Sage

Garland, D. (2002) 'The Emergence of a Positive Science of the Criminal', in Maguire, M., Morgan, R. and Reiner, R. (eds.) (2002) *The Oxford Handbook of Criminology*, Oxford, Oxford University Press

Garside, R. (2005) 'Wrong question; wrong answer', in *Crime and Society*, http://www.crimeandsociety.org.uk/articles/Wrongq.html (accessed on 5 February 2006)

Hale, C., Hayward, K., Wahidin, A. and Wincup, A. (2005) *Criminology*, Oxford, Oxford University Press

Hayward, K. and Morrison, W. (2005) 'Theoretical Criminology: a starting point', in Hale, C., Hayward, K., Wahidin, A. and Wincup, A. (2005) *Criminology*, Oxford, Oxford University Press

Heidensohn, F. (2002) 'Gender and Crime', in Maguire, M. *et al* (2002) *The Oxford Handbook of Criminology*, Oxford, Oxford University Press

Hirschi, T. (1969) *Causes of Delinquency*, Berkeley, CA, University of California Press

Houchin, R (2005) *Social Exclusion and Imprisonment in Scotland*, Edinburgh, Scottish Prison Service, http://www.sps.gov.uk/Uploads/C1D3FBFB-E123-4643-8D83-AB0F622E7755.pdf

HMCIC (2005) *Annual Report of Her Majesty's Chief Inspector of Constabulary for Scotland 2004/2005*, Edinburgh, The Stationary Office, http://www.scotland.gov.uk/Publications/ 2005/10/3192658/26589

HMCIP (2005) *Report for 2004-2005*, Edinburgh, The Stationary Office, http://www.scottishexecutive.gov.uk/Publications/2005/10/3192658/26589

Jamieson, C. (2006) *The Challenge of Reform*, Drummond Hunter Memorial Lecture, 18 January 2006, http://www.howardleaguescotland.org.uk/lecture.html

Jones, S. (2005) *Criminology* (3rd Edition), Oxford, Oxford University Press

Justice 2 Committee (2005) *Official Report 3 May 2005. Management of Offenders etc (Scotland) Bill: Stage 1*, Edinburgh, The Stationary Office, http://www.scottish.parliament.uk/business/committees/justice2/or-05/j205-1402.htm #Col1575

KPMG Forensic (2004) *Profile of a fraudster: long-serving, male executives most likely to commit company fraud*, London, KPMG, http://www.kpmg.co.uk/ news/detail.cfm?pr=1941 (accessed on 17 March 2006)

Lacey, N. (2002) 'Legal Constructions of Crime', in Maguire, M., Morgan, R. and Reiner, R . (eds .) (2002) *The Oxford Handbook of Criminology*, Oxford, Oxford University Press

Maguire, M., Morgan, R. and Reiner, R. (eds.) (2002) *The Oxford Handbook of Criminology*, Oxford, Oxford University Press

McConnell, J. (2003) *Respect, responsibility and rehabilitation in modern Scotland*, Apex Scotland Annual Lecture, 2003, http://www.scottishlabour.org.uk/ fmjusticespeech/ (accessed on 20 January 2006)

McNeill, F . (2006) *A New Paradigm for Social Work with Offenders*, CjScotland, http://www.cjscotland.org.uk/index.php/articles/desistance

Merton, R.K. (1968) *Social Theory and Social Structure*, New York, NY, Free Press

Rock, P. (1973) *Deviant Behaviour*, London, Hutchinson

Social Work Services and Prisons Inspectorates for Scotland (1998) *Women Offenders: A Safer Way. A Review of Community Disposals and the Use of Custody for Women Offenders in Scotland*, Edinburgh, The Stationary Office, http://www.scotland.gov.uk/library3/law/Wosw-00.asp

Scottish Executive (2001) *Scottish Strategy for Victims*, Edinburgh, The Stationary Office

Scottish Executive (2003) *Partnership Agreement*, Edinburgh, The Stationary Office, http://www.scotland.gov.uk/library5/government/pfbs-04.asp

Scottish Executive (2004a) *Safer, Stronger Communities: Scotland's Criminal Justice Plan*, Edinburgh, The Stationary Office, http://www.scotland.gov.uk/library5 /justice/scjp-00.asp

Scottish Executive (2004b) *Scottish Crime Survey 2003*, Edinburgh, The Stationary Office, http://www.scotland.gov.uk/library5/justice/sccs-00.asp

Scottish Executive (2004c) *re:duce re:habilitate re:form. A consultation on reducing reoffending in Scotland*, Edinburgh, The Stationary Office, http://www.scotland.gov. uk/consultations/justice/rrrc-00.asp

Scottish Executive (2004d) *re:duce re:habilitate re:form. Analysis of responses to consultation*, Edinburgh, The Stationary Office, http://www.scotland.gov.uk/ consultations/Justice/rrres-00.asp

Scottish Executive (2005a) *Criminal Proceedings in Scottish Courts 2003*, Edinburgh, The Stationary Office, http://www.scotland.gov.uk/Publications/ 2005/03/30152104/21062

Scottish Executive (2005b) *The findings and recommendations of the Expert Group report on Corporate Homicide*, Edinburgh, The Stationary Office, http://www.scotland.gov.uk/Publications /2005/11/14133559/35592

Scottish Executive (2005c) *Prison Statistics 2004-5*, Edinburgh, The Stationary Office, http://www.scotland.gov.uk/Publications/2005/08/18102211/22138

Scottish Executive (2005d) *Costs, Sentencing Profiles and the Scottish Criminal Justice System 2003*, Edinburgh, The Stationary Office, http://www.scotland.gov.uk/ Publications/2005/09/05102827/28276

Scottish Executive (2005e) *National Standards for Victims of Crime*, Edinburgh, The Stationary Office, http://www.scotland.gov.uk/library5/justice/nsvcl-00.asp

Scottish Prison Service (2005a) *Annual Report and Accounts, 2004-5*, Edinburgh, SPS, http://www.sps.gov.uk/Uploads/2071AFCD-8069-4AA2-99DC-5EBC04136 FD3.pdf

Scottish Prison Service (2005b) *Scottish Prison Service Framework Document*, Edinburgh, SPS, http://www.sps.gov.uk/Uploads/6DB901DE-8E10-401D-9169-9DBAF16F416B.pdf

Sutherland, E. (1940) 'White Collar Criminality', in *American Sociological Review*, 5

Sweeney, T., Lewis, J. and Etherington, N. (eds.) (2003) *Sociology and Scotland: An Introduction*, Paisley, Unity Publications Ltd

Tombs, J. (2004) *A unique punishment. Sentencing and the Prison Population in Scotland*, Glasgow, Scottish Consortium on Crime and Criminal Justice, http://www.scccj.org.uk/

UNHCR (1985) *Declaration of Basic Principles of Justice for Victims of Crime and Abuse of Power*, Geneva, UNHCR, http://www.unhchr.ch/html/menu3/b/h comp49.htm

Walmsley, R. (2005) *World Prison Population List* (6th Edition), London, King's College, London , http://www.kcl.ac.uk/depsta/rel/icps/world-prison-population-list-2005.pdf

Young, J. and Matthews, R. (eds.) (1992) *Rethinking Criminology: The Realist Debate*, London, Sage

Young, J. (1992) 'Ten Points of Realism', in Young, J. and Matthews , R . (eds .) (1992) *Rethinking Criminology: The Realist Debate*, London, Sage

Glossary

Absolute poverty A measure of what is required for human subsistence.

Activation policies Policies aimed at radical intervention.

Activity theory or **role theory** A theory of the role of consciousness in shaping behaviour, which emanated from the field of psychology in the former Soviet Union.

Ageism Discrimination against individuals based on age.

Anti-social behaviour orders (ASBOs) A civil order introduced by New Labour, which is placed on individuals engaging in behaviour deemed a threat to others.

'Battered Child Syndrome' Refers to injuries sustained by a child as a result of physical abuse, usually inflicted by an adult caregiver. Alternatively known as 'child abuse'.

Bed blocking A term used to describe the fact that many older people are left undischarged in NHS hospitals due to a lack of funding to provide support for them in their own homes.

Beveridgean-Keynesian A term referring to the predominant political consensus of the immediate post-war years based on the model of the welfare state as proposed by William Beveridge and the economic model associated with John Maynard Keynes.

Biological explanations of crime Explanations that assume that there are biological causes for criminality.

Black Report (1980) A government commissioned document published in 1980, which revealed significant social causes of mortality and morbidity.

Boarding Out The temporary placing of an individual under the care of those such as foster carers.

Bourgeoisie The ruling class in capitalist societies. The owners of the means of production.

Bretton Woods system A system of international management of money transactions between states, operational between 1944 and the early 1970s.

Calvinistic 'work ethic' Alternatively known as the 'Protestant work ethic', this refers to the religious notion that salvation should be found through hard work and diligence.

Casualised work Work based on temporary and occasional bases.

Children's Charter An initiative established by the Scottish Executive in 2004, which sets out what children and young people need and expect to help protect them when they are in danger of being, or already have been, harmed by another person.

Children's Hearing A lay tribunal made up of members of the **Children's Panel** (see below), which comprises trained voluntary members of the public and exists to combine justice and welfare for children in Scotland.

Children's Panels Meetings of relevant people such as parents or guardians and social workers that are held to provide support and help to children who may be experiencing difficulties in their lives.

Children's Rights Commissioner High profile independent body established by law to monitor, promote and safeguard children's human rights.

Children's Rights Officers A local council employee who offers advice and guidance on matters relating to the rights of children and young people.

Citizen's Charter A policy prerogative introduced by John Major's Conservative government in the early 1990s detailing citizen's rights.

Citizenship A term variously used to vaguely describe a drive toward more active participation in society under New Labour. Also refers to having a 'right' to live in and seek protections from the state lived in as a result of birth or naturalisation.

Civil justice Matters of justice that fall outwith criminal law, e.g. libel.

Civil rights Rights in public life such as freedom of expression and equal treatment. (See also **Rights**.)

Class consciousness A Marxist term referring to class self-awareness and the ability to act in its common interest. In other words, knowing one has common interests with all other workers and working with them to secure benefits for all workers.

Class-for-itself Marx's description of how an objectively defined 'class-in-itself' can develop subjective class awareness and become a class which is able to unite in common interest and become a 'class-for-itself'. (See **Class-in-itself**.)

Class habitus A term used by the French sociologist, Pierre Bourdieu, referring to a collective set of dispositions, or 'ways of being' that characterise a social class and created by individual members interpretation of what it means to belong to that class.

Class-in-itself Marx's interpretation of class membership as being objectively defined, i.e. regardless of whether one defines oneself as belonging to a particular class.

Class polarisation Growing inequality between the workers and the owners given that the latter are oppressive and exploitative and continually seek rising profits at the expense of the workers.

Class struggle A concept central to Marxist analyses describing the conflict forced upon the working class in capitalist societies.

Cohabitation Otherwise known as couples 'living together' outside marriage.

Communitarianism Philosophy associated with advocating the interest of community over the individual.

Community Care Caring for individuals in communities rather than institutions.

Community ownership A concept that refers to an item as belonging to the community at large rather than private enterprise or government control.

Community Planning (CP) The planning and management of the environment at the local level.

Community Planning Partnership (CPP) An agency bringing together key public, private, community and voluntary representatives with the supposed aim of delivering better public services and targeted regeneration.

Community Service Orders An alternative to a custodial sentence, which involves the offender performing some service of benefit to the community such as clearing up litter or charity work.

Compulsory heterosexuality A theoretical concept that refers to the dominant idea that heterosexuality is the 'normal' sexual preference.

Conjugal family See **nuclear family.**

Contradictory class locations A term associated with US Marxist sociologist, Erik Olin Wright, who used the term to refer to workers whose duties involve working for the owners in managing workers but having terms and conditions that reflected a class location of neither worker nor owner.

Core skills The notion that there are a number of skills central to the needs of learners and employees. These include basic levels of communication (literacy), numeracy, information technology, problem solving and working with others.

Corporate crime Breaches of the law committed by individuals in the corporation or the institution themselves at the institutional, rather than personal, level.

Criminal Law breaking.

Crown Office An independent public prosecution service that decides whether to initiate criminal proceedings. Often works alongside the Procurator Fiscal Service in Scotland. (See **Procurator Fiscal Service**.)

Cultural capital A term used by the French sociologist, Pierre Bourdieu, and closely linked to his concept of class habitus (see above). The term refers to cultural knowledge and 'know-how' and Bourdieu uses it to explain why middle class children often perform better in education. One application of it might be that these children perform better since they share cultural traits and understandings with middle class teachers, meaning that they are able to better understand what they are communicating.

Culture of dependency The politically right wing notion that 'unnecessary' welfare provision creates a situation of dependency on welfare and discourages individuals from seeking solutions to their plight.

Cycle of deprivation A sociological term referring to the difficulties facing deprived people in escaping their predicament, in that poor adults tend to have poor children, who in turn have poor children, and so on.

Deindustrialisation The widespread phenomenon occurring in many Western industrial nations from the late 1960s of a rapid and substantial decline in industrial production alongside an expansion in service sector industries.

Dementia A degenerative brain condition most common in older adults.

Demographic time bomb The arguably exaggerated and politically-charged claim that a decline in birth rates, coupled with increased life expectancy, will inevitably lead to a crisis in welfare provision.

Demunicipalisation Movement away of council services from public ownership to the private sector, often as a result of competitive tendering.

Dependency culture A politically charged and value laden term associated with right wing analysts who claim that the provision of welfare benefits above minimum levels has the effect of creating a situation where recipients become reliant on welfare and develop the view that it is the role of the state to look after them.

Deserving poor A politically charged and value laden term used by the political right to refer to those in poverty who cannot fend for themselves and thereby require state support.

Deviance Behaviour that strays from accepted norms.

Devolution Central government granting of limited rule at the national, regional or local level.

Disengagement theory The theory surrounding the concept that individual's steadily withdraw from social participation as they enter old age.

District Courts Local authority courts, which deal with small claims and minor offences.

Division of labour The specialisation of labour in specific, circumscribed tasks and roles, which is intended to increase efficiency of output. (See also **Sexual division of labour**.)

Early years' strategy A term referring to programmes developed to assess public services for children to the age of five.

Economic liberalism The branch of liberalism stemming from free market economics.

Educational attainment Performance in certificated assessments.

Elite Ruling group.

Employability A term referring to the ability to secure and maintain paid work and often used in the context of developing key skills for modern labour markets.

Employment Zones (EZ) 13 areas of high unemployment in Britain where initiatives have been set up to aid people in getting work.

English Poor Law System of welfare provision introduced at the beginning of the 16th century to address some of the issues of poverty.

Enterprise society A concept used by the Conservatives and subsequently New Labour to refer to a vision of a society based on an entrepreneurial culture.

Equality The idea that individuals have the same opportunities and life chances. (See **Life chances**.)

Ethnocentrism Viewing the world from a particular cultural position.

Exclusion The direct or indirect disinvolvement of certain individuals and groups.

Extended family A family structure including wider family, such as grandparents or other close relatives, as well as parents and children.

Families of choice A family structure where the parents or guardians may be same sex couples.

Family group conferencing Establishing formal meetings for members of the family group and relevant others to discuss issues such as what needs to be done to make sure a child or young person is safe and well cared for or, in youth justice cases, for example, to discuss with the young offender and the victim how accountability and responsibility can be taken for their behaviour.

Family values A concept promoted by recent Conservative and New Labour governments relating to a particular and value laden view of how families should be organised.

Family wage The concept that a wage was paid to the male breadwinner that provided enough to support a wife and dependent children.

Feminisation of poverty A term associated with the growing amount of lone female parents and describing how many of them are being forced into poverty through their single income.

Freedom A term that generally refers to individual decision making and sufficiency.

Free market Unregulated demand and supply transactions.

Fresh Talent An initiative particularly associated with the Scottish Executive that seeks to encourage skilled people from oversees to work and live in Scotland.

Functionalism A sociological perspective associated with Durkheim and Parsons that views society as a system of interdependent parts, where each part plays an important function in maintaining the value consensus.

Gender Notions of what is appropriate behaviour by sex (i.e. male/female).

Gendered division of labour Division of labour task founded on the patriarchal premise of the separation of paid and unpaid work between males and females.

Genetic Biologically predetermined.

Glasgow Works A waged programme designed to encourage people into work, which was replaced by Route 1 on 1 January 2005.

Globalisation A highly contested term that refers to the arranging of technology, economics, politics and culture on a global scale. Those who use the term tend to assume that it characterises the modern world.

Great Depression The widespread economic depression of the 1930s in the United States.

High Court of Justiciary Scotland's highest court.

Housing stock transfer The transfer of ownership of Local Authority housing to Housing Associations.

Human capital A term referring to the defining and categorising of individuals' skills, abilities and contributions.

Ideologically driven Influenced by motives related to political values and ideas.

Ideology Ideas and beliefs often linked to political issues.

Industrialisation The process of a society's economy becoming based on industrial production.

Industry deregulation The removal of rules, regulations and controls on the operation of firms and businesses.

Intermediate labour market (ILM) A model of waged work where temporary jobs are created in an attempt to move people out of long term unemployment.

International Monetary Fund (IMF) An international organisation that oversees the operations of the global economic system.

Interrupted learning Gaps in schooling due to illness or travelling, for example.

'Invisible hand' Adam Smith's concept that fair allocation of societal resources is achieved if consumers and sellers are left to operate uninhibited.

Jobseekers' Allowance (JSA) A form of welfare benefit in the UK that replaced Unemployment Benefit and is paid to those out of work and actively seeking work.

Juvenile delinquency A term referring to child criminality.

Knowledge economy A much debated concept that claims that modern Western economies are increasingly based on knowledge resources such as Information and Communication Technologies (ICT) and a highly educated/qualified workforce rather than economic resources.

Labelling theory Theory that highlights the processes whereby individuals and groups are labelled as different. Proponents note that the label is normally applied by powerful social groups and has negative effects on those labelled.

Labour theory of value A Marxist term describing the 'value' of a good or service as equal to the total amount of labour required to produce it.

Left realism A politically left wing version of realist theory. (See **Realism** and **Right realism**.)

Liberalism A theory that promotes a version of individual freedom, incorporating notions of individual rights, legal equality, freedom of choice and democracy.

Life chances One's opportunities in life relating to wealth, income, life expectancy and so on.

Life expectancy A term referring to a defined population's predicted average life span.

Lifelong learning A term frequently referred to by education bodies, government agencies and industrial representative organisations referring to the idea that everyone should have access to learning throughout the life cycle.

Lone parent families Families with one resident parent, typically female.

Lord Advocate The chief legal advisor to the Scottish Executive and Crown.

Managerialism A variously used term that refers to a perceived excess of administrative or 'business' type solutions or analyses.

Marginalisation The direct or indirect exclusion of individuals or groups often due to their minority status.

Market forces The influence of demand and supply transactions.

Marketisation A term referring to the trend toward viewing welfare provision in ways typically applied to private firms.

Market societies Societies built on principles of free trade and limited welfare provision.

Marxism The wide range of related approaches, theories and arguments associated with the works of the German social theorist, Karl Marx.

McCrone Report A report made to the Scottish Executive in 2001 on teachers pay and conditions.

McDonaldization a term used by the US sociologist, George Ritzer, referring to his claim that modern Western societies are taking on characteristics of fast-food restaurants, such as control and predictability.

Meals on Wheels A volunteer service delivering hot meals to the housebound.

Means of production The tools, technology, machinery and technology required for workers to produce.

Means tested Measures against criteria designed to gauge suitability for welfare provision.

Medical model The dominant model in Western medicine, which views 'problems' such as old age and mental and physical ill-health as 'illnesses' that can be treated by isolating causes and symptoms.

Medico-social problems Problems seen to require both medical and social work intervention.

Meritocracy A system whereby individuals progress in, for example, education, work and wider social life based on their own merit, i.e. demonstrated ability through qualifications, talent, etc.

Mixed economy of care A term describing the increasingly complex ways care is provided through public, private, voluntary and informal agencies.

Mode of production A term used by Marxists to refer to the way goods and services are produced. Historical modes of production include feudalist, communist and capitalist.

Monopolisation The action of large companies buying over smaller ones and thereby dominating sectors of industry.

Moral panics Episodes of perceived threat to societal norms and values often generated by media and/or politicians against minority groups, and, more recently children.

Morbidity A measure of rates of serious illness.

Mortality A measure of death rate.

National Care Standards Principles set by the Care Commission to ensure that service users receive the same standard of care wherever they live in Scotland.

Natural laws The notion that some social phenomena are naturally occurring.

'Neds' A slang and derogatory term for allegedly loutish young working class men (and women).

NEET Literally, 'Not Engaged in Employment or Training'.

Neo-liberalism A contemporary form of classical liberalism.

New Deal A New Labour initiative purportedly aimed at helping able welfare recipients to return to work.

New Right A term used to describe the type of right-wing Conservatism that emerged in many Western societies in the late 20th century.

'No order' principle The principle underpinning the rights of children when parents and/or guardians separate that no claim to rights of access need be made where both parties agree.

Normalisation and **normalisation movement** A principle based on the notion that all individuals should have access to common life experiences regardless of disability.

Norms Aspects of behaviour considered acceptable in a given culture and backed by formal and informal sanction.

Nuclear or **conjugal family** A family structure typically consisting of married spouses with their biological children.

OECD (Organisation for Economic Cooperation and Development) An international organisation of developed countries based on so-called representative democracies and 'free market' economies that exists to compare policies and strategy.

Official statistics Data gathered by agencies such as the government or police.

Parliamentary Justice Committees Committees set up to report to the Scottish Executive on matters of civil and criminal justice.

Partnership Agreement Coalition agreement between Scottish New Labour and the Scottish Liberal Democrats to govern Scotland under the terms of devolution.

Party Term used by Max Weber to describe the general moral and political outlook of individuals.

Patriarchy Male-dominated society.

Peasantry The lowest class of rural labour in pre-industrial societies.

Petite bourgeoisie Marx's term for self-employed workers such as small shopkeepers who were not wage labourers as such but who would join the proletariat when conditions were ripe for revolution.

Placing requests A request made to a local authority for a pupil to access a place on a school other than the one closest to home.

Political consensus General agreement between governments and political parties on key policies.

Poll Tax The successor to rates payments and the precursor to Council Tax, which was levied on individuals living in households for use of public services.

Poorhouse A publicly funded and maintained facility for housing the poor in Victorian Britain.

Postmodernism A theory that suggests that society has moved beyond modernity. Tends to offer a rejection of 'grand theories' as suitable explanations for different phenomena in society.

Poverty trap The notion that many welfare recipients who are willing and able to work are caught in a situation where to take on a low paid job would mean losing out on the overall level of income.

Private Finance Initiative (PFI) A method of funding public sector works where private firms secure rates of return for initial investment in service provision.

Privatisation The 'selling off' of previously state owned industries to private buyers.

Procurator Fiscal Service The representation of the Crown service once criminal proceedings are initiated.

Proletariat Marx's term for the working class in capitalist societies.

Psychological traits Identifiable and enduring characteristics in the minds of individuals.

Public Private Partnerships (PPPs) A system of provision where government works alongside a private firms with negotiated sharing of costs, and the private firms receiving negotiated rates of return on their investment.

Quasi-market A public sector institutional structure that is based on so-called free market principles.

Rationality Decision-making based on reasoned calculation.

Realist A branch of criminology that seeks to provide analyses of crime as it actually exists in modern societies. (See also **Left realism** and **Right realism**.)

Reasonable chastisement A much debated concept referring to the appropriateness of disciplining children.

Reconstituted families A family structure typically characterised by remarried parents with children from previous marriages or relationships.

Reformist socialists Socialists who advocated gradual change toward socialism, rather than the revolutionary type advocated by Marx.

Regeneration Outcome Agreements A strategic and operational framework for the achievement of programmes set by Community Planning Partnerships (see above).

Registrar-General The Head of the government body, The Office for National Statistics.

Relative deprivation A measure of lack of resources as taken against the general standard of living.

Relative poverty A measure of what is required to engage in a minimum standard of living as defined by the norm.

Reporter to the Children's Hearings The organiser and overseer of the Children's Panel.

Representative democracies The type of parliamentary system found in the UK where MPs claim to stand for the interests of their constituents.

Residualisation A term used to describe the situation arising when significant numbers move out of housing areas because they are no longer seen as desirable places to live. Those that are left are often subject to stigmatisation and decaying environments.

Respite care Temporary care provided by someone other than the primary caregiver and designed for reasons such as to provide a short break.

Responsibilities The concept that humans in return have certain obligations to society.

Restorative justice The concept that all parties affected by a criminal act should be collectively involved in restoring the associated damage.

Restriction of liberty orders The technical term for 'electronic tagging'.

Revolution The forceful overthrow of current rule.

Right realism A politically right wing version of realist theory. (See also **Realism** and **Left realism**.)

Rights The concept that humans have claim to certain societal conditions that apply to all.

Right to Buy The government scheme aimed at helping local authorities secure tenants with at least two years tenancy to buy their homes at a discount price.

Risk society A term used by sociologists such as Ulrick Beck and Anthony Giddens refering to the alleged growing preoccupation humans have with the risks associated with modern living.

Role theory See **Activity theory**.

Scottish Crime and Drug Enforcement Agency (SCDEA) An agency similar to the SDEA but with a specific focus on drug crime.

Scottish Drug Enforcement Agency (SDEA) An agency of the Scottish Executive set up to work with existing agencies such as the police in tackling drug laws.

Scottish Poor Law System of welfare provision introduced in the 16th century to address some of the issues of poverty.

Secondary victimisation Negative treatment by individuals or agencies with victims of crime, which serves to exacerbate the damage caused by the initial act.

Serfdom Enforced land labour under feudalism.

Sexual division of labour The separation of paid and unpaid work between male and female.

Sheriff Courts Courts with jury facilities for crimes and/or claims of a more serious nature.

Social closure The direct or indirect closing off of entry into a particular class or occupational group in order to protect the status attached to it.

Social construction/ism The notion that social phenomena and ideas are not 'naturally' occurring but are created by powerful groups or elites in society.

Social control The regulation of individual and group behaviour through positive and/or negative incentives.

Social democracy A set of political ideas and beliefs centred around the notion of social protection as well as tempered economic freedoms.

Social enquiry reports A report compiled by an offender's social worker detailing life history and possible mitigating factors. Such reports are often requested by courts before passing sentence.

Social exclusion A term used variously to describe how some members of society are disengaged from wider society.

Social inclusion A term preferred by the Scottish Executive to social exclusion and referring to the perceived need to have certain groups or individuals re-engage with wider society.

Social Inclusion Partnerships (SIPs) Broadly based partnerships of public agencies such as local authorities, local enterprise companies, local health boards and the voluntary and private sectors who focus on community regeneration.

Social inequality Differences between social groups in terms of aspects such as income, wealth, status or power.

Socialisation The process by which social norms and values are taught to individuals.

Socialism A broad set of ideas and beliefs that advocate social control of the economy.

Social mobility The upward or downward movement on the social hierarchy.

Social model A model of health that focuses on social causes or influences on health.

Social order A state of relative stability in society.

Social policy Governmental approached to welfare provision.

Social stratification The layering of social groups in hierarchical societies.

Solicitor-General The depute of the Lord Advocate whose role it is to advise the Crown and Scottish Executive on Scot's Law.

Solidarity Unity or togetherness. Also the name of a Scottish socialist party.

Status A term referring to social position and often characterised by differentials in wealth, power, influence and prestige.

Stigma A negative label applied to individuals and/or groups based on assumptions that they are unacceptably different.

Structural explanation An explanation that focuses on how social forces external to the individual shape their behaviour or determine their social position.

Structured dependency A term that refers to the alleged ill effects of state welfare provision.

Subcultural theory Theory that focus on how some groups such as gangs develop alternative norms and value systems.

Summary cases Claims involving money between £750-£1500, which are heard at Sheriff Courts.

Supply-side A term deriving from economics, which lays focus on labour forces and production of goods and services – the supply side of the demand/supply equation.

Sure Start A UK government initiative aimed at giving children the "best possible start in life" by improving childcare facilities, nursery provision, health and family support.

Surplus value Marx's term for 'profit'.

Thatcherism A term commonly applied to the economic and social policies undertaken by the Thatcher administration of 1979-1990 in Britain.

The Kearney Report (1992) A report of the inquiry into child care policies in Fife, which highlighted the need to improve mutual respect and co-operation between a social work department and its related Children's Hearings service.

The Reformation The split from the Roman Catholic Church of various 'protesting', or Protestant, groups in the 16th century.

The Skinner Report (1992) A report on residential care of children outlining eight key principles to ensure quality of provision.

The state A set of institutions carrying authority over defined territories, such as nation states.

Think tanks An organisation or informal group made up of people from various walks of life who meet to discuss issues of public interest. New Labour has made increasing use of such groups in an attempt to gauge public opinion.

Third sector A term describing a third sector beyond the public and private and consisting of charity and non-profit civil organisations.

Tories A term commonly used to describe members of the British Conservative Party.

UK Serious Organised Crime Agency A law enforcement agency set up in April 2006 in an attempt to protect individuals and communities from harm relating to serious crime.

UN Convention of the Rights of the Child An international convention setting out the civil, political, cultural, social and economic rights of children.

Underclass A politically right wing and value laden term applied to a wide ranging group of relatively deprived individuals and groups who, it is claimed, are detached from the generally accepted class structure.

Undeserving poor A politically right wing concept that claims that there are those in poverty who need not be if they chose otherwise.

Universal access/universalism Access to education for all, regardless of sex, class, race and ethnicity, disability, etc.

Urban renaissance agenda A government led programme for urban regeneration.

Utopian An 'ideal' and, therefore, arguably unattainable model of society.

Values Things that individuals and groups consider as important things to aim for. Examples might include working hard, saving for the future, freedom of expression.

Victimisation Where an individual is singled out for unfair treatment.

Victim Surveys Crime surveys that ask respondents to detail crimes they have been a victim of.

Wage labour The system of production whereby workers are paid more or less set pay for work done for an employer.

Wage slavery A concept commonly attributed to Marx and describing the almost complete oppression and exploitation of workers by means of (low) wage labour.

Washington Consensus A term used to broadly refer to the US version of neo-liberal economics prevalent in the early years of the 21st century.

Welfare pluralism The practice of providing welfare from a variety of sources other than the state.

Welfare state Literally, the provision of welfare services by the state.

Welfare to work A programme imported from the United States to the UK, whereby individuals are encouraged back into work, often under pain of losing benefits.

Welfarism/welfarist Usually associated with the economic aspects of welfare.

White collar crime Crime committed by workers of mid to high status in the course of their occupations.

White collar workers Salaried professionals and non-manual labourers who would have, until recent times at least, worn a shirt and tie to work.

Workfare An alternative model for welfare provision that requires recipients to work in return for welfare provision.

Workhouses Victorian facilities for the able-bodied poor who would work in the facility in return for board and lodgings.

Working Families Tax Credit (WFTC) A New Labour initiative aimed at providing financial support for working families with at least one child under the age of 16.

Working poor A term used to describe individuals and families in paid work who remain in relative poverty due to low levels of pay.

Working Tax Credits (WTC) The tax credit that replaced the Working Families Tax Credit system in 2003 that can be claimed by working individuals and childless couples as well as working families with dependent children.

Worklessness A term referring to a lack of paid employment and used as an alternative to 'unemployment', implying no blame on the individual for their status

World Bank A gro up of five international organisations that provide funding and advice for member countries.

Name Index

Subject Index